BOATOWNER'S WIRING MANUAL

BOATOWNER'S WIRING MANUAL

Charles Wing

ADLARD COLES NAUTICAL
London

First edition published 1995 by Adlard Coles Nautical
an imprint of A & C Black (Publishers) Ltd
35 Bedford Row, London WC1R 4JH

Copyright © Charles Wing 1993

First published in the USA 1994 under the title *Boatowner's Illustrated Handbook of Wiring* by International Marine, an imprint of TAB Books

ISBN 0-7136-4072-3

All rights reserved. No part of this publication may be reproduced in any form or by any means – graphic, electronic or mechanical, including photocopying, recording, taping or information storage and retrieval systems – without the prior permission in writing of the publishers.

A CIP catalogue record for this book is available from the British Library.

Printed and bound in Great Britain by
Butler and Tanner Ltd, Frome, Somerset

Contents

Introduction vii

Part I: DC

1. Basic DC Circuits — **3**
2. DC Measurements — **15**
3. Batteries — **29**
4. Alternators — **53**
5. Bonding — **73**
6. DC Standards and Practices — **103**

Part II: AC

7. AC Basics — **135**
8. Inverters and Generators — **151**
9. AC Standards and Practices — **171**

Part III: Alternate Energies

10. Conservation for Liveaboards — **221**
11. Solar Power — **231**
12. Wind and Water Power — **245**

Part IV: Projects

13. Installing Electronics — **263**
14. Fun Weekend Projects — **279**

Appendices **301**

Glossary **307**

Index **311**

Do-It-Yourself Projects

Test lamp	21
Galley battery experiment	30
Battery box	50
Galley alternator experiment	54
Alternator-regulator bypass	67
Testing for stray currents	96
Testing zinc protection	96
Make circuit diagrams	105
Install heat-shrink tubing	123
Install coaxial connectors	266
Install noise filters	274
AC-Polarity Indicator	288
LED Panel Indicators	289
AC-Frequency Meter	290
Small Battery Eliminator	291
Low-Voltage Alarm	292
Battery Monitor	293
Automatic Anchor Light	294
Cabin-Light Dimmer	295
Bilge-Water Alarm	296
Water-Tank Indicator	297
Boat-Burglar Alarm	298
Electronic Ship's Horn	299
Fan Control for Refrigeration Compressor	300

Introduction

Many of us have, at the least, a passing familiarity with electrical wiring. When a switch or socket in our home fails, we replace it. Some of us feel secure in extending a circuit, adding a new circuit, even wiring an entire house. We are able to do so because of the *National Electric Code* (NEC), and because many excellent books, based on the NEC, have been written for both the novice and the professional.

Unfortunately, a boat is not a house—a fact that many boat builders and boatyards have yet to discover.

I'll never forget the time I was working in a boatyard rigging masts. I had spent an hour trying to discover why a mast-top anchor light was not working. The blue anchor-light supply conductor disappeared into the base of the mast, yet there appeared no blue conductor at the top. I commented on the discrepancy to a co-worker who had worked as an electrician at one of this country's premier boat builders.

"Sure," he said. "We used to grab a spool of whatever, and when that ran out, we'd just splice in another. Color doesn't matter."

Or ask boat builders whether bronze skin-fittings should be bonded. Chances are good you'll get an even split.

No wonder boat owners are confused!

In fact, there *are* voluntary standards which apply to marine wiring and electrics. In the UK, the British Marine Electronics Association (BMEA) publish a *Code of Practice for Electrical and Electronic Installations in Small Craft*.

This book is an interpretation of those standards and much more.

My joy in life derives from the process of explaining how things work—first as a physics teacher at Bowdoin College, then as the founder of the first two owner-builder schools in the country, author of seven books on home building, and author and host of a PBS series on energy conservation.

Now, I live on a boat. My joy for the past year has been in discovering and bringing to this book a systematic and comprehensive view of marine wiring.

I have always felt that knowledge is useless unless based upon an understanding of principles—simply put, how things work. You will find that each subject in this book begins with a simple exploration and explanation of the hows and whys.

I also feel that books—even those of a technical nature—should be fun. We have no need for Miss Grundy to rap our knuckles to command our attention. Discovery of the things around us should be exciting. To this end, you will find dozens of simple experiments and projects designed to make your light come on, perhaps even add to the comfort and convenience of your boat.

I hope you will come away from this book with the feeling that (to paraphrase Ratty in *Wind in the Willows*), "There is simply nothing like messing about in your boat's electrical system."

I have invented nothing. I have framed no new laws of physics, discovered no principles of electricity and magnetism, and developed no products for sale. I have simply attempted to bring to the reader a lucid and clearly illustrated account of how the best minds in the field think a boat should be wired.

I would not—could not—have tackled the book without the input of individuals too numerous to recount. I must, however, acknowledge the contributions of three:

> Lysle Gray, executive director of the American Boat and Yacht Council, for reviewing the chapters based upon the ABYC standards.

> Christopher Karentz, the single greatest repository of marine technical information I have ever met, for reviewing the entire manuscript.

> Judy Wing, first mate of the PUFFIN, for giving up virtually the entire inner space of our boat and fifteen months of my companionship to see this project through.

Charlie Wing
Yarmouth, Maine
8 February, 1993

Note from the Publishers
In many instances US dollar prices have been retained in the text where they are roughly equivalent to the same sterling figure (thus for $10 read £10). Similarly readers should note the retention of some US terminology whose UK meanings are given here: hot (live), through-hull (skin fitting), receptacle (socket), range (cooker), faucet (tap).

PART I
DC

1 BASIC DC CIRCUITS

Electricity—What is it?   4

Discovery of Electricity   4

A Circuit   5

Ohm's Law   5

Using Ohm's Law   5

Loads in Series   6

Loads in Parallel   7

Loads in Series/Parallel   7

Sources in Series   8

Sources in Parallel   8

Energy and Power   9

Practice Problems   10

Basic to the ability to work with electrical wiring—be it residential or marine—is an understanding of *what electricity is*. You'll find that the *discovery of electricity*, as we now understand it, was fairly recent.

The key that unlocks the wiring puzzle is the concept of the electrical *circuit*. With this simple concept and a single formula—*Ohm's Law*—you can understand and predict the behavior of 99% of the wiring on your boat. You will be able to deal with circuits containing *loads in series*, *loads in parallel*, even *loads in series/parallel* combinations. Similarly, you will be able to predict the behavior of voltage *sources in series* and voltage *sources in parallel*. You will also discover the differences between voltage, current, *energy, and power*.

Finally I have provided a set of 18 *practice problems* on which you can cut your electric teeth.

We live in the age of electricity. Without electricity we couldn't watch television, drive automobiles, make frozen margaritas, microwave popcorn, read at night, or talk to our friends on the phone.

Many people think electricity is difficult to understand. They are wrong. Because you are surrounded by and unconsciously use electrical devices every day, little lights will go on in your head as you discover the concepts. You'll probably say, "Oooh—so that's why my boat battery is dead every morning!"

I believe you will find electricity to be fun. I am absolutely sure that, having grasped the very simple concepts behind boat wiring, you will feel more confident in both your boat and yourself.

ELECTRICITY—WHAT IS IT?

Electricity consists of electrons. The electron is the smallest quantity of electricity that exists. It is such a small quantity, however, that we use the unit *coulomb* (1 coulomb = 6.24×10^{18} electrons) in calculations.

The flow of electrons is often compared to the flow of water, so it is natural that we call electron flow "electric current." The basic unit of electric current is the *ampere* (1 ampere = 1 coulomb per second of electrons moving past a point).

What we usually refer to as electricity is the control of electrons for useful purposes. Our understanding of electron behavior allows us to predict the flow of electrons through electrical circuits. The instruments on your boat contain circuits. Indeed, a boat's wiring is little more than a collection of circuits. When we understand circuits, we will understand the behavior of electricity on a boat.

THE DISCOVERY OF ELECTRICITY

Democritus (460?–370? BC) proposes an "atomic theory" whereby all matter is made up of indivisible particles or atoms.

Charles deCoulomb (1736–1806) discovers that the force of attraction between static electric charges is proportional to the product of the two charges and inversely proportional to the distance between them.

Luigi Galvani (1737–1798) discovers that two unlike metals immersed in blood cause the muscles of a frog's legs to twitch.

Allessandro Volta (1745–1827) discovers that a current flows between two connected unlike metals in a salt solution and, thus, invents the battery.

John Dalton (1766–1827) proposes the first table of atomic weights of elements.

Hans Oersted (1777–1851) discovers a connection between electric current and magnetism and a way to measure electric current by the deflection of a magnet.

André Ampère (1775–1836) develops the theory of magnetic lines of force and quantifies electric current for the first time.

Georg Ohm (1789–1854) discovers the relationship (Ohm's Law) between voltage, current, and resistance in a circuit.

Michael Faraday (1791–1867) analyzes the chemical reactions in batteries and defines the terms "electrode," "anode," "cathode," and "electrolyte."

James Clerk Maxwell (1831–1879) develops the mathematical equations relating electricity and magnetism.

Joseph Thompson (1856–1940) proves that electricity consists of electrons.

Basic DC Circuits

A CIRCUIT

Electrons can be neither created nor destroyed, but can be transferred through conductive materials. A steady current, therefore, requires an electrical loop, or continuous path of electrically conductive material, through which to flow.

If this were not so, electrons would dribble from the end of a wire like water from a leaky faucet, and batteries would soon sit like empty water glasses with all their electrons lying around them in a pool.

We call a continuous electrical path a *circuit*. If a circuit is unbroken, we call it a *closed circuit*. If it is interrupted, preventing the flow of electricity, we say the circuit is *open*.

All materials present some resistance to electron flow, but the variation among them is so great that we call some materials *conductors* and others *insulators*.

The best conductors are gold, silver, mercury, copper, and aluminum. Copper is most often the best compromise between cost and conductivity. The best insulators are glass, ceramics, mica, and plastics. Plastic is the most often used due to its low cost, durability, and ease of manufacture.

Unfortunately for boaters, salt solutions, such as sea water, are also good conductors.

Electrical current is expressed as a rate of electron flow. In a circuit, two factors control the current (I): the electrical driving force, or voltage (V), and the resistance (R) to flow of the circuit materials.

To see just how simple electricity is, you are going to derive the basic equation of current flow in an electrical circuit. With this equation, you will be able to understand, predict, and troubleshoot more than 90% of all the electrical problems on a boat.

OHM'S LAW

Question 1. Does the flow of electrons (current, I) increase or decrease as we increase the driving force (voltage, V)?

Answer 1. Current increases with voltage.

Question 2. Does the flow of electrons (current, I) increase or decrease as we increase the resistance to electron flow (resistance, R)?

Answer 2. Current decreases with increasing resistance.

Question 3. Considering the answers to questions 1 and 2, what would be the simplest and, therefore, most likely relationship between current (I), voltage (V), and resistance (R)?

Answer 3. There are four possible "simplest" equations:

$$I = V + R, I = V - R, I = V \times R, \text{ and } I = V / R$$

If you play with the values for a minute, you'll agree that the first three equations are unlikely. For example, if we make resistance, R, infinite, current, I, becomes ∞, $-\infty$, ∞, and 0. Only the last value is reasonable, so

$$I = V / R$$

Congratulations! You have just derived Ohm's Law. If Georg Ohm hadn't beaten you to it in 1827, you might be up for a Nobel Prize.

USING OHM'S LAW

This is such an important relationship, we must be precise in its definition and the ways in which it can be used.

First, if we wish to calculate electrical quantities, we must define the units in which these quantities are measured.

$$I = V/R$$

where:

I = amperes, abbreviated as A
V = volts, abbreviated as V
R = ohms, abbreviated as Ω

Let's see how Ohm's Law is used. Ohm's Law applies to all situations, but it is useful only in circuits where electricity is flowing.

Fig. 1.1 A Simple Electric Circuit

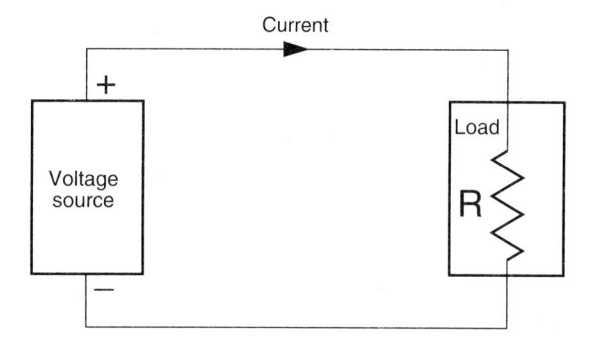

The *voltage source* in Figure 1.1 is a device that produces a voltage difference. Examples are batteries and power supplies. Unless otherwise noted, assume voltage sources are batteries. The *load* is any device or component that consumes electrical energy and, in so doing, results in a voltage drop. Examples are resistors, lamps, and motors. Unless otherwise stated, assume loads are resistances (the zigzag symbol). For a table of electrical symbols used in this book, see Appendix C.

Example: If the load is a resistance of 2 ohms, and the voltage source is a 12-volt battery, then by Ohm's Law

$$I = V/R$$
$$= 12V / 2Ω = 6A$$

We can also rearrange Ohm's Law so that we can calculate either V or I, given the other two values. The alternate forms of Ohm's Law are:

$$V = I \times R$$
$$R = V/I$$

There is more good news. Ohm's Law applies to more complex circuits as well. We can combine loads and sources in series (end-to-end), parallel (side-by-side), and series-parallel, and the equations remain the simplest possible, as you will see in the figures and examples that follow.

LOADS IN SERIES

Fig. 1.2 Series Loads

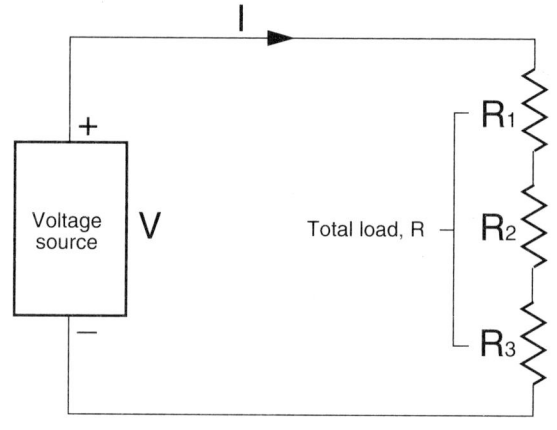

Resistive loads in series act like one continuous load of a total resistance equal to the sum of the individual resistances:

$$R = R_1 + R_2 + R_3, \text{ etc.}$$
$$I = V / (R_1 + R_2 + R_3, \text{ etc.})$$

Example:

$R_1 = 2Ω$, $R_2 = 3Ω$, $R_3 = 5Ω$, $V = 12V$
$R = 2 + 3 + 5 = 10Ω$

Basic DC Circuits

LOADS IN PARALLEL

FIG. 1.3 Parallel Loads

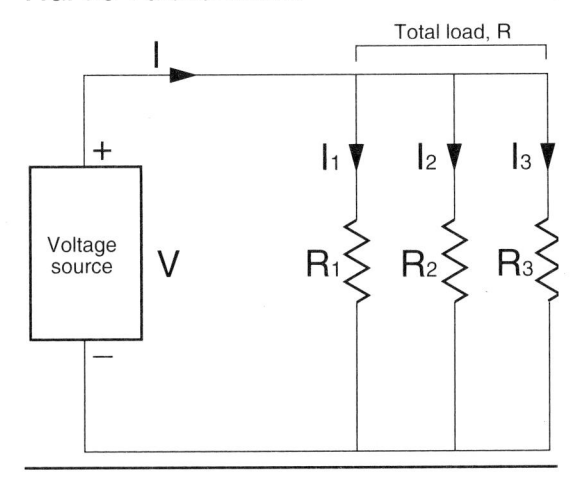

The same voltage, V, exists across each of the loads, Ohm's Law predicts that the currents through the loads are:

$I_1 = V/R_1$, $I_2 = V/R_2$, $I_3 = V/R_3$, etc.

Total current, I, is the sum of currents,

$I = I_1 + I_2 + I_3$, etc.
$= V(1/R_1 + 1/R_2 + 1/R_3$, etc.)

In other words,

$1/R = 1/R_1 + 1/R_2 + 1/R_3$, etc.

Example: $R_1 = 20\Omega$, $R_2 = 30\Omega$, $R_3 = 50\Omega$
$V = 12V$

$1/R = 1/R_1 + 1/R_2 + 1/R_3$
$= 1/20 + 1/30 + 1/50$
$= .050 + .033 + .020$
$= 1.033$

$R = 9.68\Omega$

$I = V/R$
$= 12V / 9.68\Omega$
$= 1.24A$

LOADS IN SERIES/PARALLEL

FIG. 1.4 Series /Parallel Loads

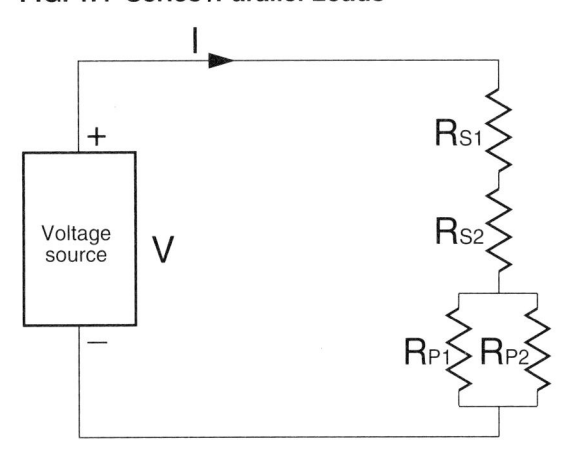

Observe that the parallel group of loads can be considered as a single resistor in series with other series loads. We first calculate the equivalent value of the parallel loads, as in the previous example, and then add the result to the other series loads.

Example: $R_{S1} = 2\Omega$ $R_{S2} = 3\Omega$, $R_{P1} = 5\Omega$, $R_{P2} = 10\Omega$, $V = 12V$

$1/R_P = 1/R_{P1} + 1/R_{P2}$
$= 1/5 + 1/10$
$= 0.20 + 0.10$
$= 0.30$

$R_P = 3.33\Omega$

$R = R_{S1} + R_{S2} + R_P$
$= 2\Omega + 3\Omega + 3.33\Omega$
$= 8.33\Omega$

$I = 12V / 8.33\Omega$
$= 1.44A$

SOURCES IN SERIES

FIG. 1.5 Series Sources

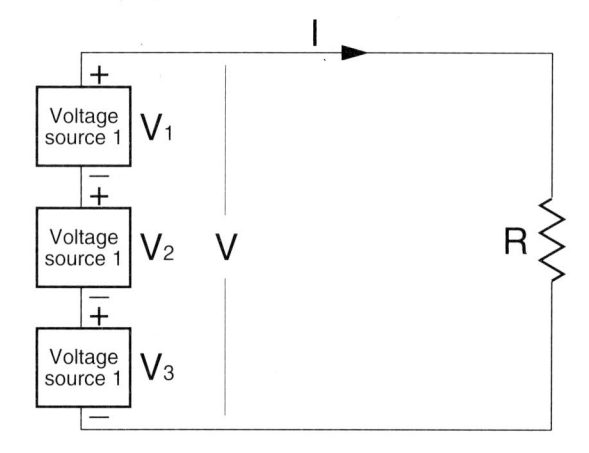

SOURCES IN PARALLEL

FIG. 1.6 Parallel Sources

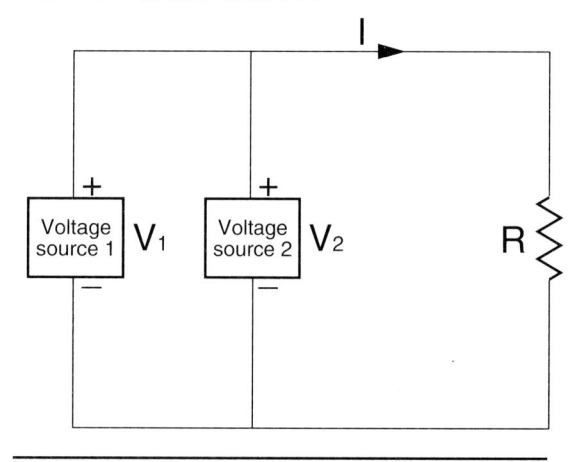

One example of a voltage source is a battery. If you've ever replaced the batteries in a flashlight, you already know that batteries can be stacked end to end, and that the total voltage equals the sum of the individual voltages. In general, then, voltages in series add.

$$V = V_1 + V_2 + V_3, \text{ etc.}$$

Therefore,

$$I = (V_1 + V_2 + V_3) / R$$

Example: $V_1 = 1.5V$, $V_2 = 1.5V$, $V_3 = 3V$, $R = 4\Omega$

$$I = (1.5 + 1.5 + 3.0)V / 4\Omega$$
$$= 1.5A$$

A caution is in order, however. If batteries are to be added in series, they must have the same capacities, and they must start with the same states of charge. If not, the battery with the greatest capacity for supplying current may drive the voltage of the weakest battery negative, which usually destroys the weaker battery.

Your boat probably has a battery selector switch. On its face it says

$$\text{OFF} - 1 - 2 - \text{BOTH}$$

In the BOTH position, both of your batteries are connected in parallel, i.e. + terminal to + terminal, and – terminal to –terminal.

Provided the batteries are of the same voltage, the net result is simply a single battery of capacity equal to the sum of the individual capacities.

If they are not of the same voltage, the higher voltage battery will discharge into the lower voltage battery, possibly overcharging and destroying it.

There is much controversy over charging and discharging marine batteries in parallel. Some experts are dead set against it, saying that the batteries will eventually destroy each other. Other experts claim it is the only way to go when charging. Both arguments and the reasoning behind them will be presented in Chapter 4.

Basic DC Circuits

ENERGY AND POWER

Energy is defined as the *ability to do work*. *Power* is defined as the *rate of doing work*. Power is, therefore, the rate at which energy is used in doing work.

Two Olympic runners exemplify the difference between energy and power. The first runner holds the record in the marathon. He is a lean, mean, efficient running machine. He burns nearly all of his stored energy resources steadily over a two-hour period. The second runner holds the record in the 100-meter dash. He uses less total energy, but consumes it in a tremendous 10-second burst. The first runner uses more energy, but the second uses energy at a greater rate, or power.

Except in nuclear reactions, energy can be neither created nor destroyed. What it can do is change between its many forms.

As an example, the water at the top of a hydroelectric dam possesses *potential energy* due to its height. As it falls and gains speed, its potential energy is converted into *kinetic* (*motion*) *energy*. When the water hits the blades of a turbine, the kinetic energy of the water is transferred to the spinning turbine. The turbine turns a generator where the kinetic energy is converted to *electrical energy*. The electricity flows into your home where a light bulb changes the electrical energy into *light energy* and *heat energy*. Ultimately, the heat escapes from your home into the atmosphere, where it causes water to evaporate into water vapor, which then turns into clouds, which then drop rain into the reservoir. And so it goes.

For the moment, we will concern ourselves only with the energy transformations occurring between your boat's batteries and its loads. The battery, as we will see in detail later, is just a box full of chemicals.

When it is connected to a closed electrical circuit, the chemicals react, sending a stream of electrons (amps) around the circuit under electrical pressure (volts). In flowing through the load (resistance), the electrons lose their pressure (the voltage drops), and the load produces heat, light, or some form of mechanical work. Chemical energy changed to electrical energy, which then changed to heat, light, or mechanical energy. You'll see later that recharging the battery involves the same steps, but in reverse order.

Power can be calculated as easily as volts, amps, and ohms.

$$P = V \times I$$

where: P = power consumption in watts
V = volts across the load
I = amps through the load

Example: What is the power of a lightbulb that draws 1.25 amps at 12 volts?

$$P = V \times I$$
$$= 12 \text{ volts} \times 1.25 \text{ amps}$$
$$= 15 \text{ watts}$$

Example: How many amps would a 20-watt lamp draw in a 12-volt circuit?

$$P = V \times I$$
$$I = P / V$$
$$= 20 \text{ watts} / 12 \text{ volts}$$
$$= 1.67 \text{ amps}$$

Electrical equipment is usually labeled with its power consumption. If you look at the back or bottom of equipment, or at the base of a bulb, you will generally find either (X) volts and (Y) amps, or (X) watts at (Y) volts.

Using Ohm's Law and the power equation, you should have no problem deducing either amps or watts, given two of the three variables in the equations.

10 DC

PRACTICE PROBLEMS

The problems below are designed to sharpen your skills in the application of Ohm's Law. They range from the simplest possible to the most complex you'll ever encounter on your boat. All you need to solve them is a simple four-function calculator, scratch paper, and a pencil.

You can make solving them a parlor game. Get your mate to play with you. Take turns making up more problems and trying to stump the other person.

Once you have mastered these examples, you are ready for real components and real circuits. The answers to these problems are listed at the end of this chapter.

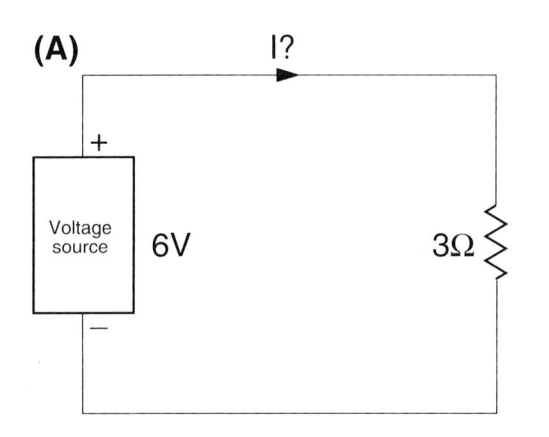

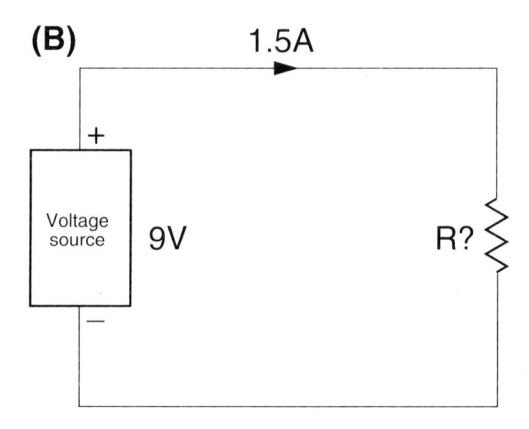

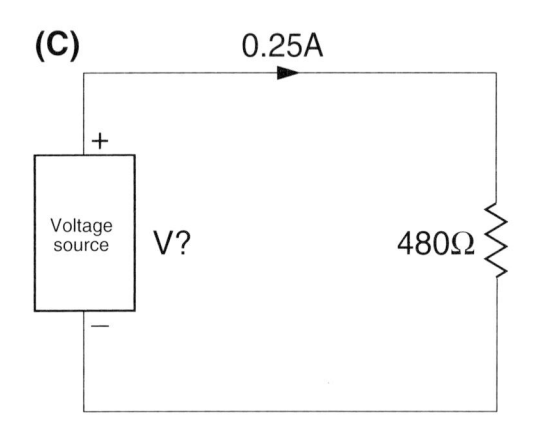

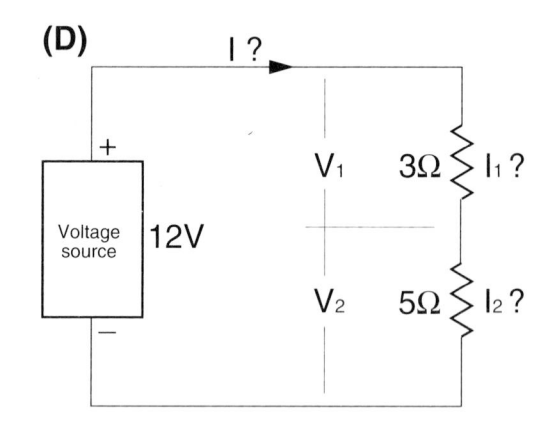

(A) Voltage source 6V, I?, 3Ω

(B) Voltage source 9V, 1.5A, R?

(C) Voltage source V?, 0.25A, 480Ω

(D) Voltage source 12V, I?, V_1 across 3Ω (I_1?), V_2 across 5Ω (I_2?)

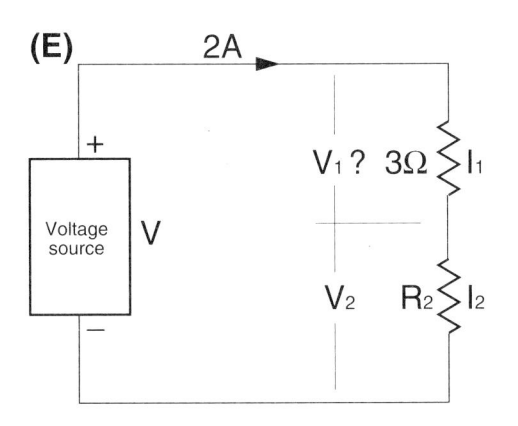

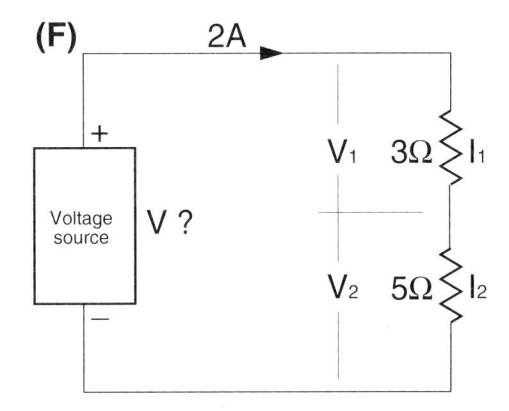

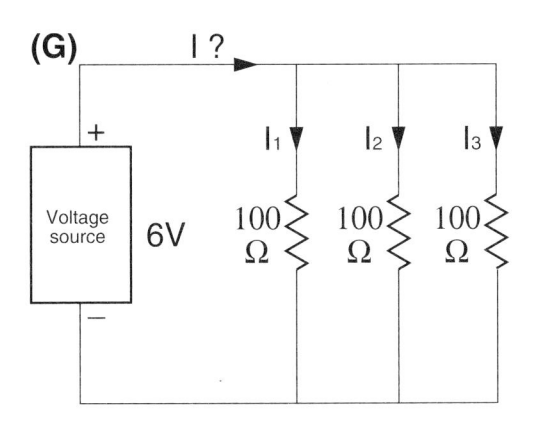

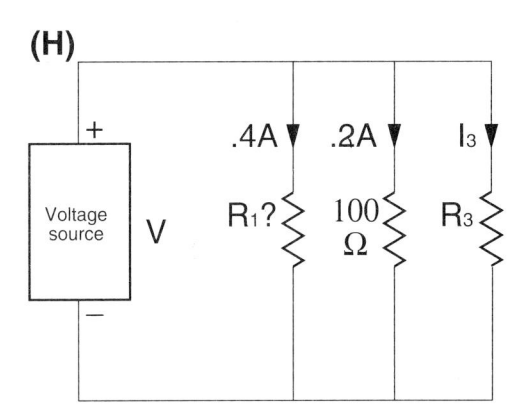

Basic DC Circuits

(E) Circuit with voltage source V, current 2A, resistor 3Ω (V_1?, I_1) in series with R_2 (V_2, I_2).

(F) Circuit with voltage source V?, current 2A, resistor 3Ω (V_1, I_1) in series with 5Ω (V_2, I_2).

(G) Voltage source 6V, current I?, three parallel 100Ω resistors with currents I_1, I_2, I_3.

(H) Voltage source V, three parallel resistors: R_1? (.4A), 100Ω (.2A), R_3 (I_3).

(I) Voltage source, 6V, 0.5A, R? W?

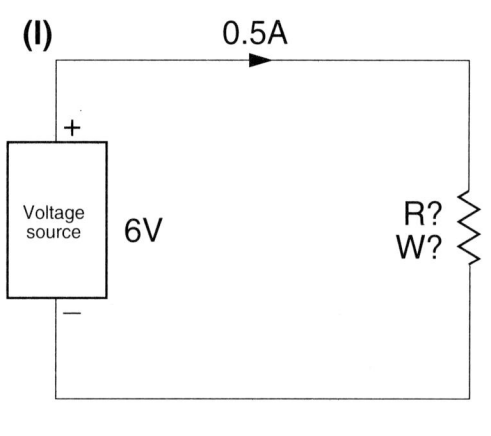

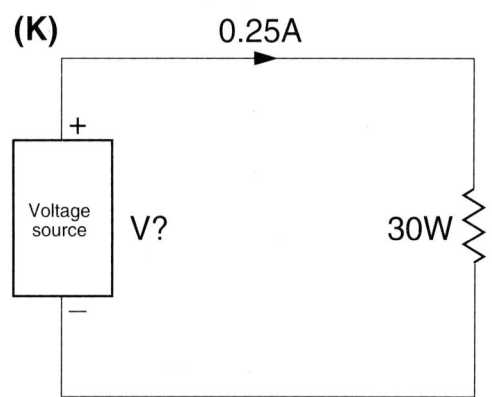

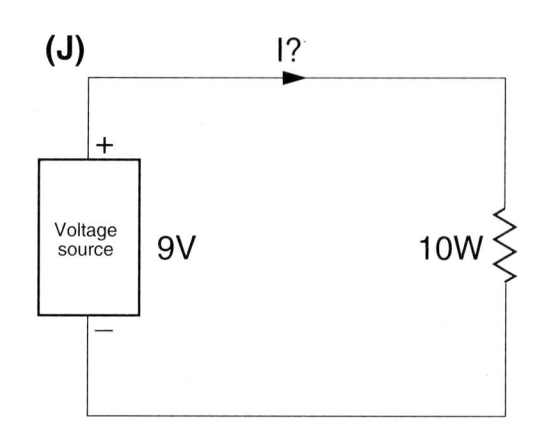

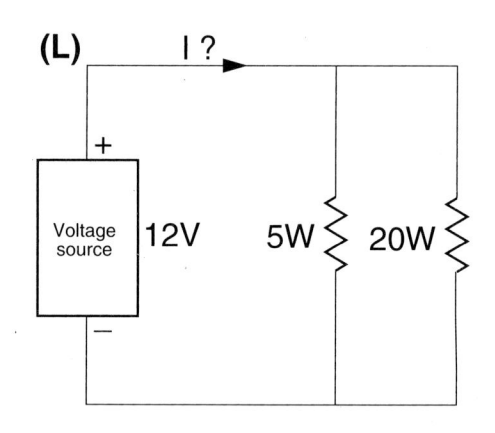

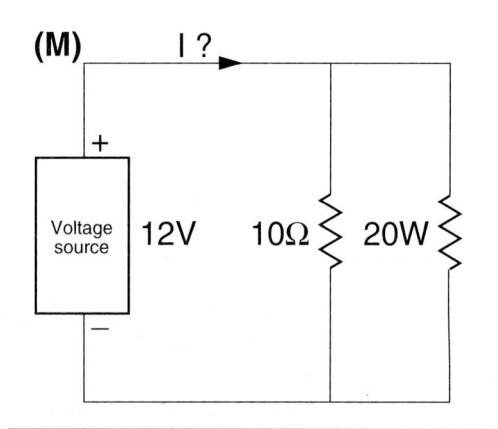

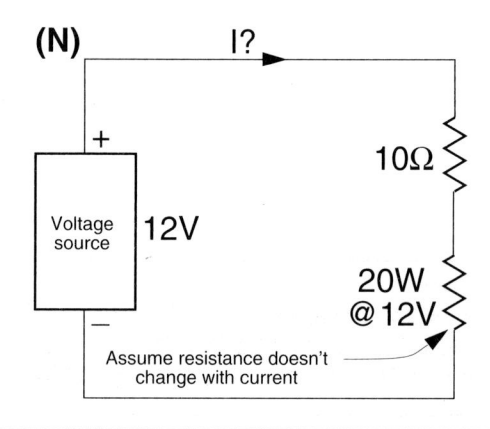

(J) Voltage source, 9V, I?, 10W

(K) Voltage source, V?, 0.25A, 30W

(L) Voltage source, 12V, I?, 5W, 20W

(M) Voltage source, 12V, I?, 10Ω, 20W

(N) Voltage source, 12V, I?, 10Ω, 20W @12V

Assume resistance doesn't change with current

Basic DC Circuits

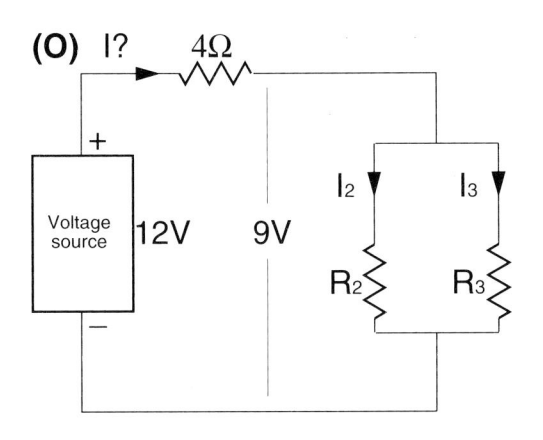

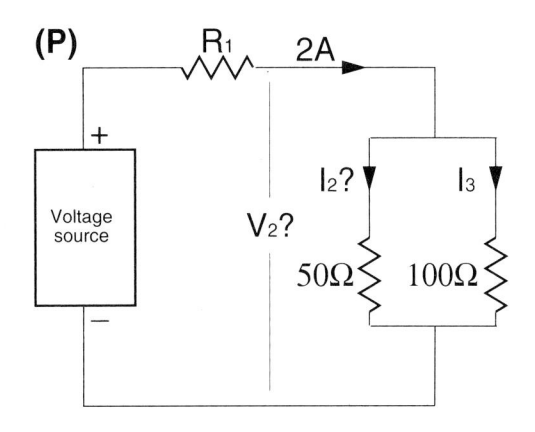

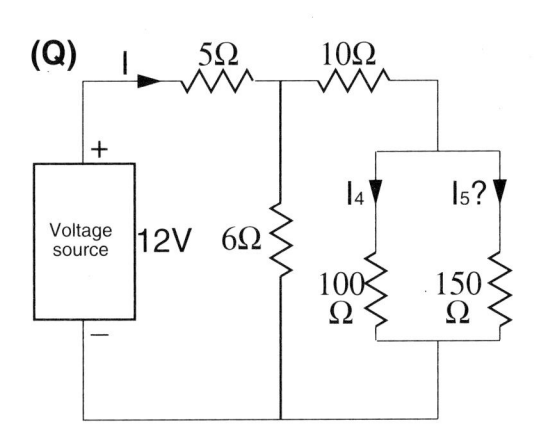

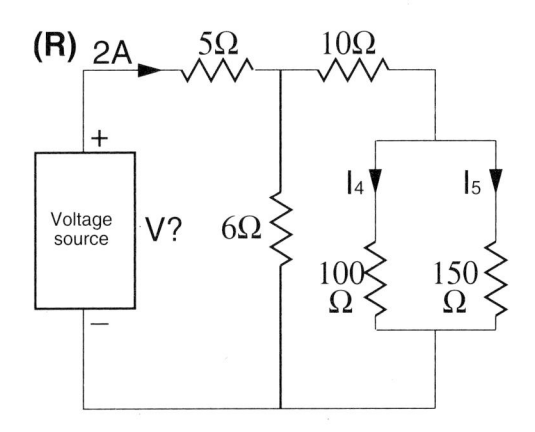

(O) Circuit with 12V voltage source, I? through 4Ω resistor, 9V branch, and parallel R₂, R₃ with currents I₂, I₃.

(P) Circuit with voltage source, R₁ with 2A current, V₂?, parallel 50Ω (I₂?) and 100Ω (I₃).

(Q) Circuit with 12V voltage source, current I through 5Ω then 10Ω, 6Ω branch, parallel 100Ω (I₄) and 150Ω (I₅?).

(R) Circuit with voltage source V?, 2A through 5Ω then 10Ω, 6Ω branch, parallel 100Ω (I₄) and 150Ω (I₅).

Answers:
(A) I = 2A, (B) R = 6Ω, (C) V = 120V, (D) I₁ = I₂ = I = 1.5A, (E) V₁ = 6V, (F) V = 16V, (G) I = 0.18A, (H) R₁ = 50Ω, (I) R = 12Ω, W = 3W, (J) I = 1.11A, (K) V = 120V, (L) I = 2.08A, (M) I = 2.87A, (N) I = 0.7A, (O) I = 0.75A, (P) V₂ = 66.7V, I₂ = 1.33A, (Q) I₅ = 0.036A, (R) V = 21.05V

2 DC MEASUREMENTS

Analog Instruments 16

Digital Instruments 19

Do-It-Yourself Testers 21

Troubleshooting with Testers 22

Practice Problems 27

Theory is fine, but we need a way to monitor electrical systems in order to see if they are working as expected. *Analog instruments*, displaying current and voltage, allow us to see, at a glance, what is happening. For the precision required to monitor batteries, however, it is better to use *digital instruments*.

Very often we need to know only whether there is voltage present. For these go-no-go tests, a simple *do-it-yourself tester* is described.

Troubleshooting with testers leads you through the deductive process of isolating electrical faults.

The *practice problems* at the end of the chapter will allow you to sharpen your troubleshooting skills.

16   DC

In Chapter 1, I asserted, "...with Ohm's Law, you will be able to understand, predict, and troubleshoot 90% of the electrical problems on a boat." I amend that to 99%.

You will recall that Ohm's Law allows us to calculate the theoretical relationships between the voltages, currents, and resistances in a circuit. What if there were instruments we could plug into circuits that would show us the actual values of voltage, current, and resistance? By comparing the theoretical and actual values, we would find that either:

1) reality agreed with theory and all was well in the circuit, or

2) reality disagreed with theory and there was something wrong in the circuit.

There *are* instruments that measure volts, amps, and ohms, and using them to compare reality with theory is what we call troubleshooting. This chapter describes the instruments and their use.

ANALOG INSTRUMENTS
Analog Ammeter

The ammeter hasn't changed much since it was developed by D'Arsonval in 1811. In Figure 2.1, current flows into terminal 1, through the spring, around the moving coil, through a second spring on the backside, and out through terminal 2. The current in the coil produces a magnetic field that interacts with the field of the permanent magnet, forcing the coil to rotate about its bearing. The needle attached to the coil displays the rotation against the calibrated scale in the background.

In order that the ammeter measure small currents, the meter movement is very delicate. The moving coil consists of many turns of fine wire, the springs are "hair springs," and the coil pivots on jewel

Fig. 2.1 The Ammeter

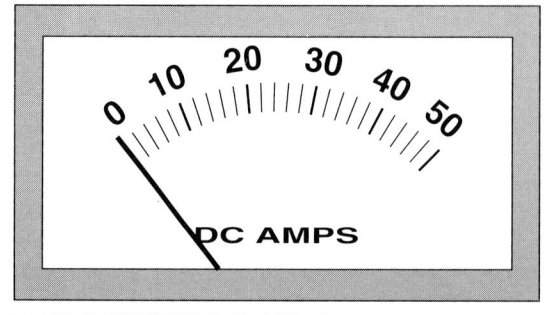

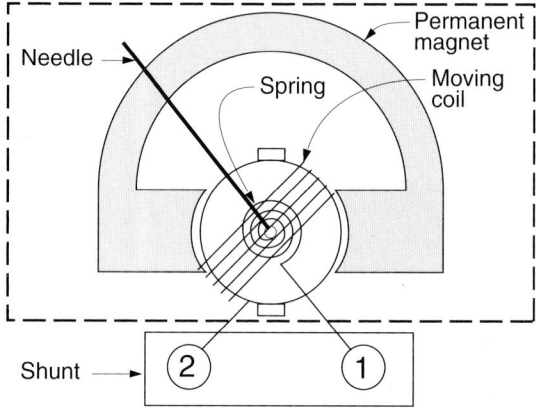

bearings. Typically, 50μA (50 x 10^{-6}A or 0.000050 amp) deflects the needle full scale.

But the currents we are interested in typically range from 0.1 to 100 amps—about one million times 50μA. You can imagine what would happen if we tried to measure the 50-amp charging current in our battery leads with the 50μA meter of Figure 2.1.

How could we modify our 50μA ammeter to measure 50 amps? Ohm's Law to the rescue! Although the perfect ammeter offers zero resistance to the current flowing through it, real ammeters are made of real wire and so have a finite resistance.

DC Measurements

Fig. 2.2 Ammeter Circuit

Fig. 2.3 Voltmeter Circuit

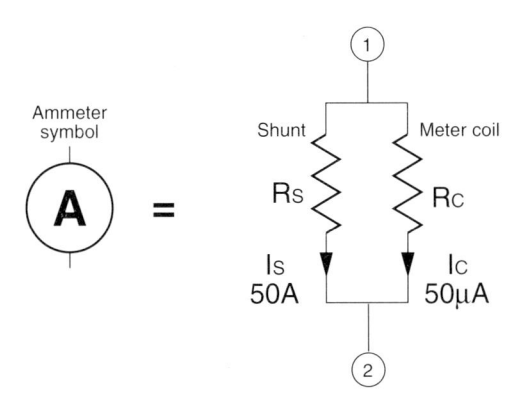

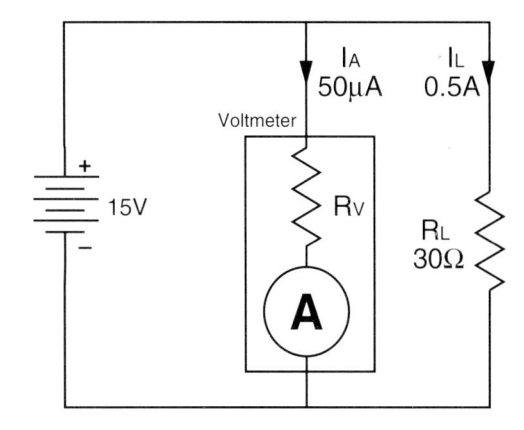

Figure 2.2 shows our ammeter as a resistance, R_C, with its full-scale current of 50μA flowing through it. In parallel with the meter, we place a shunt whose resistance, R_S, is 10^{-6} (one-millionth) of R_C. Since the voltage across both R_S and R_C is the same, Ohm's Law predicts that $I_S = 10^6$ (one million) x I_C, or 50 amps!

Using this principle, the same 50μA ammeter can be made to measure 100μA, 500μA, 30mA, 10 amps, 100 amps, or any other current merely by placing the appropriate shunt across the terminals, as shown.

Analog Voltmeter

Might we use our little 50μA D'Arsonval meter to measure voltage as well? Ideally, a voltmeter should measure the voltage across a circuit without disturbing the circuit. That means it should look like a very high resistance—much higher than any of the other resistances in the circuit.

Figure 2.3 shows a circuit consisting of a 15-volt battery and a load of 30 ohms, which results in a current of:

$$I = V / (R_L)$$
$$= 15 \text{ volts} / 30 \text{ ohms}$$
$$= 0.5 \text{ amps}$$

We have placed a series resistor, R_V, inside the case of our 50μA ammeter. If we want the ammeter to deflect full scale when the voltage is 15 volts, then Ohm's Law says that the series resistor that limits the current to 50μA must be

$$I_V = V / R_V$$
$$R_V = V / I_V$$
$$= 15 \text{ volts} / 0.00005 \text{ amps}$$
$$= 300,000 \text{ ohms}$$

The load imposed on the circuit by our voltmeter—one ten-thousandth of the 30-ohm circuit load—is clearly negligible. If the circuit load, R_L, had been 30,000, instead of 30 ohms, then our voltmeter would have siphoned off 10% of the current, giving a result 10% in error, as well as altering the performance of the circuit.

Voltmeters are simply ammeters with internal series resistors of 5,000 to 100,000 ohms per volt of full scale.

Analog Ohmmeter

By now you are probably expecting me to tell you that our 50μA ammeter can be modified to measure resistance as well. You are correct.

To measure the resistance of a resistor or other circuit load, we must isolate that component from the rest of the circuit. (Review the practice problems of Chapter 1, if you don't remember why.)

Sometimes we can open a switch; sometimes we can disconnect a terminal; sometimes we have to unsolder one end of the component. Regardless of how we isolate the component, we measure its resistance indirectly by applying a test voltage and measuring the resulting current. Since zero resistance (a distinct possibility in case of a short inside the component) would draw a destructive infinite current, we place a series current-limiting resistor in the test circuit, as well.

Figure 2.4 shows our ohmmeter. Inside its case are our old standby 50μA ammeter, a 1.5-volt battery, and a series resistor, R_R. Maximum current will flow, and the meter will deflect full scale, when the resistance being tested, R_L, is zero. From Ohm's Law

$$I = V / R_R$$
$$R_R = V / I$$
$$= 1.5 \text{ volts} / 0.00005 \text{ amps}$$
$$= 30{,}000 \text{ ohms}$$

At the other end of the scale, the current drops to zero, and the needle shows no deflection. Thus, we have a meter with 0 ohms on the right, ∞ ohms on the left, and all other values on a logarithmic scale in between. Near 0 ohms the meter will be very sensitive, and, as R_L approaches ∞ ohms, the meter will be less sensitive.

Fig. 2.4 Ohmmeter

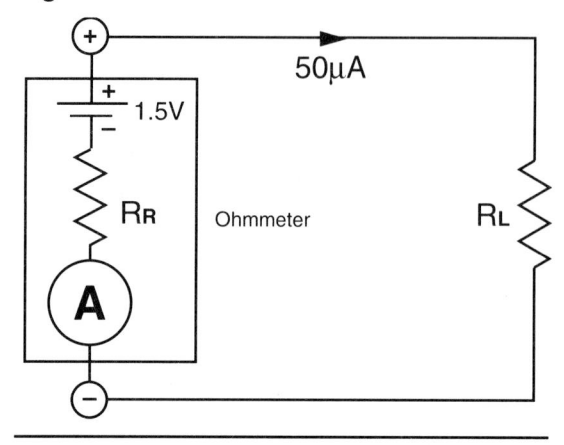

Analog Panel Meters

Ammeters and voltmeters (Fig. 2.5) are used in distribution panels to monitor battery voltage and rate of charge/discharge. A "battery charge indicator" is a voltmeter with the needle tensioned and held at the left until the voltage reaches approximately 8 to 10 volts.

Fig. 2.5 DC Panel Meters

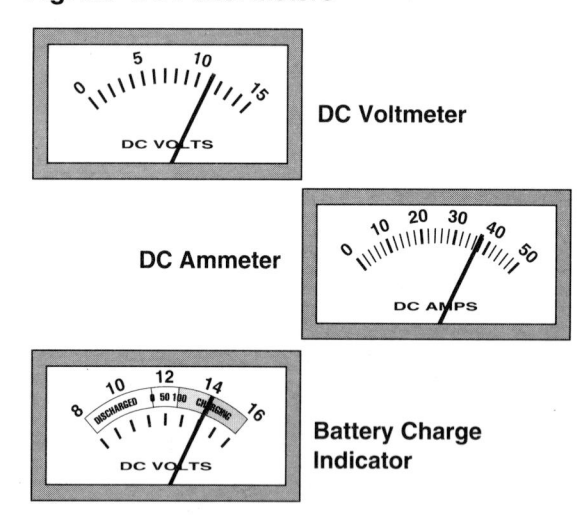

DC Voltmeter

DC Ammeter

Battery Charge Indicator

DC Measurements

Volt-Ohm Meters

To troubleshoot a circuit, you may need an ammeter, a voltmeter, an ohmmeter, or all three. You may also need a variety of ranges. As you have probably come to expect, it is a simple matter to combine all of these functions into a single meter called a volt-ohm meter (VOM), as in Figure 2.6 below.

To the 50µA ammeter, we add a battery, assorted precision resistors and shunts, and a multipole, multiposition switch. More expensive VOMs have input amplifiers that increase input resistance and decrease current drawn by the VOM. In this way, the VOM has less effect on the tested circuit.

Fig. 2.6 Typical Volt-Ohm Meter (VOM)

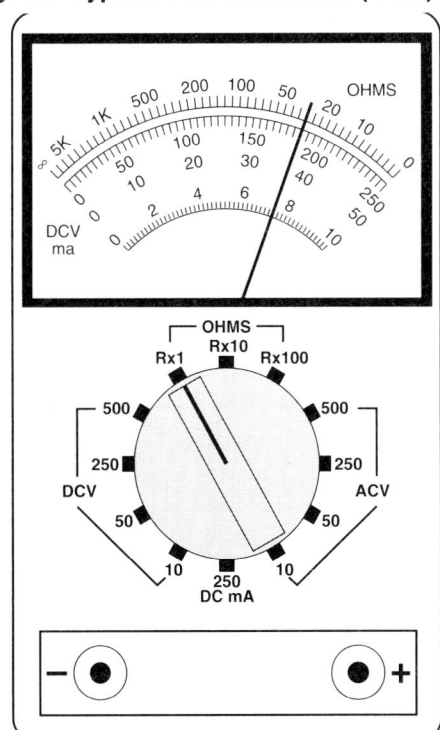

DIGITAL INSTRUMENTS

One of the very first clocks was a "water clock." Water dripped into a cup. When the cup was full, it tipped over, spilling its contents and starting over. In tipping, it advanced a counter mechanism that indicated the number of times it had tripped and thus the passage of time.

A digital ammeter is exactly the same, except that it uses electrons instead of water. The cup is a capacitor. As current flows into the capacitor, the voltage across the capacitor increases. When the voltage of the capacitor reaches a predetermined level, the capacitor is discharged, and the charging begins again.

The greater the current, the more rapidly the capacitor charges and discharges. The charge/discharge cycles are electronically counted, and the number of cycles per second are directly proportional to current.

The analogy between analog and digital ammeters, voltmeters, ohmmeters, and multimeters is similar. Given a digital ammeter, we just add shunts, resistors, batteries, and rotary switches. Figure 2.7 shows typical digital panel meters. Figure 2.8, on the next page, shows a digital multimeter.

Fig. 2.7 Digital Panel Meters

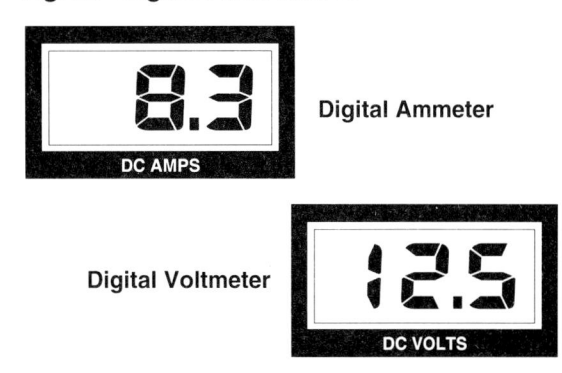

DC

Fig. 2.8 Typical Digital Multimeter

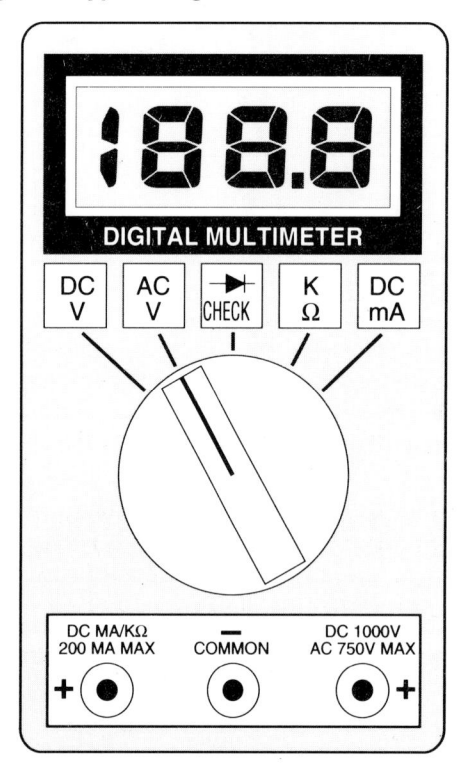

Table. 2.1 Typical Analog and Digital Multimeter Specifications

Specification		Analog Multimeter	Digital Multimeter
DC volts	lowest range	250 mV	300 mV
	highest range	1,000V	1,000V
	accuracy*	±3%	±0.2%
AC volts	lowest range	5V	3V
	highest range	1,000V	750V
	accuracy*	±4%	±0.5%
DC amps	lowest range	50µA	300mA
	highest range	10A	10A
	accuracy*	±3%	±0.5%
Resistance	lowest range	2KΩ	300Ω
	highest range	20MΩ	30MΩ
	accuracy*	±3%	±0.2%
Input resistance		25KΩ/V	10MΩ

* Accuracy, as percent of full scale

A glance at an old-fashioned watch gives you a sense of the approximate time very quickly. A digital watch, however, first requires recognition of the numbers displayed, then an interpretation of the significance of the numbers. The same is true of analog and digital multimeter displays.

If you wish to know only whether your battery is charging or discharging (roughly 14 versus 12 volts), the analog meter with ±4% accuracy (±0.6 volt on 15-volt scale) will do the job. But if you want to know the percentage of charge remaining in your battery, where the same ±0.6 volts represents ±50% of battery capacity, you'd better use a digital meter with its ±0.2% (±0.03 volt on 15-volt scale) accuracy.

Digital vs. Analog Multimeters

So which are better—analog or digital multimeters? Both are available in a range of sizes, from shirt-pocket to bench-top, and both can be had for as little as £20 to as much as £500. To help you decide which is better for you, Table 2.1 lists the specifications of two typical mid-priced units.

The specifications use several prefixes:

$\mu = 10^{-6}$ — multiply by 0.000001
$m = 10^{-3}$ — multiply by 0.001
$K = 10^{+3}$ — multiply by 1,000
$M = 10^{+6}$ — multiply by 1,000,000

DC Measurements

DO-IT-YOURSELF TESTERS

Most of the wiring problems on a boat are of the go, no-go variety. All DC circuits start at the 12-volt battery. As you check a suspect circuit farther and farther from the battery, there either is or isn't voltage present. At the first point you find no voltage, you know the problem lies between this point and the last point where voltage was present.

The most common marine wiring problems are due to corrosion of connections and contacts. When copper corrodes, it forms green copper oxide—an excellent electrical insulator. As corrosion progresses, more and more of the contact surface through which current flows is eliminated. Eventually, there is so much resistance and voltage drop across the contact that the reduced voltage affects the load. If the load is a lamp, for example, the lamp will dim. If the load is a motor, the motor will slow down or not start at all.

There are two simple, do-it-yourself, troubleshooting devices you will probably end up using more than your fancy multimeter. The first is nothing more than an automotive bulb with leads; the second is a piezoelectric alarm buzzer with leads.

Figure 2.9 shows a typical 10-watt, 12-volt-DC automotive bulb you can purchase at any auto parts or hardware store. Get a pair of high-quality "test leads" at an electronics store. These will be rubber-insulated, very-fine-stranded #14 to #18 wire with alligator clips, banana plugs, or minitest tips attached. Solder the test leads to the side and base of the bulb, as shown, or to a socket. Don't worry about ever having to replace the bulb. It is rated 5,000 hours at 13.5V, so the only way it should fail is if you step on it or try to test a 110V circuit with it.

Fig. 2.9 Do-it-Yourself Test Light

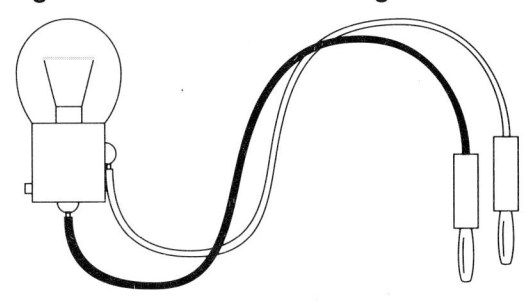

The second tool is similar but produces a noise instead of a light. As in Figure 2.10, solder test leads to a 3V–16V piezoelectric buzzer, which can be found at an electrical or radio shop for under £10.

If you want to get fancy, assemble both the light and the buzzer in a small box with a switch that allows you to use either the light, the buzzer, or both, simultaneously.

Fig. 2.10 Do-it-Yourself Test Buzzer

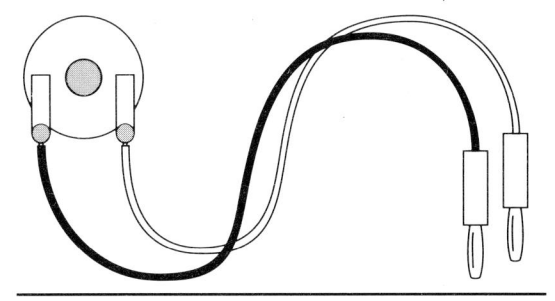

When connected to 12 volts, the bulb will glow brightly. If the voltage is low, the bulb will glow, but dimly. If there is no voltage, the bulb will not glow. Similarly, at 12 to 16 volts, the buzzer will screech; at 3 to 12 volts, the buzzer will sound fainter; at less than 3 volts, the buzzer will not sound at all. In a noisy environment, the light works best. In bright sunlight, the buzzer is best.

Fig. 2.11 Interchangeable Test Lead Tips

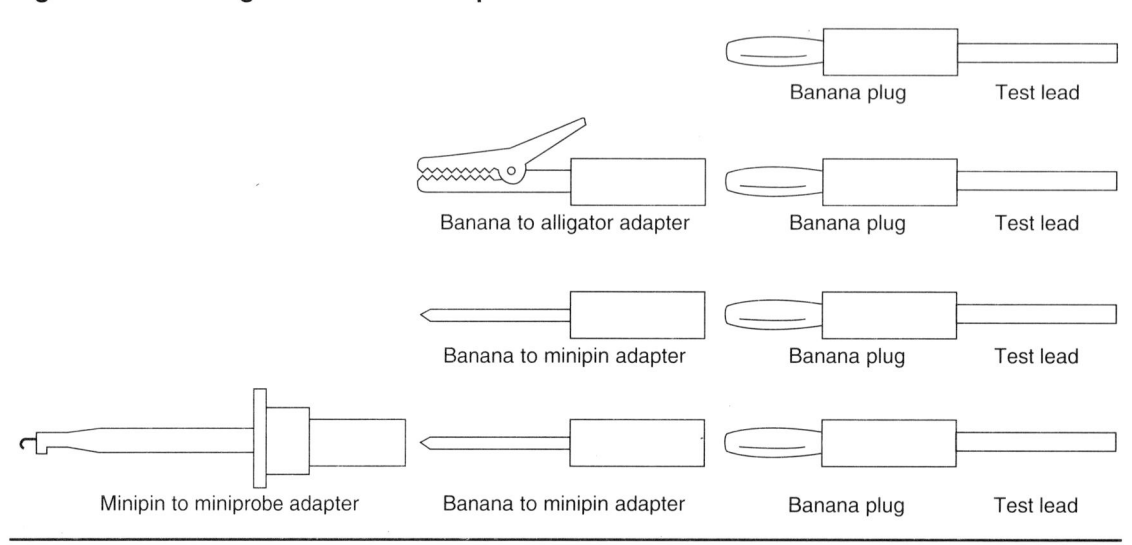

Next pick your tips. I find a set of interchangeable tips, as shown in Figure 2.11, very useful. Permanently attached to the test leads are banana plugs. These can be plugged into banana-to-alligator adapters, banana-to-minitip adapters, and minitip-to-miniprobe adapters. I choose the adapters based on wire size and whether I'm using one hand or two. Also handy is a single 50-foot extension lead with male and female banana plugs, so that I can extend one test lead the length of a boat or a mast.

TROUBLESHOOTING WITH TESTERS

Multimeters, test lights, and test buzzers are all useful in troubleshooting circuits. Only where a precise voltage or a precise resistance is needed will the multimeter be more useful than the simpler light or buzzer, however. For simplicity, the examples and illustrations that follow will show only the simple test light. Just remember that where the test light is on, the buzzer would sound, and the multimeter would show a voltage, but where the test light is off, the buzzer would be silent, and the multimeter would show no or low voltage.

Figure 2.12 (next page) shows a simple cabin light circuit. The positive side of battery 1 is connected to terminal 1 of the battery-select switch. The common terminal of the battery switch feeds the positive bus bar in the distribution panel. The cabin light circuit branches at the "cabin lights" circuit breaker (or fuse) connected to the positive bus and then runs out of the panel to the cabin lights, which are connected as parallel loads.

At the light fixture, the positive wire feeds the on-off switch, which then controls the bulb. The other terminal of the bulb connects to the negative wire, which runs back to the negative bus in the distribution panel and the negative terminal of the battery, completing the circuit.

DC Measurements

Fig. 2.12 A Simple Cabin Light Circuit

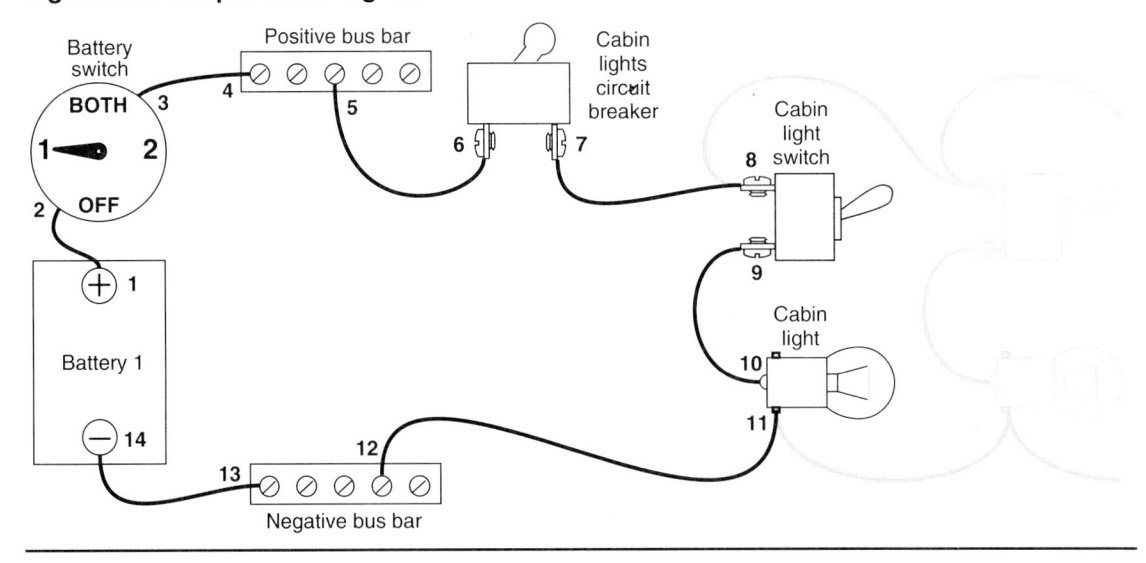

Figure 2.13 shows the same cabin light circuit in the form of a wiring diagram, using the standard component symbols listed in the Appendix. Note that the circuit load consists of lamps, which are nothing more than resistances that glow white hot. We could equally well have shown the load as parallel resistors, as in previous examples. In both Figures 2.12 and 2.13, fourteen points to which we could connect test leads are numbered. As we troubleshoot the circuit, we will connect our test light to pairs of these points to see whether voltage is present.

Fig. 2.13 Cabin Light Wiring Diagram

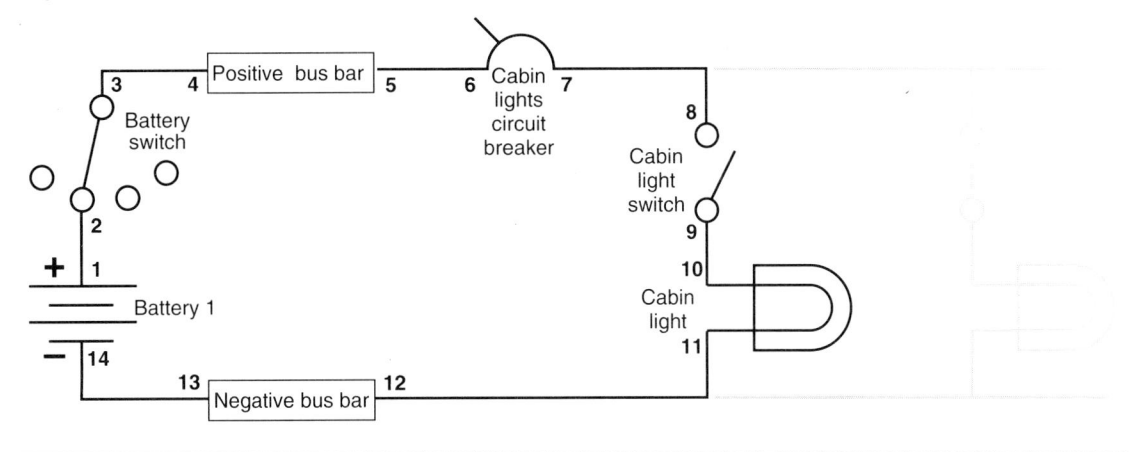

Fig. 2.14 A Circuit with No Faults

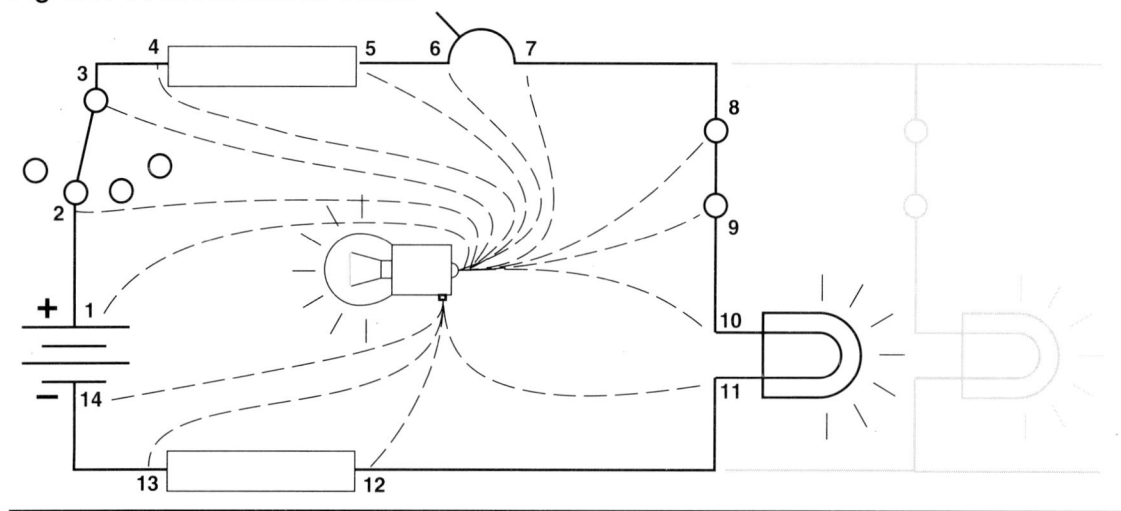

Turn all circuit switches to their on positions. The cabin lamps light up, meaning there is nothing wrong with the circuit. Since the wire and switches are designed to have near-zero resistance, we expect there to be no voltage drop at points 1–10.

There should also be no voltage change from points 11–14. With one test lead on any of points 1–10 and the other lead on points 11–14, the test light should light, but with both leads on either the positive or negative side, the test light should not light.

Fig. 2.15 Finding a Burned-out Lamp

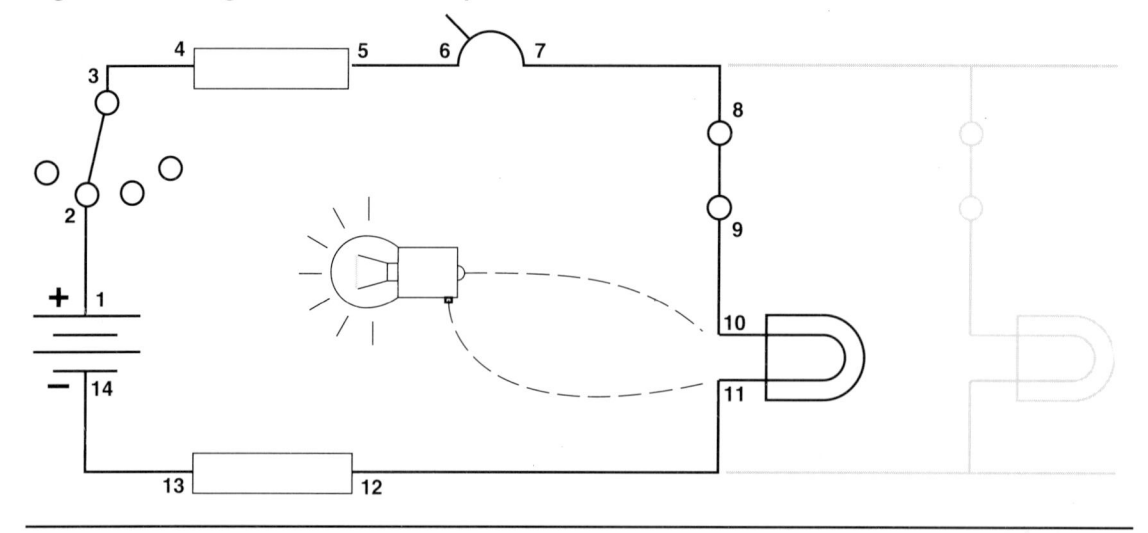

DC Measurements

In Figure 2.15 (previous page) we investigate a cabin lamp that will not light. All of the switches in the circuit are on, yet the light remains off. Furthermore, all of the other cabin lights in the same circuit do work.

We could start testing at points 1 and 14 and work our way toward the light. If we do, we'll find that the test lamp lights at every point, just as it did with the previous example of a normal circuit. If we suspect a burned-out bulb, however, we can save a lot of time by applying the test leads to points 10 and 11 immediately and discover that the circuit is OK all the way to the bulb holder.

At this point I'd simply replace the bulb. If you want to be sure it's the bulb and not the bulb holder, however, get out your multimeter and measure the resistance between the bulb contacts. If the multimeter reads infinite ohms, you know you have the culprit—a burned-out filament.

In Figure 2.16, we uncover a broken switch in the cabin light. We start as in the previous example with a cabin light that will not light up with all switches in the on position.

We suspect that the bulb has burned out, so we place our test lamp leads between points 10 and 11. The test lamp does not light. We therefore know that 12 volts is not reaching point 10. Next we place the test leads between 8 and 11. Now the test lamp lights up. The problem must be either in the switch or the short wire between the switch and the bulb holder.

We place the test leads across 8 and 9. Now both the test lamp and the cabin light glow dimly. What's going on? Our test lamp has bridged the broken switch, but acts like a load in series with the cabin light. This reduces the current and brightness of both bulbs. The bulb is OK, but the light switch must be replaced.

Fig. 2.16 Finding a Defective Switch

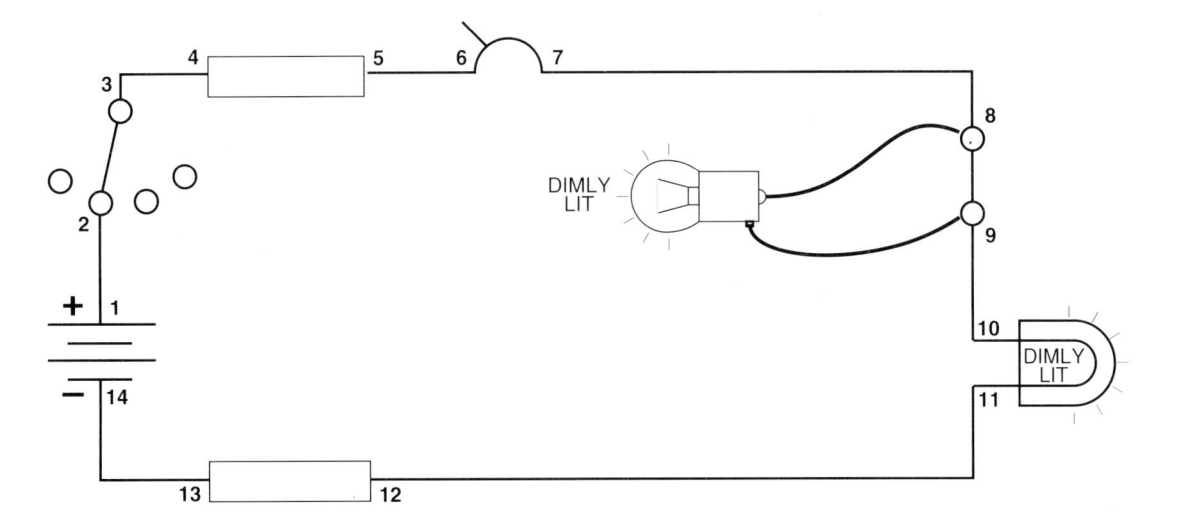

Fig. 2.17 Use of the Multimeter

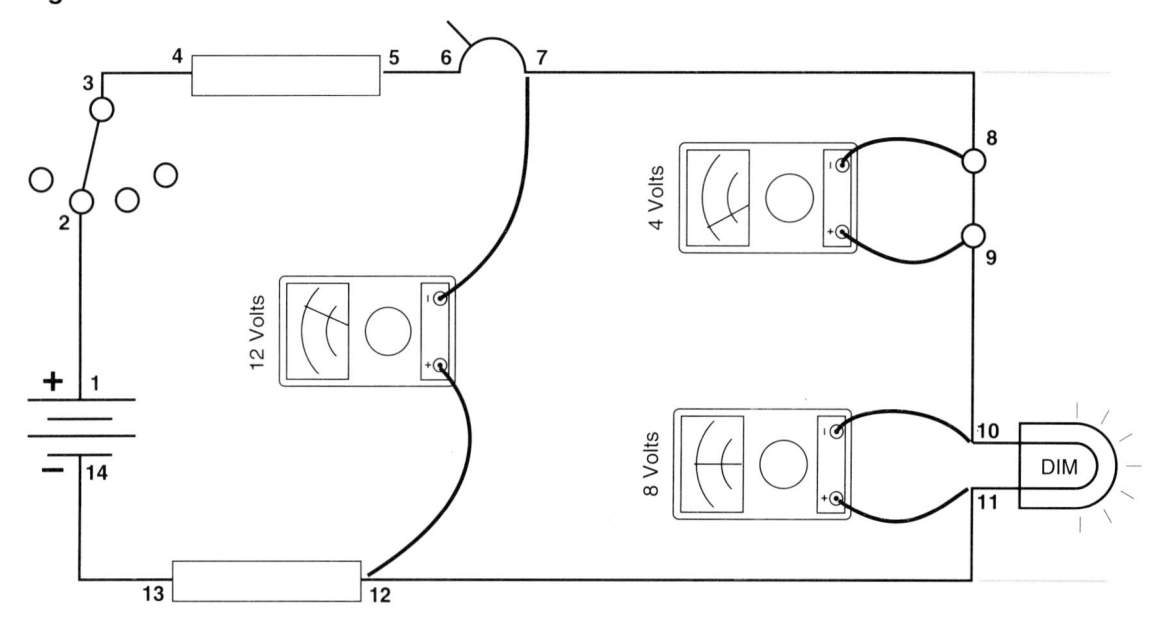

In the previous two examples, a component in the circuit had failed, resulting in an open circuit and zero current.

In Figure 2.17, we know the circuit is closed because the lamp is lit. But the lamp is dim. This is a very familiar phenomenon with flashlights—the light dims, but when we shake or hit the case the light becomes bright again.

The problem is due to poor contact. In a boat, poor contact is usually caused by corrosion of switch contacts or connectors. We will use this example to demonstrate the use of the multimeter.

Just to be sure our battery isn't low, we measure between points 7 and 12, which are easily accessed behind the distribution panel. The meter reads 12 volts, so we know the battery is charged, and the circuit is OK up to the point where it leaves the panel for its run to the cabin lights.

Next, we try the other cabin lights in the circuit. They light normally, so we know our problem lies inside the dim light fixture. We remove the fixture base, exposing the internal switch and lamp holder wiring. We measure the voltage across the lamp itself, points 10 and 11—the meter reads only 8 volts. Next, we measure the voltage across the switch, points 8 and 9 —the meter reads 4 volts.

We have found the missing electrons. The bad switch contacts are a resistance in series with the lamp, resulting in a voltage drop. In fact, one-third of the power in the circuit is being consumed within the switch, which is hot to the touch.

DC Measurements

If we suspected internal resistance in the switch, why didn't we simply place the multimeter in the ohms mode and measure the resistance of the switch directly between points 8 and 9?

We could have, provided (*and this is an extremely important provided*) we opened the circuit by turning off either the battery switch or the circuit breaker.

If we tried measuring the resistance without opening the circuit, the 12-volt battery would still be in the circuit. Figure 2.4 showed that an ohmmeter consisted of a delicate 50µA ammeter in series with an internal resistor and 1.5-volt battery. By placing the ohmmeter circuit in series with the cabin light circuit, we have effectively added or subtracted (depending on polarity) the 12-volt battery from the 1.5-volt battery. In the best case, the resistance reading will be grossly in error. At worst, the 50µA ammeter will be burned out.

In general, to measure the resistance of a circuit component, remove the component from the circuit by disconnecting one of its leads. Never try to measure resistance in a circuit with a live voltage.

A similar caution applies to measuring current in a circuit directly with a multimeter. Many multimeters are designed to measure currents of up to 250mA (0.25 amps). Others contain an internal shunt that allows measurements up to 10 amps. Make sure the current in a circuit is less than the maximum your meter can handle. Otherwise, you may blow the fuse or, worse, the meter itself.

A common accident is to think you are measuring a voltage when, in fact, the multimeter is in the Amps position. The result is the same—something will blow.

PRACTICE PROBLEMS

Table 2.2 below is intended to give you practice troubleshooting a circuit. First, cover column three, "Likely Cause." Then, referring to Figure 2.12, see if you can guess the cause of the problem, given the symptons listed in columns one and two. Column three lists my best guesses.

Table 2.2 Symptoms and Causes

Test Light ON Between	Test Light OFF Between	Likely Cause
—	1 and 14	Dead battery
1 and 14	2 and 14	Positive battery cable
2 and 14	3 and 14	Battery switch off or defective
3 and 14	4 and 14	Bad connection or broken cable between battery switch and positive bus
6 and 14	7 and 14	Breaker off, defective breaker, or blown fuse
7 and 14	8 and 14	Broken wire from breaker to light switch
8 and 14	9 and 14	Switch off or defective
9 and 14	10 and 14	Broken wire between light switch and lamp holder
10 and 14	11 and 14	Burned-out lamp or poor contact between bulb and holder
10 and 14	10 and 13	Negative battery cable
10 and 13	10 and 11	Bad connection at negative bus or broken wire from bus to bulb holder

3 BATTERIES

What is a Battery? 30

A Few Messy Details 33

Electrical Model of the Battery 34

Monitoring Batteries 36

Discharge Characteristics 38

Battery Discharge Ratings 40

Charging Characteristics 41

Charging Recommendations 42

Choices 44

Sizing Storage Batteries 45

Series or Parallel? 49

Installation 50

BMEA Standards 51

Except for the diesel engine, the greatest mystery to most boaters is the black box called the ship's battery.

What is a battery? Exactly what is going on inside that black box? In this chapter, you'll find the simple answers and *a few messy details* as well.

Although it is more complex than simple conductors and resistors, it is useful to have an *electrical model of the battery.*

Monitoring batteries is the key to performance. Monitoring the discharge/charge cycle requires an understanding of *discharge characteristics, battery-discharge ratings,* and *charging characteristics.* You'll discover that *charging recommendations* vary between battery types.

In selecting batteries for your boat, you have several *choices.* In addition, you have to *size the batteries* to your load and decide whether to install multiple batteries in *series or* in *parallel.*

Safe *installation* involves electrical and mechanical considerations. Both of which are covered by *BMEA standards.*

Probably no aspect of a boat is less well understood by its owner than its batteries. The perceptions we hold of these mysterious boxes have been formed by perhaps a high school chemistry course, experience with our own boats and automobiles, and, unfortunately, a barrage of advertising hype.

As with most of today's mass marketed products, engineering has taken a back seat to marketing. Meaningful specifications and instructions have been replaced by words such as "heavy-duty," "marine-grade," "deep-cycle," and "die-hard." Some manufacturers have gone so far as to promise boating Nirvana—a world where you can stick a battery anywhere in your boat and never give it another thought.

This is most unfortunate because (1) it is not true, and (2) nothing is more important to today's cruising boat than an adequate and reliable 12-volt system. Without a reliable source of 12 volts, most of us would have no lighting, refrigeration, navigation, or communication. In fact, we couldn't even start our engines.

This chapter explains what you need to know in order to select and then maintain the batteries that are the heart of your boat's electrical system.

WHAT IS A BATTERY?
To read Madison Avenue's revised history, one would think that today's batteries represent recent technological breakthroughs. The truth is that the chemistry of Thomas Edison's batteries of 100 years ago is identical to the chemistry of today's batteries. But what about the new, sealed, gelled-cell batteries you can store under your bunk? You are right—they are newer. They were patented in 1933.

Most of what you need to know about lead-acid batteries can be observed in a simple galley experiment. All you need is a glass containing a cup of battery acid (borrow some from your battery, or buy a quart at the auto parts store), two lengths of lead solder (the type used to make electrical connections), two D cells from a flashlight, a battery holder, and a voltmeter.

Place the D cells in the battery holder as in Figure 3.1. Connect one length of solder to the negative end and the other length to the positive end of the battery holder. Do not let the lengths of solder touch, but dip their ends into the acid.

Fig. 3.1 A Galley Battery: Step One

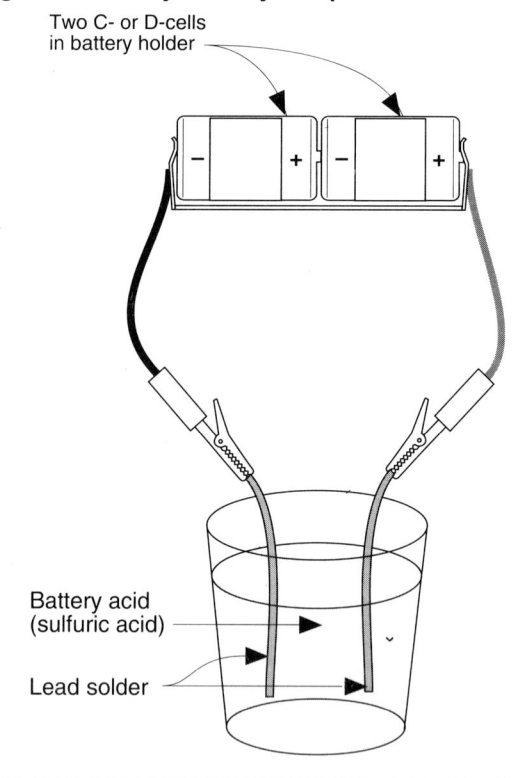

Two C- or D-cells in battery holder

Battery acid (sulfuric acid)

Lead solder

Batteries

Bubbles will form and rise in the acid. Soon you'll notice one of the lengths of solder turning brown. Remove the batteries and connect the voltmeter to the solder, as shown. The voltmeter will read about 2 volts.

Fig. 3.2 A Galley Battery: Step Two

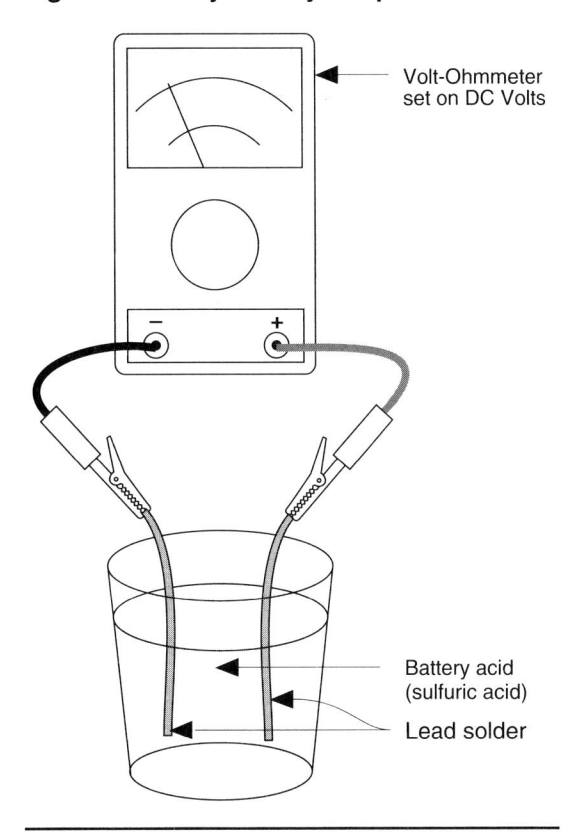

You have just manufactured and witnessed the operation of a lead-acid cell—the very same thing that is in your boat's batteries. Figure 3.2 shows how six such cells are connected in series to make a 12-volt battery, as well as the obvious derivation of the schematic symbol for the multicell battery.

Fig. 3.3 A Battery of Cells

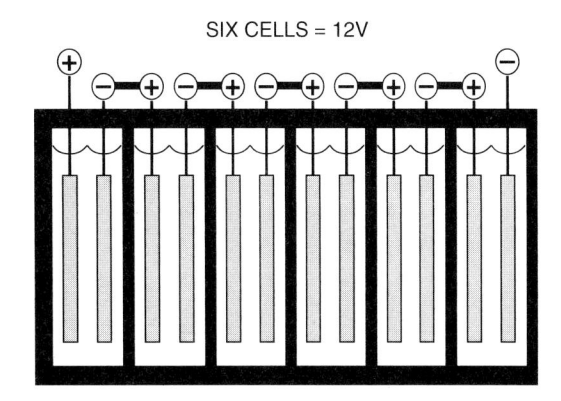

SIX CELLS = 12V

CIRCUIT SYMBOL FOR BATTERY
(number of plates variable)

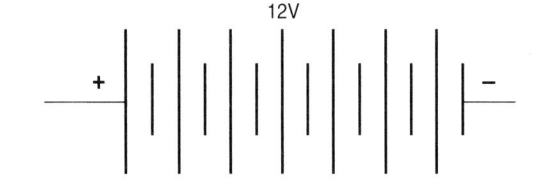

12V

WHAT IS GOING ON?

What you have just witnessed is the reversible chemical reaction found in all lead-acid batteries:

$$\text{PbO}_2 + \text{Pb} + 2\text{H}_2\text{SO}_4 \underset{\Rightarrow}{\overset{\Leftarrow}{=}} 2\text{PbSO}_4 + 2\text{H}_2\text{O}$$

(charging ⇐ / ⇒ discharging)

Figure 3.4 on the next page shows the four phases of a lead-acid cell charge/discharge cycle.

Fig. 3.4 The Charge/Discharge Cycle

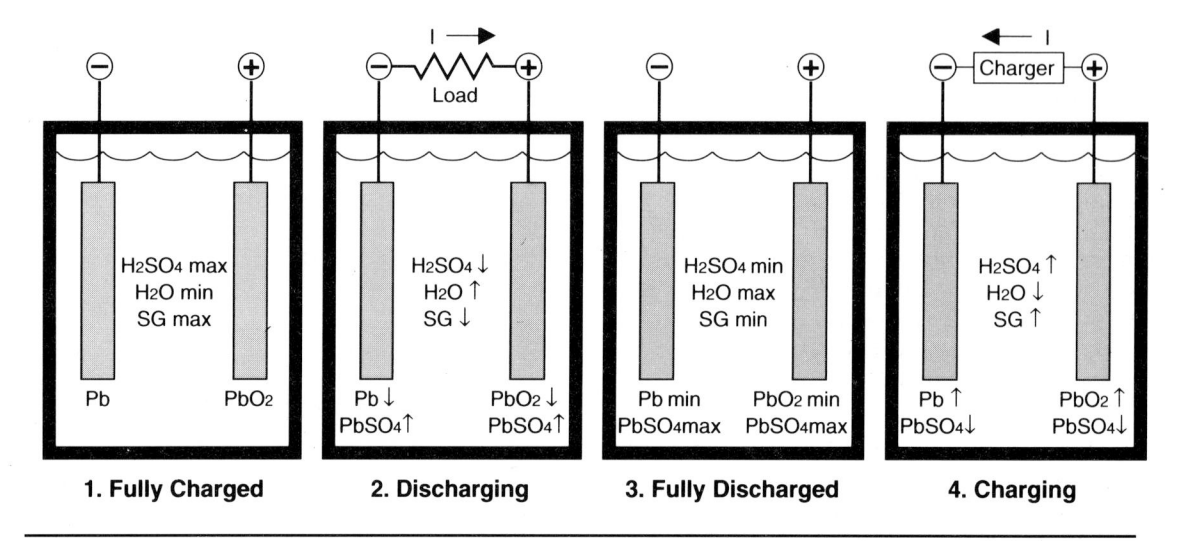

1. Fully Charged	2. Discharging	3. Fully Discharged	4. Charging
H₂SO₄ max H₂O min SG max Pb / PbO₂	H₂SO₄ ↓ H₂O ↑ SG ↓ Pb ↓ / PbO₂ ↓ PbSO₄ ↑ / PbSO₄ ↑	H₂SO₄ min H₂O max SG min Pb min / PbO₂ min PbSO₄ max / PbSO₄ max	H₂SO₄ ↑ H₂O ↓ SG ↑ Pb ↑ / PbO₂ ↑ PbSO₄ ↓ / PbSO₄ ↓

1. *Fully Charged.* In the equation, application of an external charging voltage has driven the reaction all the way to the left. The negative electrode has become pure lead (Pb), the positive electrode is now pure lead dioxide (PbO$_2$), and the sulfuric acid electrolyte (H$_2$SO$_4$ + H$_2$O) is at its maximum concentration.

2. *Discharging.* By connecting a load (shown as a resistor in Figure 3.4), we complete the electrical circuit, allowing the chemical reaction to proceed to the right in its natural direction. The H$_2$SO$_4$ breaks into H and SO$_4$ ions (molecules with either extra or missing electrons). The H is attracted to the positive electrode where it steals the O$_2$ from the PbO$_2$ and forms water, H$_2$O. The now free Pb combines with the SO$_4$ ions to form PbSO$_4$ in place of the PbO$_2$. At the negative electrode, SO$_4$ ions also combine with the pure Pb to form more PbSO$_4$. Thus, both electrode materials are converted to lead sulfate, PbSO$_4$, while the electrolyte loses sulfuric acid, H$_2$SO$_4$, gains water, H$_2$O, and becomes more dilute.

3. *Fully Discharged.* The cell is fully discharged when it runs out of one of the necessary ingredients. Either the PbO$_2$ has been totally converted to PbSO$_4$, or all of the SO$_4$ ions in the electrolyte have been used up, reducing it to pure water. In either case, PbO$_2$ and electrolyte strength have been minimized and PbSO$_4$ maximized.

4. *Charging.* By connecting a charging voltage to the cell, we drive it in the reverse direction of the reaction. Ideally, the negative electrode is restored to pure PbO$_2$, the positive terminal to pure Pb, and the acid electrolyte to its maximum strength.

Batteries

A FEW MESSY DETAILS

The good news is that the chemistry of the lead-acid battery is always the same and always simple. The bad news is that the physics, or the way in which it actually happens, is a bit more complex.

Figure 3.5 shows a cross-section of a small bit of a cell. As in Figure 3.4, both positive and negative electrodes are immersed in electrolyte. The reactive materials, lead and lead peroxide, are suspended on lead grids that serve to both support the materials and conduct electric current. So far, so simple. Now for the complications:

• Batteries in automobiles and boats are bounced around. In order that the plates do not touch each other and short circuit the cell, the many closely-spaced plates (electrodes) are interleaved with porous fiberglass separators.

• The lead that forms the grid is chemically and electrically compatible with the active materials that it supports, but it is not very strong. To increase strength, it is alloyed with either antimony (conventional wet, deep-cycle batteries) or calcium (sealed, maintenance-free batteries).

• When the discharge reaction starts, the lead sulfate is first formed at the electrode surfaces. As the reaction continues, the already-formed sulfate acts as a barrier between the electrolyte and the unreacted material beneath. This slows the reaction and limits the currents that can be drawn. The greater the surface area and the thinner the plates, the greater the possible current flow. Batteries whose primary purpose is engine starting have many very thin plates in order to provide large currents for short periods. The electrodes are also "sponged"

Fig. 3.5 Cross-Section of a Lead-Acid Cell

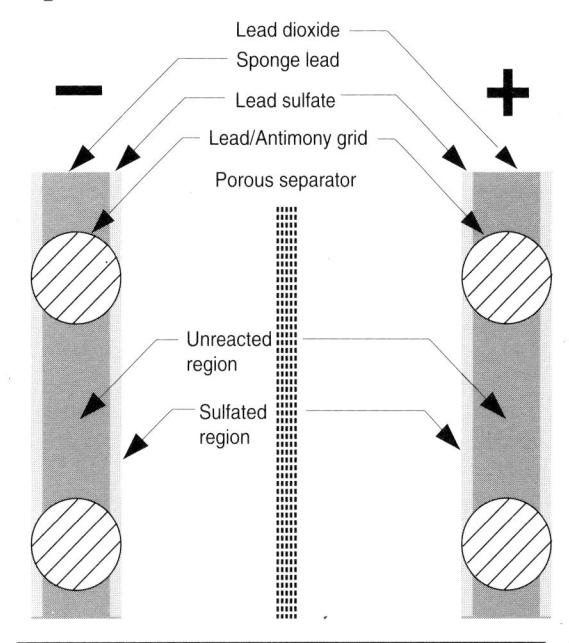

(made full of minute holes) in order to further increase their surface areas.

• But lead, lead dioxide, and lead sulfate are not of the same density. When one replaces the other, expansion and contraction cause stresses that tend to dislodge the materials from the grids. The result is that each time a cell is cycled, a small amount of lead sulfate is shed from the electrode and falls to the bottom of the cell. If enough material is shed, the accumulation at the bottom may short out the plates. The more complete the reaction (the deeper the discharge), the greater the loss. Batteries designed for deep-cycling have fewer but thicker plates.

• When a battery is fully charged, all of the lead sulfate of the positive plate has been oxidized to lead dioxide. What happens if we continue to charge (actually overcharge) the battery? Some of the electrical energy goes into oxidizing the lead of the grid, turning it, also, into lead dioxide. While good for battery capacity, lead dioxide has little mechanical strength, and the grid will ultimately fall to the bottom of the cell.

- The rest of the charging energy goes into hydrolysis—separation of the water of the electrolyte into H_2 and O_2—which we saw as bubbles in our galley experiment. Various tricks are employed in sealed batteries to recombine the gases into water, but, if overcharging and gassing are too vigorous, *all* batteries will vent the gas and lose electrolyte. Lost water can be replaced in a conventional wet-acid battery. In a sealed- or gelled-cell battery, it cannot.

- As we have seen, charging a battery regenerates the H_2SO_4 electrolyte. Pure H_2SO_4 is 1.83 times as dense as water. As the H_2SO_4 is generated, it tends to sink to the bottom of the cell. Since it is the H_2SO_4 that makes the electrolyte conductive, its absence at the top of the cell limits the acceptance of charging current. In a conventional wet-acid battery, acceptance will be low until gassing begins. The rising gas bubbles then mix the electrolyte, and acceptance increases.

- Gelled electrolyte batteries (also known as immobilized electrolyte batteries) capture the electrolyte in a gel, preventing stratification and increasing initial charge acceptance rates. "Starved electrolyte batteries" accomplish the same goal by limiting the electrolyte just enough to saturate the porous separators.

- Last, but perhaps most serious, is the phenomenon called *sulfation*. If a battery is left in a discharged state, i.e., with much of its electrodes in the form of $PbSO_4$, the initially fine and soft deposits grow into larger, harder crystals that clog the holes in the sponged electrodes. The crystals are relatively difficult to reconvert and so the battery is difficult to charge and displays reduced capacity. Vigorous overcharging and bubbling can break up and dislodge the crystals, resulting in recovery of much of the capacity. However, each time it is done, the plates shed more material and get closer to the end of their useful lives.

So you see that, although the basic chemistry of all lead-acid batteries is the same, there are enough variations in construction to allow battery company marketing departments a field day.

ELECTRICAL MODEL OF THE BATTERY

An ideal voltage source would supply unlimited current, with no drop in voltage. Considering the construction of the battery, as shown in Figure 3.5, it is obvious that the lead-acid battery is not such a source.

For current to flow, SO_4 and H ions must migrate through the electrolyte. Resistance to their movement manifests itself as an internal electrical resistance, R_i.

And when the battery is disconnected from an external circuit so that no current should flow, there is still the electrochemical force inside the cell ready to supply current to anything that might bridge the gap between the electrodes. Slight impurities in the electrolyte, as well as dirt on the surface of the battery, provide that path. They result in a parallel resistance, R_p, that acts to self-discharge the battery. This explains why you should never add anything but distilled water to your battery and why it is a good idea to keep its top surface clean.

Batteries

Fig. 3.7 Electrical Model of the Battery

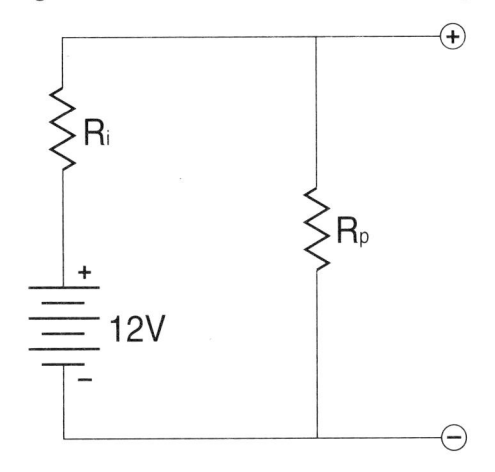

Fig. 3.8 Self-discharge vs. Temperature

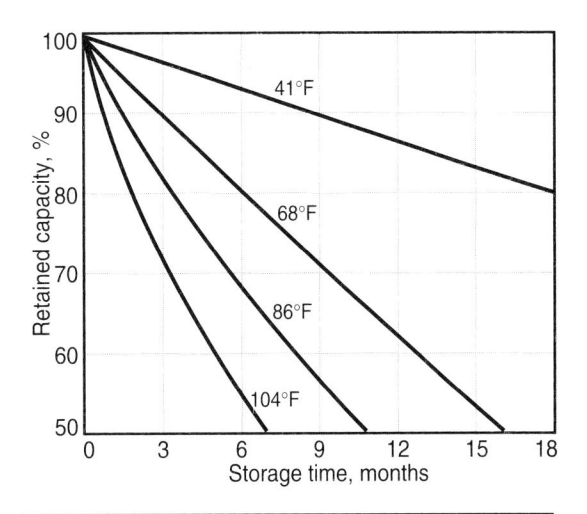

Figure 3.7 shows the electrical model of a battery consisting of an ideal voltage source with a series internal resistance, R_i, and a parallel self-discharge resistance, R_p. Since chemical reactions always speed up with temperature, both resistances decrease with increasing temperature.

R_i in a new battery is very small—of the order 0.01 ohms. It can be determined by drawing a known current and observing the drop in voltage at the terminals.

Example: We monitor the current drawn by a starter motor as 200 amps. As soon as we switch on the starter, we observe that the battery voltage drops from 12.5 to 9.5 volts. The battery's internal resistance, R_i, is then

$$R_i = V/I$$
$$= (12.5 - 9.5) \text{ volts}/200 \text{ amps}$$
$$= 0.015 \text{ watts}$$

The voltage must be measured at the battery terminals to eliminate the drop in the battery cables.

R_p is typically quite large—of the order 1,000 to 10,000 ohms. It can be deduced by observing the drop in battery stored capacity over time.

Figure 3.8 shows the self discharge of a typical new battery at different temperatures.

Example: At 68°F, the battery lost the first 10% of charge in three months. If this were a 100 Ah battery, it lost 10% of 100Ah, or 10Ah over a period of 90 days. Since there are 24 hours in a day, the discharge period was 90 x 24, or 2,160 hours. The average discharge current was thus 10Ah / 2,160 hours = 0.0046 amps. Using Ohm's Law,

$$R_p = V/I$$
$$= 12 \text{ volts}/0.0046 \text{ amps}$$
$$= 2{,}600 \text{ ohms}$$

The effect of temperature on R_p is evident from the discharge curves. Performing the same calculations as above, we find that R_p at 40°F is 7,900 ohms, while at 104°F it has dropped to 930 ohms.

MONITORING BATTERIES

Short of taking a battery apart and weighing the amounts of chemicals present, how can we determine the state of charge?

Recently, there have appeared expensive instruments (basically dedicated computers) that keep track of amperes flowing into and out of a battery. For now, we will consider the more basic methods that have been used since batteries were invented.

First, in what units do we measure the energy stored in a battery? As stated in Chapter 1, electrical energy is measured in watt-hours—the watts of power dissipated in a load times the duration in hours. Again, as in Chapter 1, watts equals current times voltage,

$$W = I \times V$$
where I = amps through the load
V = volts across the load

However, since the voltage of a battery is always near 12 volts, it is customary to drop the volts and refer to the amount of energy stored in a battery as Ah.

As an example, we charge a battery at 50 amps for two hours. We put 50 x 2, or 100 Ah, into the battery. Then we draw 5 amps from the battery for ten hours. We took 5 x 10, or 50 Ah, out of the battery. There are, thus, 100Ah – 50Ah, or 50Ah, still in the battery.

Battery electrolyte is a mixture of water (density 1.000 grams/cubic centimeter) and sulfuric acid (density 1.830 grams/cubic centimeter). Since the flow of electricity into and out of a battery results in either generation of sulfuric acid or loss of sulfuric acid, it is not surprising that the amount of stored energy in a battery is a direct, linear function of the density of the electrolyte.

The density of the electrolyte is expressed as its specific gravity, SG—the ratio of its density to the density of water.

SG is measured with a battery hydrometer calibrated for the range of electrolyte densities normally found in a battery, 1.000–1.300. Do not confuse it with an antifreeze hydrometer, which is designed to measure SG's of less than 1.000.

When a sample of electrolyte is drawn into the hydrometer, a float indicates the SG. However, SG must be corrected to what it would be at 80°F, in order to show the battery state of charge. Figure 3.9 shows the corrections to make.

Fig. 3.9 Electrolyte SG Corrections

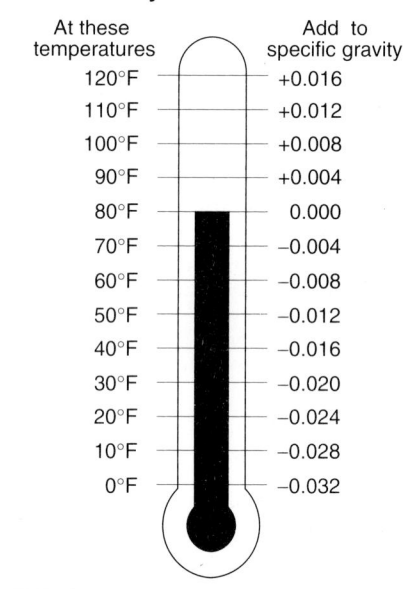

At these temperatures	Add to specific gravity
120°F	+0.016
110°F	+0.012
100°F	+0.008
90°F	+0.004
80°F	0.000
70°F	–0.004
60°F	–0.008
50°F	–0.012
40°F	–0.016
30°F	–0.020
20°F	–0.024
10°F	–0.028
0°F	–0.032

Example: A battery is located in an engine compartment. The temperature of the electrolyte is 95°F. The hydrometer reads 1.250. What is its SG, corrected to 80°F? Answer: 1.250 + 0.006 = 1.256.

Batteries

Fig. 3.10 Remaining Capacity vs SG

Fig. 3.11 SG vs Open Circuit Voltage

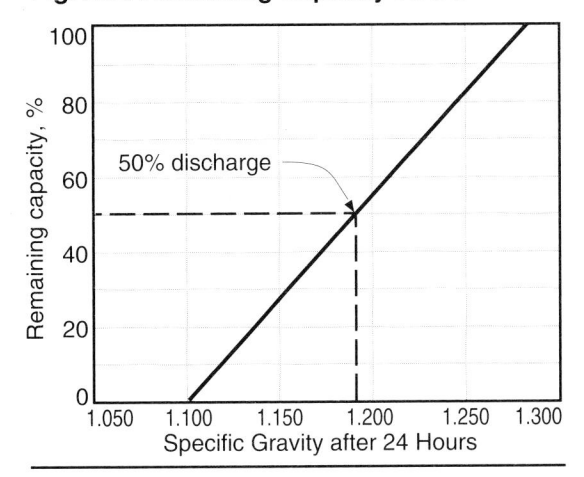

Figure 3.10 shows the relationship between state of charge and electrolyte SG for a typical new lead-acid battery. The form of the relationship is always correct, but:

1. The high and low SG end points are particular to the individual battery, depending on age, condition, and the preferences of the manufacturer. High SG is more often between 1.265 and 1.280.

2. The SG has been measured only after the battery has rested for a time sufficient for the electrolyte to become homogeneous through diffusion, usually considered to be 24 hours.

3. The SG has been corrected to the standard temperature of 80°F.

Battery manufacturers can make the high SG any value they wish. The tradeoff of using a more concentrated electrolyte is higher voltage and increased capacity versus shorter battery life. SGs are higher in colder climates. Most new battery high SGs fall in the range 1.265—1.280.

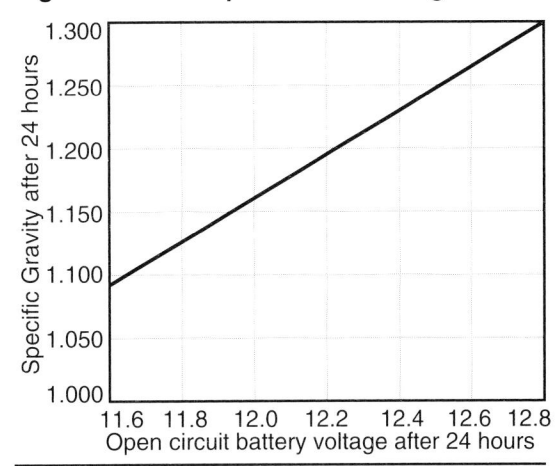

Figure 3.11 shows a second electrochemical relationship—this time between SG and voltage. The open circuit (no current being withdrawn) voltage of a single lead-acid cell is determined by the homogeneous, temperature-corrected electrolyte SG as:

$$V = 0.84 + SG$$

For a 12-volt (six-cell) battery the relationship becomes that in Figure 3.10:

$$V = 6 \times (0.84 + SG)$$

Using either Figure 3.10 or Figure 3.11 requires that we actually measure the SG of the electrolyte. This operation is messy, destructive of clothing, awkward in the spaces where batteries are usually stowed, and impossible with a sealed battery.

Fortunately, Figures 3.10 and 3.11 can be combined, resulting in the convenient relationship between state of charge and open-circuit voltage shown in Figure 3.12.

38 DC

Fig. 3.12 Remaining Charge vs Voltage

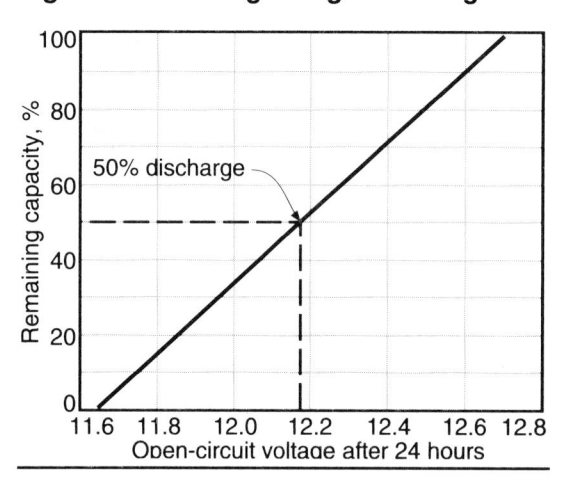

Figure 3.12 shows that, after 24 hours of rest, this battery would read 11.6 volts when fully discharged, 12.8 volts when fully charged, and 12.2 volts when 50% discharged.

If we can wait 24 hours, determining the remaining capacity of a battery is simple using an accurate voltmeter. The 24-hour rest period is provided by switching between two battery banks daily.

Why do we say the battery is fully discharged at 11.6 volts when the battery obviously has some amount of charge remaining? It is destructive to discharge a multicelled, lead-acid battery to 0 volts. With even small differences between cells, as 0 volts is approached, the stronger cells will drive the weaker cells into reversed polarity. Their grids will be damaged by being converted to $PbSO_4$. To avoid damage, "fully discharged" is defined as 10.5 volts at the 20-hour discharge rate. For example, for a 100 Ah battery, full discharge is the point where the closed-circuit voltage is 10.5V, while the current is 100 Ah/20 hours = 5 amps.

DISCHARGE CHARACTERISTICS

Earlier we noted the custom of measuring battery capacity in Ah. At small charge and discharge rates, the voltage drops due to internal resistance is small, and the number of Ah we can withdraw very closely approximates to the number of Ah we have put in.

When discharging at high currents, however, there is an apparent loss of battery capacity. As discharge current increases, the internal voltage drop through the battery's internal resistance increases, so the 10.5-volt cutoff point is reached sooner. Because of this misleading effect, cutoff voltage for starter-motor applications is reduced to 7.2 volts.

Fig. 3.13 Battery Discharge Characteristics

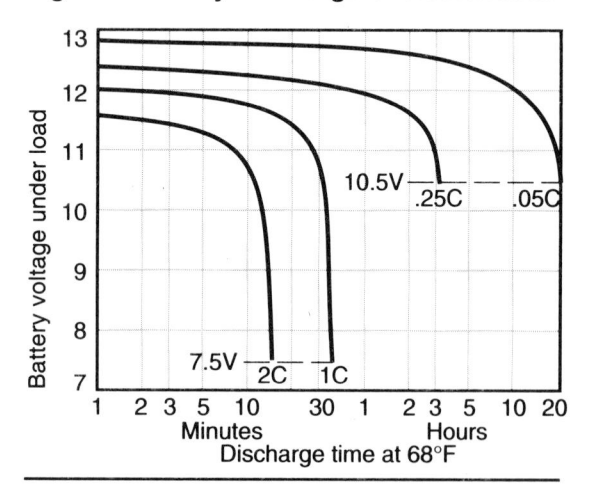

Figure 3.13 shows the discharge characteristics—voltage vs. time at different constant currents—for a typical new battery. Currents are shown as fractions of 20-hour Ah capacity, C, rather than amps, so that the curves can represent a whole family of batteries of similar construction.

Batteries

If a certain battery's capacity, C, is 200 Ah at the 20-hour discharge rate, then when discharged at a constant rate of .05C (.05 x 200 = 10 amps), the output voltage will fall to the zero-capacity cutoff of 10.5 volts in 20 hours. If the draw is increased to .25C (50 amps), however, it will fall to 10.5 volts in about 3 hours. In the first case, 10 amps x 20 hours = 200Ah. In the second case, 50 amps x 3 hours = 150Ah. Discharged at .25C, the battery seems to have only 75% of its rated capacity.

The apparent loss of capacity vs. discharge rate is clearly shown in the more general curve of Figure 3.14. Note, that if we discharge at less than the 20-hour rate, the apparent capacity is greater than 100%. If this doesn't surprise you, it shows that you understand the effect of battery internal resistance.

Fig. 3.14 Capacity vs Discharge Time

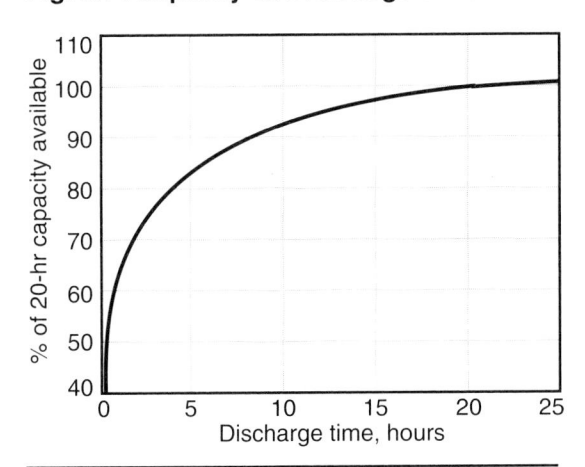

Since internal resistance is strongly affected by electrolyte temperature, one would expect a family of such discharge curves for different temperatures.

Figure 3.15 shows available capacity vs. both discharge rate and temperature. As in Figure 3.14, at 80°F, a battery discharged at five times the 20-hour rate (5 × .05C = .25C) gives us 75% of its rated capacity. At 0°F and .25C, however, only 45% of the rated capacity is available.

Fig. 3.15 Capacity vs Temperature

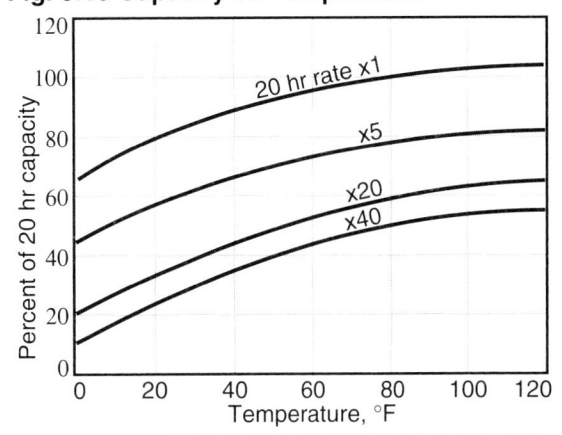

If you have a good memory, you may now be wondering how this loss of Ah squares with the principle that electrons are neither created nor destroyed. Where did all those electrons go?

They are still there in the battery—they just got left behind. With the heavy current, the electrolyte in the plates was temporarily depleted. If we allow the battery to rest a while, electrolyte ions will diffuse into the plates, and, when we start drawing current again, we'll find the voltage has recovered to more than 10.5 volts. This is a familiar phenomenon to those of us who have had to start balky automobiles in sub-zero weather. If we are, in fact, willing to withdraw the current at a much lower rate, we will succeed in retrieving nearly 100% of our invested Ah.

BATTERY DISCHARGE RATINGS

Because batteries are used in widely varying applications, several standard capacity ratings have evolved.

  1. *Ah at 20-Hour Rate*—amps a battery will supply for 20 hours at 80°F, before dropping to 10.5 volts, times 20 hours.

  2. *Cold Cranking Amps (CCA)*—minimum number of amps a battery can supply for 30 seconds, at a temperature of 0°F, before dropping to 7.2 volts.

  3. *Reserve Capacity*—number of minutes a battery will supply a specified constant current (usually 25 amps) at 80°F, before dropping to 10.5 volts.

The first two ratings are of most interest to boatowners. When running on battery power, the "house" batteries are usually required to run from the time the engine is turned off until it is turned on again. For a cruising boat, the period is likely to last from 16 to 24 hours, so the 20-hour Ah rating is an appropriate specification.

Extremely large currents are drawn by engine starting motors. You can obtain the CCA required by any engine from its manufacturer. Small diesels, in the 10- to 50-hp range, require from 200 to 500 CCAs.

Batteries

CHARGING CHARACTERISTICS

Charging a battery is the process of driving the lead-acid chemical reaction backward through application of an external voltage. To fully charge a battery, we must convert 100% of the $PbSO_4$ back to Pb and PbO_2.

The usual goal is to recharge the battery as quickly as possible without damaging the battery. Damage can occur due to overheating, excessive gassing, and overcharging.

Overheating. A battery should never be charged when its temperature is over 120°F. Internal heat is generated by the internal resistance of the battery. With a charging current of 100 amps and an internal resistance of 0.01 ohms, the heat generated would be:

$$Watts = I \times V$$

where: I = charging current in amps
V = voltage across R_i

so, Watts = $I \times I \times R_i$
= 100 amps x 100 amps x 0.01 ohms
= 100 watts

In a hot engine compartment, the internal temperature rise is on top of the ambient temperature of the space. Fast charging while the engine is running in the tropics is a good way to kill batteries.

Gassing. When the desired chemical reaction, conversion of $PbSO_4$ to Pb and PbO_2, cannot keep pace with the charging current, the excess current goes into hydrolysis, splitting the water molecules of the electrolyte into gaseous hydrogen and oxygen. Wet-acid batteries vent the gasses and so lose water. Through various tricks, including internal pressure, sealed batteries recombine small amounts of gas and prevent water loss. Even the best sealed batteries, including those with gelled electrolyte, can be overcharged to the point where they vent gas, however. No battery is totally immune to loss of electrolyte and subsequent loss of capacity.

Overcharging. A battery is fully charged when all $PbSO_4$ has been converted. Charging beyond that point is overcharging. As current continues to flow, gassing continues, as above, with the same destructive effect. Even more damaging, however, is oxidation of the positive grids into PbO_2, a relative nonconductor. The increase in internal resistance decreases both the battery's charge acceptance rate and its ability to supply large discharge currents.

Optimal fast charging of a battery (charging as rapidly as possible without damage) involves three phases (Figure 3.16).

Fig. 3.16 Optimal Fast Charging

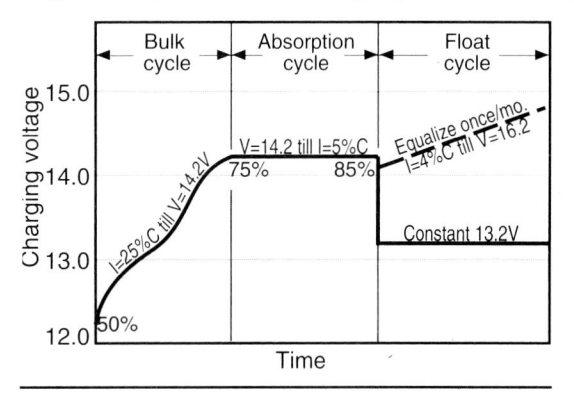

Bulk Cycle. If a healthy wet-acid battery is discharged more than 25%, it will readily accept charges of 0.25C or more, up to the point where it is about 75% charged. Gelled-electrolyte batteries do not suffer from electrolyte stratification and will typically accept charges of 0.5C.

Absorption Cycle. When the battery reaches 75% charge, charging voltage has increased to around 14.4 volts, and gassing begins. To avoid gassing, voltage is held constant at less than 14.4 volts, while the battery absorbs current at its own decreasing rate. When current drops to .05C, the battery is approximately 85% charged; at .02C about 90% charged; at .01C nearly 100% charged. How far the absorbtion cycle is carried depends on whether the engine is being run for the sole purpose of charging (.05C cutoff recommended), or whether the boat is underway or on shore power (.01 – .02C cutoff recommended).

Float Cycle. The final stage, provided the battery is still on a charger, is designed to hold the battery in its fully charged condition. If the battery is removed from all loads, such as in winter storage, the ideal float voltage is about 0.1 volts above its rested, open-circuit voltage, or approximately 13.0 volts. The float charger should be a pure DC source with no ripple. The common battery charger found in auto parts stores puts out unfiltered, rectified AC pulses, which appear to the battery as a lower voltage. If the battery is in a float cycle, but on-line so that current is occassionally withdrawn, either the charger should be capable of supplying the entire draw, or the float voltage should be increased to between 13.2 and 13.5 volts.

Equalization. Each cell of a battery has its own R_p, as well as slight differences in composition. In the conventional wet-acid battery, electrolyte SGs may change through sulfation, gassing, addition of water, or all three. As a result, after cycling many times, the charge states of the cells may get out of balance. Since the battery may only be discharged as low as the weakest cell, overall battery capacity is effectively reduced. Equalization is a controlled overcharge, during which all of the cells are brought back to their fully charged states. A constant current of .04C is applied for four hours, or until battery voltage rises to 16.2 volts, whichever occurs first. Overcharging forces all of the $PbSO_4$ in each cell to be converted, so that, except for material previously lost by shedding, each cell is restored to its original condition. After equalization, the cells should be topped off with distilled water.

Equalization will not bring a battery back to its factory-fresh condition, but it will maximize its capacity. Equalization should not be performed too often, since overcharging also oxidizes the positive plates. It should be performed whenever the cell SGs differ by 0.030, indicating a difference in capacity of 15% – 20%. Alternatively, for batteries cycled daily, an equalization schedule of once per month is recommended.

CHARGING RECOMMENDATIONS

Each manufacturer has a recommended method for recharging its products. Sealed batteries are less likely to need equalization because they ordinarily neither lose nor gain electrolyte. Furthermore, they would gas excessively and lose electrolyte if subjected to 16.2 volts. Constant-current charging is a possibility with wet-acid batteries because limited accidental overcharging will probably result only in loss of replaceable water. Sealed-battery manufacturers, however, fear such an accident and so recommend constant-voltage with limited-current charging.

Figure 3.17 compares charging recommendations of the manufacturers of the four most popular marine batteries—two wet-acid and two gelled-electrolyte.

Batteries

Fig. 3.17 Recommended Charging Procedures

WET-ACID

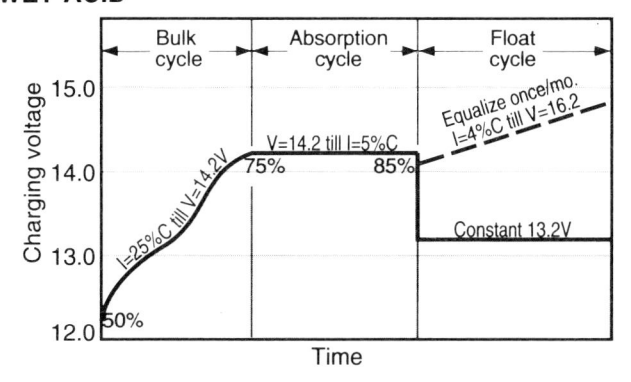

CHARGING ROUTINE

1. Bulk cycle: charge with constant current of 25% of Ah rating from 12.2V up to 14.2V.

2. Absorption cycle: charge at constant 14.2V until current falls to 5% of Ah rating.

3. Float cycle: maintain at constant 13.2V.

4. Equalization: once per month finish charge with constant current of 4% of Ah rating until V=16.2, or 4 hours, whichever occurs first.

GELLED ELECTROLYTE

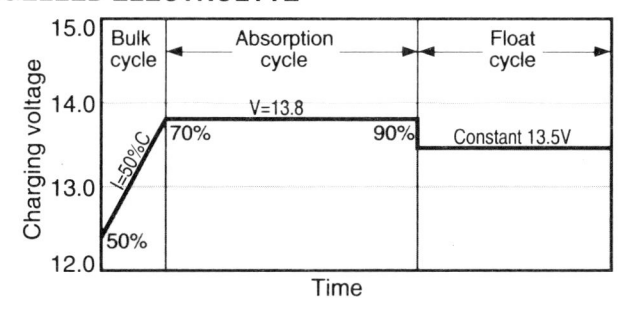

CHARGING ROUTINE

1. Bulk cycle: charge at constant 13.8V with current limited to 50% of Ah rating

2. Absorption cycle: charge at constant 13.8V for 1 hour or until current falls to 2% of Ah rating.

3. Float cycle: maintain at constant 13.5V.

GELLED ELECTROLYTE

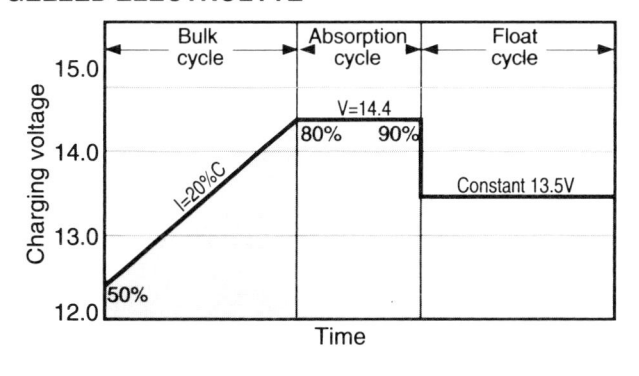

CHARGING ROUTINE

1. Bulk cycle: charge at constant 14.4V with current limited to 20% of Ah rating

2. Absorption cycle: charge at constant 14.4V for 1 hour or until current falls to 2% of Ah rating.

3. Float cycle: maintain at constant 13.5V.

CHOICES

Forget the marketing terminology you have seen in battery advertisements. Batteries can be divided into four general categories:

1. Conventional, wet-acid automotive
2. Maintenance-free automotive
3. Deep-cycle, wet-acid
4. Gelled-electrolyte

Conventional, wet-acid automotive batteries are characterized by low price, short warrantees, and electrolyte-fill caps. They are not recommended for marine applications.

Maintenance-free automotive do not vent gas unless seriously overcharged. They are designed for engine starting. The thin, porous plates that yield high currents do not stand up well to deep cycling. Because so many of these batteries are sold, however, competitive pricing makes them very attractive. Provided discharge is limited to around 50%, they are suitable for the seasonal boater who expects to replace his batteries every other year.

Deep-cycle, wet-acid batteries have fewer but thicker plates designed for regular discharge to 50% or less of capacity. The largest users of such batteries are not boats but golf carts and forklifts, requiring large currents and capacities, in addition to the ability to cycle many times. Such batteries have the maximum cycling potential and are ideally suited to cruising boats with heavy loads and long seasons, provided their owners are willing to spend the time monitoring and maintaining them.

Gelled-electrolyte batteries were developed for applications where acid spills and gas venting were prohibited, such as military tanks and wheelchairs. Recently freedom of location and freedom from maintenance have made them popular on boats. They can be deep cycled fewer times than the wet-acid, deep-cycle type, but they are less subject to damage, if left in a discharged state, and accept higher recharge rates. They are ideally suited to boats with large loads, long seasons, and owners who are unwilling to monitor and maintain wet-acid batteries.

Figure 3.18 shows the nominal sizes of the most popular batteries. Actual sizes vary, so assume an extra 1/2 inch all around, or get actual specifications.

Fig. 3.18 Nominal Battery Sizes

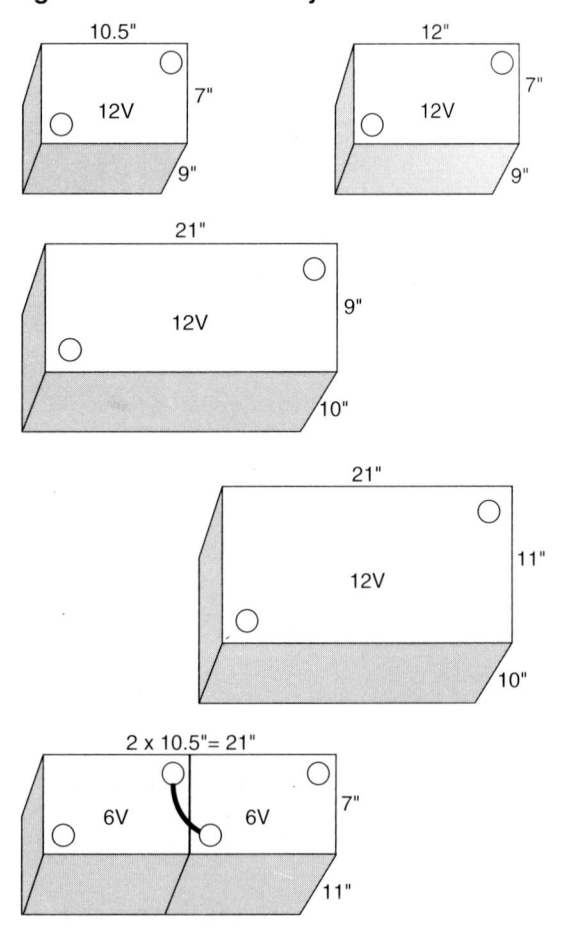

Batteries

SIZING STORAGE BATTERIES

The first step in selecting storage batteries is to determine the daily consumption of electricity in Ah. Table 3.3 lists equipment commonly found on boats. Power ratings can usually be found somewhere on the device, either in watts or amps. Add to or modify Table 3.3 to make your own table.

To calculate daily Ah requirement, first convert all ratings to amps by dividing watts by 12. Next multiply by the average hours of use to get Ah. Finally, add the Ah for all the devices for the total Ah/day.

For many of the devices, two ratings have been listed: 1) the typical consumption and 2) the consumption of the most efficient models. The table shows the total Ah/day for two cruisers: 1) with standard equipment and 2) with the most efficient models.

The boat with standard equipment consumes 100 Ah/day, while the more efficient boat consumes only half as much. The more efficient boat will require only half as large a battery system, or, alternatively, will go twice as long before recharging.

Table 3.3 Power Consumption for Cruising Boats at Anchor

Area	Device	Watts	÷ 12 = Amps	Ave. Hours per Day	Standard Amp Hr	Energy Eff. Amp Hr
Galley	Microwave (9 minutes/day)	550	45.8	0.15	6.9	6.9
	Toaster (5 minutes/day)	800	66.7	0.04		
	Blender (30 seconds/day)	175	14.6	0.01	0.15	0.15
	Coffee Grinder (15 seconds/day)	160	13.3	0.005		
	Refrigerator – 2" insulation	60	5.0	10	50.0	
	– 4" insulation	60	5.0	5.0		21.9
Head	Hair Dryer (2 minutes/day)	1200	100	.033		
Lighting	Reading – 2 incandescent 15-watt	30	2.5	2	5.0	
	2 halogen spots 5-watt	10	0.8	2		1.6
	Galley – 2 incandescent 25-watt	50	4.2	2	8.4	
	2 fluorescent 8-watt	16	1.4	2		2.8
	Anchor – manual 1-watt	10	0.8	14	11.2	
	automatic 10-watt	10	0.8	11		8.8
Fans	Typical 6", 100 cfm	12	1.0	5.0	5.0	
	Most efficient, 100 cfm	4	0.3	5.0		1.5
Entertainment	Stereo, 20-watt/channel	60	5.0	1.0	5.0	
	7-watt/channel	35	3.0	1.0		3.0
	Television, 19-inch color	80	6.7	4.0		
	10-inch color	36	3.0	2.0	6.0	
	6-inch color	20	1.7	4.0		3.4
	VCR, typical 110 volt-AC	28	2.3	1.0	2.3	
	12 volt-DC play only	10	0.8	1.0		0.8
				Totals	100.0	50.8

The next step in determining the size of storage batteries is to specify the discharge/charge cycle, i.e. how deeply we will discharge the batteries and at what point we will consider them recharged.

Discharge Depth. Figure 3.19 shows cycles vs. depth of discharge under laboratory conditions. The shape of the curves was established with one set of data each for wet-acid and gelled-electrolyte batteries. The golf cart curve was assumed to be of the same shape and adjusted to the single published 100% discharge point.

Fig. 3.19 Battery Life Cycles

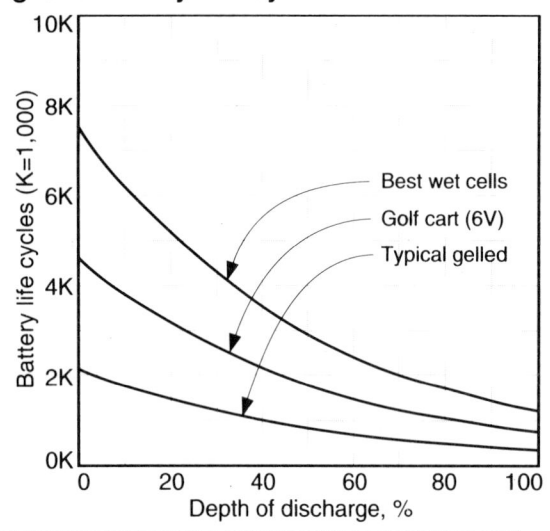

Since a boat is far from an ideal laboratory environment, you should probably count on getting about a third of the cycles shown. Thus, instead of 3,000 discharges to 50% for the best wet-acid battery, you should assume 1,000 cycles. Alternating banks daily, and recharging the banks in parallel in order to minimize engine run time, you can project 1,000 recharges x 2 days = 2,000 days, or 5 to 6 years.

On the same 50% discharge and two-day cycle, the best golf cart batteries should last about 3 years, and the typical gelled-electrolyte batteries about 2 years.

Figure 3.20 plots cost per kilowatt-hour versus depth of discharge assuming half of the life cycles shown in Figure 3.19. To calculate costs, it was assumed the batteries were size 220Ah and were bought for list price. The wet-acid and gelled-electrolyte batteries cost £270 each. The equivalent pair of 6-volt golf cart batteries cost £90.

Fig. 3.20 Battery Cost per KWh

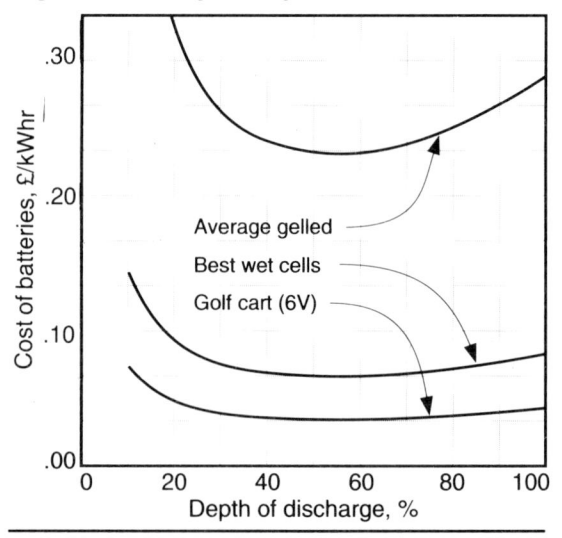

Figure 3.20 leads to two conclusions:

1. Considering the cost of the batteries alone, the optimum depth of discharge is approximately 50%, although the differences in the range from 30% to 80% are minimal.

2. Due to a remarkably lower cost, the golf cart battery is the most economical battery by far.

Batteries

Charge Cutoff. Figure 3.16 showed that charging current must be decreased once a battery has been recharged to 75% of capacity. To stop at 75% runs the risk of sulfation over the long run. If the engine is run for the sole purpose of charging, run time becomes uneconomical beyond 85% – 90%. When charging underway or with wind or solar, run time is not an issue, and recharge to above 90% is desirable.

We will assume a boat at anchor, a discharge limit of 30% – 50%, and a recharge cutoff of 85% – 90%. Since a battery is usually defined as "dead" when it has permanently lost 40% of its rated capacity, we will also derate our batteries by 20%.

Example: Our daily load is 75Ah. We decide to discharge to 30% and charge to 85%. The required derated battery size is

$$75Ah / .80(.85-.30) = 170Ah$$

Figure 3.21 allows easy determination of nominal battery size, given daily load and charge–discharge range.

Fig. 3.21 Battery Size Selection

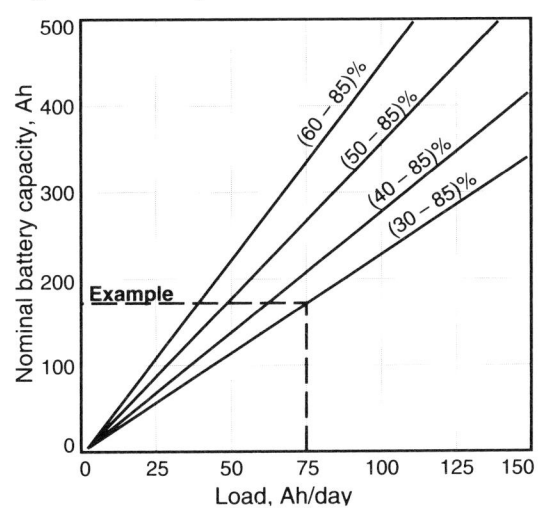

Alternator Size. When deeply discharged, batteries accept high rates of charge. Gelled-electrolyte batteries typically accept 0.5C (50% of capacity per hour), while healthy wet-acid batteries safely accept 0.25C. Once a battery has recovered to 75%, charge rates must be reduced in order to prevent gassing in all batteries, as was shown in Figure 3.17.

The total cost per kilowatt-hour produced and stored is the sum of battery cost (Figure 3.20) and engine/fuel costs. Figure 3.22 compares battery and engine/fuel costs.

The example is American and costs are given in dollars, but the purpose of the graphs is to compare different battery and charging systems.

The three curves show the dramatic savings that can be realized by matching the alternator to its load. Minimum engine/fuel cost is achieved by deep discharge of gelled-electrolyte batteries and recharge at 0.5C (220A for the example of parallel 8D batteries). For a pair of 8D wet-acid batteries, the matched alternator would be rated at 110A.

No discussion of charging would be complete without inclusion of solar and wind power. These will be fully discussed in Chapter 10, but costs per kilowatt-hour for solar and wind-produced power have been included in Figure 3.22 for comparison.

The solar system is assumed to cost $500 per 50-watt panel, last 10 years, and be used all year. The wind machine has a 5-foot blade, costs $1,500, lasts 10 years, and is used all year in 10-knot average winds.

Solar and wind costs per kilowatt-hour are independent of discharge depth, assuming the systems are matched to the daily load.

DC

Fig. 3.22 Costs per Kilowatt-hour Associated with Battery Power

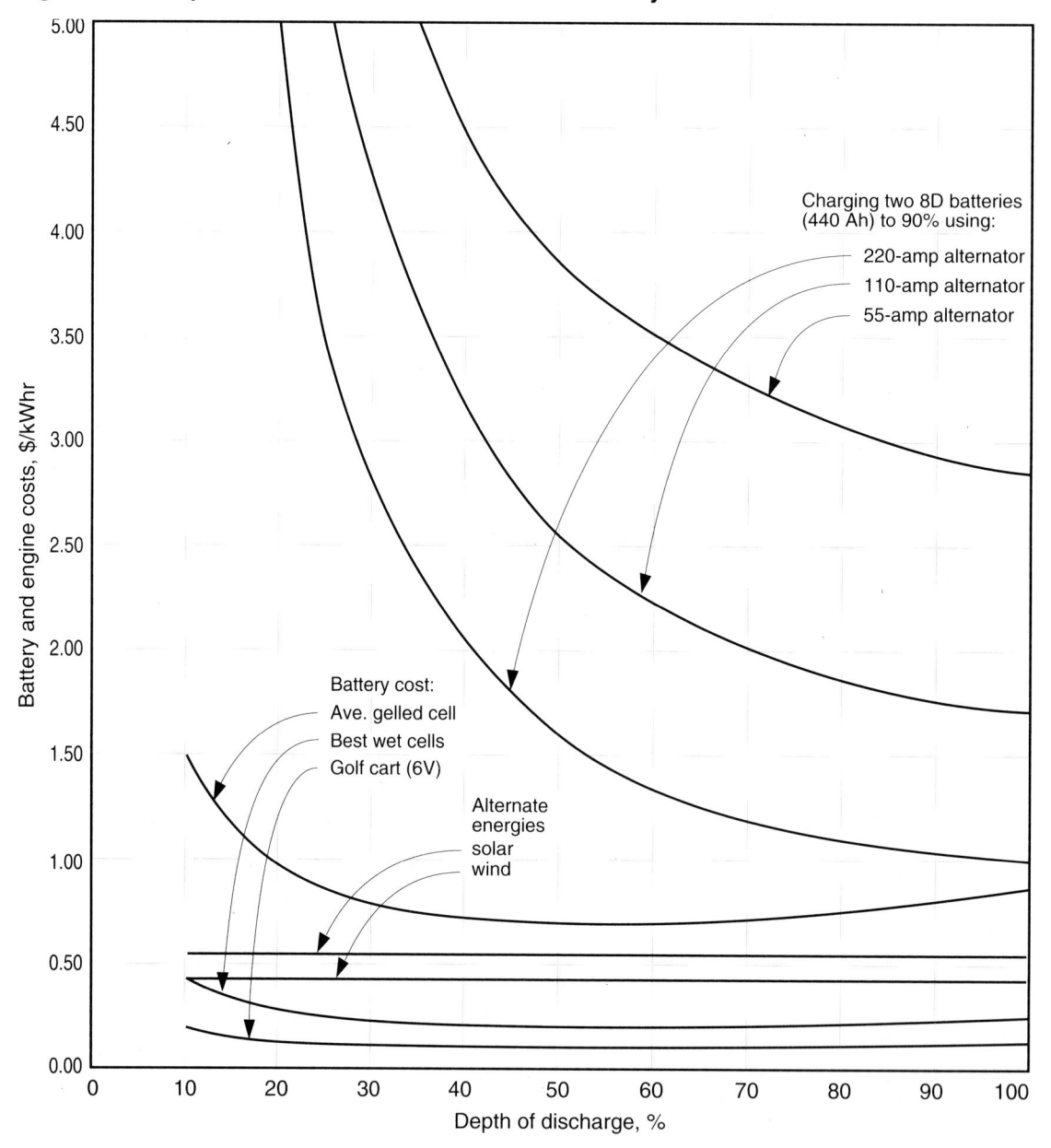

Batteries

SERIES OR PARALLEL?

A battery bank is one or more batteries, connected to act as a single 12-volt unit. It is wise to have two or more battery banks for redundancy. A common question is whether large banks should be made up of parallel 12-volt batteries or series 6-volt batteries. Also, should both banks be on, or should they be alternated?

First, how large a bank do you need? Some say that one's batteries can never be too large, but consider two facts:

1. Batteries should not be left in even a partially discharged condition any longer than necessary.

2. The cost of charging batteries is greater than the amortized cost of any battery. Unless a battery is discharged to at least 50%, recharging currents are limited and charge times elongated.

These are both reasons to size each battery bank to a single day's load. Even if your daily load is 100Ah, you can get by with an 8D battery (220 Ah) by cycling between 85% and 30%. An exception is the use of two 6-volt golf cart batteries, which cost less than half as much for the same capacity.

Otherwise, here are the pros and cons of series versus parallel battery connections.

Reasons series connection is better:

• Failure of a single cell will be apparent as a sudden 2-volt drop, but voltage will still be sufficient for engine starting.

• Failure of a single cell will not draw charge from the second unit.

• 6-volt golf cart batteries are the cheapest sources of battery power.

Reasons parallel connection is better:

• Assuming isolation diodes are used, the bad battery can be removed, and the remaining battery still has full voltage at half capacity.

• The strong battery cannot drive a weaker battery into cell reversal.

The second question was whether to leave the battery selector switch permanently in the "both" position.

Reasons "both" is better:

• Current drain from each battery is less, so less energy is lost to internal resistance. This is important when using an electric windlass or a microwave oven.

• Each battery receives only half of the charge currents, so both batteries can be charged in half of the time. If using solar or wind, charging near 100% capacity will less likely cause gassing.

Reasons switching banks is better:

• A catastrophic short circuit, or leaving the anchor light on for a week, will not result in total loss of capacity. The reason for two banks is redundancy.

• Without an expensive Ah meter, battery condition can be accurately measured only after a 24-hour rest period. Switching banks allows better monitoring of capacity and performance.

Recommendation: alternate banks daily. Switch to "both" when charging (including solar and wind), starting the engine, hauling the anchor with an electric windlass, or running other high loads, such as microwave ovens.

INSTALLATION

Building a battery box is an excellent way to learn basic fiberglass techniques. No curved surfaces are required, appearance is not critical, and the plywood core forms the mold.

Figure 3.23 shows the construction of a box large enough to hold two 12-volt 330 Ah to four 6-volt golf cart batteries (440 Ah total).

Batteries weigh about 0.75 pound and contain 2 ounces of acid per Ah. While you are making the box, consider the consequences of 330 pounds of batteries and 28 quarts of battery acid breaking loose in a storm. Also picture installing or removing batteries weighing up to 165 pounds each.

1. Mark cuts on 3/4-inch Ext. plywood.

2. Apply fiberglass to both sides of the plywood using epoxy or polyester resin.

3. Cut panels and apply resin to edges.

4. Glue and nail the box together.

5. Round all outside edges and fill inside corners with an epoxy paste.

6. Apply at least three overlapping strips at each inside and outside corner, making sure there are no voids.

7. Apply two complete layers of fiberglass cloth over the entire outside and paint with epoxy.

8. Fasten box firmly to boat with countersunk stainless, flat-head bolts.

9. Apply two layers of fiberglass to inside and paint with white epoxy.

10. Insert batteries using 1/4-inch nylon line, leaving the line for later extraction.

Fig. 3.23 Build a Battery Box

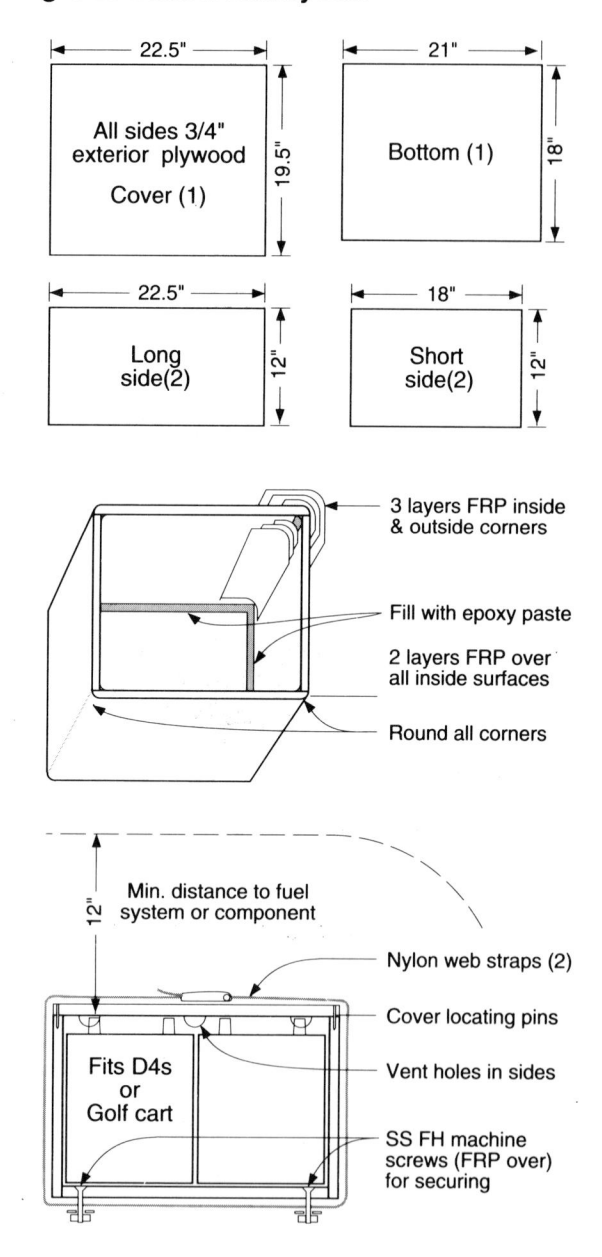

Batteries

Extract from the BMEA Code of Practice for Electrical and Electronic Installations in Boats.

1.13 BATTERIES

This section applies to lead acid batteries of the vented or valve-regulated type. Vented batteries are those that permit the gases evolved during charging to be vented to the atmosphere through the top of the battery. Valve regulated batteries (sometimes called sealed batteries) have a valve on the top of the battery to reduce the gas evolution by about 95%. The hydrogen and oxygen produced are recombined within the battery. Valve regulated batteries cannot be topped up as the electrolyte reduces.

These guidelines are not intended to cover power systems for electrically propelled boats.

1.13.1

a) To calculate the battery capacity required it is necessary to establish the likely current demand and its duration that will be required when the alternator is not in use. If the boat is to have only one battery set, then the capacity calculation must include sufficient power to start the engine.
The formula to arrive at the demand is: $1 = 1.2 \times (C/t)$
1 = Discharged current (amps)
t = Time stated by the manufacturers (hours)
C = Battery capacity stated by the manufacturer (Ah)
Generally when charging, the batteries will need 1.2 times the discharge rate, to return them to their fully charged state.
b) Each battery should be provided with a durable label bearing manufacturer's name, type number and battery capacity.
c) Batteries should be fitted so that they can be easily removed and the top of vented batteries should be readily accessible for checking electrolyte level.
d) Batteries should be installed so as to restrict movement horizontally and vertically. A battery should not move more than 10 mm in any direction when exposed to a force corresponding to twice the battery weight.
e) Batteries should be fitted in boxes or trays of non-corrosive material so that leakage of all the electrolyte from every battery in the box should be contained within the box to a level not exceeding 75% of the height of the box.
f) Batteries should be capable of an inclination of 45 degrees without electrolyte spillage.
g) All fittings should be corrosive resistant and treated with protective material such as petroleum jelly or silicone grease.

1.13.2

a) Batteries should be located where they are not exposed to excessive heat, cold, spray or physical damage.
b) Batteries should be installed, or protected so that metallic objects cannot come into unintentional contact with the battery terminals.
c) Batteries should not be installed directly above or below fuel tank or fuel fitters, or in the bilges.

1.13.3

a) Any metallic component less than 300 mm directly above a battery shall be protected with insulating material.
b) Battery cable terminals should not depend on spring tension for attachment to the battery terminals, but should be of the pillar bolt or double screw type. Aluminium road vehicle type terminals are not recommended.
c) Batteries should be fitted in well ventilated areas so that no build up of hydrogen gas can accumulate in any space adjacent to or above the batteries. If the area is not naturally well ventilated then an extractor fan should be fitted to remove hydrogen gas from the battery compartment.

d) Batteries connected to a charging device of more than 2kW output rating should be mounted in a battery box with sealed lid and separately forced or naturally ventilated.
e) Ventilated batteries should not be mounted under a bunk unless the battery box is sealed and fitted with ventilation trunking. This arrangement allows hydrogen gas to leave the compartment.
f) Batteries should not be mounted so that adjacent equipment is adversely affected by battery gas emissions.

1.13.4
a) Engine starter batteries should be located as close as practicable to the engine so as to minimise voltage drop. Any added distance should be compensated by increasing the cross sectional area of the conductors. Connections should be made using compression terminals.
b) Switches, fuses or other electrical equipment should not be mounted in a confined battery compartment or immediately adjacent to batteries within a machinery space unless ignition protected.
c) Light fittings within a battery compartment should be of a design suitable for flammable gases, i.e. ignition protection.

1.13.5
The charge current and voltage should be chosen to be compatible with the batteries. They must not exceed the manufacturer's recommendations otherwise damage to the batteries could occur.

1.13.6
The battery charger should be designed for marine service and capable of automatically charging the battery or batteries to the required level. Its rating should be selected by reference to manufacturer's recommendations.
The essential features are:
a) Automatic voltage regulation
b) Regulation of output current
c) The charger should be inhibited when there is no battery connected to the output.
d) No discharge with mains supply 'off'
e) Correct output voltage to be maintained with input varied due to supply volts drop.

1.13.7
a) It is preferable to consider a battery coupling switch between engine and service batteries system. This type of system should ensure that power is uninterrupted to vital navigation aids during engine starting. A make before break switch arrangement must be used.
b) Battery disconnection switches are normally inserted in the positive conductor. However they may be placed in the negative conductor, in which case the typical diagram would be amended. They should be located in a readily accessible position as close as possible to the batteries.
c) Battery disconnect switches should be capable of carrying the maximum current of the system including the intermittent load of the engine or generator starter.
d) If the battery disconnect switch is equipped with a remote control, it should also be capable of manual operation at the switch.

1.13.8
Suitable warning instructions on how to isolate batteries before working on them must also be placed in a visible location adjacent to the batteries.

4 ALTERNATORS

Rotary-Current Machine   54

Three-Phase Current   56

Diodes & Rectification   56

Controlling the Alternator   61

Type-P and Type-N Alternators   64

Powering the Regulator   64

Excitation   66

Bypass Controls   67

Troubleshooting   68

An alternator is a *rotary-current machine* that transforms mechanical rotation into AC current. The *three-phase current* produced by the alternator coils is *rectified by diodes* into DC current for charging the ship's batteries.

In order not to overcharge the batteries we need a regulator for *controlling the alternator*. Whether the regulator field-coil wire is connected to the positive or negative battery terminal determines whether it is a *P-type* or *N-type alternator*. The methods of p*owering the regulator* and supplying *excitation* current to the field coil vary as well.

Regulator *bypass controls*, allowing more rapid battery charging, are popular among cruisers.

Despite the plethora of alternator models, the basic principles and components are largely the same, allowing for a simple *troubleshooting* guide.

If you enjoyed making the galley battery in Chapter 3, you will certainly enjoy making the galley alternator in Figure 4.1. All you will need are an analog voltmeter or ammeter (a multimeter with many ranges would be best), a large steel nail or bolt, several feet of insulated copper wire, and a magnet.

Wrap half a dozen turns of the insulated wire around the nail and connect the bare ends of the wire to the meter. If you are using a multimeter, start with the highest amps scale. Hold the magnet as close to the head of the nail as possible without actually touching it. Now move the magnet rapidly back and forth, as shown in the illustration. The needle of the meter should jump back and forth across zero.

If the needle doesn't move, switch the meter to a lower amps scale. If the needle doesn't move even on the lowest amps scale, increase the number of turns of wire until it does move.

What's going on? As Hans Oersted discovered in 1820, an electric current is induced in a wire whenever the magnetic field around the wire changes. Our moving magnet induces magnetism in the nail. As the permanent magnet moves back and forth, the magnetism in the nail alternates in direction, so the magnetic field through the coiled wire alternates as well. The alternating field produces pulses of current of alternating polarity as shown in the graph at the bottom of Figure 4.1.

The scale of the graph is not important to our experiment, but you should know that the current is directly proportional to the strength of the magnetic field, the speed that the magnet is moved, and the number of turns in the coil.

Fig. 4.1 A Galley Alternator

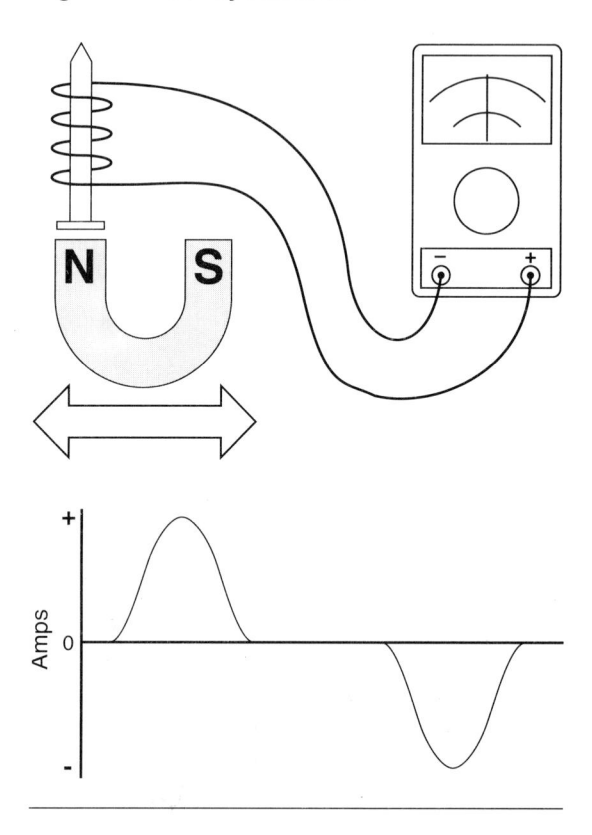

A ROTARY-CURRENT MACHINE

Instead of tediously passing the magnet back and forth across the head of the nail, we can make a rotating machine to do the same thing. Figure 4.2, on the next page, shows a straight bar-magnet pivoted about its center between two series-connected coils. The coils are wound in opposite directions, so that the opposite poles of the magnet produce current in the same direction. As the magnet turns, however, each coil sees alternating poles, so the current changes polarity as shown in the graph.

Alternators

Fig. 4.2 A Rotary-Current Machine

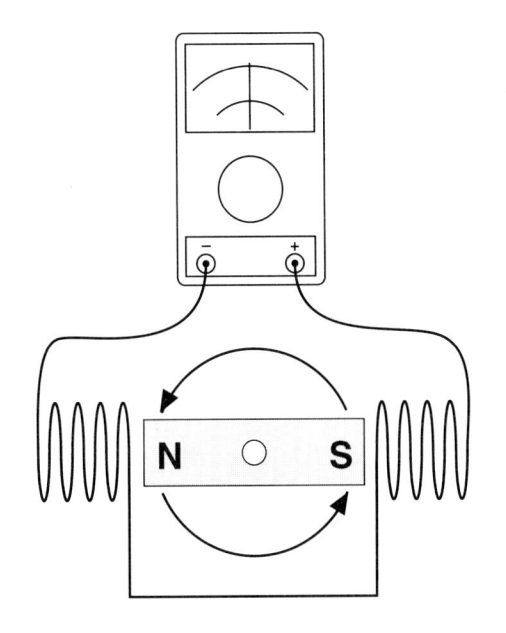

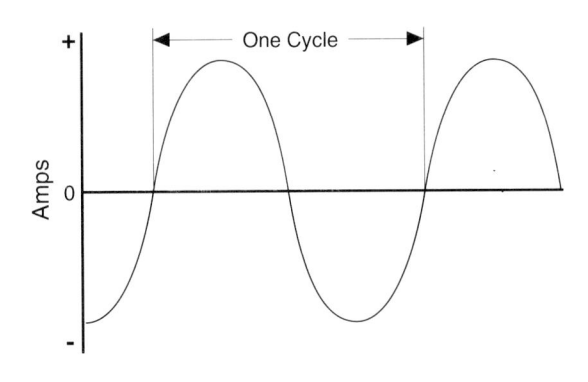

This type of current is called alternating current, or AC. Part II of this book deals with AC power on boats. All we need to know about AC at this point is that both voltage and current reverse, usually many times per second. One complete swing from plus to minus and back to plus again is called a cycle. The number of cycles per second is the frequency, measured in hertz (hz). Utility power in the U.S. is delivered at 60 hertz; in Europe, at 50 hertz.

We can make our rotary-current machine more efficient by placing more magnets on the rotating shaft, and by adding a corresponding number of coils of wire as shown in Figure 4.3. With three times as many magnets and coils, the result is three times as much generated power.

With three times as many magnet poles, each revolution of the shaft produces three times as many cycles. All of the coils still produce current in synchronism, however, so the forms of the output current and voltage remain the same as before.

Fig. 4.3 Multiple Poles and Coils

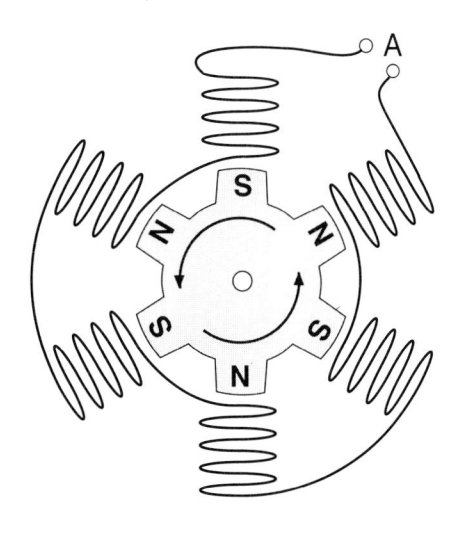

DC

THREE-PHASE CURRENT

Let's call the entire series-connected coil of Figure 4.3, coil A. Now let's add coils B and C, identical in form to coil A, but rotated one-third and two-thirds of the gap between the small coils of coil A, as shown in Figure 4.4.

Figure 4.4 Three Sets of Poles and Coils

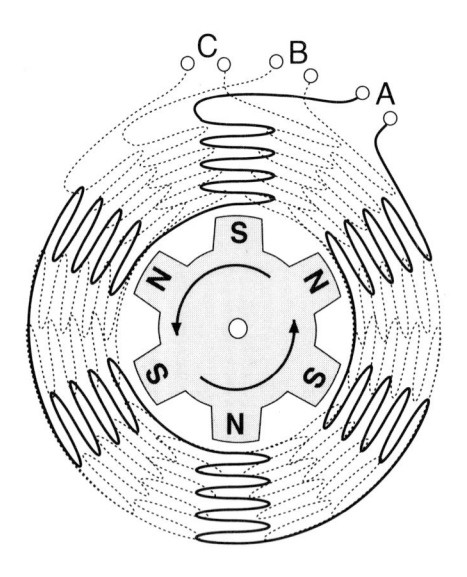

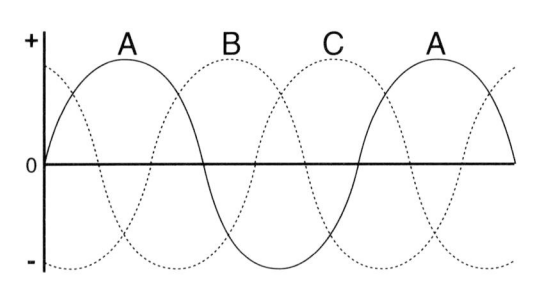

The poles of the rotating magnet will pass each set of small coils in the order: A, B, C, A, B, C, etc. The currents induced in coils A, B, and C will therefore be offset by one-third and two-thirds of a cycle as shown at the bottom of Figure 4.4. We now have three identical alternating currents, offset in phase by 120° (one complete cycle equals 360°). We call this *three-phase AC*.

Why would we want to complicate our rotary-current machine in this way?

1. We can triple power output without increasing the size of the wire in the coils.

2. It is easier to wind closely spaced coils than to increase the number of magnetic poles.

3. The three phases result in a better (smoother) output, as we'll see later.

DIODES AND RECTIFICATION

As we saw in Chapter 3, batteries produce direct current (DC), which is always of the same polarity or sign. In order to recharge batteries, we need DC. Our rotary-current machine is of no use in charging batteries or powering DC electronics unless we convert its three-phase AC output to DC.

Enter the diode. As its circuit symbol (Figure 4.5, top) indicates, the diode allows current to flow only in the direction of the arrow. If you like analogies, you can think of a diode as the equivalent of a check valve in a water-supply system, allowing water to flow in one direction but not the opposite.

Of course nothing is perfect, so we have to consider the limitations of the diode in real applications. All diodes have the following three ratings:

Alternators

maximum forward current—the maximum current in the forward direction

peak inverse voltage—the maximum voltage at which the diode will block current flow in the reverse direction

forward voltage drop—the voltage in the direction of the arrow at which the diode begins to conduct current

Diodes come in different sizes and shapes, depending on their intended uses. The top three (below the circuit symbol) in Figure 4.5 are signal diodes intended for low-current applications. The bottom two, with heavy metal cases, are rectifying diodes, which are used in high-current applications such as alternators.

A typical alternator diode might have ratings of 50 amps, 50 volts, and 0.6 volt.

Fig. 4.5 Typical Diodes

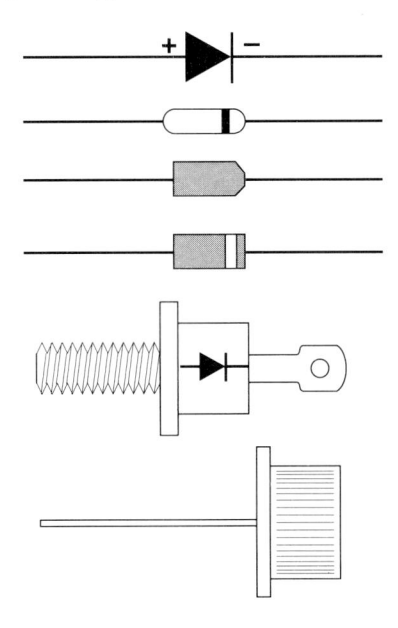

If you haven't put away your galley experiment, insert a diode into the circuit as shown in Figure 4.6. Now when you pass the magnet back and forth, the needle should deflect only in the positive direction. If you get a negative deflection, either the meter leads are reversed, or the diode is pointing in the wrong direction. As the current plot shows, the magnet and wire coil are still producing negative pulses, but the pulses are blocked by the diode.

Fig. 4.6 Effect of Adding a Diode to the Galley Alternator

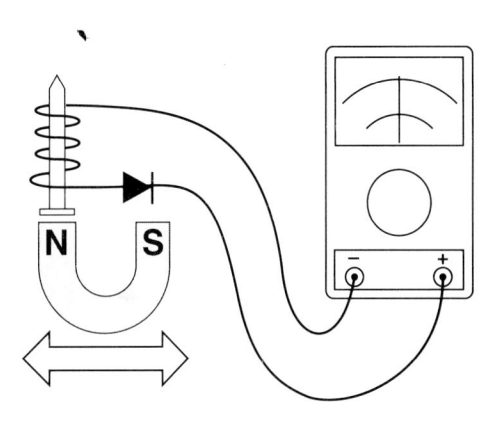

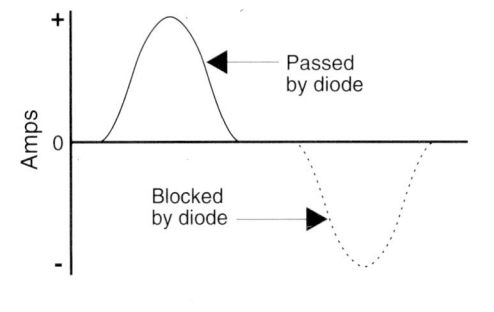

Figure 4.7 shows how a diode would similarly block negative current in our rotary current machine. The process of passing current of one polarity but blocking current of the opposite polarity is called *rectification*. Passing only the positive halves of an AC wave is called *half-wave rectification*.

Rectification would be twice as efficient if we could somehow pass both halves of the AC wave. This is done in Figure 4.8 by arranging four diodes in a full-wave rectifier. With a given polarity of current and voltage through the wire coil, two of the four diodes see reverse voltage and act as if they were open circuits.

Fig. 4.7 Half-wave Rectification

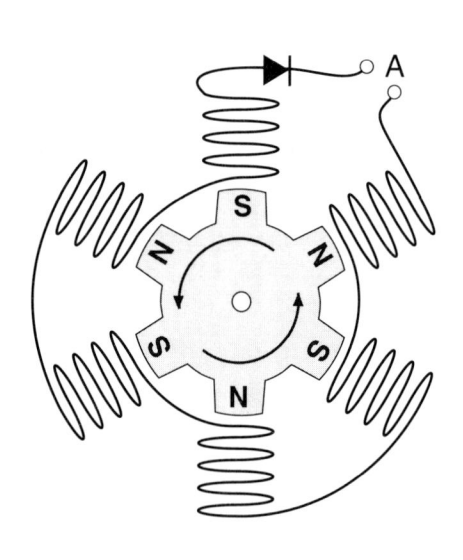

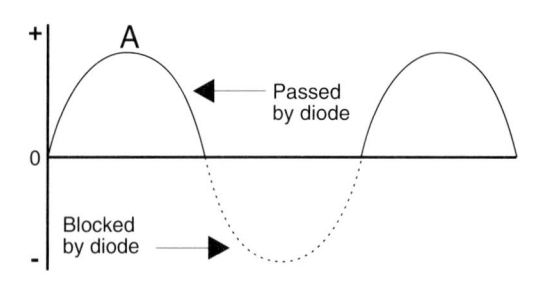

Fig. 4.8 Full-wave Rectification

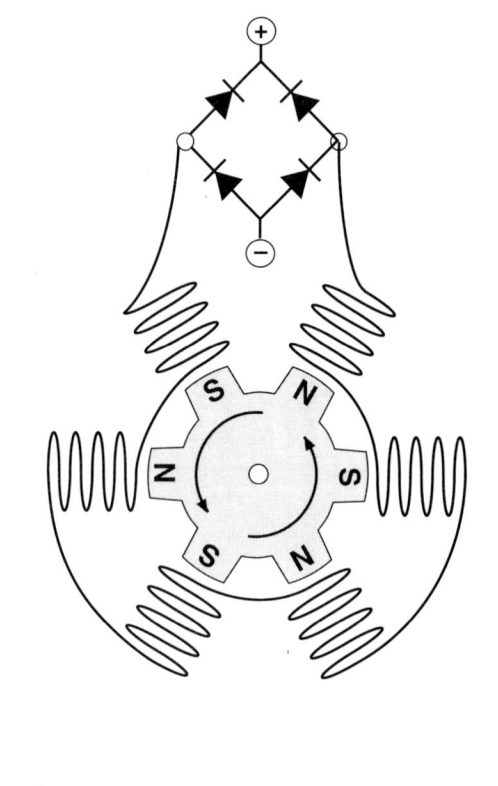

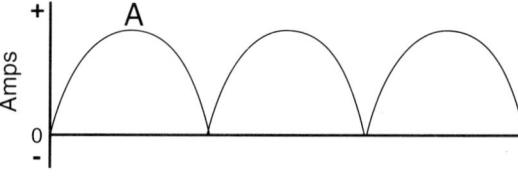

Alternators

Follow the currents in Figure 4.9 as they flow through the coil, the diodes of the rectifier, and the externally connected load in the alternating closed circuits labeled Path 1 and Path 2.

Fig. 4.9 Rectifier Current Paths
PATH 1   PATH 2

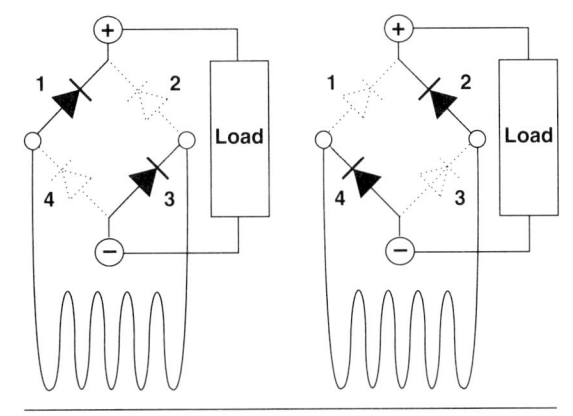

The first half-wave travels Path 1: from the coil, through diode 1, into the positive terminal, through the external load, into the negative terminal, through diode 3, and back to the coil.

The second half-wave travels Path 2: from the coil, through diode 2, out the positive terminal, through the external load, into the negative terminal, through diode 4, and back to the coil.

An obvious extension would be to provide each of the coils in Figure 4.4 with their own full-wave rectifiers, as shown in Figure 4.10. This would be fine if we wanted three separate outputs to recharge three separate batteries or to power three independent DC circuits, but we don't. We'd rather have a single DC system, and, although we might have three batteries, we'd rather charge them in parallel from a single source.

Fig. 4.10 Three Sets of Rectifiers

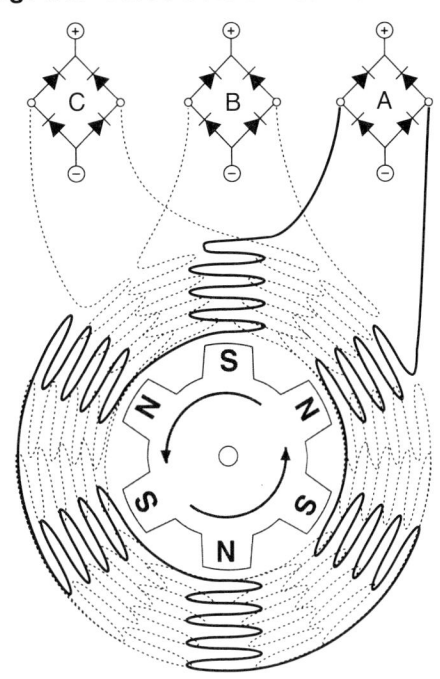

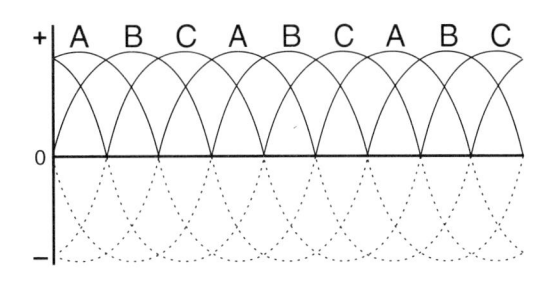

It would be needless torture to force you through the logic, but it turns out that connecting the ends of the three coils produces a felicitous simplification. (If it didn't, alternator technicians would be as highly paid as brain surgeons.)

60   DC

Figure 4.11 shows the two common ways to connect the coils: the *Delta* and the *Y*. With the coils connected, half of the 12 diodes can be eliminated. With either configuration, we are left with only three coil terminals, each of which is connected to a pair of diodes.

Figure 4.12 shows the ends of the coils connected to a single pair of output terminals. The currents combine in such a way that total output current approximates steady DC. Our rotary-current machine has evolved into a DC-output alternator.

Fig. 4.11 Common Coil Configurations

DELTA Configuration

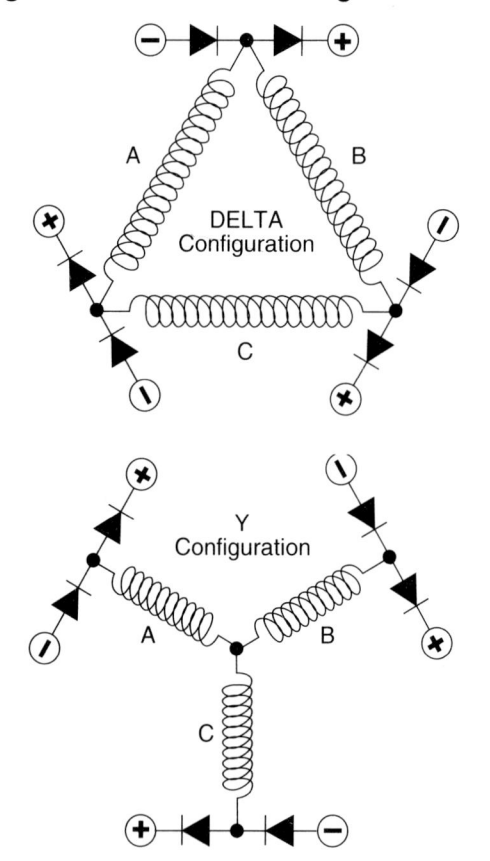

Y Configuration

Fig. 4.12 Alternator Configurations

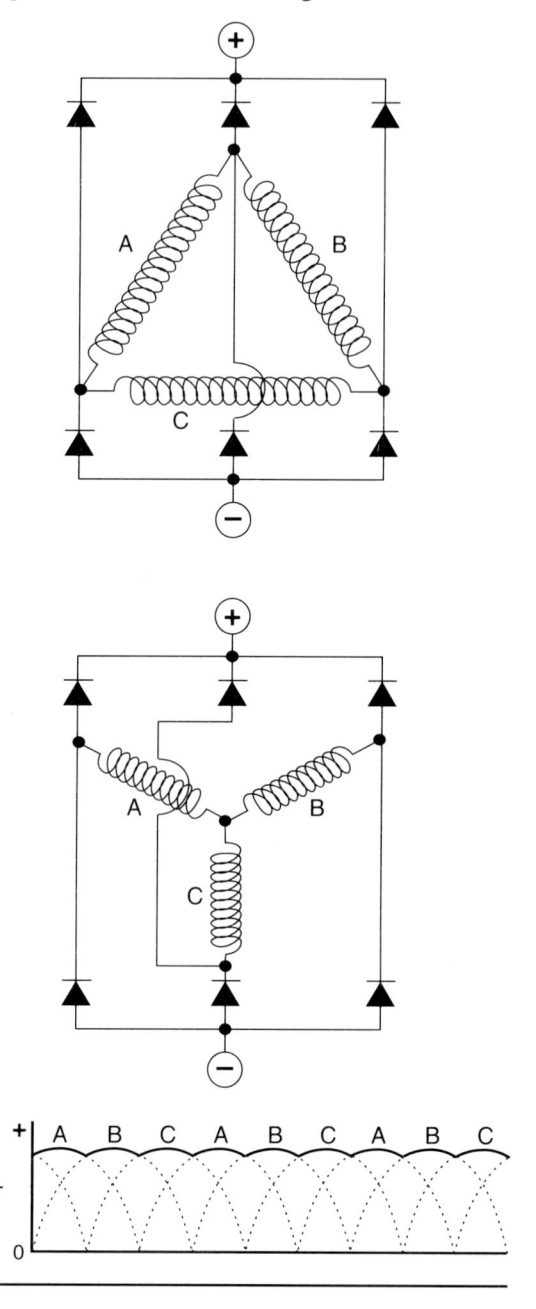

Alternators

CONTROLLING THE ALTERNATOR

The output of the galley alternator in Figure 4.1 depended on three variables:

1. Strength of the magnet
2. Number of turns of wire
3. Speed of magnet movement

The alternators in Figure 4.12 are similar. We can vary their outputs only by changing engine rpm, which is inconvenient.

The problem of control is solved by varying the strength of the magnet. Instead of the permanent magnet in Figure 4.1, we use an electromagnet as in Figure 4.13. The iron core concentrates the magnetic field, which is generated by the current in the coil. The strength of the field generated is proportional to the current flowing in the *field coil*. Thus, alternator output can be controlled by varying current through the field coil.

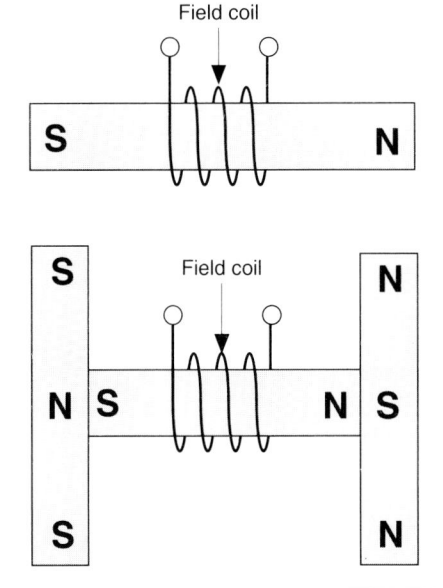

Figure 4.13 also demonstrates a phenomenon you can verify with your galley magnet and two or more nails: A magnet will induce magnetism of opposite polarity in any piece of iron in close proximity. For example, in Figure 4.13, two additional iron bars placed at the ends of the core also become magnets. This can be verified with either iron filings or a small compass.

Figure 4.14 shows the added iron bars replaced by iron disks with fingers that have been bent around and interleaved. In this way, current through a single field coil wrapped around the shaft results in alternating magnetic fingers around the circumference. It also shows how current can be fed to the field coil through carbon brushes riding on copper slip-rings fixed to the shaft.

Fig. 4.13 Electromagnets

Fig. 4.14 Alternator Rotor and Brushes

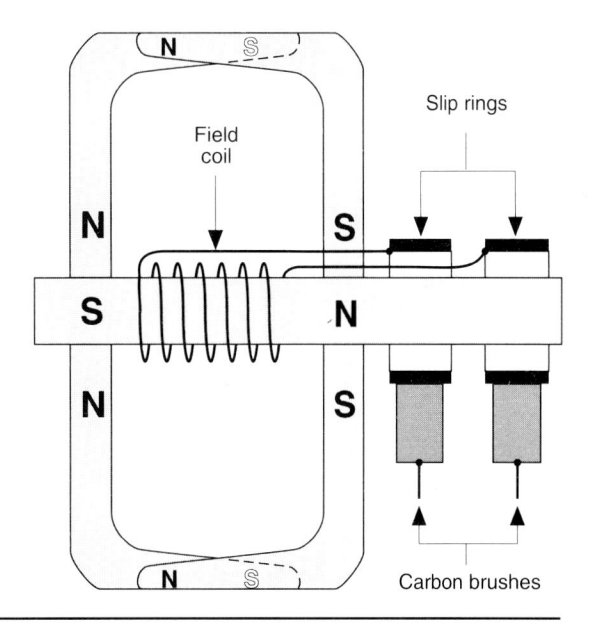

Figure 4.15 shows a typical alternator *rotor* with its interleaving magnetic poles, slip rings, and field coil wrapped around the inside shaft. The rotor assembly rotates inside the collection of stationary coils, known as the *stator*.

Fig. 4.15 Typical Alternator Rotor

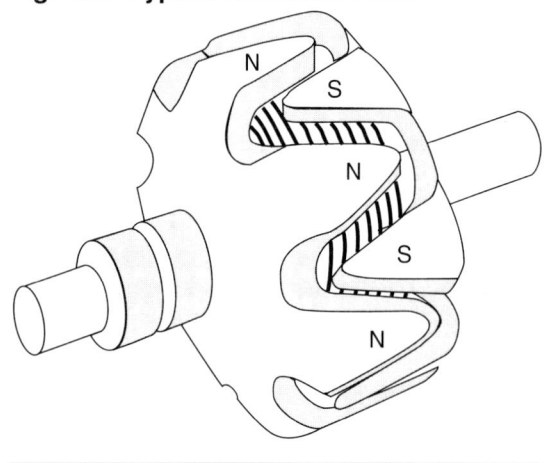

The device that controls field-coil current, and thus alternator output, is known as a *voltage regulator.* How it came to be known as a voltage—rather than a current—regulator, is lost in history. We will not change its name. Just remember that it controls output current, not voltage.

Because it is simple to understand, we'll start with the electromechanical voltage regulator which is used in some older boats. It is shown in Figure 4.16. The field current flows through the relay arm that pivots about F and contacts the points labeled ignition and ground at left. Ignition is connected to the battery + terminal through the engine ignition switch, so you can think of it as battery +.

Fig. 4.16 Electromechanical Regulator

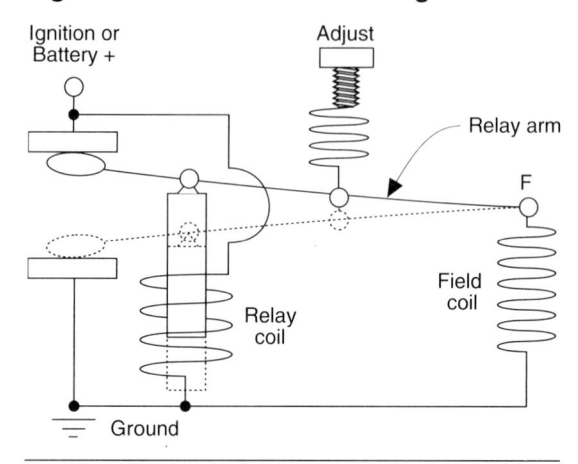

Before the alternator starts producing current, the arm is held up against the ignition contact by the tension in the adjust spring. With full-field current flowing, the alternator quickly begins to put out its maximum current. If the battery voltage is low enough, the alternator continues to pump out maximum current. As soon as battery voltage recovers to a predetermined value (somewhere between 13.8 and 14.2 volts), the increased current flowing from ignition to ground through the relay coil pulls the arm down and opens the contact. Field current drops to zero, alternator output drops to zero, battery voltage drops, and the contact arm is pulled up to the ignition contact to start the whole cycle again.

The greater the voltage of the battery, the greater percentage of time the contact remains pulled down into the open position. Alternator output actually switches between full and zero output hundreds of times per minute. When read by a meter, the average voltage approaches a constant voltage, while average charging current

Alternators

smoothly falls toward zero (plus whatever load is being drawn at the same time). The constant battery voltage can be adjusted by turning the adjust spring.

It is easy to check the operation of a voltage regulator. While the engine is running, and after output current has dropped to a trickle, turn on a heavy load, such as all of your cabin lights. If the regulator is doing its job, the battery voltage will remain the same, but alternator current will immediately increase by the amount of the newly imposed load.

Electromechanical regulators have been replaced by regulators containing transistors. Although destroyed by reversing battery and ground leads and by excessive heat, they never wear out from use and operate at much higher switching speeds. Figure 4.17 shows a solid-state equivalent of the electromechanical regulator of Figure 4.16.

Fig. 4.17 Solid-state Regulator

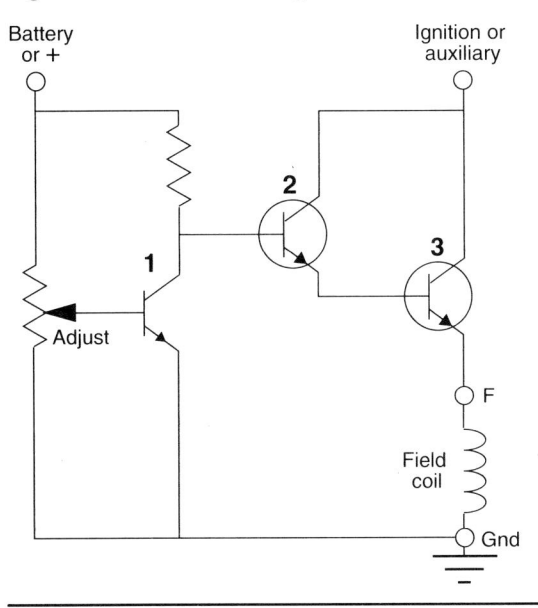

Fig. 4.18 NPN Transistor

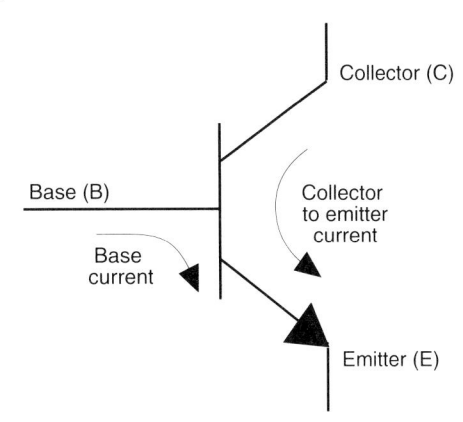

The operation of a solid-state regulator is easily understood if you understand how a transistor works. Figure 4.18 shows the most common type of transistor—the NPN. It has three leads: base (B), emitter (E), and collector (C). It can be thought of as an amplifying valve. The current flowing into the base controls the current flowing from the collector to the emitter. Because the junction between base and emitter is essentially a diode in the direction of the arrow, no current flows until the base-to-emitter voltage reaches 0.5 to 1.0 volt. Above that voltage, the current is about 20 to 100 times the base current. Thus the transistor can be used as an electronic switch, an amplifier, or both.

In Figure 4.17 assume battery voltage is low. The base of transistor 1 is therefore at a low voltage and transistor 1 is off. With transistor 1 acting as a high resistance between the base of transistor 2 and ground, the voltage of transistor 2 base is high and transistor 2 is on. Transistor 3 simply amplifies the collector-to-emitter current of transistor 2 by a factor of 20 or more. Thus, a large current flows through the field coil, and the alternator puts out maximum current.

Soon battery voltage increases, however, and transistor 1 switches on. The resistance from the base of transistor 2 to ground decreases, and transistors 2 and 3 switch off, cutting off the current to the field coil. With no field current, alternator output ceases.

The transistors switch on and off hundreds of times per second, with the ratio of on-to-off times controlling the average field current and alternator-output current. The analogy between electromechanical and solid-state voltage regulators is obvious.

Note that the solid-state regulator of Figure 4.17 had two positive terminals:

1. Battery or + is for sensing the voltage of the battery so that it can be charged at the correct voltage.

2. Ignition or auxiliary supplies the majority of the field current.

TYPE-P AND TYPE-N ALTERNATORS

Not to be confused with NPN and PNP transistors, alternators and regulators can be connected in two different ways called type P and type N (Figure 4.19).

In type-P alternators, the voltage regulator goes on the positive end of the field coil. In type-N alternators, the voltage regulator is located between the negative end of the field coil and ground.

Type-P and type-N alternators can be physically identical except for internal connections. In fact, if these connections are accessible, you can change a type-P to a type-N and vice-versa.

Fig. 4.19 Type-P and Type-N Regulators

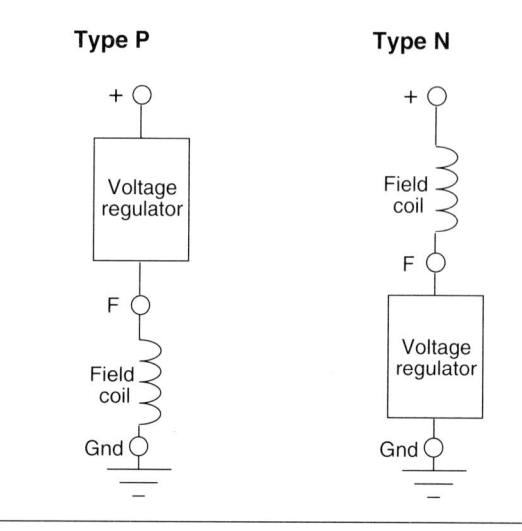

POWERING THE REGULATOR

Both type-P and type-N voltage regulators close the circuit between battery + and ground. If this circuit is not interrupted when the engine stops running, the voltage-regulator/alternator coil will slowly drain the battery. There are several methods of supplying power to the regulator, so that it doesn't drain the battery while the engine is off.

Figure 4.20 on the next page shows three small diodes (the diode trio) connected to the three coil terminals in a type-N alternator. These diodes function in the same way as the larger charge diodes, except that they feed a terminal labelled Aux. instead of the alternator-output terminal, +. When the alternator is not turning, there is no current to power the regulator, so there is no drain on the battery. Reverse current flow from the battery to the auxiliary terminal is prevented by the charge diodes.

Alternators

Fig. 4.20 Diode Trio

Fig. 4.21 Isolating Diode

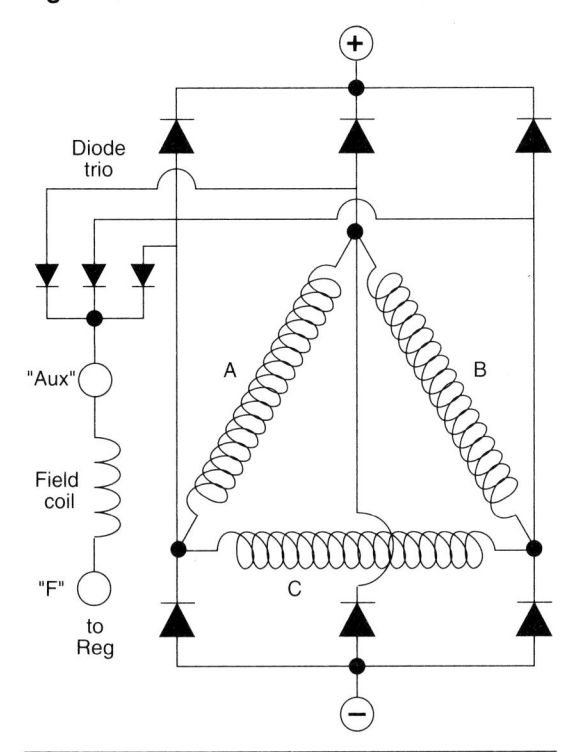

Figure 4.21 shows a second method of supplying regulator current. A large isolating diode is placed between the three charge diodes and the alternator + output terminal. This isolating diode prevents reverse current flow from the battery to the regulator.

Do not confuse the diode trio or the alternator-isolating diode with battery-isolating diodes. The first two are part of an alternator and will not be seen unless the case is opened. Battery-isolating diodes (Figure 4.22) are visible as large diodes mounted on a finned heat sink. Their purpose is to prevent paralleled batteries from discharging each other. Not all systems have battery-isolating diodes.

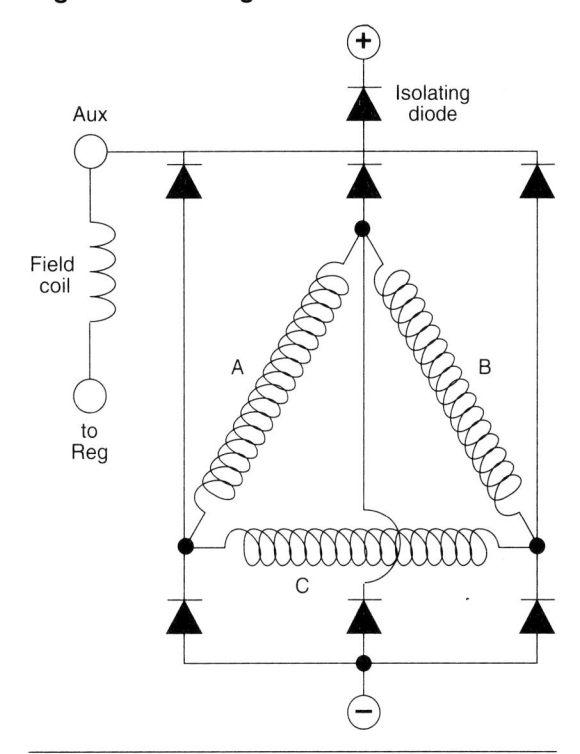

Fig. 4.22 Battery Isolating Diodes

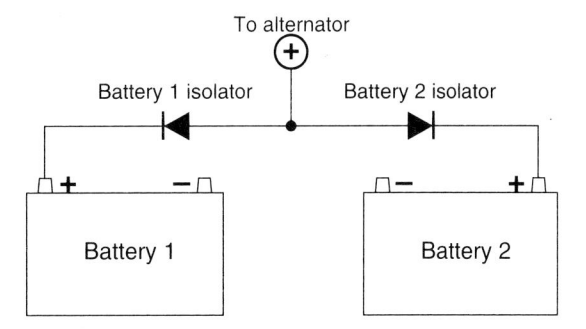

EXCITATION

Have you spotted a problem with the circuits of Figures 4.20 and 4.21? If we wired an alternator and regulator as shown in either of the figures, the alternator would never come on unless the field magnet retained a sufficient degree of permanent magnetism. The alternator will not generate current without field current, but there will not be field current until there is an alternator output! To solve this chicken-and-egg dilemma, alternators that derive their field currents from internal-diode trios or isolation diodes need a temporary source of field current called *excitation current*.

Figure 4.23 shows a typical excitation circuit added to the alternator of Figure 4.21. Its operation will be familiar to anyone who owns an automobile.

When the ignition switch is turned on, current flows from the battery, through the light and paralleled resistor, to the alternator auxiliary terminal, and then through the field coil. As soon as the engine starts, however, the alternator begins generating current, which then makes the voltage at the auxiliary terminal 0.5 to 1.0 volt higher than the battery voltage. With only 0.5 to 1.0 volt across its terminals, the 12-volt charge-indicator light goes out. If it stays on or comes on again, you know that the alternator has stopped producing current. A resistor is placed in parallel with the light to provide excitation current in case the light burns out.

An alternative scheme is to feed the light from the engine oil-pressure switch rather than the ignition switch, so that the alternator is excited as soon as oil pressure climbs.

Fig. 4.23 Alternator Excitation Circuit

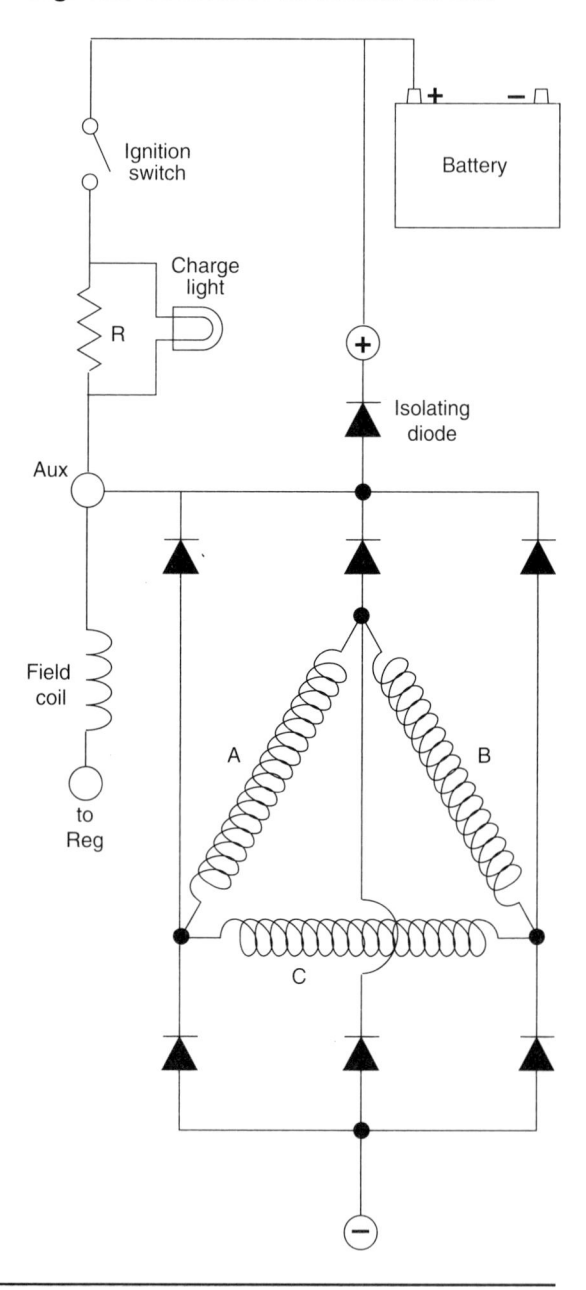

Alternators

REGULATOR BYPASS CONTROLS

The standard alternator with fixed-voltage regulation is a simple and reliable device. It is not an ideal marine battery charger, however. Without modification, it is simply a current-limited, fixed-voltage charger set at a compromise voltage between 13.8 and 14.2 volts. As we saw in Chapter 3, 13.8 to 14.2 volts is higher than the recommended float voltage, (13.2 to 13.5 volts) and lower than the recommended absorption voltage (14.4 volts). An alternator controlled by a standard regulator will never fully charge a battery in typical operation, yet will overcharge the same battery if run for days.

Cruising boats, particularly sailboats, impose large loads on their batteries but run their engines only a few hours per day. Worse, when a boat is at anchor the engine is usually run for the sole purpose of charging the batteries. What is needed is a way to control the alternator output for optimum fast charging as shown in Figure 4.24. The optimum charge cycles include:

1. Bulk —constant current to 14.4 volts
2. Absorption—constant 14.4 volts
3. Float—constant 13.2 to 13.5 volts

Fig. 4.24 Optimum Fast Charging

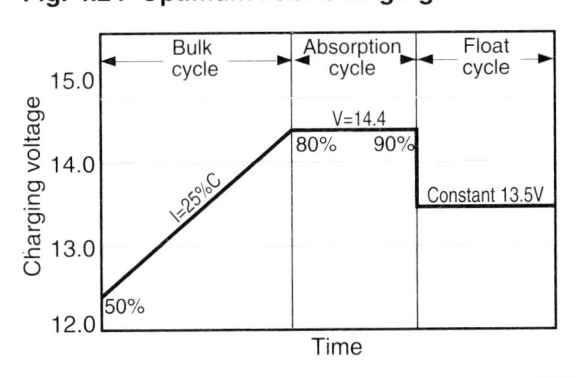

Fig. 4.25 Regulator Bypass Hookups

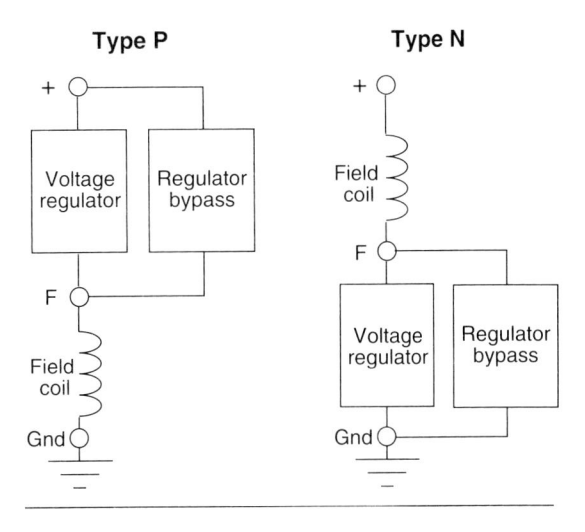

Figure 4.25 shows regulator bypasses installed across both type-P and type-N voltage regulators. Note that the original voltage regulators remain in place. The bypass regulators simply increase field current in order to increase alternator output. After the regulator bypass has accomplished its task and is switched off, the original voltage regulator resumes control of the alternator.

Some regulator bypasses are strictly manual, requiring diligent monitoring of battery-charge current and voltage. The simplest of the automatic bypasses come on when the engine is started, provide a constant-current bulk charge, then switch off when the battery reaches a preset voltage. More sophisticated (and much more expensive) regulator bypasses automatically cycle through constant-current bulk charge, constant-voltage absorbtion charge, and constant-voltage float charge. An equalization charge can also be selected whenever desired.

Figure 4.26 shows a simple manual-control regulator bypass you can build yourself. Note that the bypass circuit is the same whether used with type-P or type-N alternator. The on/off switch allows the bypass to be switched into or out of the circuit. The 2–ohm, 25-watt fixed resistor limits the maximum field current. The 20–ohm, 100-watt rheostat (variable power resistor) allows the field current to be varied over a wide range.

Fig. 4.26 A Manual Regulator Bypass

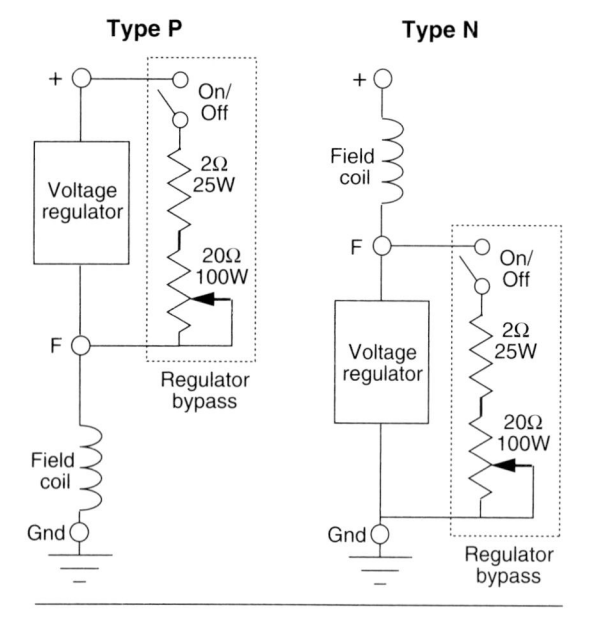

Warning. Manual regulator bypasses should never be used without diligent monitoring of both battery charging current and voltage. It is easy to destroy a $300 battery with a $30 homemade regulator bypass. If you do not have the discipline to continuously monitor the charging process, you should either forego the fast-charge option or invest in one of the commercially available automatic models.

TROUBLESHOOTING

An alternator is an alternator, and, whatever its name, it works on the principles above. Variations in outward appearance, arrangement of terminals, and internal connections number in the hundreds, however. It is beyond the scope of this book to detail the differences.

There are two basic approaches to alternator repair. The first is to carry replacements for all of the components likely to fail in the field: charge diodes, diode trio, isolating diode, brushes, bearings, and voltage regulator. The second is to carry an exact replacement for the entire alternator, including the voltage regulator if it is external. I favor the second approach for the following reasons:

1. There will be no spare part you might have overlooked. For example, what if the problem were a broken mounting flange?

2. You don't have to carry special tools such as a bearing puller, press, or heavy-duty soldering iron.

3. Replacement takes minutes; repair takes hours.

4. The cost of the whole alternator (with trade-in) is probably no greater than the cost of a complete set of spare components.

When your alternator fails to fully charge your batteries, the fault may lie with the alternator, or it may lie entirely outside the alternator in the wiring or an external regulator. To replace an alternator without first identifying the problem is to risk immediate failure a second time. The troubleshooting guide on the next page should help you to discover whether the problem is with the wiring, the alternator, or the regulator.

Alternators

Alternator to Battery Wiring
— no Battery Isolating Diodes (Figure 4.27)
Turn the engine off and the battery-select switch on. The multimeter should read:

>   Alternator + to Battery +, 0 volts
>   Alternator - to Battery -, 0 volts

On the resistance scale the multimeter should read:

>   Alternator + to Battery +, 0 ohms
>   Alternator - to Battery -, 0 ohms

If not, suspect corrosion or a broken wire.

Turn the engine on and the battery-select switch on. The multimeter should read:

>   Alternator + to Battery +, < 0.5 volt
>   Alternator - to Battery -, < 0.5 volt

If not, suspect corrosion or a broken wire.

— with Battery Isolating Diodes (Figure 4.28)
Turn the engine off and the battery-select switch off. The multimeter should read:

>   Battery + to Ground, 12 volts or more
>   Alternator + to Ground, 0 volts

If Alternator + to Ground reads 12 volts, suspect a shorted diode.

Turn the engine on with the battery-select switch on. The multimeter should read:

>   Alternator + to Battery +, 0.5 to 1.0 volt
>   Battery + to Ground, about 1 volt higher than with the engine off.

If not, suspect the diode feeding the battery.

To check a battery-isolating diode, disconnect batteries and read resistance across the diode, reversing leads. An open-circuit diode reads ∞ ohms in both directions; a shorted diode reads near 0 ohms in both directions; a healthy diode reads near ∞ ohms in one direction and 0 ohms in the other direction.

Fig. 4.27 Wiring with No Isolating Diodes

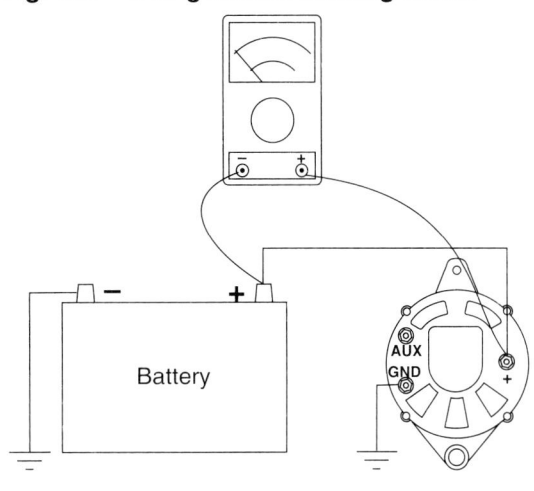

Fig. 4.28 Wiring with Isolating Diodes

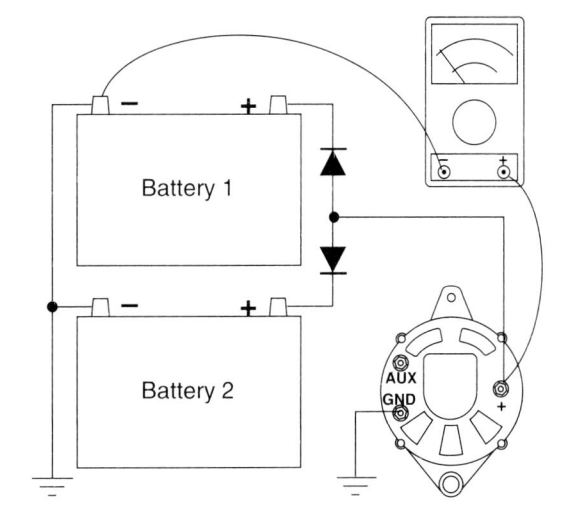

Alternator and Battery Voltage
— no Battery Isolating Diodes (Figure 4.29)
Turn the engine off and the battery-select switch on to the battery being tested (repeat tests for other batteries). On the voltage scale the multimeter should read:

> Battery + to Ground, 12 to 13 volts. If not, the battery may be bad.

> Alternator + to Ground, 12 to 13 volts. If not, Alternator + to Battery + wire is bad.

Turn the engine on and the battery-select switch on to the battery being tested (repeat tests for other batteries). On the voltage scale the multimeter should read:

> Battery + to Ground, about 1 volt higher than with the engine off.

> Alternator + to Ground, at least 1 volt higher than with the engine off. If not, the alternator is not charging.

— with Battery Isolating Diodes (Figure 4.30)
Turn the engine off and the battery-select switch on to the battery being tested (repeat tests for other batteries). On the voltage scale the multimeter should read:

> Battery + to Ground, 12 to 13 volts. If not, the battery may be bad.

> Alternator + to Ground, 0 volts. If not, suspect a shorted isolating diode.

Turn the engine on and the battery-select switch on to the battery being tested (repeat tests for other batteries). On the voltage scale the multimeter should read:

> Battery + to Ground, should be about 1 volt higher than with the engine off. If not, the alternator is not charging.

> Alternator + to Ground, should be 0.5 to 1.0 volt higher than Battery + to Ground. If not, suspect a shorted isolating diode.

Fig. 4.29 Alternator and Battery Voltage

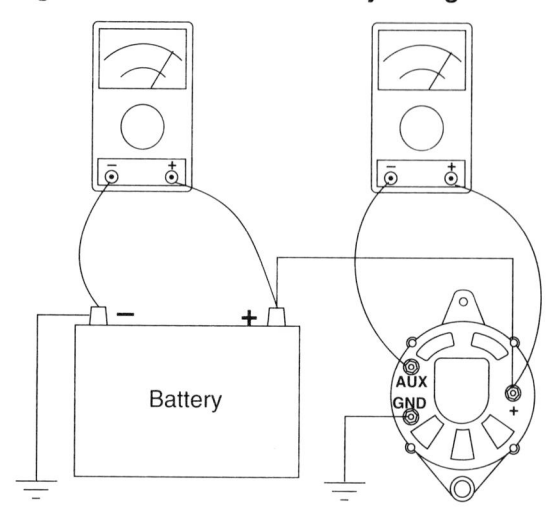

Fig. 4.30 Voltages with Isolating Diodes

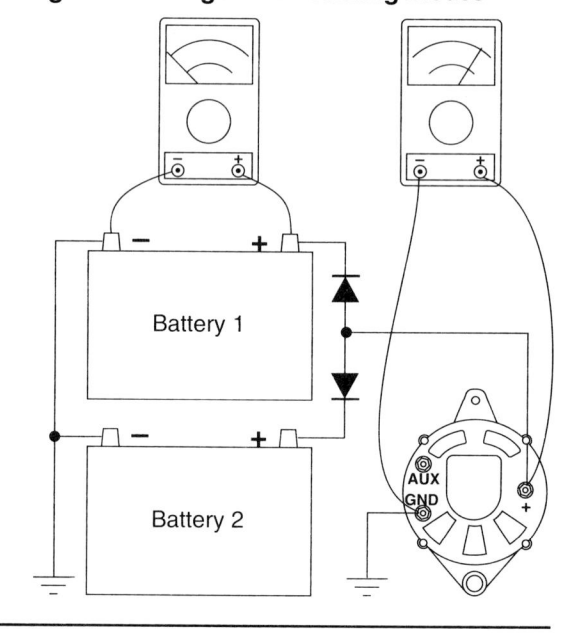

Alternators

Alternator and Regulator

P-type (Figure 4.31)
Turn the engine off. Measure the voltage from battery + to ground and note its value. Remove the wire from alternator terminal, F. Connect test light (minimum 12-watt, such as anchor light) from terminal F to battery +. Start the engine and measure the voltage from battery + to ground again. If the voltage is about 1 volt higher than with the engine off, then the alternator is good, but the regulator is bad (see Flashing P-Type Alternator, below).

N-type (Figure 4.32)
Turn the engine off. Measure the voltage from battery + to ground and note its value. Remove the wire from alternator terminal F. Connect a test light (minimum 12-watt, such as an anchor light) from terminal F to battery +. Start the engine and measure the voltage from battery + to ground again. If the voltage is about 1 volt higher than it was when the engine was off, then the alternator is good, but the regulator is bad.

Flashing P-type Alternator (Figure 4.33)

If the P-type regulator tested bad as above, the problem may lie in the excite circuit.

To test the excite circuit, turn on the engine and measure the voltage from battery + to ground. Then momentarily connect the test light between battery + and alternator terminal F. If the voltage from battery + to ground is now about 12 volts higher than with the engine off, the alternator and regulator are good, but the excite circuit is bad.

You can either repair the excite circuit, or you can create an excite circuit temporarily by placing a 12-watt lamp between the engine oil-pressure switch and alternator terminal F.

Fig. 4.31 Checking P-type Alternator

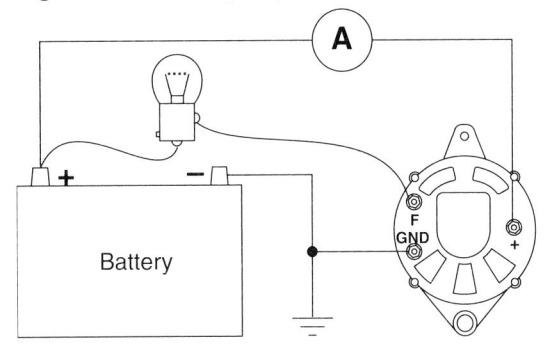

Fig. 4.32 Checking N-type Alternator

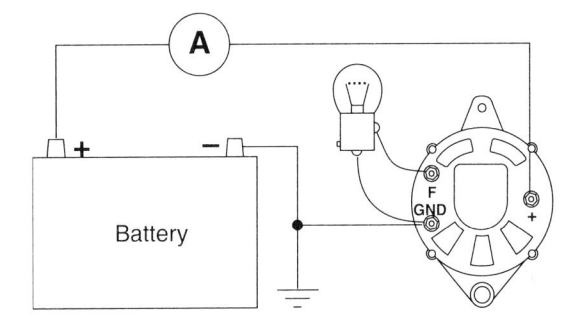

Fig. 4.33 Flashing P-type Alternator

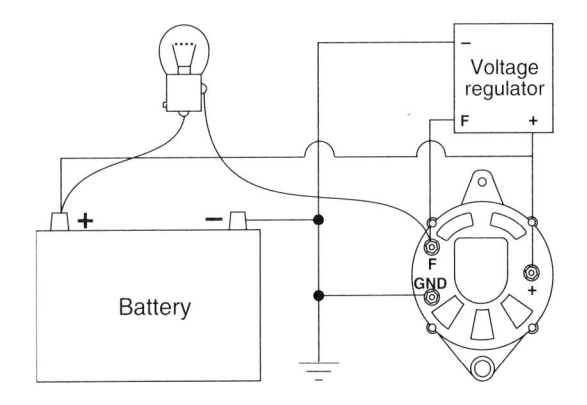

5

BONDING

What is Bonding? 74

Electrical System Grounding 76

Lightning Protection 78

Corrosion Protection 86

Stray-Current Corrosion 92

To Bond or Not to Bond 95

Testing Your Protection 96

General Application of Cathodic Protection 98

Other Types of Corrosion 99

Bonding is a controversial, and often poorly understood, wiring practice. As usual, we start by answering the basic question—*what is bonding?*

The purposes of bonding are threefold: 1) *electrical system grounding*, 2) *lightning protection*, and 3) *corrosion protection*.

The bonding controversy stems from the possibility of its encouraging *stray-current corrosion*. So—*to bond, or not to bond*—that is the question we address in detail.

Fortunately, there are simple methods for *testing your protection* against corrosion. These, and the ABYC standards for the *general application of cathodic protection*, should protect your boat's underwater metals.

Though neither caused nor prevented by bonding, *other types of corrosion* are explained as well.

No marine wiring topic causes more confusion than bonding. That is because there are at least three separate and compelling reasons for electrically connecting, or bonding metal objects, aboard a boat:

1. Electrical system grounding
2. Lightning protection
3. Corrosion protection

At the same time, there are reasons for not bonding certain items. As they occur, the exceptions will be discussed.

You will note that the grounding of AC electrical systems is not discussed in this chapter. In keeping with my opinion that marine DC and AC systems are best treated and installed as separate systems, AC grounding will be covered in *Chapter 9, Part II, AC Standards and Practices.* You will be relieved to find that AC grounding is related to DC bonding in a simple way.

WHAT IS BONDING?

Bonding is the electrical connection of the exposed, metallic noncurrent carrying parts to the ground side of the direct-current system.

Ground is a surface or mass at the potential of the earth's surface, established by a conducting connection (intentional or accidental) with the earth, including any metal area that forms part of the wetted surface of the hull.

Bonding Conductors are normally noncurrent-carrying conductors used to connect the noncurrent-carrying metal parts of a boat and the noncurrent-carrying parts of direct-current devices on the boat to the boat's bonding system.

Common Bonding Conductor is an electrical conductor, usually running fore-and-aft along the boat's centerline, to which all equipment bonding conductors are connected.

Ground

In practical terms, ground is the potential, or voltage, of the water in which the boat is immersed. As we will later see, the voltage in the water may vary slightly due to stray currents. The purpose of the bonding system is to force this voltage to be as uniform as possible through the use of low-resistance conductors and connections.

Bonding Conductors

Individual bonding conductors are separate from, and in addition to, the DC (and AC) grounded conductors, which are defined below. They should ideally take as short and as direct routes as possible to the common-bonding conductor, which usually runs near the fore-and-aft centerline of the boat. Each bonding conductor should be at least as large as the current-carrying positive and negative conductors that protect equipment in case of a short circuit.

The engine-bonding conductor should be at least as big as the largest bonding conductor in the rest of the bonding system and large enough to carry starter-motor cranking current. In multiengine installations with cross-over starting systems (ability to parallel batteries), the engines should be bonded together with a conductor large enough to carry cranking current and separate from all current-carrying conductors.

Bonding

Fig. 5.1 DC Bonding System

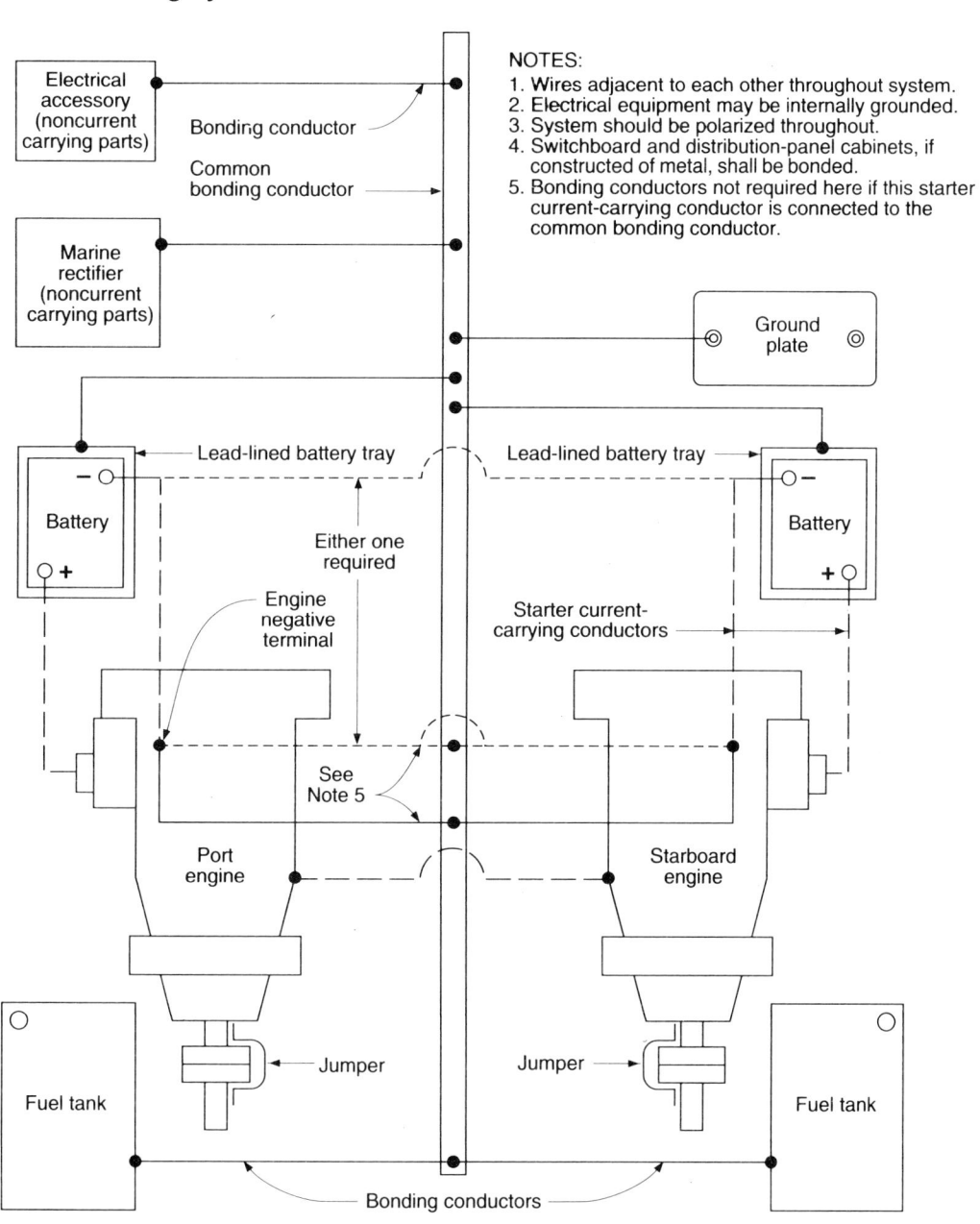

NOTES:
1. Wires adjacent to each other throughout system.
2. Electrical equipment may be internally grounded.
3. System should be polarized throughout.
4. Switchboard and distribution-panel cabinets, if constructed of metal, shall be bonded.
5. Bonding conductors not required here if this starter current-carrying conductor is connected to the common bonding conductor.

Common-Bonding Conductor

The large common-bonding conductor is normally blue coated. If wire, it may consist of bare, stranded, tinned copper or insulated stranded wire of minimum size 8 AWG. If solid, it may be uninsulated copper, bronze strip, or copper pipe at least .030 inch thick and 0.5 inch wide. The copper, bronze strip or pipe may be drilled and tapped, provided it is thick enough to provide at least three full threads for terminal screws. It may, in any case, be through-drilled for connections using machine screws and locknuts.

Although the only practical location for the common-bonding conductor is often the bilge, care should be taken that it never be submerged due to the likely corrosion of its connections.

Equipment to be connected to the boat's bonding system includes:

- Engines and transmissions
- Propellers and shafts
- Metal cases of motors, generators and pumps
- Metal cabinets and control boxes
- Electronics cabinets
- Metal fuel and water tanks, fuel-fill fittings, and electrical fuel pumps and valves
- Metal battery boxes
- Metal conduit or armoring
- Large non-electrical metal objects as recommended under lightning protection below

Note that electrically isolated through-hull fittings may or may not be connected to the bonding system. The subject of bonding metal through-hulls is controversial, especially in the case of wooden hulls. The question will be discussed further under bonding for corrosion protection.

ELECTRICAL SYSTEM GROUNDING

DC Grounding Conductors are normally noncurrent-carrying conductors. They are used to connect metallic noncurrent-carrying parts of direct current devices to the engine negative terminal or its bus for the purpose of minimizing stray-current corrosion.

DC Grounded Conductors are current-carrying conductors connected to the side (usually negative) of the source, which is intentionally maintained at boat ground potential.

Ground is established by a conducting connection with the earth, including any conductive part of the wetted surface of a hull.

Engine Negative Terminal is the point on the engine at which the battery negative terminal is connected.

Panelboard is an assembly of devices for the purpose of controlling and/or distributing power on a boat. It may include devices such as circuit breakers, fuses, switches, instruments, and indicators.

DC grounding conductors are the same as the bonding conductors defined and shown in Figure 5.1. Why the difference in terms? Bonding is an all-inclusive term serving safety, lightning protection, and corrosion protection. Grounding, although sharing the same conductors, refers specifically to electrical grounding for safety and prevention of stray currents. For the purpose of grounding only, grounding conductors should be no less than the smaller of either 18 AWG

Bonding

Fig. 5.2 DC Negative/DC Grounding System

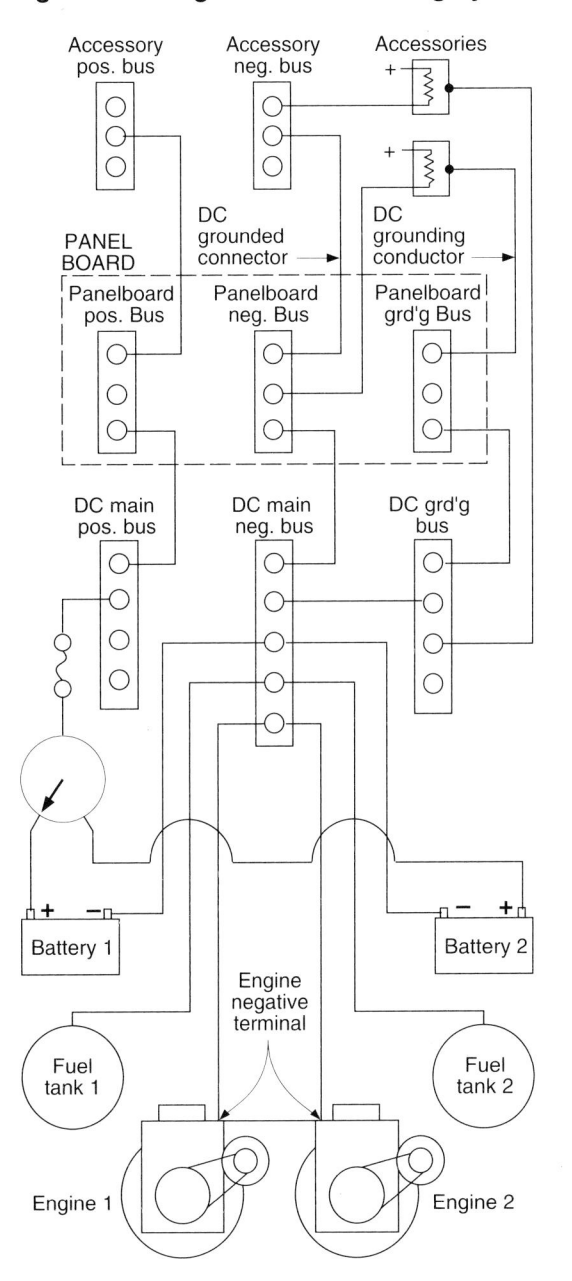

or one size smaller than the current-carrying conductors to a device. They may be routed as separate conductors or together with the positive and negative conductors as a third wire. They also may be connected to the engine negative terminal, the DC main-negative bus, or to a DC grounding bus, which is then connected to either the engine negative terminal or DC main-negative bus.

Note that the common bonding conductor of Figure 5.1 is also a DC grounding bus.

DC grounding conductors, like bonding conductors, may be either bare, green, or green with a yellow stripe.

DC grounded conductors, or negative-supply conductors, are subject to the recommendations in *Chapter 6, DC Standards and Practices*.

Grounding serves three purposes:

1. If a positive (+ 12-volt) wire inside a piece of electrical equipment were to short by accidentally contacting the metal case, the case would become dangerous, either as a source of shock or of ignition. A grounding wire to the case holds the case at ground potential by providing a low-resistance return path for the accidental current.

2. By providing a low-resistance return path for electrical current, the grounding wire prevents stray currents. As we'll see, these can result in damaging corrosion.

3. Grounding a metal electrical case prevents emission from inside or absorption from outside of radio frequency noise (RFI).

LIGHTNING PROTECTION

We have all been awed by the power of this natural electrical phenomenon. There are several theories as to the exact mechanism of lightning production. The mechanism doesn't matter, but the result does.

At any moment, there are approximately 10,000 lightning storms in progress on earth, producing 100 strikes every second. In some regions, lightning is a rarity. In others, such as Florida in summer, it is an almost daily occurrence.

To put the danger in perspective, there are approximately 100 lightning deaths per year in the U. S. Over a 20-year period recorded deaths were:

• Florida	253
• North Carolina	133
• Texas	120
• Maryland	101
• Virginia	33
• Alaska & Hawaii	0

The deaths occurred:

• In or around the home	20%
• In vehicles (mostly open)	19%
• Taking refuge under trees	15%
• In boats	13%
• Everywhere else	33%

Considering the great percentage of deaths occurring in boats and the low percentage of people in boats at any given time, it is apparent that lightning strikes on boats is a serious matter.

What is Lightning and How Does It Act?

In all lightning theories, the combination of vertically moving water droplets and air currents results in the buildup of large quantities of oppositely charged particles within clouds and between clouds and the ground (Figure 5.3). The electrical potential differences between charges may be as high as 100,000,000 volts. By comparison, the voltage on the power lines running along a street is 12,000 volts.

Fig. 5.3 Lightning Cloud and Charges

In particular, the base of a cloud becomes negatively charged. Since opposite charges attract, the surface of the earth directly beneath the cloud becomes positively charged. People standing in this positively charged area, under a cloud, sometimes report feeling their hair standing on end due to the static charge just before a lightning strike. What prevents the two charges from combining is the very high electrical resistance of air. The voltage ultimately

Bonding

builds to the point, however, where electrons are stripped from air molecules, turning the air molecules into positively charged ions. Ionized air *is* electrically conductive.

Ionization proceeds in steps of about 100 feet. Electrons flow downward through the ionized path and cause a faint blue-white glow, similar to the flow of electrons in the ionized gas of a neon sign. Each step requires only about 0.00005 second to ionize and fill, so that the stepped leader traverses a distance of 10,000 feet, from cloud base to ground, in about 0.005 second.

The final step to ground is of most interest to a boater. Up to that point, the presence of the boat has had no influence on either the location or the direction of the discharge. When looking for the final connection to earth, however, the lightning will head for the closest accumulation of positive charge. That generally means the highest point within a radius of 100 feet. If that point is you, chances are you will be struck. If it is the tip of your mast, your boat will be struck.

After the ionized column has been completed by the leader, we have an electrical short circuit from the cloud to earth. The resulting rush of accumulated charge from the cloud to the earth is what we see as a lightning bolt—an ionized column of air, heated to 50,000°F, conducting a typical current of 50,000 amps. The rapid heating of the air produces a supersonic air-pressure wave that we hear as thunder. The entire 0.005-second process may be repeated several or even dozens of times during the following second, depending on the initial size of the accumulated charge.

A direct strike is the most dangerous. Consider that the largest circuit breaker on your boat is probably rated at less than 50 amps, and that the cranking current to your starter motor is probably on the order of 200 amps. Now consider what 50,000 to 200,000 amps might do to that same wiring. Although the peak current lasts only 0.0001 second, the resistive heating is often sufficient to burn insulation, melt components—even vaporize conductors, if small enough.

Much lightning damage occurs from near hits, however. It is not uncommon for one boat to suffer a direct strike and for boats in adjacent slips to lose electronic equipment. Just as a current-carrying wire produces a magnetic field, and a varying magnetic field produces current in a conductor (the principle behind the alternator), lightning currents produce tremendous magnetic fields, which then induce currents in nearby wires. These induced currents are often sufficient to destroy sensitive electronic circuits.

Just any copper conductor will not suffice to conduct currents of 50,000 amps. The conductor must be large (conductive) enough to present the path of least resistance to ground (the surrounding water in the case of a boat). Small diameter wire, corroded connections, and too small a ground plate (area of metal in contact with the water) may cause the lightning to seek additional paths to ground, resulting in dangerous side flashes to other metal in and on the boat.

Zones of Protection

Metal masts tend to draw the final step of a leader to themselves within a radius equal to their height. The conical zone beneath is known as the zone of protection. A person or object entirely within this zone is substantially protected from a direct strike.

Figure 5.4 shows the zone of protection for a sailboat mast of height above the water less than 50 feet. A sailboat hull will lie entirely within the zone of protection. To qualify as a lightning-protective mast, the mast must either be metal or be equipped with an air terminal and conductor to ground.

Figure 5.5 shows zones of protection for a powerboat with a lightning-protective mast and with the mast extended by a grounded air terminal. Powerboat hulls do not generally fall entirely within their zones of protection unless their masts are extended by grounded antennas or outriggers, or they have more than one grounded mast.

Figure 5.6 shows how the zone of protection is calculated for a sailboat with a lightning-protective mast of height in excess of 50 feet. If there is more than one mast, zones are drawn for each mast. The combined protective zone includes all areas under one or more of the individual zones.

To qualify as lightning protective masts, each mast must be grounded. Multihulls require grounding plates in each hull.

Fig. 5.4 Lightning-Protective Zone for a Sailboat with a Mast Height Less Than 50 Feet

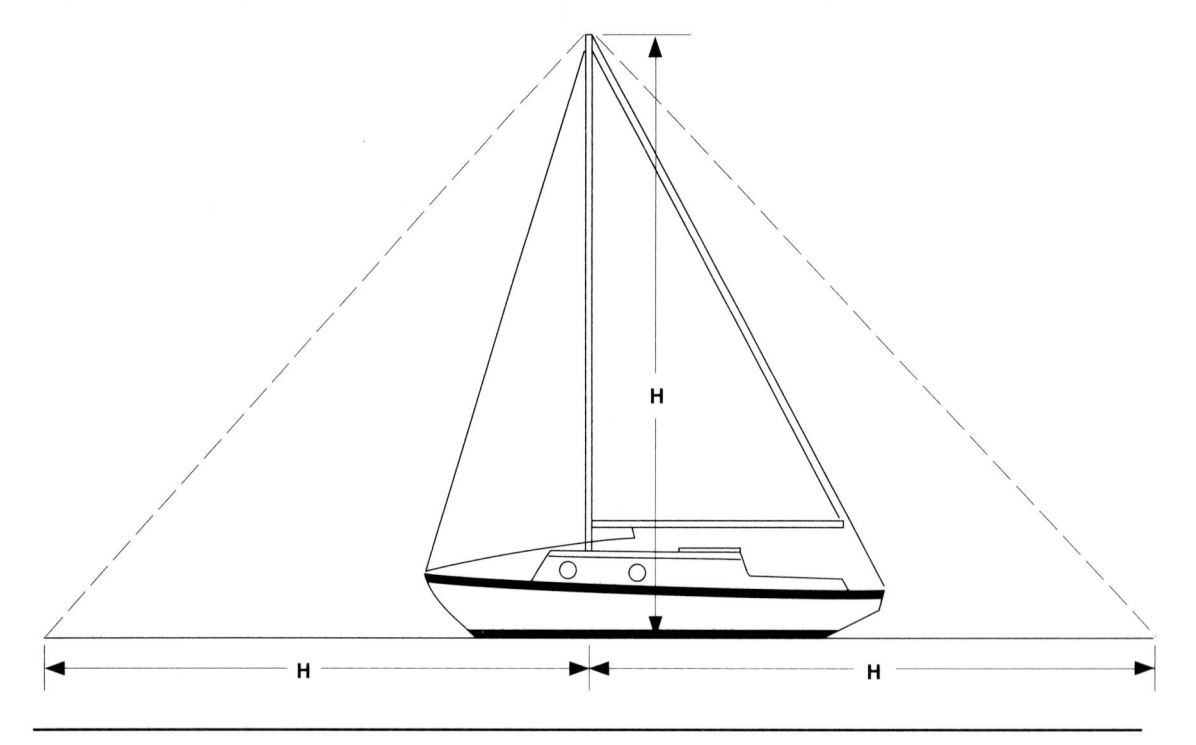

Bonding 81

Fig. 5.5 Lightning-Protective Zone for a Motorboat with a Lightning-Protective Mast or a Mast and Approved Extension

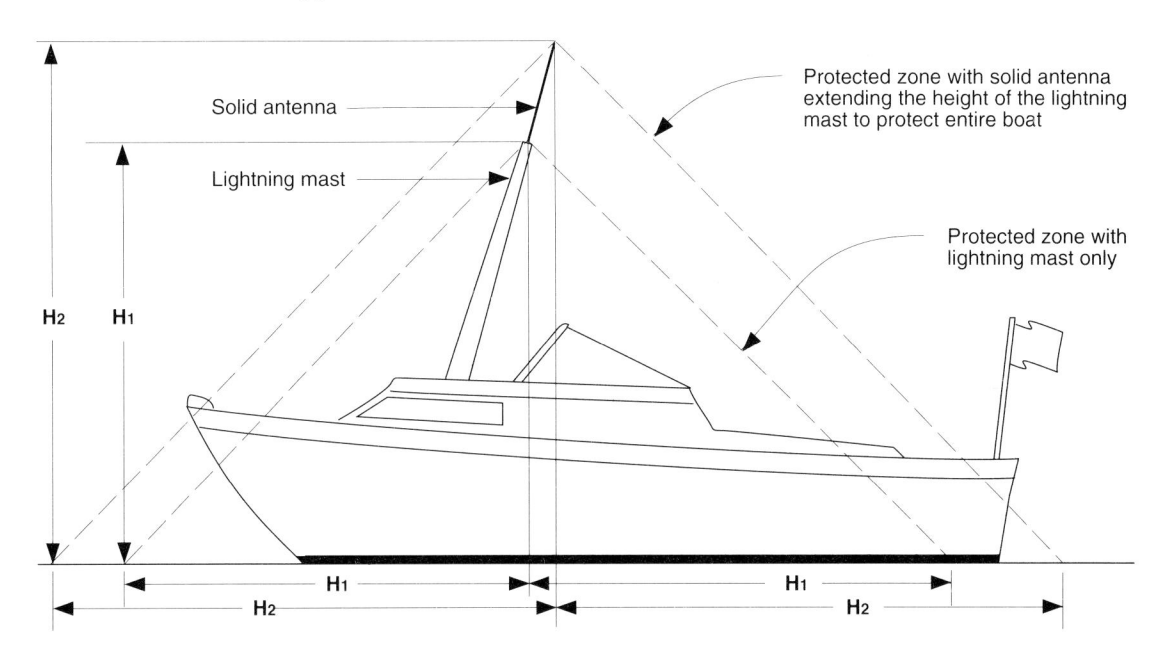

- Solid antenna
- Lightning mast
- Protected zone with solid antenna extending the height of the lightning mast to protect entire boat
- Protected zone with lightning mast only

H_2 H_1

H_1 H_1
H_2 H_2

Fig. 5.6 Lightning-Protective Zone for a Sailboat with a Mast Over 50 Feet or Multiple Masts

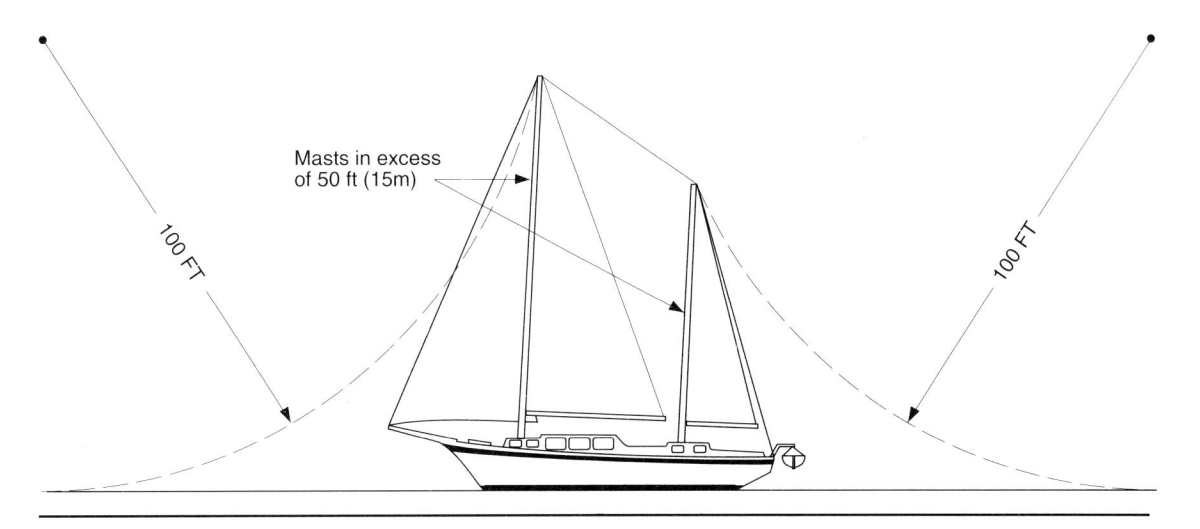

Masts in excess of 50 ft (15m)

100 FT   100 FT

The Safe Path to Ground

The intent of the safe path to ground is to provide an electrical path to ground (water) that is as short and straight as possible and sufficiently conductive to prevent side flashes to alternate routes. The safe path to ground consists of two parts: the lightning-protective mast and the lightning-ground connection.

Lightning-Protective Mast

Metal masts qualify as protective masts. If nonconductive, a mast must be provided with a grounding conductor running from an air terminal 6 inches above the mast in as straight a line as possible to the lightning-ground connection. The conductor must be securely fastened to the mast and consist of either a stranded-copper wire of minimum size 8 AWG (with no strand smaller than 17 AWG), or a metal strip of conductivity equal to that of 8 AWG copper wire and thickness of at least .030 inch.

Conductive joints, including the connection to the lightning-ground connection, must not be subject to immersion or damaged during fabrication. In the case of 8 AWG wire, the connection must be strong enough to support a 45 pound weight for one minute. To avoid corrosion, all bolts, nuts, washers, and lugs must be galvanically compatible with the conductor.

A radio antenna or outrigger may serve as a lightning-protective mast or extension if its conductivity is equal to that of 8 AWG copper wire, and it has either a means for direct connection to ground, or a lightning-protective gap (closely spaced electrodes which lightning will easily jump).

If not disconnected when the antenna is grounded, the antenna feed line should also have a lightning arrestor, or transient-surge suppressor.

Lightning-Ground Connection

A lightning-ground connection may be any underwater metal surface of at least one square-foot area. Metal hulls, centerboards, and external keels all are excellent for the purpose. Metal rudders may qualify in terms of area, but the connection from mast to rudder is far from short and direct.

It is common practice to bond all metal through-hulls on the assumption that the sum of the wetted areas would provide sufficient conduction to ground. If the bonding conductor were broken, leaving but one through-hull to serve as the lightning ground, the area would not be sufficient. Furthermore, bonding of through-hulls, particularly in wooden boats, is questionable from a corrosion standpoint, as you'll see later in this chapter.

It is also commonly thought that the large surface areas of the propellor and shaft provide adequate lightning grounding. This is probably true, but the common practice of bonding to the engine block and relying on the conductivity of the engine, transmission, and shaft may lead to extremely large currents through main-engine- and transmission-output bearings, to their detriment. If the shaft and propellor are to be bonded, it should be through a brush riding on the shaft.

Most controversial are the sintered-bronze plates intended to serve as ground plates for both SSB radios and lightning. Due to their porosity, these plates have wetted areas of many times the areas of their envelopes. Recent evidence, however, suggests that they are not much more effective than plain copper plate of the same area. In fact, it is theorized that edge length is more important than area in lightning-

Bonding

ground plates. A 12' x 1" x 1/4" copper strap would be six times more effective than a 1' x 1' square copper plate.

I feel that the best lightning-ground connections are (in order):

1. Metal hull
2. External metal keel
3. External 1" x 1/4" copper strap
4. Large sintered-bronze plate

For a fiberglass or wooden boat with encapsulated keel, I feel the best lightning ground is the largest available sintered-bronze plate. It should be mounted as close as possible to the termination of the lightning-protective mast conductor, with the conductor connected to each of the plate's through-hull bolts.

Interconnection of Metallic Masses

Comprehensive lightning protection calls for the interconnection of permanent metallic masses aboard a boat with the lightning-conductor system. The concept behind interconnection is shown in Figure 5.7.

On the left of the illustration is what physicists call a *Faraday cage*. The cage consists of a conductive mesh or membrane completely enclosing a volume of space. Metal automobile and airplane bodies are practical examples. The interior of a Faraday cage is immune to lightning strike because the conductivity of the cage forces the potential of the interior to be uniform. Without a potential difference across the cage, a person touching the interior of the cage would not receive a shock.

Fig. 5.7 Faraday Cage and Its Approximation through Interconnection of Metallic Masses

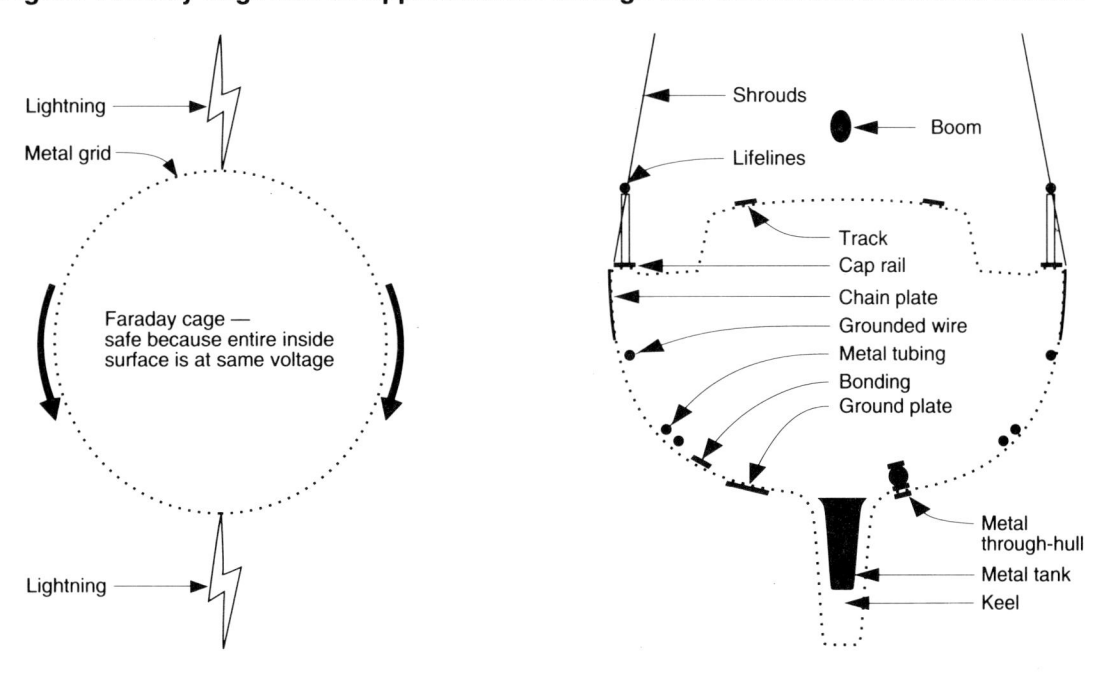

Figure 5.7 shows how the hull of a boat may be transformed into an approximate Faraday cage through the bonding of all large metallic objects to the lightning conductor. Objects to be bonded include:

Exterior – spars, shrouds, stays, lifelines, handrails, smoke stacks, electric winches and windlasses, davits, tracks, and hatch frames.

Interior – engines, generators, shafts, engine and steering control rods and cables, and all large metallic masses within 6 feet of the lightning conductor, including metal fuel and water tanks.

Stays and shrouds should be grounded at their lower ends and, if penetrating the hull, at their lowest interior points.

Exception: Metal-hulled boats require only grounding of masts and rigging to the hull.

The theory is that lightning will flow through the bonding conductors rather than through the highly resistive air as side flashes, or the hull to water as with the lower ends of interior chainplates. Interconnection of metallic masses is a good idea, but it is doubtful that one boat in one hundred conforms. It would be less expensive to improve the mast/lightning-ground connection than to protect against its deficiencies by interconnection of masses.

Protecting Electronics

Even a well-protected boat may suffer loss of electronics due to lightning. The problem is that today's solid-state electronics are very intolerant of voltage surges. It doesn't matter if they come from a direct hit, a nearby strike, or come in on an antenna lead, a microphone cord, or power leads.

There are two basic approaches to the protection of electronics:

1. Shorting the surge
2. Disconnecting leads

Fig. 5.8 Alternatives for Protecting Electronics from Lightning Surges

Short the Surges

- Solid whip
- Lightning bypass gap bridging loading coil
- Long coax run
- Transient voltage suppressor (TVS)
- 2' – 3' distance
- Electronic equipment
- MOV
- Battery

Disconnect Leads

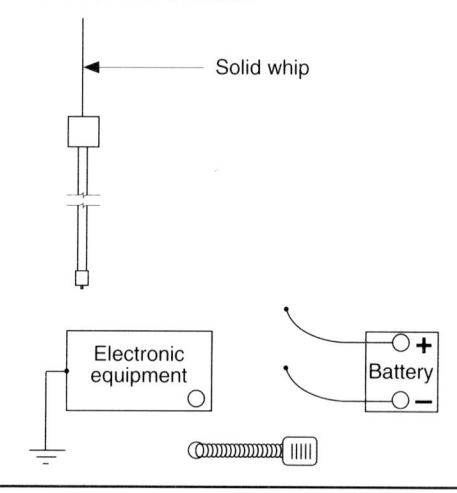

- Solid whip
- Electronic equipment
- Battery

Bonding

Shorting the Surges

Figure 5.8 shows a radio (it could equally well be a loran or GPS). At the top of the mast is the antenna. If we intend to make a solid-wire antenna with base-loading coil into an effective air terminal, we must install a lightning-bypass gap between the solid wire and the antenna base. Otherwise, the base coil resists lightning current, and the lightning-protective mast effectively originates at the base of the antenna. If the antenna is fiberglass, its conductivity is insufficient to be considered an air terminal, and the lightning protection begins at the top of the mast.

A coaxial conductor from the antenna to the radio will pick up current, either as part of a direct strike, or induced by the magnetic field of a nearby strike. This surge is shorted to ground by a coaxial transient voltage suppressor (TVS) installed several feet from the electronics enclosure. The TVS typically contains a one-shot cartridge and costs about $70.

Surges on the power supply line are shorted to ground by a metal-oxide varistor (MOV), which acts in less than one microsecond. Both TVSs and MOVs are available at most ham- and marine-radio dealers.

Apart from the nominal cost, there are several problems with the approach:

1. Insertion of the TVS in the antenna-feed line results in some loss of transmitted power.

2. By shorting the cable to ground, the TVS makes it more likely that the coaxial line will be damaged by a strike.

3. By shorting the antenna feed to ground, the TVS leads current closer to the electronics than if the cable were disconnected and placed out of the way.

Disconnecting Leads

In discussing lightning protection with both radio and TVS manufacturers, I jokingly told them I wished I had retained the original equipment cartons. I said that whenever I heard the distant rumble of thunder I would place my electronics in the cartons and attach notes saying, "Dear Lightning, there is nothing of interest in this box."

They all laughed and agreed. The best thing you can do to protect your electronics is to remove all leads, including the microphone. Just turning off the circuit breaker is not sufficient because the lightning will easily bridge the small breaker gap.

If any of your electronics have aluminum cases, place them in a steel box, such as an Army-surplus ammunition case, which will shield them from magnetic fields. Don't, however, do this while the lightning is crashing about your boat!

Protecting People

Assuming all of the protective measures above are in place, you can minimize the lightning danger to personnel aboard your boat by following these rules:

1. Keep everyone inside the boat (certainly within the zone of protection).

2. Do not allow any part of anyone's body in the water.

3. Keep everyone at least 6 feet from the lightning-protective mast.

4. Do not allow anyone to touch any part of the spars, standing rigging, metal rails or metal lifelines.

5. Do not allow anyone to touch any two grounded objects with two hands, which could result in a current flow through their chest.

DC

CORROSION PROTECTION

Everyone who owns a boat knows about corrosion. That is, they know it happens. Everywhere they look they see staining, pitting, powdering and disintegration. Corrosion is so pervasive on a boat that it's easy to throw up one's hands and accept it, like death, as inevitable. But corrosion is not inevitable. Corrosion can be prevented.

As with most complex problems, solution comes only after understanding, and understanding requires an investment of mental energy. If you wish to stop the corrosion on your boat, get a cup of tea or coffee, find your spot and clear your mind.

What is Corrosion?

In general terms, *corrosion* is the deterioration of a material by chemical or electrochemical reaction with its surroundings. As boat owners, we are most interested in *galvanic corrosion*—the deterioration of the anode of a galvanic couple resulting from the flow of ions from the anode to the cathode through an electrolyte.

Whoa! Those are fancy words to describe a very familiar phenomenon—the chemical reaction inside a battery.

Figure 5.9 shows a common carbon-zinc flashlight battery (the cheap kind that comes with electrical toys).

If we were to slice the battery in half, we would see a carbon rod in an electrically conductive paste, all inside a zinc-coated can. At A we measure the voltage between the carbon rod and the zinc can as 1.5 volts. At B, placing a 1.5-volt lamp in series with the meter + lead, we find that current is flowing from the + terminal to the – terminal as expected. Since electrons are negative, the electrons are flowing in the opposite direction, from – to +.

Fig. 5.9 A Battery— Useful Corrosion

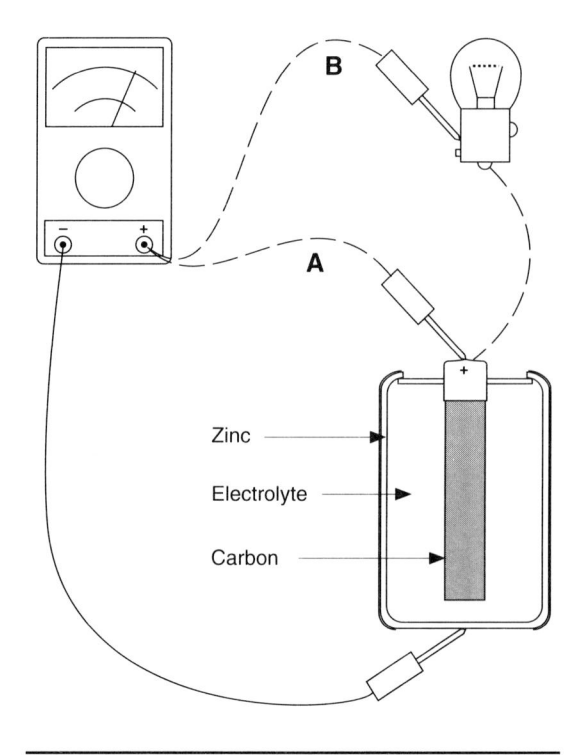

If we were to leave the lamp connected to the battery, the battery voltage and current would eventually drop to zero. Upon examination, we would find that all of the zinc coating had disappeared (corroded). On the other hand, if we disconnected the lamp so that there was no electrical connection between the carbon and the zinc, the zinc would not corrode, and the battery would retain its voltage for a very long time.

You have just witnessed galvanic corrosion in a galvanic cell. The common carbon-zinc battery is a convenient example, but it is just one example of a common phenomenon.

Bonding

Another Galley Experiment (Figure 5.10)

Let's continue our experimentation. Actually performing the following series of experiments will do wonders for your understanding of corrosion on your boat.

Gather a bucket of fresh water, a tablespoon of salt, a volt-ohmmeter (VOM), several test leads with alligator clips, and an assortment of metal items. I used a stainless bolt, a bronze bolt, a piece of ordinary unpainted steel, four pieces of aluminum flashing, and a shaft zinc.

Fig. 5.10 Testing Galvanic Potential

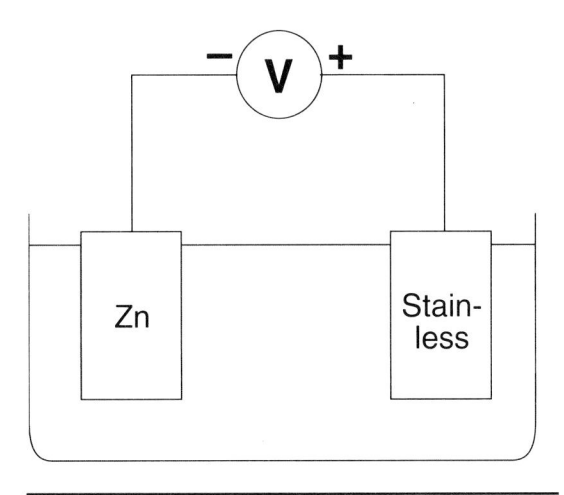

Switch the VOM to volts. Using the test leads, connect the – meter lead to the zinc and the + meter lead to the piece of stainless and lower both pieces (the electrodes) into the water. Surprised? The meter will indicate over 0.5 volt.

Now switch the meter to amps (Figure 5.11). You may or may not read any current but hold on. Get a bucket of sea water or dump the tablespoon of salt into the fresh water and stir. Wow! Depending on the sizes of the electrodes, you will now probably measure a current of from 10 to 100 milliamps flowing from the stainless piece to the zinc.

Fig. 5.11 Testing Galvanic Current

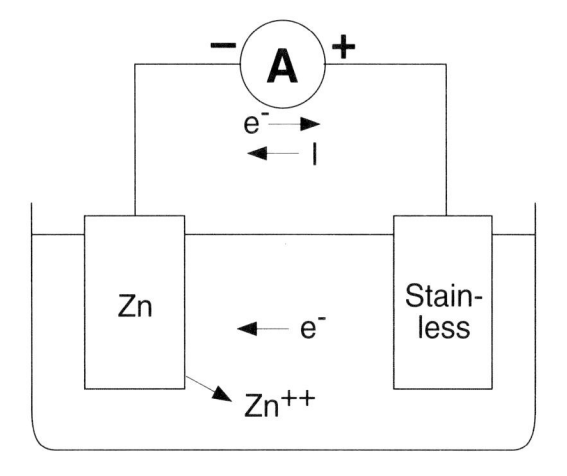

What's going on? When two dissimilar metals are placed together in an electrolyte (electrically conductive fluid, gel, or paste), one metal will assume a higher potential than the other. In Chapter 1 we learned that current flows only in closed circuits. Two isolated electrodes, immersed in electrolyte, form an open circuit and no current flows. But when we electrically connect the two electrodes, either with a wire or by letting them physically touch, we complete the circuit and current flows.

In this case, the current flow through the wire is from the stainless into the zinc. Since electrons are negatively charged, electron flow is in the opposite direction, from zinc to stainless.

Fig. 5.12 Corrosion of Zinc

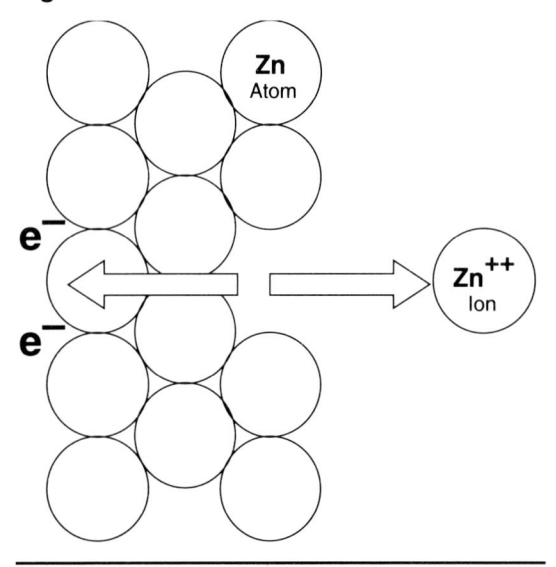

Figure 5.12 shows what is happening to the zinc on an atomic level. The zinc atoms are breaking down by giving up two electrons each. The released electrons are flowing from the zinc to the stainless through the wire, and the newly formed zinc ions are departing the crystalline structure of the zinc and flowing into the electrolyte (the zinc is corroding).

Continue the experiment by substituting other pairs of dissimilar metals. As long as the metals are different, they will always generate a potential difference, and current will always flow into the lower voltage metal. The voltage will be the same, whether the water is salt or fresh. The currents, however, will be much greater in salt water due to its lower resistance.

The potential difference between any two dissimilar metals can be predicted by consulting a galvanic potential table. To form such a table, potential differences are measured between various metals and a reference eletrode, such as silver-silver chloride. Table 5.1 reproduces the values for metals and alloys in sea water flowing at 8 to 13 feet per second (4.7 to 7.7 knots) and at temperatures of 50°F to 80°F.

The values in the table are between a metal and a silver-silver chloride electrode. Values between any two metals are found as the difference between table values for the two metals.

Example: What is the corrosion potential between silicon bronze and zinc? From Table 5.1 we find the corrosion potentials of silicon bronze vs. the reference and zinc vs. the reference to be –0.26 to –0.29 volt (average –0.28 volt) and –0.98 to –1.03 volt (average –1.00 volt) = 0.72 volt.

By now you may be thoroughly alarmed at the thought of all the underwater metallic components on your boat—stainless bolts, stainless or bronze shaft, brass cutless-bearing shell, and aluminum outboard drive. And well you should be with all that potential (no pun intended) for corrosion. But let's press on.

Before continuing our galley experiment, let's review what we have learned. We have found that any two dissimilar metals or alloys immersed in water will generate a potential difference. We have also found that if the two metals are isolated (neither physically touching nor electrically connected by wire), no current or corrosion will occur. Good. But what if they cannot be separated (a bronze prop on a stainless shaft), or what if we have bonded them for lightning protection (a steel rudder, several bronze through-hulls, and a sheet-copper ground plate)? Have we shot ourselves in the foot?

Bonding

TABLE 5-1, GALVANIC SERIES OF METALS IN SEA WATER
(Sea water flowing at 8 to 13 ft./sec. (4.8 to 7.8 kn.), temperature range 50°F to 80°F – except as noted)

Metals and Alloys (Anodic or Least Noble—Active)	Corrosion-Potential Range in Volts
Magnesium and Magnesium Alloys	-1.60 to -1.63
Zinc	-0.98 to -1.03
Galvanized Steel or Galvanized Wrought Iron	NA
Aluminum Alloys	-0.76 to -1.00
Cadmium	-0.70 to -0.73
Mild Steel	-0.60 to -0.71
Wrought Iron	-0.60 to -0.71
Cast Iron	-0.60 to -0.71
13% Chromium Stainless Steel, Type 410 (active in still water)	-0.46 to -0.58
18-8 Stainless Steel, Type 304 (active in still water)	-0.46 to -0.58
Ni-Resist	-0.46 to -0.58
18-8, 3% Mo Stainless Steel, Type 316 (active in still water)	-0.43 to -0.54
78% Ni – 14.5% Cr – 6% Fe (Inconel) (active in still water)	-0.35 to -0.46
Aluminum Bronze (92% Cu – 8% Al)	-0.31 to -0.42
Naval Brass (60% Cu – 39% Zn)	-0.30 to -0.40
Yellow Brass (65% Cu – 35% Zn)	-0.30 to -0.40
Red Brass (85% Cu – 15% Zn)	-0.30 to -0.40
Muntz Metal (60% Cu – 40% Zn)	-0.30 to -0.40
Tin	-0.31 to -0.33
Copper	-0.30 to -0.57
50–50 Lead – Tin Solder	-0.28 to -0.37
Admiralty Brass (71% Cu – 28% Zn – 1% Sn)	-0.28 to -0.36
Aluminum Brass (76% Cu – 22% Zn – 2% Al)	-0.28 to -0.36
Manganese Bronze (58.5% Cu – 39% Zn – 1% Sn – 1% Fe – 0.3 MN)	-0.27 to -0.34
Silicon Bronze (96% Cu Max – 0.8% Fe – 1.5% Zn – 2% Si – 0.75% MN – 1.6% Sn)	-0.26 to -0.29
Bronze-Composition G (88% Cu – 2% Zn – 10% Sn)	-0.24 to -0.31
Bronze-Composition M (88% Cu – 3% Zn – 6.5% Zn – 1.5% Pb)	-0.24 to -0.31
13% Chromium Stainless Steel, Type 401 (passive)	-0.26 to -0.35
90% Cu – 10% Ni	-0.21 to -0.28
75% Cu – 20% Ni – 5% Zn	-0.19 to -0.25
Lead	-0.19 to -0.25
70% Cu – 30% Ni	-0.18 to -0.23
78% Ni – 13.5% Cr – 6% Fe (Inconel) (passive)	-0.14 to -0.17
Nickel 200	-0.10 to -0.20
18-8 Stainless Steel, Type 304 (passive)	-0.05 to -0.10
70% Ni – 30% Cu Monel 400, K-500	-0.04 to -0.14
18-8, 3% Mo Stainless Steel, Type 316 (passive)	-0.00 to -0.10
Titanium	-0.05 to +0.06
Hastelloy C	-0.03 to +0.08
Platinum	+0.19 to +0.25
Graphite	+0.20 to +0.30

(Cathodic or Most Noble —Passive)

To find out if we are in trouble, let's continue our galley experiment. First repeat the aluminum vs. stainless test. Next add the piece of zinc as a third electrode. Connect the aluminum, stainless and zinc electrodes together, as shown in Figure 5.13. Now, one at a time, place the meter in each of the leads to detect current flow.

Fig. 5.13 Testing Sacrificial Zinc Anode

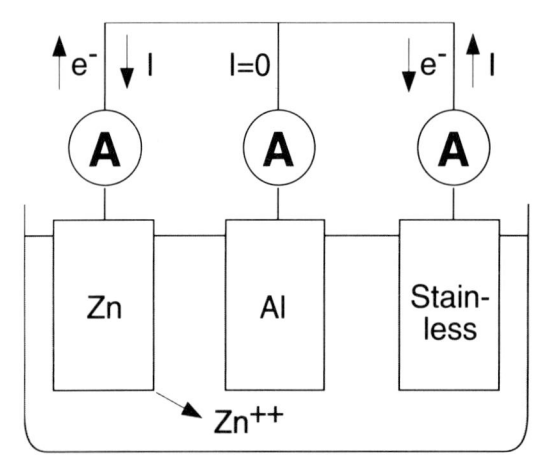

Amazing! Electric current is flowing out of the stainless electrode and into the zinc electrode, but no current is flowing either into or out of the aluminum electrode. Since metal is lost only by an electrode that receives current, it seems that the zinc is protecting the aluminum by sacrificing itself!

You can repeat this experiment with any three metals you wish, and the results will be the same: When dissimilar metals in an electrolyte are mechanically or electrically bonded, the only metal to corrode will be the least noble (highest in the galvanic series) of the group. The metal most used in boats for this purpose is zinc.

The phenomenon you observed is called *cathodic protection*, and the zinc masses are called *zinc anodes* or just *zincs*.

Figure 5.14 shows two examples of cathodic protection using zincs. At top is an outboard engine mounted on the transom of a boat. A large zinc is bolted directly to the transom underwater, and a wire is run from the mounting bolts of the zinc to the outboard. The zinc protects all of the other metals.

At the bottom of Figure 5.14, is a sailboat with a zinc on the shaft. The zinc is mechanically (and thus electrically) connected to the shaft. Protection is extended to the rudder shaft by a conductor from rudder to engine block. Rudder, rudder shaft, engine, transmission, prop shaft, and prop are all connected and thus protected by the zinc. A nonconductive, flexible shaft coupling would require a jumper strap across the coupling or a brush riding on the shaft.

Fig. 5.14 Two Uses for Zinc Anodes

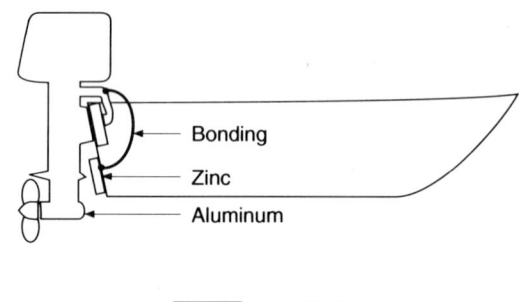

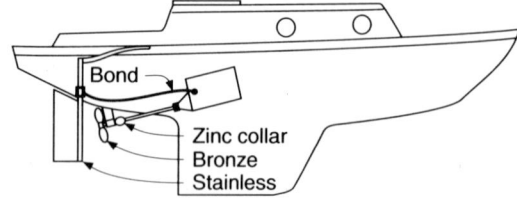

Bonding

Figure 5.15 shows a variety of zincs commonly found in chandleries. Many more shapes and forms are available from specialty suppliers. Engine zincs are mounted inside the cooling systems of engines. The guppy is used at anchor or in a slip and will be discussed below.

Fig. 5.15 Commonly Available Zincs

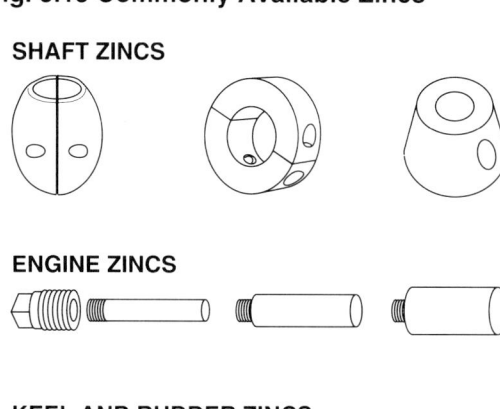

SHAFT ZINCS

ENGINE ZINCS

KEEL AND RUDDER ZINCS

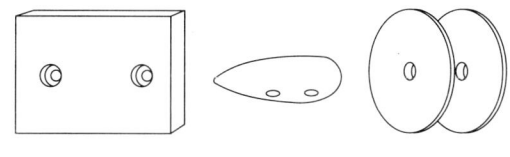

TRANSOM ZINC

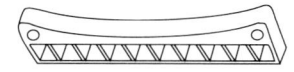

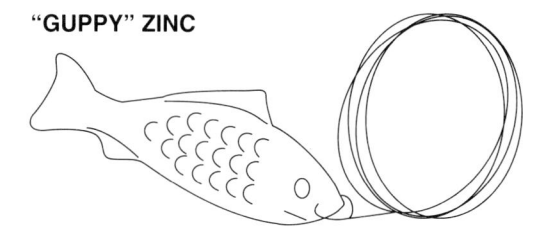

"GUPPY" ZINC

Impressed-Current Systems

Galvanic corrosion occurs due to the natural potential differences between dissimilar metals. But what if we were to force a potential difference by connecting an external voltage source to one of the electrodes? As Figure 5.16 shows, with a high enough voltage, the current will be forced to flow into the impressed-current electrode.

If the voltage of the impressed-current electrode is higher than the natural galvanic voltage of the other underwater metals, underwater current will flow out of the electrode and into the other metals, thus preventing corrosion of those other metals.

As a rule of thumb, the impressed-current electrode is maintained 0.2 volt higher than the highest-voltage galvanic component it is designed to protect.

Impressed-current systems are common on large metal hulls. Systems for small boats are available, but installation and regulation are tricky and best left to professionals.

Fig. 5.16 An Impressed-Current Electrode

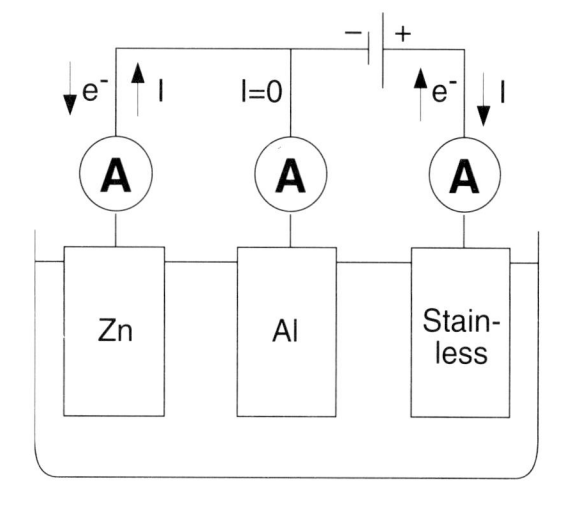

STRAY-CURRENT CORROSION

Even if flushed with recent mastery of the subject of galvanic corrosion, I suggest you take a break at this point. We have an even larger dragon to slay—stray-current corrosion.

Galley Experiment Continued

As a refresher, place two identical aluminum electrodes in the sea water, as in Figure 5.17. Measure both voltage and current between the electrodes. The results should be zero in both cases.

Fig. 5.17 Testing Identical Electrodes

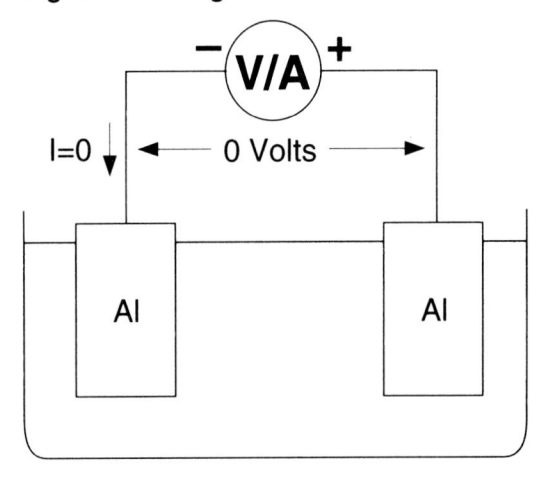

Fig. 5.18 Impressing Stray Current

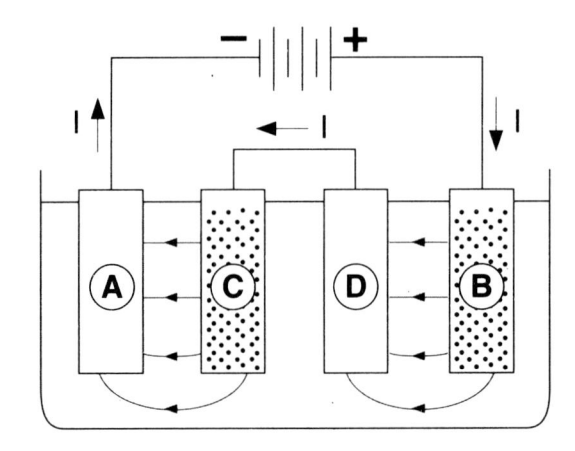

Next place a 1.5-volt battery between the two electrodes, A and B, as in Figure 5.18. Now you will measure 1.5 volts across the electrodes and, with the meter placed in series with the battery, a current flowing from the battery + terminal into its electrode. If you let the experiment go on long enough, you'll find that the electrode into which the current flows will corrode, just as it did with galvanic corrosion. It makes no difference whether the potential difference is inherent due to dissimilar metals or impressed from an outside source—the current-receiving electrode always corrodes. When the impressed voltage is accidental (as from a poorly insulated connection), the corrosion is termed stray-current corrosion. Since stray, or accidental, voltage sources can be much greater (up to 12 volts, compared to a few tenths of a volt), stray-current corrosion is often many times more damaging than the natural variety.

Finally, we'll use all four aluminum electrodes. We'll use the previous two electrodes, A and B, to force a current in the sea water. Now, insert the connected pair, C and D, between A and B. Measure the current between C and D. It will be approximately the same as in the previous experiment. Likewise, electrode C will eventually show signs of corrosion. Now you see why this insidious phenomenon is termed stray-current corrosion. Two perfectly innocent metallic objects, if electrically bonded, will pick up stray currents in the electrolyte and participate in the corrosion process!

Bonding

Figure 5.19 (top) shows a boat floating in an external voltage and current field (perhaps due to an adjacent boat). The voltage difference, from left to right across the illustration, is 1.0 volt.

Since the electrical resistance of the path from ground plate to bonding wire to engine to shaft to prop is less than that of the water path, electric current flows into the ground plate, through the bonding system and out of the prop. And since the current is flowing into the prop from the bonding system, the prop will corrode.

Figure 5.19 (bottom) shows that a sacrificial zinc on the shaft will divert the current flow to itself and save the prop.

Fig. 5.19 Stray-Current Corrosion and Protection with Zinc Anode

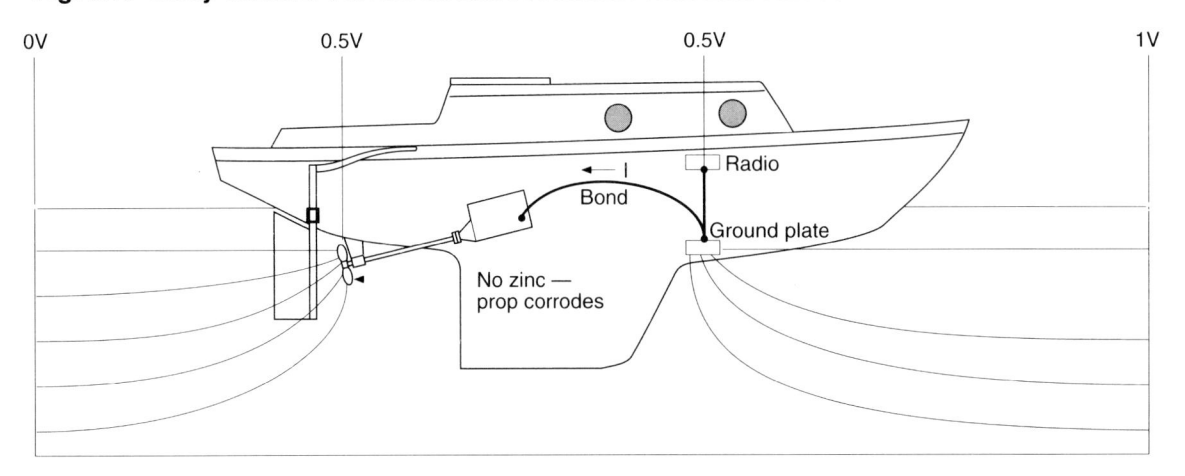

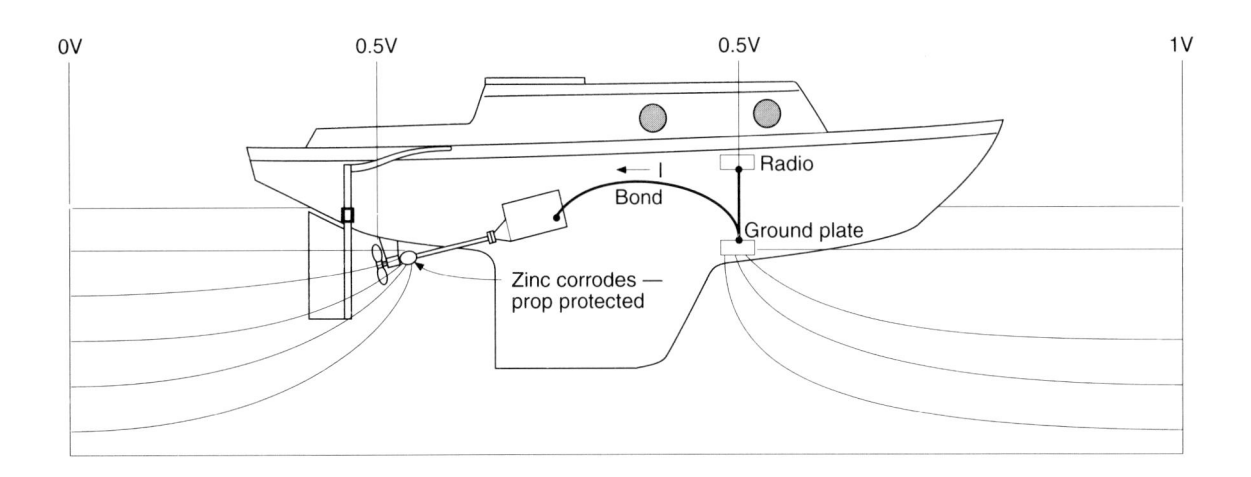

Figure 5.20 shows a stray current originating entirely inside the boat. Both a bilge pump and a bronze through-hull are sitting in bilge water. The unbonded pump develops a short from its positive power lead to its housing, establishing the pump housing at 12 volts. Current flows from the electrified housing, through the bilge water, into the through-hull, to the water outside the hull, and back through the prop, shaft, and engine path to ground. The through-hull will corrode. If the pump housing had been electrically bonded, the stray current would have found the bonding conductor the lowest resistance path back to ground, thus preventing corrosion.

Fig. 5.20 Stray Current from Shorted Bilge Pump

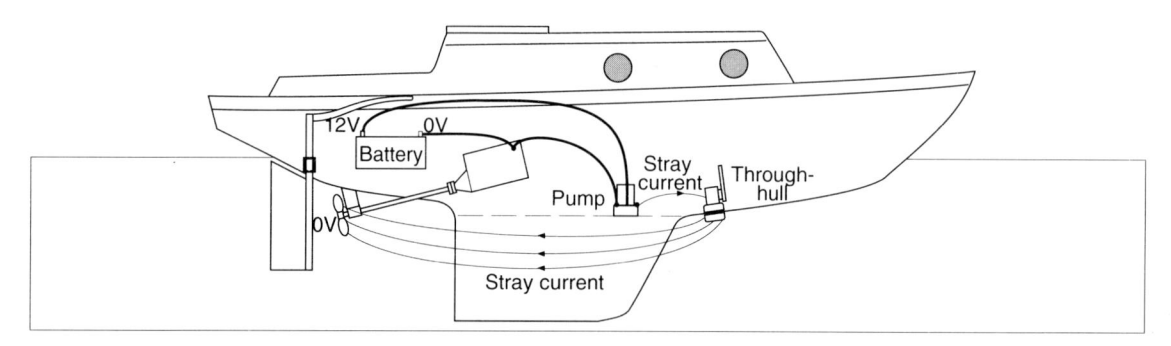

Figure 5.21 shows stray current originating from a terminal strip in the bilge. A single 12-volt/ground pair is shown here, but there are usually several pairs, serving anchor light, steaming light, and spreader lights on the mast.

The terminal strip is wet, and some of the stray current finds its way back to ground by way of the through-hull seawater connection. If the through-hull were bonded to ground, the stray current would flow back to ground by way of the bonding.

Fig. 5.21 Stray Current from Wet Terminal Strip in Bilge

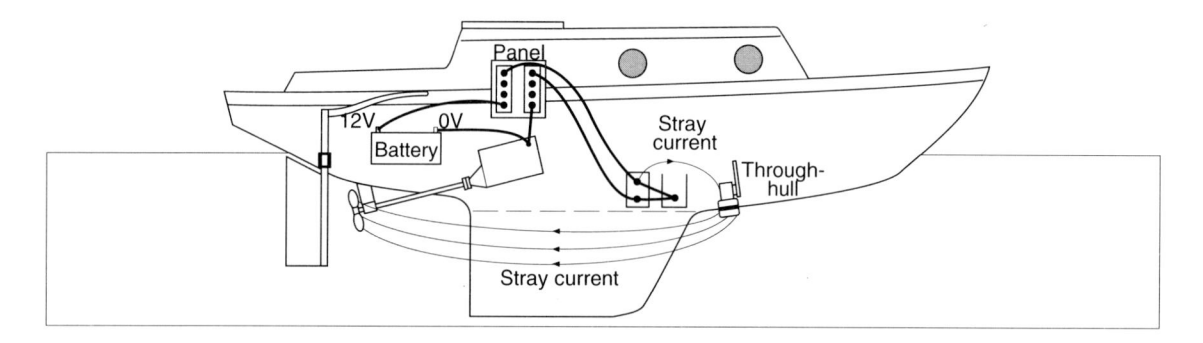

Bonding

TO BOND OR NOT TO BOND

We have just seen three examples of stray current corrosion. Two would have been prevented by bonding, but one was, in fact, caused by bonding. *In general, bonding of immersed metal components prevents corrosion due to stray currents inside the hull, but it causes corrosion due to stray currents outside the hull.*

There are two solutions to this dilemma:

1. Bond everything and protect
2. Unbond everything and isolate

Bond and Protect

Figure 5.22 shows the bond and protect principle. Every underwater mass is connected to the boat's bonding system. To protect against stray currents outside the hull, sacrificial anodes are connected to the bonding system and placed where they may best protect all underwater masses.

Fig. 5.22 Bond and Protect Principle

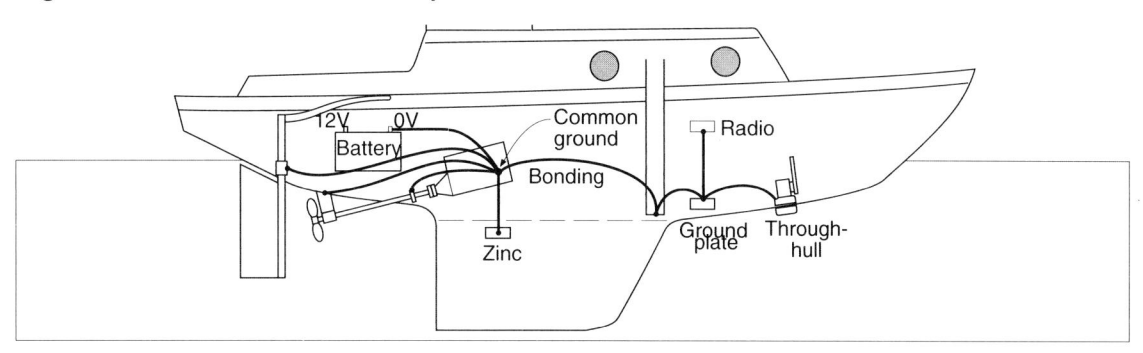

Unbond and Isolate

Figure 5.23 shows the alternative unbond and isolate principle. Underwater masses are isolated so neither galvanic nor outside stray current can flow between them. The only bonded underwater mass is the lightning and radio ground. Masses entirely within the hull (engine, transmission, metal tanks, and mast) are bonded to the boat's bonding system. The shaft is isolated by an insulating flexible coupling. The prop is protected by a shaft zinc, if necessary.

Fig. 5.23 Unbond and Isolate Principle

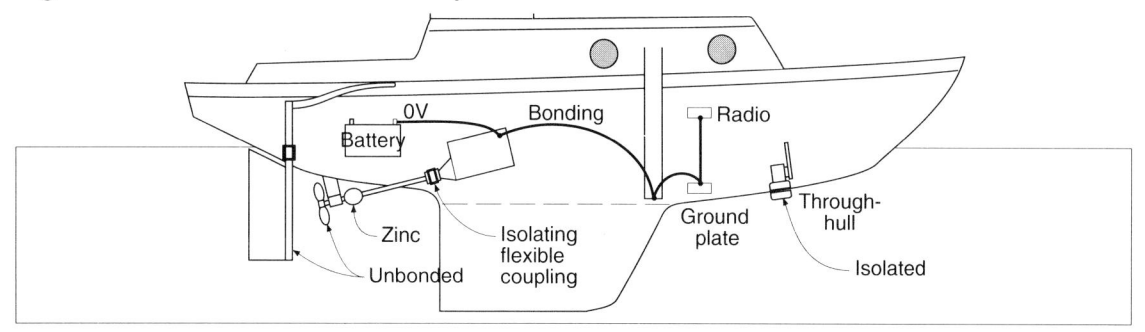

DC

Pros and Cons of Bonding

The bond and protect approach offers the advantage of greater wetted surface area for the lightning and radio grounds.

On the other hand, proponents of the unbond and isolate approach claim that the largest sintered-bronze ground plate provides adequate ground for both lightning and SSB radio, and that electrochemical reactions at bonded wooden-hull through-hulls dangerously soften the surrounding wood. The BMEA seems to favor the bond and protect approach, but suggests that electrically isolated through-hull fittings need not be bonded.

TESTING YOUR PROTECTION

If you have implemented the unbond and isolate approach correctly, there is no need to electrically test for corrosion. The best and only meaningful test is periodic visual inspection of underwater metals.

With a bonded system, there are two simple tests you can perform using a VOM.

Test 1: Stray Currents (Figure 5.24)

In a bonded system, any stray current will be captured by the boat's bonding conductor. Stray current through an individual or other accessible underwater mass can be measured simply as shown in Figure 5.24.

Disconnect the bonding conductor and place the meter between the bare end of the conductor and the metal of the through-hull. Current into or out of the through-hull will now flow through the meter. Repeat the test with each fitting, as well as rudder shaft, prop shaft, and strut or shaft log. Remember that current flowing out of the through-hull is harmless, and current flowing into it is causing corrosion of the fitting.

Fig. 5.24 Testing for Stray Currents

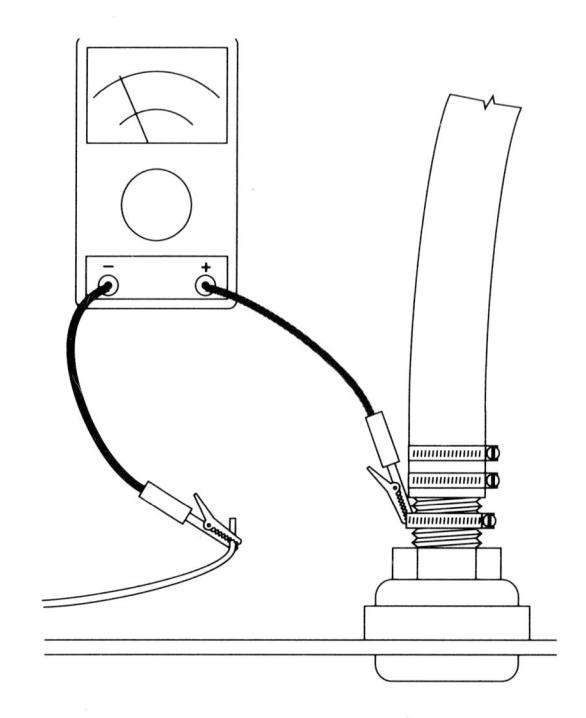

Test 2: Corrosion Potentials (Figure 5.25)

This test will determine whether the boat's sacrificial zincs are doing an adequate job of protecting the boat's underwater metallic masses.

First connect the + lead of the voltmeter to the boat's bonding system. A bonded shroud or stay will work; otherwise, connect to the engine negative terminal making sure that the electrical connection is clean and sound.

Next, connect the – lead to a zinc "guppy" or other large zinc mass, and lower the zinc into the water. Note the voltage reading.

Bonding

Repeat the measurement near all underwater metal masses. If the boat's zincs are doing their job, the readings should all be less than 0.2 volt. Readings of 0.5 volt to 0.8 volt indicate a complete lack of zinc. Readings in excess of 0.8 volt indicate a voltage field in the water surrounding the boat. If you can't eliminate or reduce the external field, consider moving your boat or unbonding and isolating its underwater fittings, as shown in Figure 5.23.

Hanging one or more large zinc masses (the large rectangular ones are the best buy) over the side is a good idea whenever the boat is not underway, as at anchor, on a mooring, or in a slip. The large zinc surface area provides excellent protection and will reduce the consumption of shaft collars or other zincs on the boat. Make sure that the electrical connection from the zinc to the boat's bonding system is clean and sound.

Fig. 5.25 Testing Zincs and Corrosion Potentials

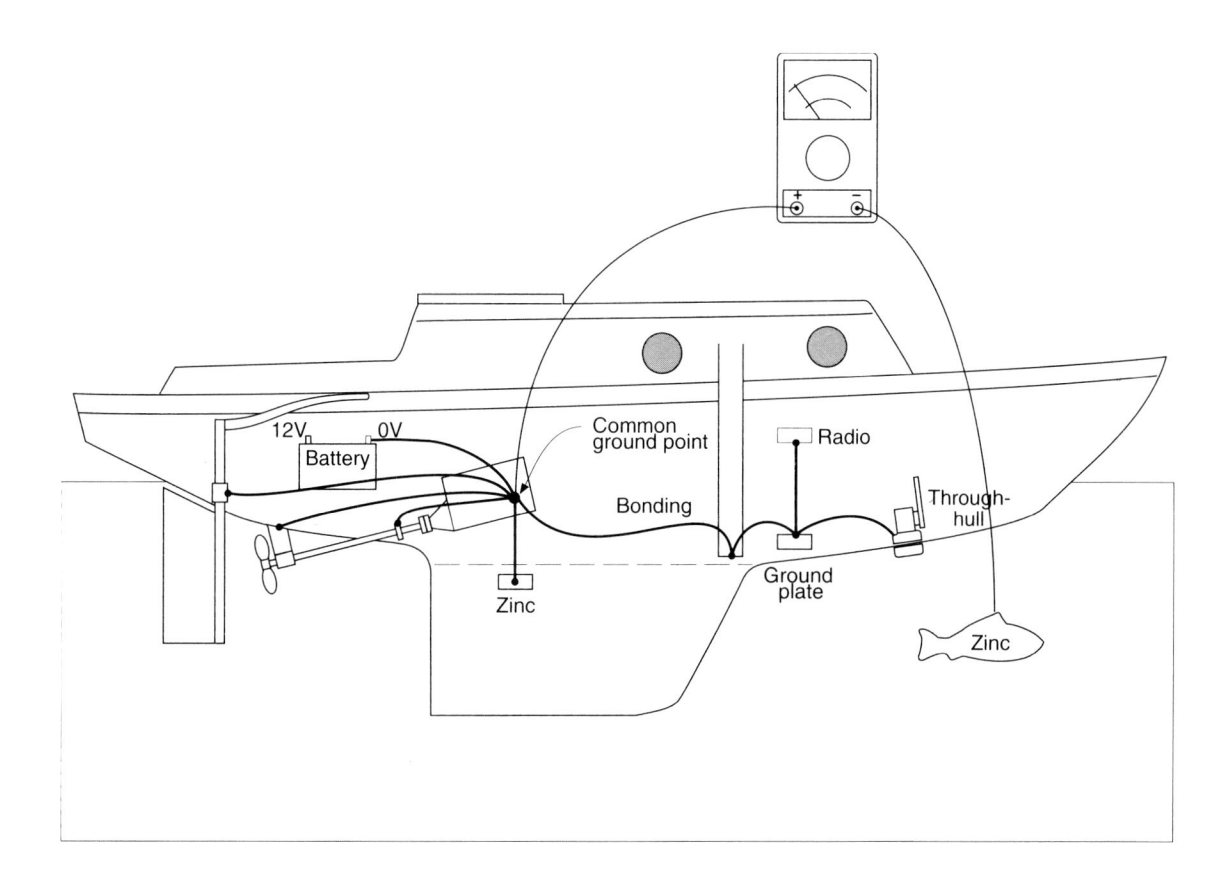

GENERAL APPLICATION OF CATHODIC PROTECTION

a. Although cathodic protection will, depending on the current capability of the system, help to minimize stray-current corrosion when it exists, stray-current corrosion should be controlled by:

   (1) Minimizing DC and AC electrical leakage levels from electrical products, and

   (2) The use of a bonding system such as shown in Fig 5.22.

b. Factors that affect the type and degree of cathodic protection required:

   (1) Water velocity—Cathodic protection current requirements increase with water velocity past the hull. The current requirements can be as high as 30 times that required in still water.

   (2) Boat Usage—More frequently operated vessels require more cathodic protection than vessels infrequently used.

   (3) Fresh and Sea Water—Current requirements increase with salinity but higher driving potentials are required in fresh water.

   (4) Deterioration of Protective Coatings—Current requirements increase as protective coatings deteriorate.

c. The need for a cathodic protection system for metal appendages on nonmetallic hulls may not be justified if the metals coupled are galvanically compatible.

d. Hull-mounted metallic trim tabs may be electrically isolated from the boat's bonding system to reduce the load on the boat's cathodic protection system, providing the trim tabs are also electrically isolated from their electrical actuating mechanism. If the trim-tab system is connected to the boat's bonding system the cathodic protection system's milliampere rating will have to be increased to provide the additional protection.

e. A cathodic protection system shall be capable of inducing and maintaining a minimum negative shift of 200 millivolts in the potential of the composite cathode being protected.

f. Since the area relationship of metals in a galvanic cell will affect current density and therefore corrosion rate, the immersed cathodic metal surfaces may be coated to obtain a more favorable anode to cathode area relationship. Coatings shall not contain pigments that will form galvanic couples with the substrate. Coatings on substrate and coatings on surfaces must be able to tolerate alkali generated by the cathodic reaction.

g. Impressed-current anodes shall have the words "DO NOT PAINT" on a visible surface when installed.

   NOTE: Anodes are ineffective if painted.

h. In general, the use of several anodes instead of one large anode will tend to provide better distribution of the protective current. Sacrificial anodes may be mounted remotely, the best current distribution will be obtained with the anode(s) positioned to be as equidistant as possible from the metals to be protected.

i. Anodes should be faired and, if possible, arranged in a longitudinal row to minimize drag. After installation, peripheral crevices should be sealed.

j. Anodes shall be mounted on a sloping surface that cannot entrap gas bubbles.

k. If anodes are located near through-hull fittings they shall be positioned forward of discharge fittings and aft of intake ports. Anode locations that disturb the flow of water past the propeller should be avoided.

l. All metals which are to receive cathodic protection from the cathodic protection system must have good electrical continuity to the boat

Bonding

bonding system. Galvanic anodes, if used, must be affixed in a manner that electrical continuity is maintained with the metals they are to protect, either through their mounting means or through the boat's bonding system.

(1) Propeller shafts do not provide reliable electrical continuity to the boat's bonding system without brushes and/or slip rings and brushes.

(2) Rudder posts shall be grounded with slip rings and brushes, or by means of a flexible bonding strap positioned to allow full rudder movement without stressing the bonding strap or its connections.

m. In general, sacrificial anodes may be mounted directly on the metal to be protected, but the best current distribution will be obtained by remote mounting with the anode(s) positioned to be as equidistant as possible from the metals to be protected.

n. The negative potential (over 1,000 millivolts as compared to silver-silver chloride) that can be achieved by some corrosion control systems will result in some decrease in the effectiveness of antifouling paints. Because the decrease in the effectiveness increases with higher negative voltages, the negative potential should be kept as close to the optimum value as possible. A reference potential reading in excess of 1,000 millivolts indicates excessive cathodic protection.

o. Anodes and reference electrodes shall be positioned to avoid contact with lifting slings and chocks when the boat is hauled.

p. The electrical interconnection that occurs via shore-power cables or metal mooring cables between two vessels or between a vessel and submerged metal or the dock may result in galvanic corrosion of steel or aluminum hulls and aluminum underwater appendages. An isolator or an isolation transformer can break this couple.

OTHER TYPES OF CORROSION

We have addressed the types of corrosion that can be eliminated by cathodic protection. There are further annoying types of corrosion on a boat that must be addressed by other means.

Dezincification

Figure 5.26 shows the dezincification of brass screws. Brass consists of a mixture of copper and zinc. Common yellow brass contains 65% copper and 35% zinc. In the presence of moisture (an electrolyte and very common around boats), the zinc and copper react galvanically, just as they would underwater, although slower. The result is a loss of zinc and loss of strength. When a badly dezinced screw is removed, the screw head often snaps off. Moral: use only stainless or bronze screws around a boat.

Fig. 5.26 Dezincification of Brass

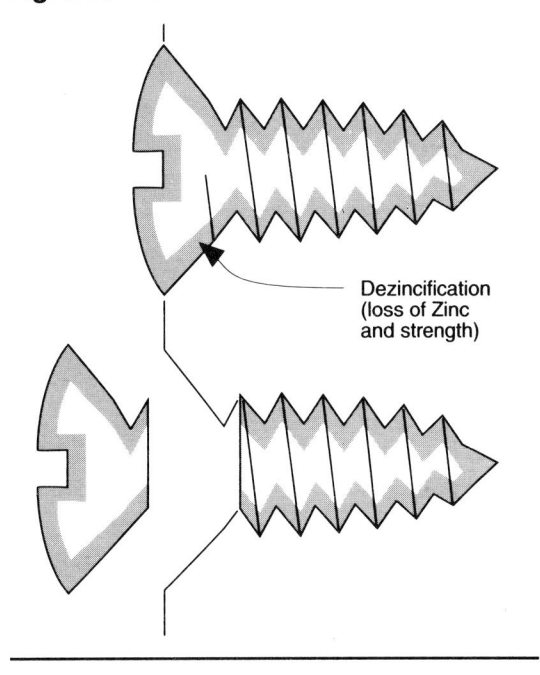

Stainless Screws in Aluminum

Figure 5.27 shows what happens when a fitting is attached to an aluminum mass with stainless screws. When water finds its way into the capillary spaces between the stainless and aluminum threads, an ideal galvanic cell is set up with resulting loss of aluminum in the area of the threads. Ultimately, the stainless screw seizes in the hole or, worse, falls out under load. Filling both sets of threads with silicone sealant or grease before fastening will reduce the corrosion by sealing out water.

Stainless Pitting

Figure 5.28 shows how stainless (it should be spelled "stain-less") steel develops corrosion pits. Stainless steel is principally an alloy of iron and chromium. In the presence of oxygen, the chromium quickly oxidizes and forms a shiny protective skin (the stainless is then said to be passivated). The chromium oxide is also very noble in the galvanic series (see Table 5.1, entry 18-8, 3% Mo Stainless Steel, Type 316 (passive)), so it resists corrosion and protects the iron below.

Fig. 5.27 Stainless Screws in Aluminum

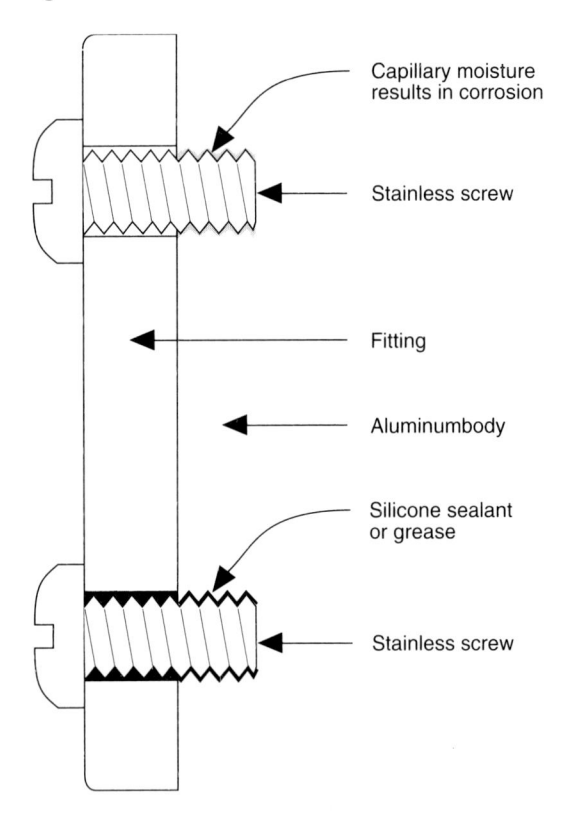

Fig. 5.28 Pitting of Stainless Steel

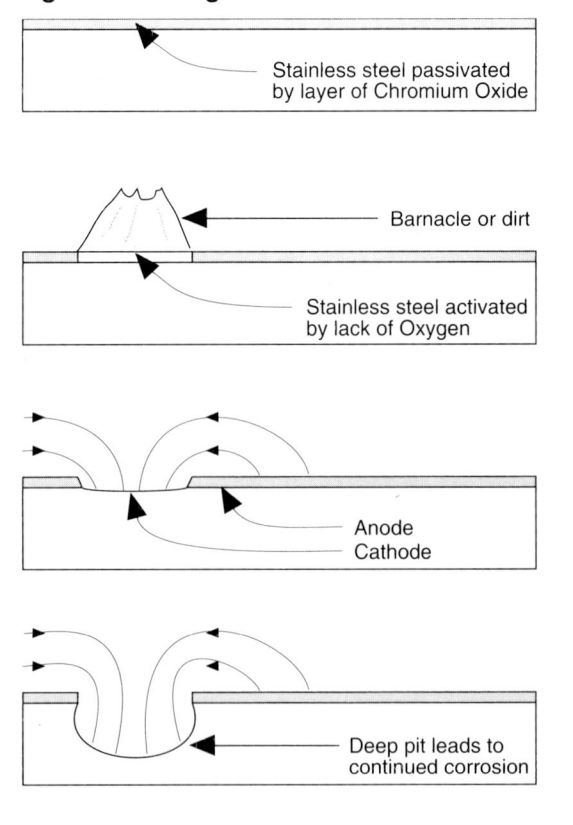

When the surface is immersed or covered with an oxygen-free liquid, however, the chromium loses its oxygen, the passive skin is lost, and the iron is free to rust. In Figure 5.28 a barnacle has attached itself to a stainless surface, depriving the chromium-oxide skin of its oxygen. The unpassivated area and the surrounding passivated area act as a galvanic couple, resulting in corrosion under the barnacle.

The same sort of corrosion occurs between stainless stanchions and their water-retaining bases, explaining the rust stains seen in these areas.

Cavitation Erosion

Finally, Figure 5.29 shows cavitation erosion of the trailing edge of a propeller. Cavitation is the rapid formation and collapse of vacuum bubbles just behind propeller blades. Cavitation is not galvanic corrosion. Instead, the propeller is turning so quickly that the water immediately forward of the blade is left behind, forming vacuum bubbles. As these bubbles collapse, the water hits the blade like thousands of tiny hammers. You can hear the sharp sound underwater when a boat passes. The result is a mechanical erosion of the metal at the trailing edge of the blade. The solution is a larger area of blade, which reduces the pressure difference across the blade.

A bronze propeller, or any other bronze fitting, suffering from galvanic corrosion would display a rosy-pink color instead of its normal brassy-yellow color. Corrosion selectively removes the zinc from the bronze, leaving the reddish copper behind.

Fig. 5.29 Cavitation Erosion

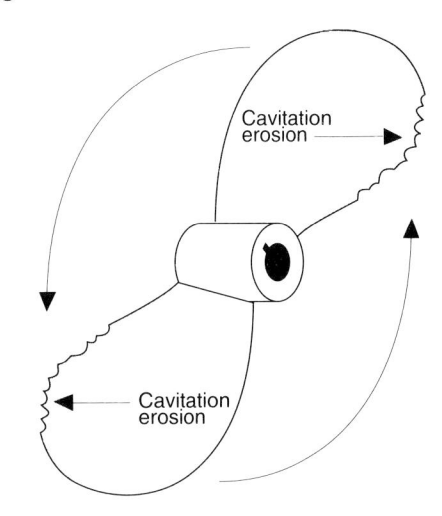

6

DC STANDARDS AND PRACTICES

Wiring Diagrams   104

Marine Wire   108

Load-calculation Method   110

Allowable Amperage of Conductors   111

Conductor Sizes for Allowable Voltage Drops   112

Identification of Conductors   113

Installation of Wire Runs   114

Over-current Protection   116

Making Connections   120

Ignition Protection   127

Standards and recommended practices for the wiring of boats are promoted by the British Marine Electronics Association and the American Boat and Yacht Council. This chapter explains and expands upon these standards. Preliminary to the standards, however, we first explain the wisdom of creating *wiring diagrams* for your boat's electrical systems.

The standards and practices start with the specification of acceptable *marine wire*. The *load calculation method* allows you to calculate the maximum current expected to flow in a conductor and to use the tables for *allowable amperage of conductors* and *conductor sizes for allowable voltage drop*.

Wiring and later troubleshooting are both facilitated by the proper *identification of conductors*, as well as the proper *installation of wire runs*.

As in a house, *over-current protection*, in the form of fuses and circuit breakers, guards against overheating and possible fire.

The marine environment, characterized by moisture, salt, and vibration, makes *conductor connections* critical.

The lethal mixture of gasoline vapors and open flame or electric spark dictates the recommended requirements for *ignition protection*.

WIRING DIAGRAMS

When you first bought your boat, you probably judged its wiring on appearances. Either it looked good or it did not. You never gave it another thought—until something went wrong. Then you discovered whether or not it had a wiring diagram. Chances are, if your boat was American made, it did not.

The person who wired your boat didn't need a wiring diagram. First, yours was probably one of dozens, if not hundreds, he had wired just like it. Second, he assumed he would not be there when something went wrong. Troubleshooting would be your problem.

One summer I worked in a boatyard rigging and stepping masts. One of my jobs was to check the mast wiring before the mast was stepped. Some masts had combined tricolor, anchor, and strobe light (4 conductors), masthead or steaming light (2 conductors), spreader lights (2 conductors), windvane light (2 conductors), plus a windspeed indicator (6 wires in a cable) and a VHF coaxial cable—a total of 10 conductors plus 2 cables.

It seemed like every other mast had a problem. A bulb was burned out or not properly seated, connectors were corroded, or a wire was broken. The symptoms were obvious—a light at the top of the mast did not come on. Finding the cause, however, was an art. Without a wiring diagram, labeled terminals and color-coded conductors, finding the fault sometimes required an hour of labor for two workers: one at the top end reading voltage or watching the light, the other at the bottom applying voltage to successive pairs of conductors. Did you know that the number of possible pairs of n wires is $n(n-1)/2$? For 10 wires we had to check up to 45 pair combinations!

Sometimes we found that a light that had worked on the ground no longer worked with the mast up. Now there were even more possibilities! Something could have happened inside the mast during stepping, or the problem could lie between the distribution panel and the base of the mast. It was here that we sometimes encountered the case of the disappearing color. A wire would leave the distribution panel with blue insulation, disappear into the bilge or behind a liner, and emerge at the base of the mast with yellow insulation!

One of my associates had worked for one of the best boat builders in the U.S. Over lunch I related the strange case of the chameleon wire.

"Oh, sure," he said, "we used to run wires until the spool ran out. Then we'd grab another spool of whatever color and splice it in."

A proper wiring diagram shows every electrical device: circuit breaker, fuse, switch, terminal and conductor, and wire size, color, and label. Such a diagram makes troubleshooting simple. If a light doesn't come on, the diagram shows exactly where to check for voltage, all the way from the lamp back to the distribution panel. A circuit diagram also shows the best place to tie in additional electrical equipment, what spares to carry, and whether or not you are fused correctly.

Best of all, if you create your circuit diagram by visual inspection of your existing wiring, you will get a systematic look at every component and may be able to spot potential problems before they become real problems.

DC Standards and Practices

Creating Wiring Diagrams

Circuit symbols are, like international road signs, intended to convey meaning at a glance. Unlike international signage, however, there is no rigorous standard for electrical symbols.

Figure 6.1 shows commonly used symbols for most of the simple devices encountered in a boat. If these don't work for you, feel free to invent your own. For example, you may elect to show a fan as a fan blade and a fuse as a simple rectangle.

Figure 6.1 Common Circuit Symbols

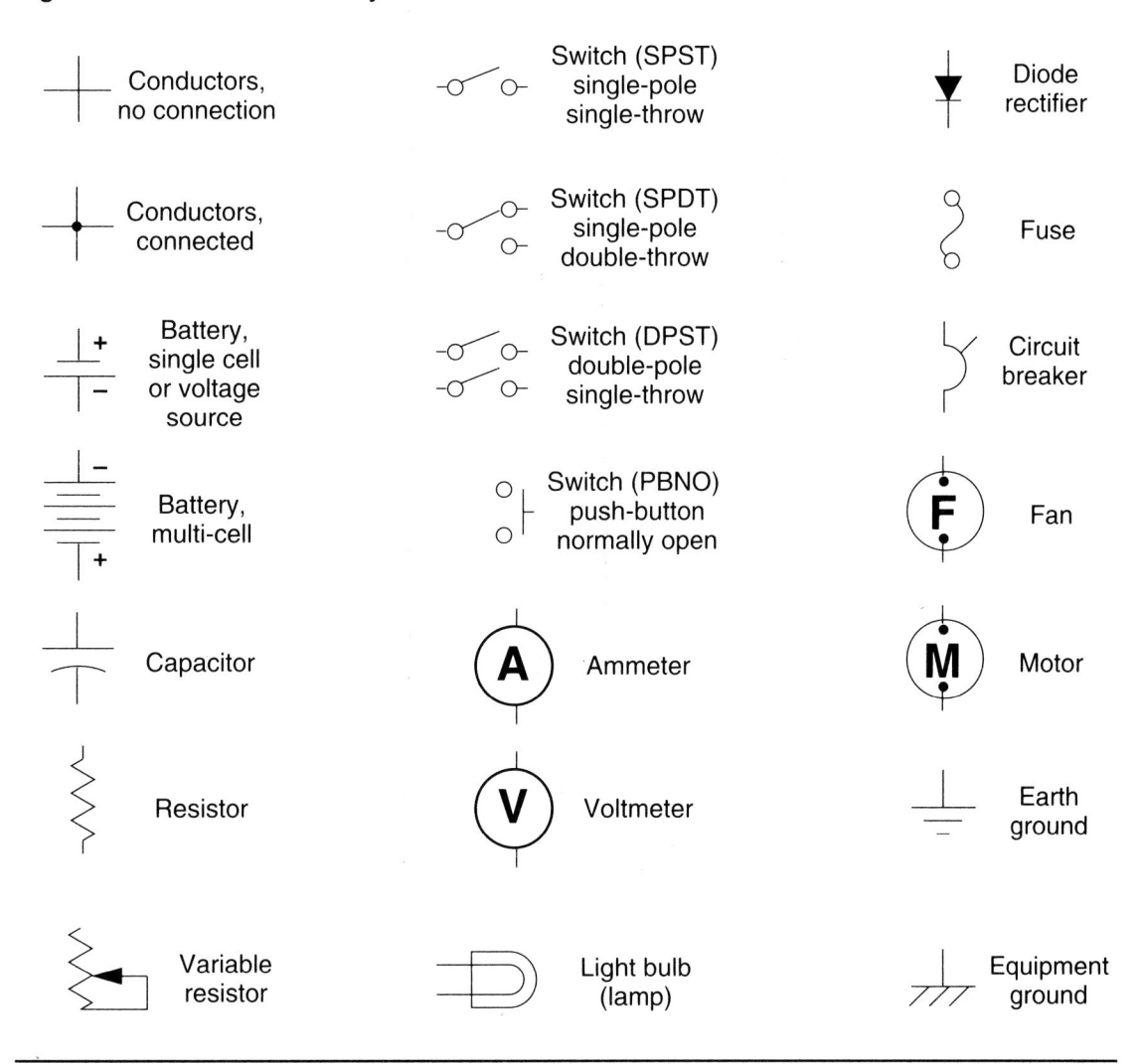

	Conductors, no connection
	Conductors, connected
	Battery, single cell or voltage source
	Battery, multi-cell
	Capacitor
	Resistor
	Variable resistor
	Switch (SPST) single-pole single-throw
	Switch (SPDT) single-pole double-throw
	Switch (DPST) double-pole single-throw
	Switch (PBNO) push-button normally open
	Ammeter
	Voltmeter
	Light bulb (lamp)
	Diode rectifier
	Fuse
	Circuit breaker
	Fan
	Motor
	Earth ground
	Equipment ground

If you have the repair manual for your engine (a minimal and wise investment), it probably contains a wiring diagram for the starting motor, alternator, and instrument panel. If so, you are in luck; you are already halfway there. Consider the engine diagram to be the first of your circuit diagrams and adopt its style and symbols for the rest of your diagrams.

Breaking the total system into a set of smaller systems has the added advantages of smaller sheets of paper, less confusion, and the ability to make changes without redrawing the entire system.

A complete set of circuit diagrams for a typical pleasure boat might include:

- Engine wiring (complete)
- Engine starting circuit
- Cabin lights and accessories
- Navigation lights
- Instrumentation and radios
- 240V or 110 VAC system
- Main distribution panel
- Mast wiring
- Water pumps

Don't worry if several of your diagrams overlap. The intent is to locate the general area of a fault and then to isolate the exact location within that area.

A Starter-Motor Circuit

Figure 6.2 shows a very simple diagram of an engine starter motor circuit. If one day you turn on the ignition switch, push the start button and nothing happens, this is the circuit diagram you will need. The more complete engine wiring diagram would probably contain the same information, but it would also contain all of the meters, idiot lights and alternator wiring. It would also add considerable visual confusion.

Figure 6.2 A Typical Starter Motor Circuit

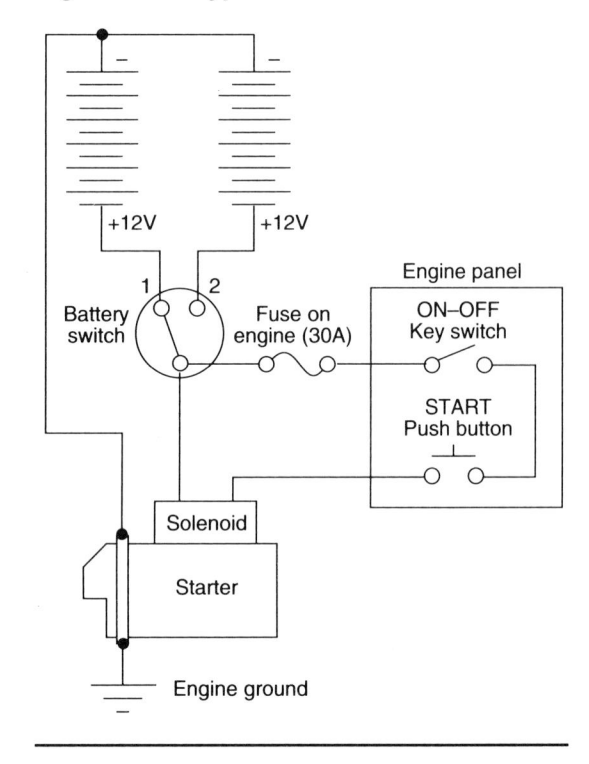

All we need to see are the

- Battery-select switch
- Fuse between battery-select switch common terminal and engine panel
- On-off switch
- Momentary start switch
- Wire from start switch to solenoid
- Heavy positive cable from battery-select common terminal to solenoid
- Heavy negative cable from battery negative terminal to engine-negative terminal

If it is a diesel engine and it won't turn over, the problem probably lies somewhere in this diagram.

DC Standards and Practices

A Cabin Lighting Circuit

Although it shows 15 separate lights and fans, the cabin lighting diagram of Figure 6.3 is even simpler in concept than the engine starter circuit. The diagram consists of two similar but separate branch circuits.

On the right is the starboard-cabin lighting circuit, originating at a 10-amp circuit breaker in the DC distribution panel and running forward to serve all lights and fans on the starboard side. The positive conductor is a brown AWG 14 wire labeled "27." The negative conductor is a blue AWG 14 wire labeled "28." Except for the two paralleled main cabin lights, each light and fan is controlled by an individual single-pole, single-throw switch. You may wish to include model numbers and specifications for each device so that you can calculate current draws and find replacement parts.

The devices are drawn on paper as laid out in the boat so that we can physically pinpoint a problem. For example, if the *chart-table* light failed, but the *main-aft* light still worked, the circuit diagram would allow us to immediately isolate the problem to either the *chart-table* light or the lamp's controlling switch.

On the other hand, if the *main-aft*, *main-forward*, and *V-berth* lights failed as well, we would suspect the problem to be in either the positive or negative conductors or the connections between the *night light* and the *chart-table* light.

On the left is the similar port-cabin lighting circuit, originating at a 10-amp circuit breaker in the DC distribution panel and running forward to serve all lights and fans on the port side. The positive conductor is a brown AWG 14 wire labeled "29." The negative conductor is a blue AWG 14 wire labeled "30."

Figure 6.3 A Cabin Lighting Circuit

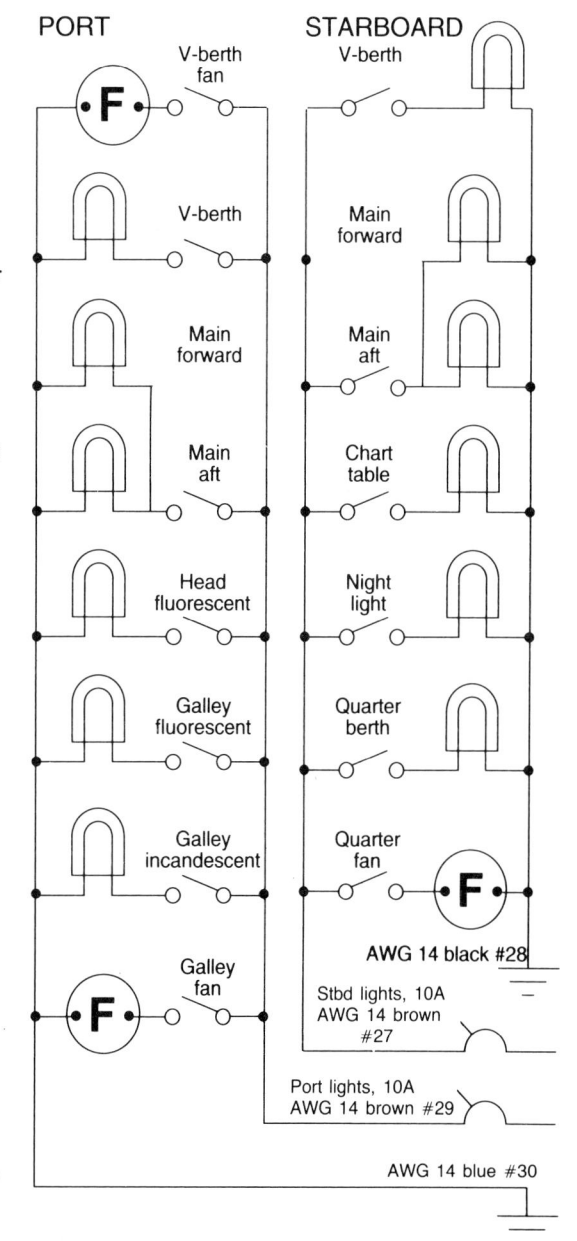

PORT	STARBOARD
V-berth fan	V-berth
V-berth	Main forward
Main forward	Main aft
Main aft	Chart table
Head fluorescent	Night light
Galley fluorescent	Quarter berth
Galley incandescent	Quarter fan
Galley fan

AWG 14 black #28
Stbd lights, 10A AWG 14 brown #27
Port lights, 10A AWG 14 brown #29
AWG 14 blue #30

MARINE WIRE

Real circuits consist not of pencil lines on a sheet of paper but of real metal conductors having electrical resistance. The conductors and their installations should satisfy a number of criteria:

1. Construction should be such that the conductor will not break under continuous vibration or accidentally imposed force.

2. Insulation should be appropriate for the expected maximum ambient (surrounding air) temperature and degree of exposure to sunlight, moisture, and air.

3. Ampacity (current-carrying capacity) should be sufficient to avoid dangerous overheating.

4. Conductor size should be selected considering conductor length and current in order that voltage drop not impair the functioning of the loads.

Construction

The ABYC calls for all conductors to be stranded and of size AWG 16 minimum. The single exception is sheathed AWG 18 conductors that do not extend more than 30 inches beyond their sheath.

Because copper wire becomes brittle under repeated flexing, solid wire is not allowed at all. Type II stranding is the minimum allowed for general boat wiring, and Type III stranding should be used wherever frequent flexing is expected, such as on an engine.

Table 6.1 shows minimum circular-mil areas (a circular mil is the area of a circle of diameter one mil, or .001 inch), overall diameters, and minimum numbers of strands specified by the ABYC for AWG 18 through 4/0 conductors.

Table 6.1 Circular-Mil Area and Stranding

Size AWG	Dia., in.	Minimum Circular Mils	Minimum Strands Type 2	Minimum Strands Type 3
18	.044	1537	16	–
16	.055	2336	19	26
14	.069	3702	19	41
12	.086	5833	19	65
10	.109	9343	19	105
8	.137	14810	19	168
6	.182	25910	37	266
4	.218	37360	49	420
2	.282	62450	127	665
1	.315	77790	127	836
0	.355	98980	127	1064
2/0	.399	125100	127	1323
3/0	.449	158600	259	1666
4/0	.512	205500	418	2107

Insulation

All single conductor and cable insulations should be one of the types listed in Table 6.2, appropriate to its expected exposure to temperature, moisture, and oil. The letters in the designations indicate:

- T means thermoplastic
- M means oil resistant
- W means moisture resistant
- H means heat resistant to 75°C
- HH means high-heat resistant to 90°C.

An insulated jacket or sheathing may qualify for more than one rating and be labelled as such. The most commonly available cable suitable to all applications in the typical boat is probably UL1426-Boat Cable.

DC Standards and Practices

Table 6.2. Acceptable Insulation Types

Type	Description
CONDUCTORS	
THW	Moisture and Heat Resistant, Thermoplastic
TW	Moisture Resistant, Thermoplastic
HWN	Moisture and Heat Resistant, Thermoplastic
XHHW	Moisture and Heat Resistant, Cross-Linked Synthetic Polymer
MTW	Moisture, Heat and Oil Resistant, Thermoplastic
AWM*	Moisture, Heat and Oil Resistant, Thermoplastic, Thermosetting
UL1426	Boat Cable
SAE CONDUCTORS	
GPT	Thermoplastic Insulation, Braidless
HDT	Thermoplastic Insulation, Braidless
SGT	Thermoplastic Insulation, Braidless
STS	Thermosetting Synthetic-Rubber Insulation, Braidless
HTS	Thermosetting Synthetic-Rubber Insulation, Braidless
SXL	Thermosetting, Cross-Linked Polyethylene Insulation, Braidless
FLEXIBLE CORDS	
SO	Hard-Service Cord, Oil Resistant
ST	Hard-Service Cord, Thermoplastic
STO	Hard-Service Cord, Oil Resistant, Thermoplastic
SEO	Hard-Service Cord, Oil Resistant, Thermoplastic
SJO	Junior Hard-Service Cord, Oil Resistant
SJT	Hard-Service Cord, Thermoplastic
SJTO	Hard-Service Cord, Oil Resistant, Thermoplastic

Ampacity

Branch circuit conductors should be sized to carry the maximum currents drawn by their loads. In the case of motors, maximum current should be for the locked-rotor or stalled condition.

Main feed conductors for distribution panels and switchboards should be determined using the ABYC procedure, shown in Table 6.3 (an example calculation is shown).

With the maximum-load current in amps and the temperature rating of the conductor insulation, the minimum-required conductor size is selected from Table 6.4.

Voltage Drop

All wire has resistance. As current flows through the wire, voltage drops according to Ohm's Law. If power is supplied to a circuit by a 12.0-volt battery and the voltage drops 0.5 volt in the positive conductor going to the load and another 0.5 volt in the negative conductor back to the battery, then the voltage across the load is not 12.0 volts, but 12.0 - 0.5 - 0.5 = 11.0 volts. The voltage drop in the total length of conductor to-and-from the load is 1.0/12.0 = 8.3%.

The ABYC specifies two allowable percentage drops, depending on the effect on safety:

- 3% for panelboard feeds, bilge blowers, electronics, and navigation lights
- 10% for general lighting and other noncritical applications

Conductor size may be determined from:

$$CM = K \times I \times L / E$$

where:
  CM = conductor circular mils (Table 6.1)
  K = 10.75
  I = current in amps
  L = round-trip length in feet
  E = voltage drop in conductor, volts

Table 6.3 Load Calculation Method
For Total Electrical Loads for Minimum Sizes of Panelboards, Switchboards, and Main Conductors.

NOTE: Calculations are based on the actual operating amperage for each load and not on the rating of the circuit breaker or fuse protecting that branch circuit.

Column A
List the loads that must be available for use on a continuous-duty basis.

Equipment	Amperes
Navigation lights	5.5
Bilge blower(s)	2.0
Bilge pump(s)	4.2
Wiper(s)	0.0
Largest radio (transmit mode)	2.5
Depth sounder	0.9
Radar	7.5
Searchlight	12.0
Instrument(s)	2.3
Alarm system (standby mode)	0.5
Refrigerator	5.5
Other: Autopilot	3.5
Total of column A	46.4
Enter value from same line of Column B	80.0
Add two above lines (total load)	122.9

Column B
List the intermittent loads. The largest load or 10% of the total, whichever is greater, will be carried to column A.

Equipment	Amperes
Cigarette lighter	0.0
Cabin lighting	10.0
Horn	6.3
Additional electronic equipment	10.0
Trim tabs	0.0
Power trim	0.0
Toilets	0.0
Anchor windlass	80.0
Winches	0.0
Fresh water pump(s)	5.8
Other: Microwave	60.0
Total of column B	172.1
10% of column B	17.2
Largest item in column B	80.0
Larger of two above lines— Enter in both column A and column B	80.0

DC Standards and Practices

Table 6.4. Allowable Amperage of Conductors for Under 50 Volts

Conductor Size, AWG	60°C (140°F)	75°C (167°F)	80°C (176°F)	90°C (194°F)	105°C (221°F)	125°C (257°F)	200°C (392°F)
			Outside Engine Spaces				
18	10	10	15	20	20	25	25
16	15	15	20	25	25	30	35
14	20	20	25	30	35	40	45
12	25	25	35	40	45	50	55
10	40	40	50	55	60	70	70
8	55	65	70	70	80	90	100
6	80	95	100	100	120	125	135
4	105	125	130	135	160	170	180
2	140	170	175	180	210	225	240
1	165	195	210	210	245	265	280
1/0	195	230	245	245	285	305	325
2/0	225	265	285	285	330	355	370
3/0	260	310	330	330	385	410	430
4/0	300	360	385	385	445	475	510
			Inside Engine Spaces				
18	5.8	7.5	11.7	16.4	17.0	22.3	25.0
16	8.7	11.3	15.6	20.5	21.3	26.7	35.0
14	11.6	15.0	19.5	24.6	29.8	35.6	45.0
12	14.5	18.8	27.3	32.8	38.3	44.5	55.0
10	23.2	30.0	39.0	45.1	51.0	62.3	70.0
8	31.9	48.8	54.6	57.4	68.0	80.1	100.0
6	46.4	71.3	78.0	82.0	102.0	111.3	135.0
4	60.9	93.8	101.4	110.7	136.0	151.3	180.0
2	81.2	127.5	136.5	147.6	178.5	200.3	240.0
1	95.7	146.3	163.8	172.2	208.3	235.9	280.0
1/0	113.1	172.5	191.1	200.9	242.3	271.5	325.0
2/0	130.5	198.8	222.3	233.7	280.5	316.0	370.0
3/0	150.8	232.5	257.4	270.6	327.3	364.9	430.0
4/0	174.0	270.0	300.3	315.7	378.3	422.8	510.0

Table 6.5. Conductor Sizes for Allowable Voltage Drops

Current, Amps	\multicolumn{10}{c}{Length of Conductor, in feet, from Source of Current to Device and Back to Source}
	10	20	30	40	60	80	100	120	140
\multicolumn{10}{c}{3% Voltage Drop}
1	18	18	18	18	16	14	14	14	12
2	18	18	16	14	14	12	10	10	8
5	18	14	12	10	10	8	6	6	6
10	14	10	10	8	6	6	4	4	2
15	12	10	8	6	6	4	2	2	1
20	10	8	6	6	4	2	2	1	0
25	10	6	6	4	2	2	1	0	2/0
30	10	6	4	4	2	1	0	2/0	3/0
40	8	6	4	2	1	0	2/0	3/0	4/0
50	6	4	2	2	0	2/0	3/0	4/0	—
60	6	4	2	1	2/0	3/0	4/0	—	—
70	6	2	1	0	3/0	4/0	—	—	—
80	6	2	1	0	3/0	4/0	—	—	—
90	4	2	0	2/0	4/0	—	—	—	—
100	4	2	0	2/0	4/0	—	—	—	—
\multicolumn{10}{c}{10% Voltage Drop}
1	18	18	18	18	18	18	18	18	18
2	18	18	18	18	18	18	16	16	14
5	18	18	18	16	14	14	12	12	10
10	18	16	14	14	12	10	10	8	8
15	18	14	12	12	10	8	8	6	6
20	16	14	12	10	8	8	6	6	6
25	16	12	10	10	8	6	6	4	4
30	14	12	10	8	6	6	4	4	2
40	14	10	8	8	6	4	4	2	2
50	12	10	8	6	4	4	2	2	1
60	12	8	6	6	4	2	2	1	1
70	10	8	6	6	2	2	1	1	0
80	10	8	6	4	2	2	1	0	2/0
90	10	6	6	4	2	1	0	0	2/0
100	10	6	4	4	2	1	0	2/0	2/0

DC Standards and Practices

Example: What size conductor is required for an anchor light drawing 0.9 amp at the top of a 50-foot mast with a 15-foot run from panelboard to base of the mast?

The light is a navigation light, so the allowed voltage drop is 3% of 12 volts or 0.36 volts. The length of the conductor from panelboard to the light and back to panelboard is 15' + 50' + 50' + 15' = 130'. The minimum circular-mil area of the conductor is thus

CM = 10.75 x 0.9 x 130 / 0.36 = 3,494

Table 6.1 tells us we need a #14 AWG conductor. If you don't like to calculate, consult Table 6.3 for the approximate answer.

IDENTIFICATION OF CONDUCTORS

It is recommended that each electrical conductor that is part of the boat's electrical system shall have a means to identify its function in the system.

Two means of identification are insulation color (alternate color applied to the insulation) and labels (numbers and/or letter) applied near the terminal points. The use of both is recommended.

Color Code

In general, DC conductor insulation should follow the color scheme:

DC Positive	– Red or Brown
DC Negative	– Black
DC Grounding	– Green or Green with Yellow

There are no absolute rules or strict conventions for the colour coding of DC wiring in the UK. Table 6.6 lists some common wiring colour uses found in the UK marine industry, although many UK manufacturers adopt their own colour codes.

Table 6.6 Common UK wiring colour uses for DC

Colour	Conductor use
Green with yellow stripe	Oil pressure switch to oil pressure warning light
Blue with yellow stripe	Water temperature switch to warning light
Brown with yellow stripe or brown with black stripe	Charge warning light to alternator
Black with blue stripe or slate	Tachometer to sender
White with brown stripe	Oil pressure gauge to sender
Green with blue stripe	Water temperature gauge to sender
Brown	Main positive feed
White	Auxiliary feeds from ignition switch
Black	Main negative feed
White with red stripe	Starter solenoid to starter switch
Red	Key switch heat position to glow plugs
White with black stripe	Stop/run fuel solenoid
Green with black stripe	Fuel gauge to sender
Brown with white stripe	Ammeter to alternator
Blue	Feed to instrument lights
Green	General ground DC

INSTALLATION OF WIRE RUNS
AC and DC Bundles
When both AC and DC conductors are run in the same area and direction, the AC conductors should be kept separate from the DC conductors by bundling, sheathing, or other means.

Continuous Support (Figure 6.4)
In order to minimize flexing from vibration, conductors should be supported continuously or every 18 inches minimum by clamps or straps. Nonmetallic clamps and straps should not be used in locations where failure would result in a hazard, such as over engines, shafts or passageways.

Metal clamps should be lined with moisture, gasoline and oil-resistant material, or have smooth, rounded edges. The cable beneath should be protected by a wrapping to protect the conductors.

Figure 6.4 Cable Support Devices

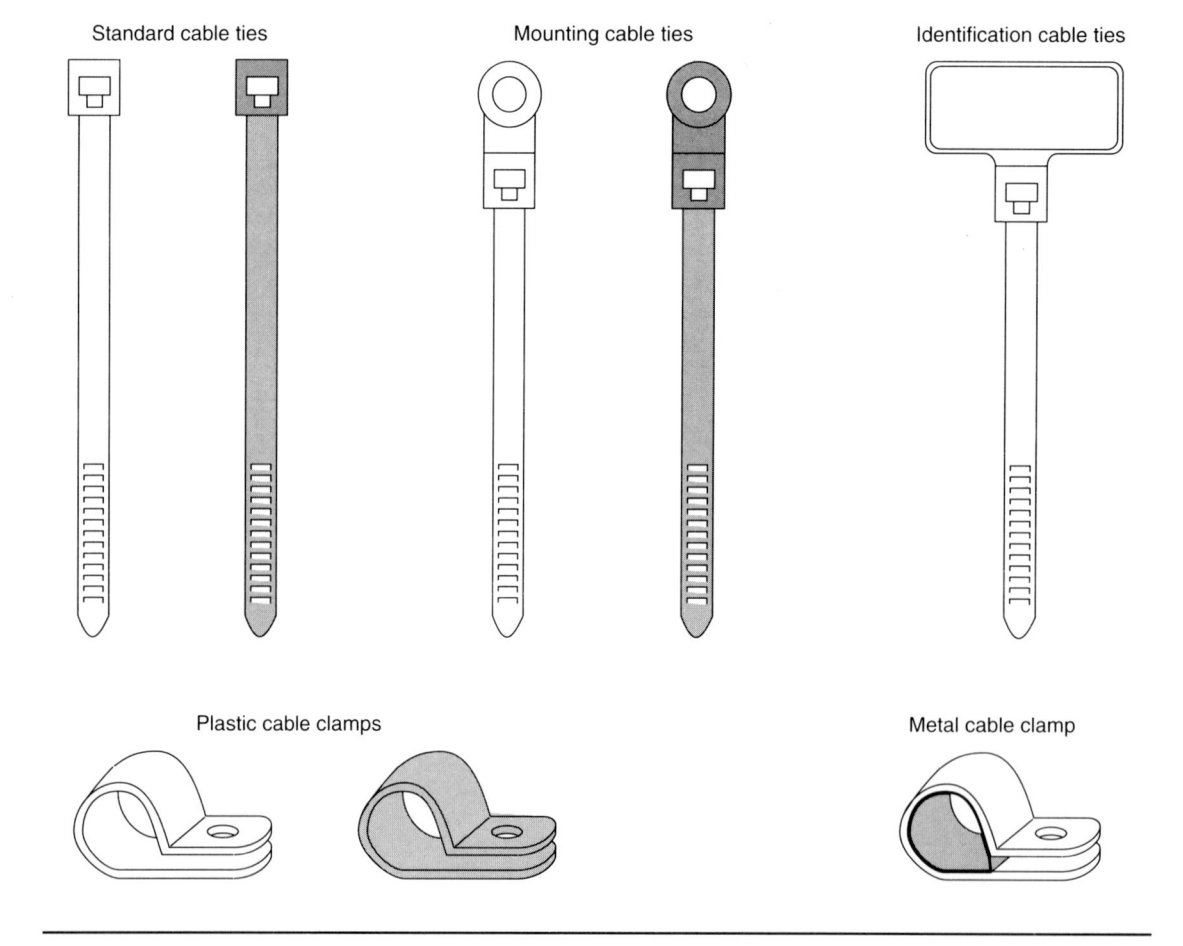

Standard cable ties

Mounting cable ties

Identification cable ties

Plastic cable clamps

Metal cable clamp

DC Standards and Practices

Exposure to Damage (Figure 6.5)
Conductors should be protected from chafing or other accidental damage by routing clear of engine and steering shafts and control linkages. In exposed areas, conductors should be protected by conduit, raceway or equivalent wrap. Holes in panels, bulkheads or other structural members should be lined to reduce chafing.

Protecting Connections
Enclosures containing electrical connections should either be in dry locations or be weatherproof. If wet locations cannot be avoided, nonmetallic enclosures are preferred, but metal enclosures may be mounted to prevent accumulation of moisture between the enclosure and adjacent surfaces, such as providing a space of at least 1/4".

Figure 6.5 Chafe Protection Materials

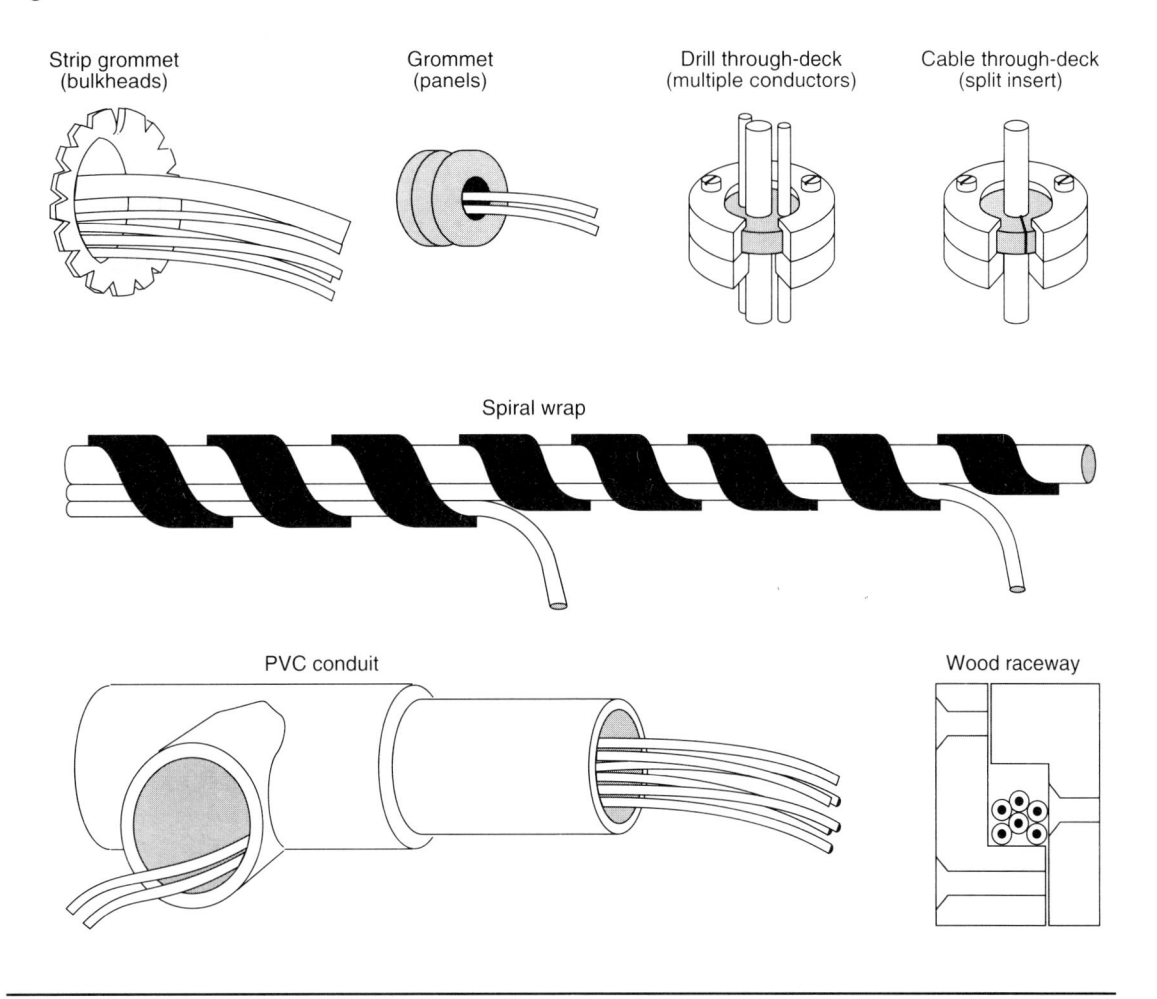

Wiring in the Bilge

It is unfortunate that the simplest routing of conductors is often through the bilge. More than 90% of all electrical problems on a boat are due to corrosion, and nothing leads to corrosion more quickly than a dip in water—particularly of the salt variety. Current-carrying conductors should be routed as high as possible above bilge water. If routing through the bilge can not be avoided, connections must be watertight.

Sources of Heat

Conductors should be kept away from—and never run directly above—engine exhaust pipes and other similar sources of heat. Minimum recommended conductor clearances are 2 inches from wet-exhaust pipes and components and 9 inches from dry-exhaust components, unless equivalent thermal insulation is provided.

Battery Cables

Unless battery cables are over-current protected, they should be run above bilge water level, away from metal fuel-system components, such as fuel line and fuel filters, and away from the engine, transmission and shaft. The grounded battery cable is excepted because contact between the grounded engine and a grounded conductor does not pose a danger.

Wiring near Compasses

Direct current flow through a wire produces a concentric magnetic field, which may disturb a compass if too close. The direction of the magnetic field changes with change in current direction, so twisting positive and negative conductor pairs negates the overall magnetic field. All conductor pairs within 24 inches of a compass should be twisted, unless they are of the coaxial variety.

OVER-CURRENT PROTECTION

Circuits Requiring Protection

Distribution Panels and Switchboards (Fig. 6.6)
A distribution panel or switchboard should be protected at its source of power by a fuse or trip-free circuit breaker of capacity not exceeding the capacity of the panel or the ampacity of the feed conductors.

If there is also a sub-main fuse or breaker on the panel that does not exceed the panel or feeder ampacity, then the protection at the power source may be rated up to 150% of the feeder capacity.

Branch Circuits.
Every ungrounded conductor should be protected at its point of origin in the panel unless its rating is the same as the main or sub-main protection. The over-current protection rating should not exceed 150% of the conductor ampacity.

Motor-Operated Equipment
Except for engine-starter motors, all motors should be protected either internally or at the panel. The over-current protection rating should be low enough to prevent a fire, in the case of a stalled motor rotor, for up to seven hours.

Fuse and Breaker Location

Sources of power for positive-feed conductors can be a battery terminal, battery-select common terminal, or unswitched feed to the starter. The maximum allowed unprotected lengths of positive feeder conductors are shown below and in Figure 6.7:

- Connected directly to a battery terminal —72 inches

- Connected to other than a battery terminal, but contained entirely within a sheath or enclosure—40 inches

- All others—7 inches

DC Standards and Practices 117

Figure 6.6 Protection of Panelboards and Switchboards

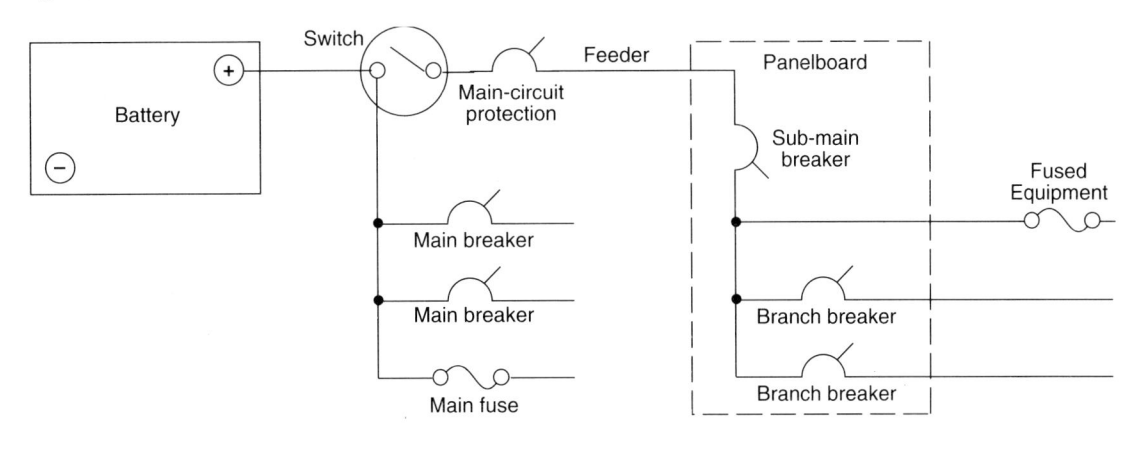

Figure 6.7 Maximum Unprotected Lengths of Positive-Feeder Conductors

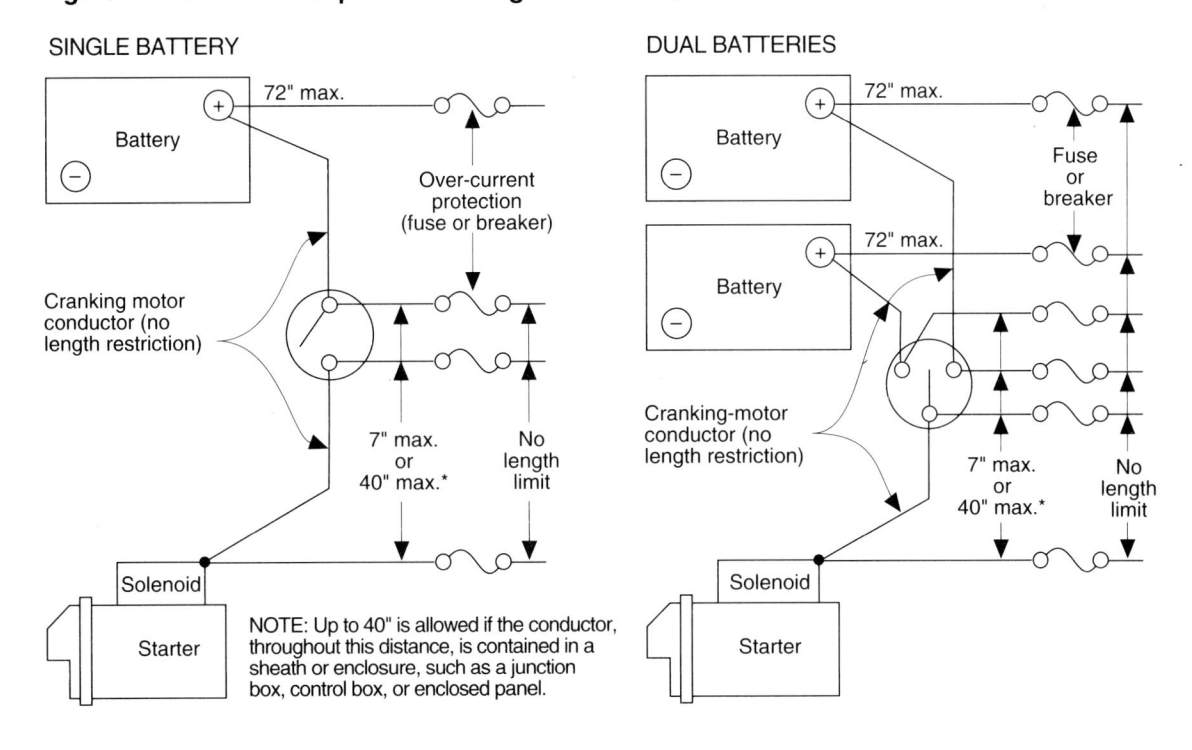

SINGLE BATTERY

- Battery
- 72" max.
- Over-current protection (fuse or breaker)
- Cranking motor conductor (no length restriction)
- 7" max. or 40" max.*
- No length limit
- Solenoid
- Starter

NOTE: Up to 40" is allowed if the conductor, throughout this distance, is contained in a sheath or enclosure, such as a junction box, control box, or enclosed panel.

DUAL BATTERIES

- Battery
- 72" max.
- Battery
- 72" max.
- Fuse or breaker
- Cranking-motor conductor (no length restriction)
- 7" max. or 40" max.*
- No length limit
- Solenoid
- Starter

Circuit Breakers

As shown in Figure 6.6, by definition the first breaker or fuse in a circuit connected in series with the battery is considered to be the *main* circuit breaker or fuse. All other breakers or fuses in the circuit, including sub-main breakers and fuses, are considered to be *branch* circuit breakers and fuses. Note that breakers and fuses may be mixed in the same circuit. It is possible, for example, to use a main fuse ahead of a panel containing branch circuit breakers.

If installing a circuit-breaker panel, purchase the circuit breakers from the panel manufacturer to insure compatibility. Most manufacturers offer two sizes of breaker—small for up to 50 amps, and large for over 50 amps. Either size may be used for main or branch breakers, although many of the larger panels are designed to accept the larger size breaker for the main and the smaller breaker for the branches. Figure 6.8 shows the dimensions and available current ratings for Ancor brand breakers.

Figure 6.8 Ancor Circuit Breakers

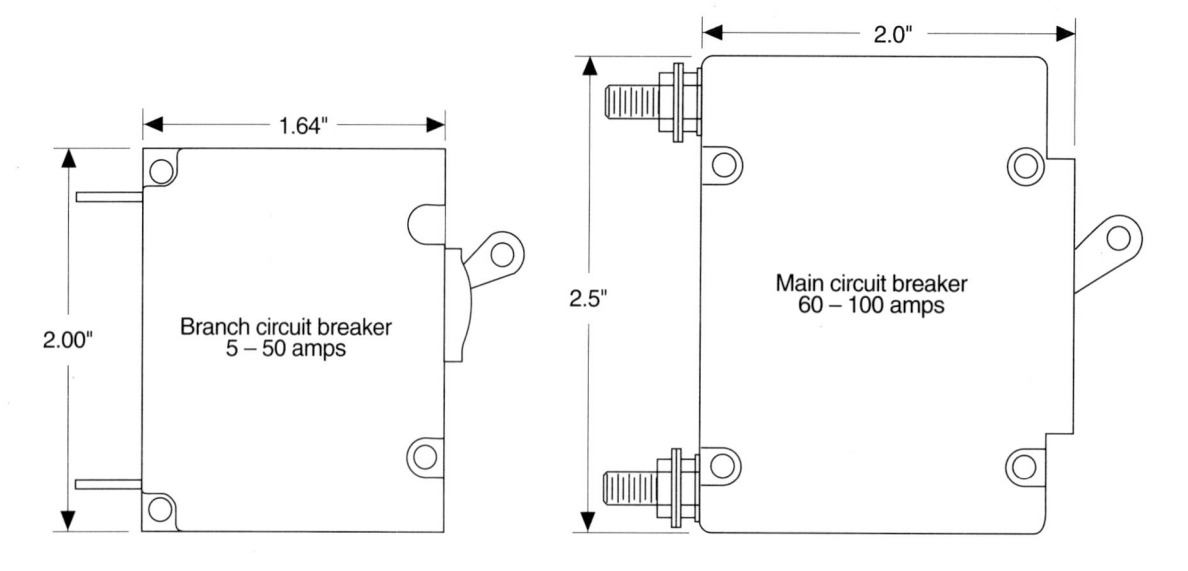

Small Circuit-Breaker Ratings, Amps

5	25
10	30
15	40
20	50

Large Circuit-Breaker Ratings, Amps

60
80
100

DC Standards and Practices

Table 6.7 Common Ratings of Fuse Types

Rating. Amps	mains	fast	delay	short	metric	spade
1/8		●				
1/4		●				
1/2		●	●			
3/4		●				
1		●	●		●	
1-1/2		●	●			
2		●	●		●	
2-1/2		●	●			
3		●	●		●	
4		●				
5	●	●	●		●	●
6		●				
6-1/4		●	●			
7		●			●	
7-1/2		●	●			
8		●				
10	●	●	●		●	●
15	●	●	●		●	●
20	●	●	●	●		●
25	●	●	●			●
30	●	●	●	●		●
40	●					
50	●					
60	●					

Fuses

Fuses may be mounted in equipment, fuse blocks, distribution panels with switches, and in-line fuse holders.

Fuse blocks may contain multiple fuses, and the individual fuse holders may be electrically isolated or they may share a hot bus bar. Figure 6.9 shows a variety of fuse holders.

Table 6.7, on the previous page, shows the actual sizes and available ratings of the most commonly used fuse types.

Figure 6.9 Common Fuse Holders

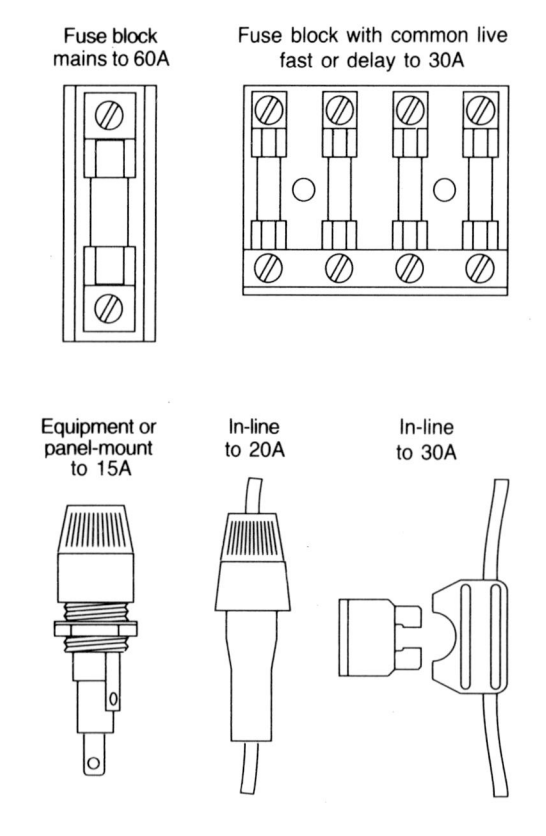

Fuse block mains to 60A

Fuse block with common live fast or delay to 30A

Equipment or panel-mount to 15A

In-line to 20A

In-line to 30A

MAKING CONNECTIONS

Most wiring failures occur at connections. When copper corrodes it forms a layer of greenish copper oxide. Because it is thin, the oxide does little to the conductivity of the wire, but, because it is nonconductive, it forms a resistive barrier at surface-to-surface connections. Most of the remaining failures are due to physical stresses on connections (the constant vibration from the engine, or a pull on the conductor when an object or person accidentally strikes it).

Most boat owners spend as little as possible on specialized electrical tools. Instead, they attempt to make do with what they have. This is false economy. Although it is possible to make bad connections with good tools, it is virtually impossible to make good connections with the wrong tools.

Figure 6.10 shows a variety of special wiring tools. The *cut, strip and crimp tool* at upper left should be your minimal investment. This tool is found in both hardware and electronics stores in a wide range of qualities. Two key considerations are:

> **1.** The stripper holes should line up perfectly (try stripping a few wires before purchasing).
>
> **2.** The tool should match the brand of terminals you will be crimping. (The tool is often sold in a kit with terminals.)

Professional electricians use ratcheting crimp tools. A *single-crimp ratchet* (top center) crimps just the barrel. A *double-crimp ratchet* crimps both barrel and sleeve. The advantage of the ratchet is that the tool will not release until the terminal has been crimped the proper amount. It is almost impossible to under- or over-crimp the terminals made to be used with this tool.

DC Standards and Practices

Figure 6.10 Special Tools for Wiring

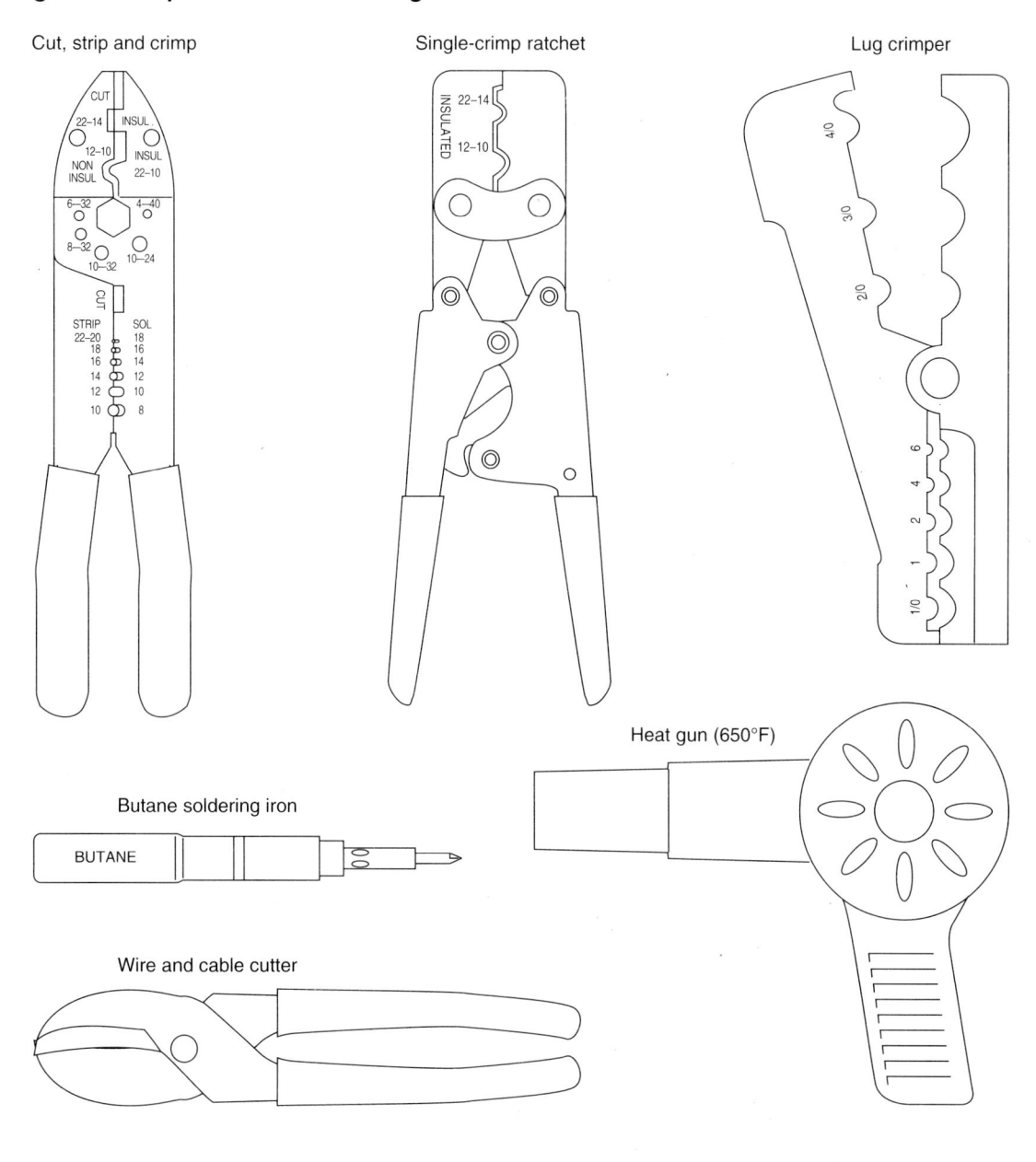

Lugs are terminals for large conductors. The *lug crimper* at top right in Figure 6.10 is actuated either by squeezing in a vise or by striking with a hammer.

Most soldering problems are due to insufficient heat. It is better to get in and out quickly than to linger on a connector while the iron struggles to reach 400°F. The pocket-size *butane soldering iron*, at lower left, can produce all the heat you'll need—short of soldering battery lugs, will burn for several hours on a filling, and free you from trailing cords.

Diagonal wire cutters ("diagonal pliers") distort the cut end, making it difficult to insert into the proper size connector barrel. The *wire and cable cutter*, at bottom left, shears the wire, resulting in a cleaner cut.

Heated to 275–300°F, heat-shrink tubing shrinks to one-third or less of its original diameter, thus gripping the conductor tightly. If the tubing contains adhesive, the melted adhesive seals and strengthens the connection.

Heat guns, such as the one at lower right, achieve temperatures in excess of 500°F and shrink the shrink-tubing quickly.

Approved Connectors

Marine connectors differ from residential wiring connectors in being subject to vibration and other stresses. Figure 6.11 is self-explanatory and shows both approved and disapproved types of connector. Note specifically that the ubiquitous wire nut, so popular in household wiring, is not approved for marine use.

Figure 6.11 Approved and Disapproved Connectors for Marine Use

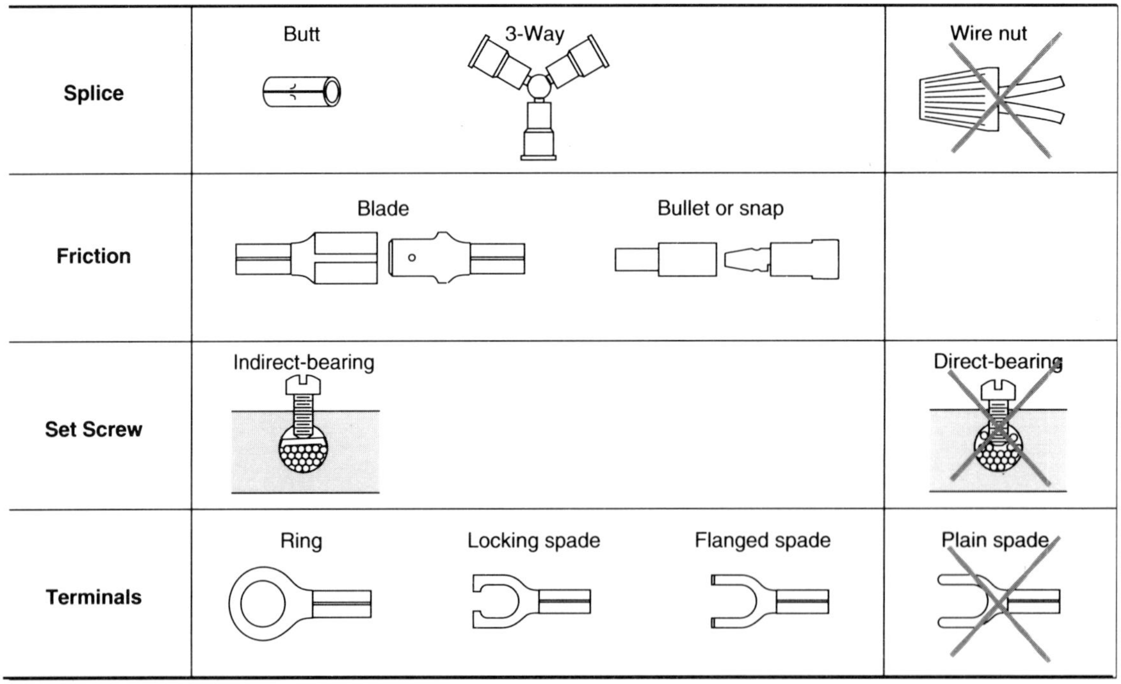

Splice	Butt	3-Way	Wire nut ✗
Friction	Blade	Bullet or snap	
Set Screw	Indirect-bearing		Direct-bearing ✗
Terminals	Ring	Locking spade / Flanged spade	Plain spade ✗

DC Standards and Practices

Strength of Connections

Friction-type connectors (blade and bullet shown in Figure 6.11) can be used provided they resist a pull in the direction of the conductor of at least 6 pounds for one minute. The other connectors in Figure 6.11 must resist the tensile forces shown in Table 6.8 for at least one minute.

Table 6.8 Tensile Test Values for Connections

Conductor Size, AWG	Force, Lb.	Conductor Size, AWG	Force Lb.
18	10	4	70
16	15	3	80
14	30	2	90
12	35	1	100
10	40	0	125
8	45	2/0	150
6	50	3/0	175
5	60	4/0	225

Solder

The use of solder in marine connections is controversial. Some experienced electricians feel that soldered connections are the most secure and best at eliminating terminal corrosion. Others point out that the solder in an overheated terminal may melt and allow the conductor to pull out of the terminal. A further problem is wicking of solder into the stranded conductor, resulting in a rigid portion which is liable to break like a solid conductor.

Solder should not be the sole means of mechanical connection in any circuit, with the single exception of battery lugs having a solder-contact length of not less than 1.5 times the conductor diameter.

Fortunately, terminal systems are now available that resolve all of the above problems (Figure 6.12, below). Although expensive (about twice the price of the usual automotive-grade materials), anything less in the hostile marine environment is false economy.

1. *Pretinned, stranded conductors* are available in all gages and recommended colors. Pretinning (coating with solder) prevents oxidation of the conductor strands, eliminates the need to cut the conductor back several inches when repairing, and makes soldering easier if desired.

2. *Heat-shrink tubing with adhesive coating*, applied over both terminal and conductor, seals out moisture, makes the connection more secure, and insulates the terminal shank all at the same time. The shrink tubing may be purchased separately or already attached to terminals.

Figure 6.12 Adhesive-Lined Heat-Shrink Tubing (Ancor)

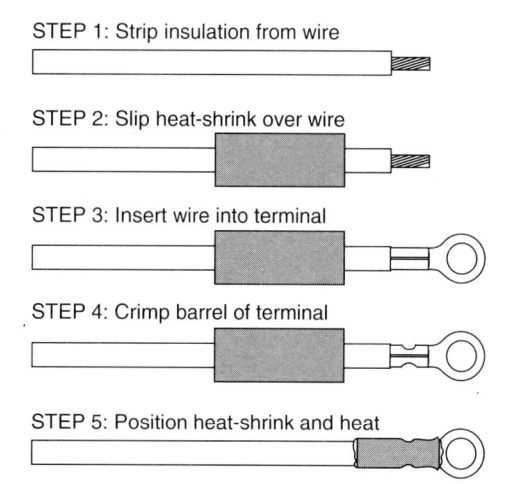

STEP 1: Strip insulation from wire

STEP 2: Slip heat-shrink over wire

STEP 3: Insert wire into terminal

STEP 4: Crimp barrel of terminal

STEP 5: Position heat-shrink and heat

Other Considerations

1. The throats of ring and captive-spade terminals should be of the same nominal size as the stud.

2. An extra length of conductor should be provided at terminations to relieve tension, permit fanning of multiple conductors, and allow for future repairs.

3. Except for grounding conductors, terminal shanks should be insulated to prevent accidental shorting.

4. Connections should be in locations protected from weather or in weatherproof enclosures. If exposed to immersion, connections should be watertight.

5. Terminal studs, nuts, and washers should be corrosion resistant and galvanically compatible with the conductor and terminal lug. Aluminum and unplated steel are unsuitable.

6. No more than four conductors should be attached to a single terminal stud. If necessary, two or more terminal studs can be connected by jumper straps.

Figure 6.13 Proper Terminations

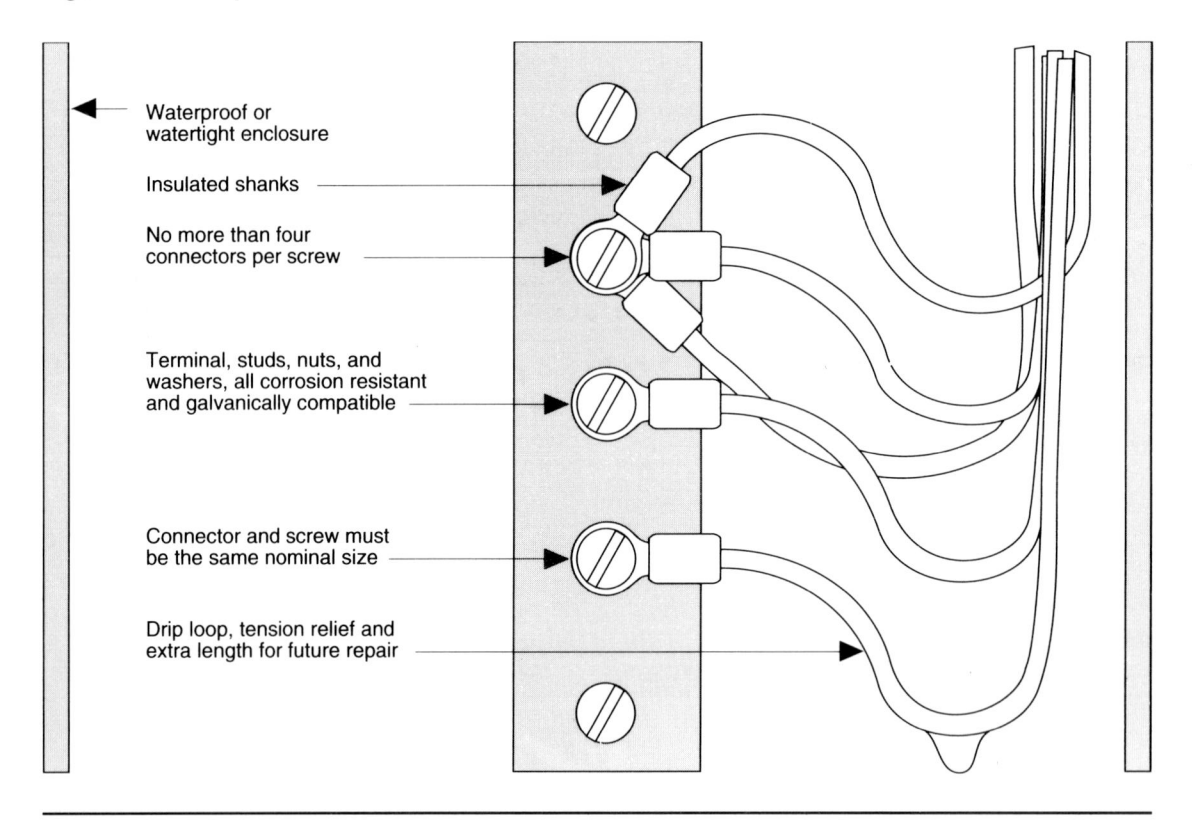

- Waterproof or watertight enclosure
- Insulated shanks
- No more than four connectors per screw
- Terminal, studs, nuts, and washers, all corrosion resistant and galvanically compatible
- Connector and screw must be the same nominal size
- Drip loop, tension relief and extra length for future repair

DC Standards and Practices

Coaxial Connectors

Coaxial cable consists of an insulated center conductor, surrounded by a concentric (coaxial) grounded-shield conductor (either fine, braided strands or foil), all protected by an outer insulating jacket. Because the outer conductor (the shield) is grounded and completely surrounds the center conductor, coaxial cables neither radiate nor pick up much electrical noise. "Coax" is primarily used to connect antennas to electronic equipment, such as VHF and HF transceivers, and loran, SatNav and GPS receivers.

Like the wire used for DC wiring, coaxial cable for marine use should have pre-tinned center conductor and braid.

Table 6.9 lists the characteristics of five types of coaxial cable found on a boat.

Conductor size is important only for heavy current flows, such as the output of SSB and ham-radio transmitters.

Impedance is the high-frequency equivalent of resistance and must match the output impedance of the transmitter in order to achieve maximum output power. (All VHF and SSB radios are designed with 50Ω output impedance.)

Attenuation is the loss of transmitted power between the radio and the antenna, where each 3 decibels (db) represents a 50% loss of power.

- *RG58U* is very thin and is typically used only for interconnecting electronics where lengths are short and attenuation is not a problem.
- *RG59U* is used to connect television antennas and cable service.
- *RG8X* is typically used to connect VHF and HF antennas up to lengths where attenuation becomes excessive.
- *RG8U* and *RG213* are both used to conduct maximum power to VHF and HF antennas.

Marine coaxial cables are usually terminated at both ends with PL-259 male-UHF connectors. It is important to know how to install this type of conductor, which has so many applications on a boat.

Table 6.9 Coaxial Cables

Specification	RG58U	RG59U	RG8X	RG8U	RG213
Nominal O.D.	3/16"	1/4"	1/4"	13/32"	13/32"
Conductor AWG	#20	#23	#16	#13	#13
Impedance	50Ω	75Ω	50Ω	52Ω	50Ω
Attenuation per 100'					
@ 50 MHz	3.3 db	2.4 db	2.5 db	1.3 db	1.3 db
@ 100 MHz	4.9 db	3.4 db	3.7 db	1.9 db	1.9 db
@ 1000 MHz	21.5 db	12.0 db	13.5 db	8.0 db	8.0 db

Figure 6.14 demonstrates the simple four-step process for the large diameter RG8U and RG213 cables. Although there are solderless connectors available, they are not recommended except in protected locations (inside cabin) due to corrosion. After assembly, it is a good idea to apply a moisture-displacing lubricant. If the connection is exposed to weather, the connection should be wrapped in a good quality plastic electrical tape to exclude moisture.

Figure 6.15 shows the similar but slightly more complex assembly with the smaller diameter RG58U, RG59U, and RG8X cables.

Figure 6.14 Installation of Coaxial Connector on RG8U and RG213 Cable

STEP 1: Slip on shell and strip to center of conductor and back 3/4"

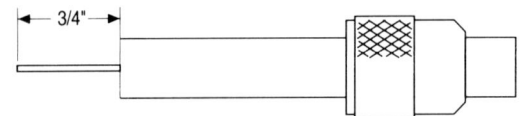

STEP 2: Strip outer jacket additional 5/16"

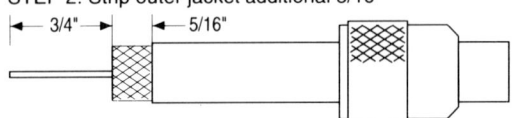

STEP 3: Slip on body, making sure shield does not contact center conductor, and solder tip and shield through holes

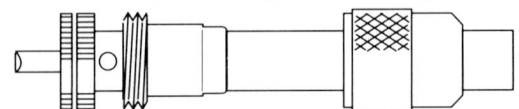

STEP 4: Screw shell onto body

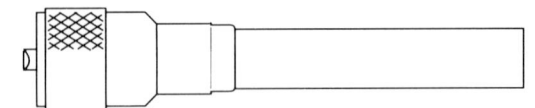

Figure 6.15 Installing Coaxial Connector on RG58U, RG59U and RG8X Cable

STEP 1: Slip on shell and adapter; strip outer jacket back 5/8"

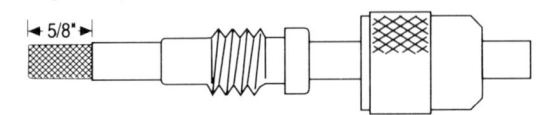

STEP 2: Bend back braided shield

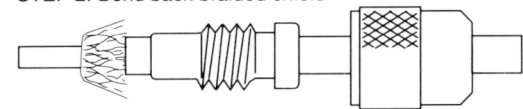

STEP 3: Slip adapter under braided shield

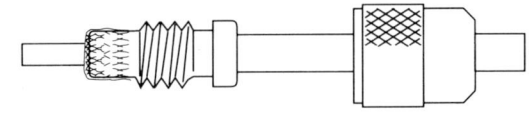

STEP 4: Strip center conductor 1/2" and tin

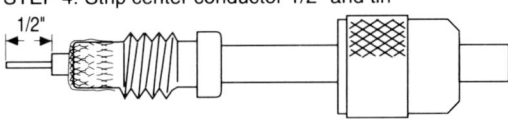

STEP 5: Screw on body and solder tip and braid through holes in body

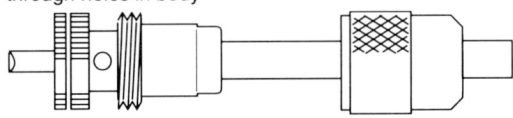

STEP 6: Screw shell onto body

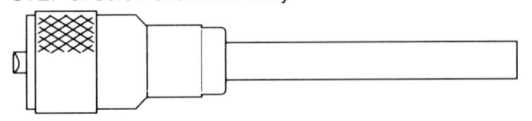

DC Standards and Practices

Figure 6.16 Adaptors

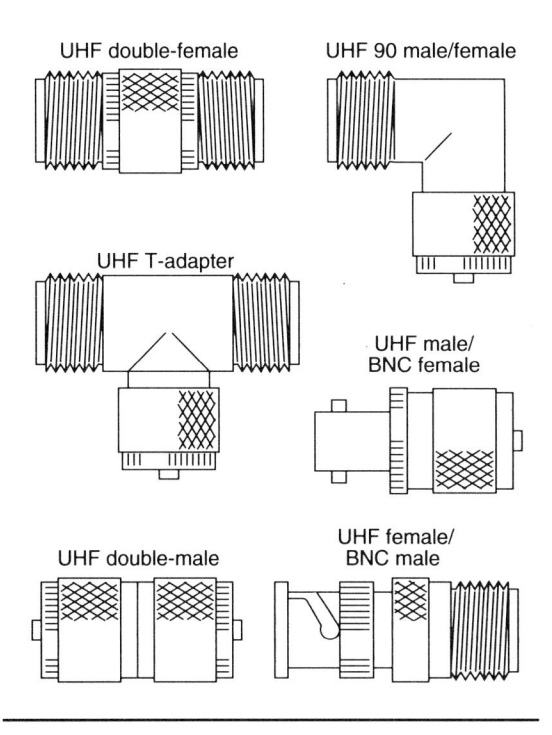

- UHF double-female
- UHF 90 male/female
- UHF T-adapter
- UHF male/BNC female
- UHF double-male
- UHF female/BNC male

IGNITION PROTECTION

Gasoline and propane explosions are among the leading causes of marine loss of life. For this reason, rigorous ignition protection precautions should be taken aboard boats.

Recommended Standards for Ignition Protection

Fuels

1. Gas tank connections and regulators are outside of the hull or are located in an enclosure which is vaportight to the interior of the boat and vented overboard.

2. The gas supply can be shut off at the tank by a control that is part of or located near the appliance. Manual controls must provide a warning when the supply valve at the tank is open.

Boats using petrol as a fuel for either propulsion or auxiliary generator should always adopt these standards.

Isolation of Ignition Sources

Ignition sources located in the same spaces as petrol engines, petrol tanks, and petrol fuel joints and fittings must be ignition protected unless the components are isolated from the fuel sources. An electrical component is considered isolated from a fuel source if:

1. It is separated by a bulkhead of full width and height that leaks no more than 1/4 oz. of water per hour with a water height of 12 inches or one-third the bulkhead height (whichever is less), and has no higher opening with greater than 1/4-inch gap around its perimeter.

2. The electrical component is separated by a floor, deck, or other type of enclosure.

3. The distance between electrical component and fuel source is at least 2 feet, and the space between is open to the atmosphere, where "open" means 15 square inches of open area per cubic foot of net compartment volume.

Figure 6.17 delineates the requirements for an acceptable bulkhead.

Figures 6.18 through 6.20 illustrate application of the requirements for a variety of installations.

Figure 6.17 Requirements for Isolation Bulkheads

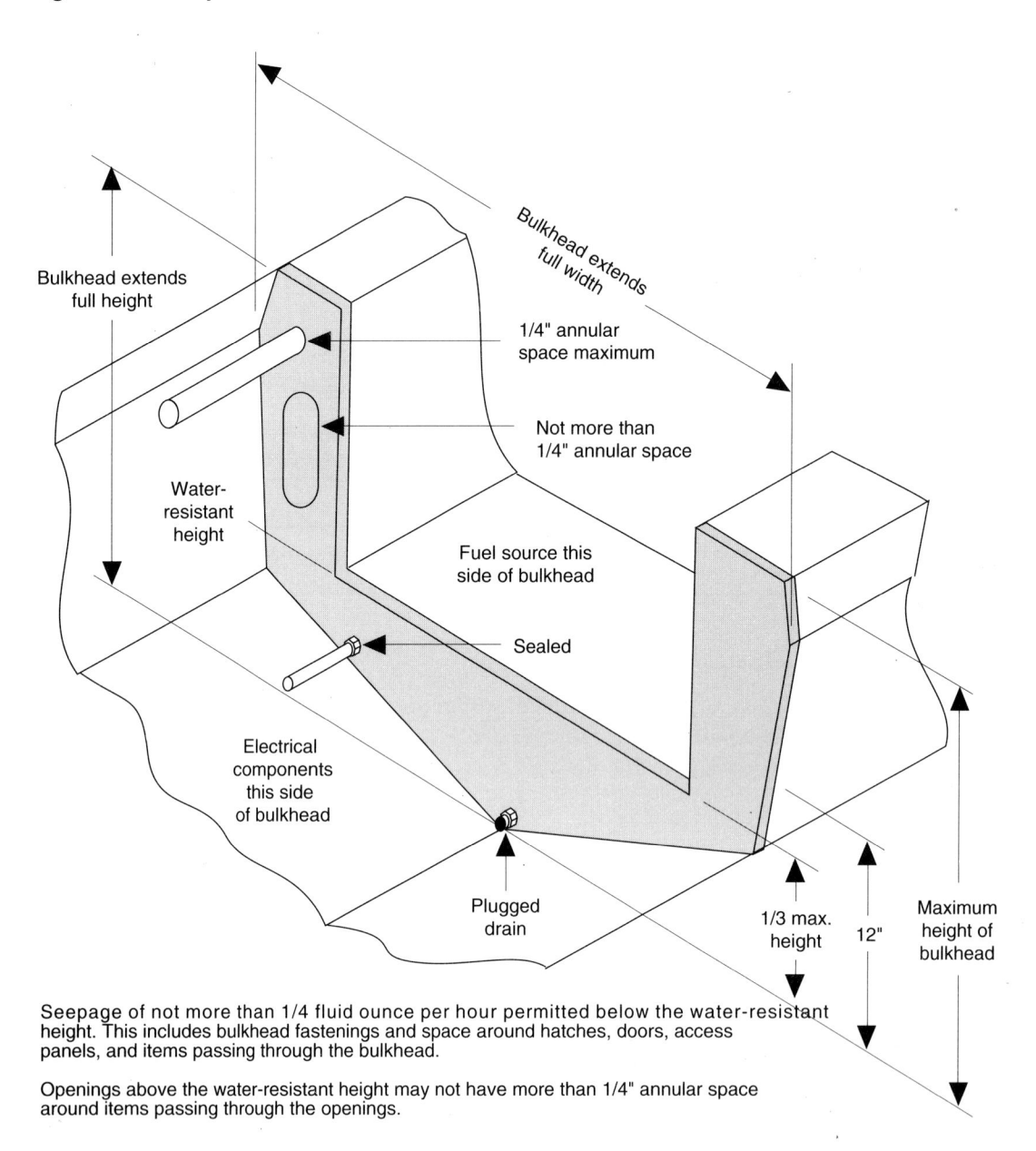

Bulkhead extends full height

Bulkhead extends full width

1/4" annular space maximum

Not more than 1/4" annular space

Water-resistant height

Fuel source this side of bulkhead

Sealed

Electrical components this side of bulkhead

Plugged drain

1/3 max. height

12"

Maximum height of bulkhead

Seepage of not more than 1/4 fluid ounce per hour permitted below the water-resistant height. This includes bulkhead fastenings and space around hatches, doors, access panels, and items passing through the bulkhead.

Openings above the water-resistant height may not have more than 1/4" annular space around items passing through the openings.

DC Standards and Practices

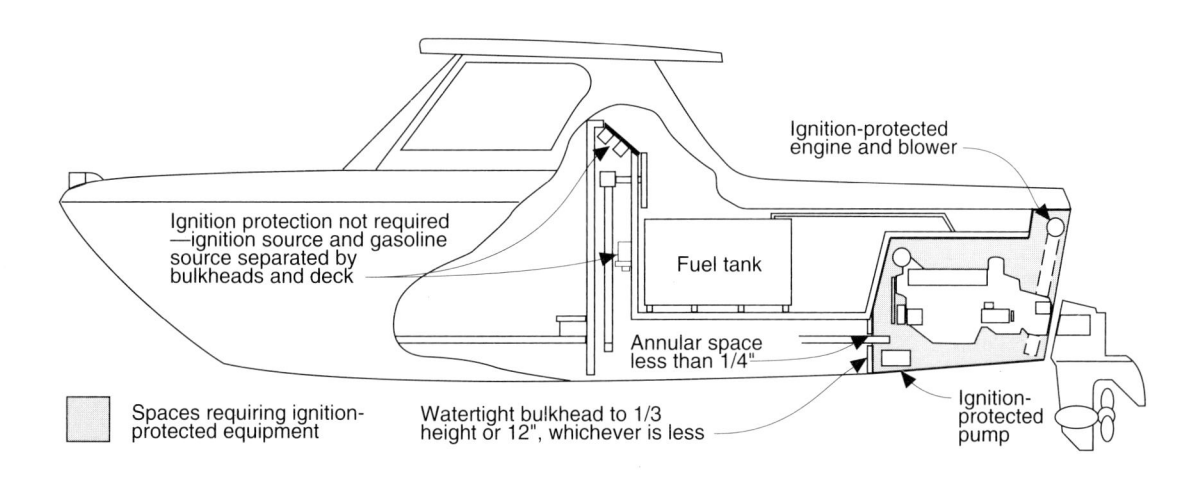

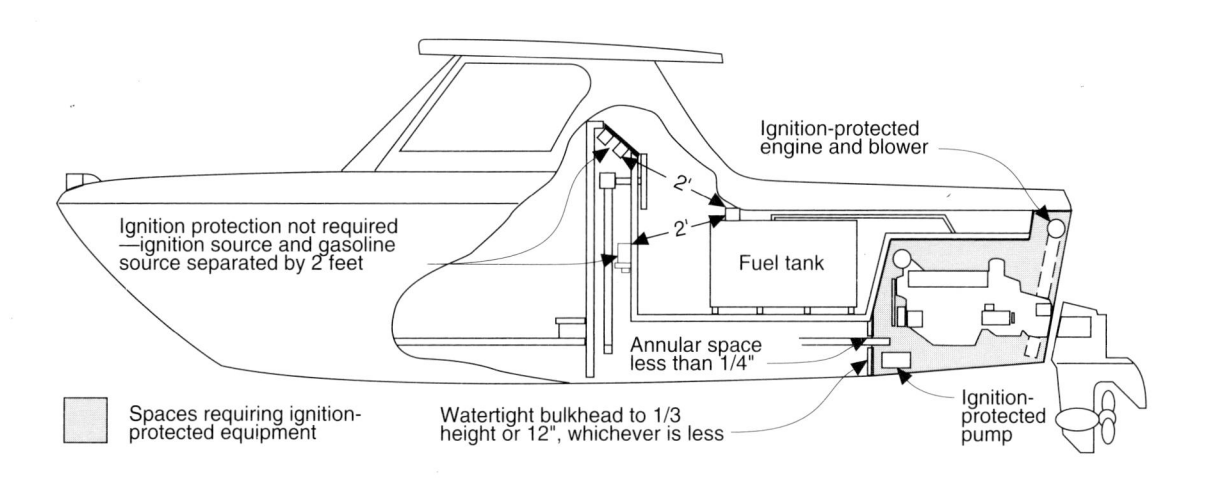

Figure 6.18 Isolation of Electrical Components

130   DC

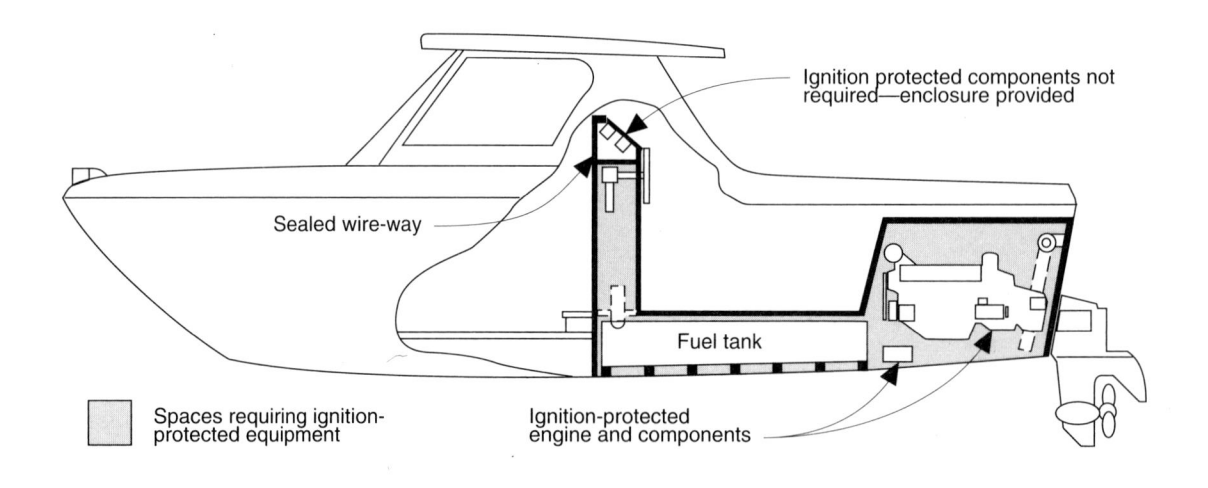

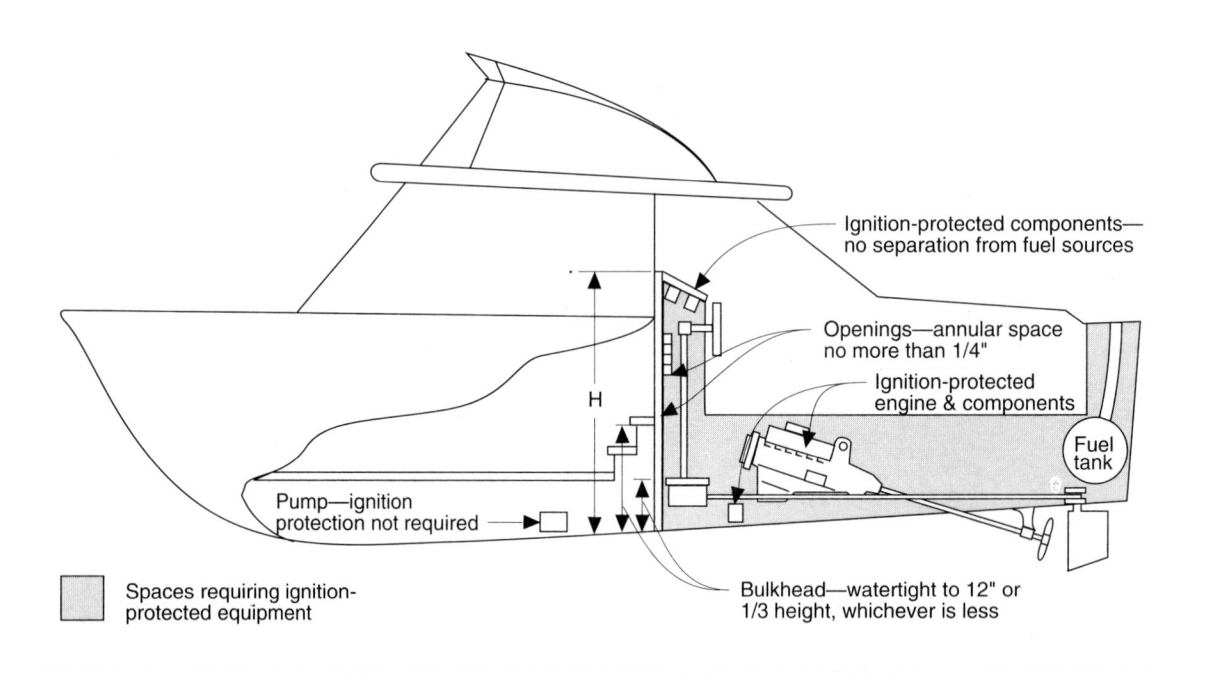

Figure 6.19 Isolation of Electrical Components

DC Standards and Practices 131

Figure 6.19 Isolation of Electrical Components

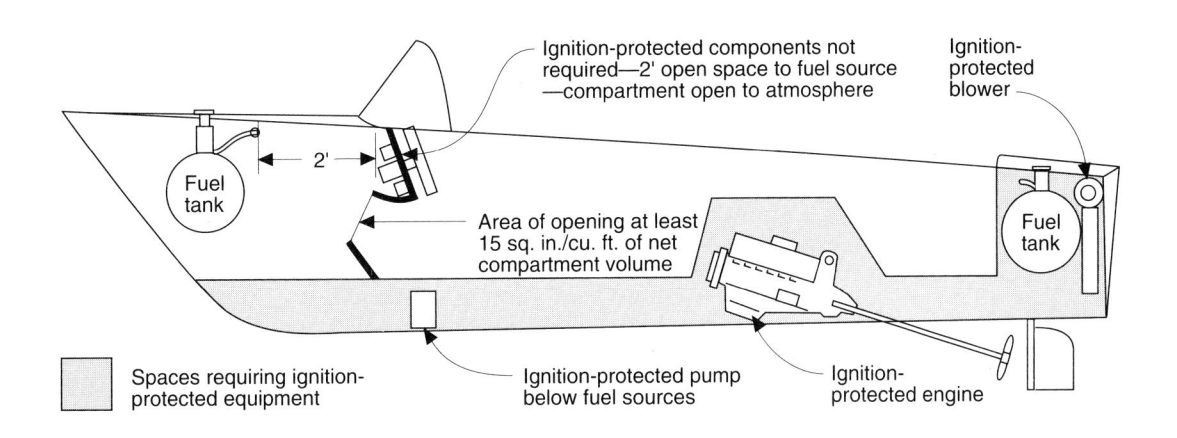

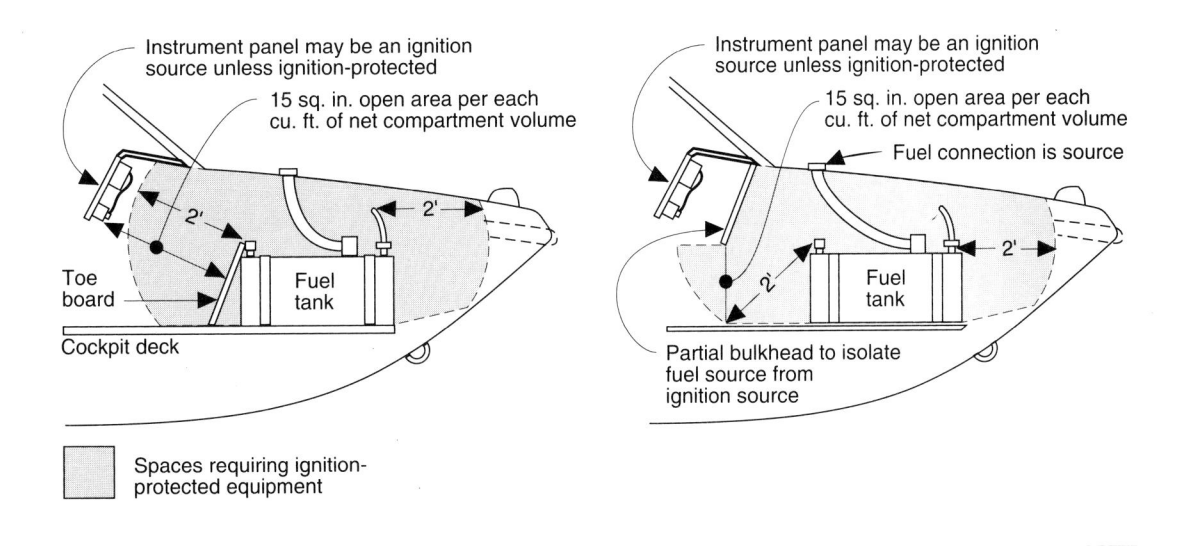

Figure 6.20 Isolation of Electrical Components

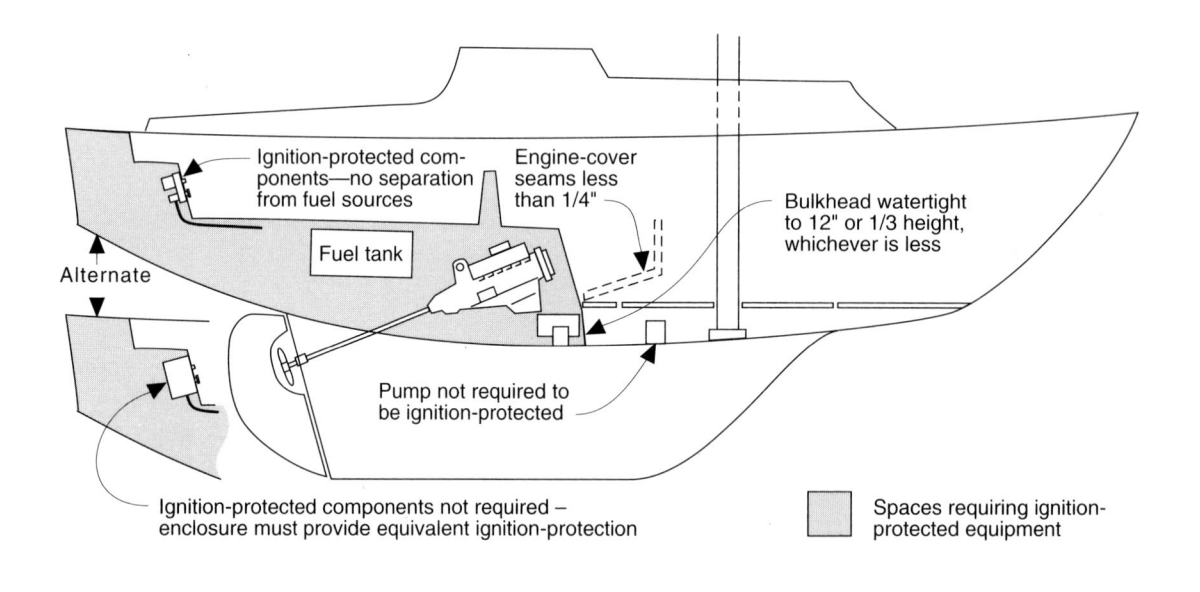

PART II
AC

7

AC BASICS

Alternating Current 136

Will the Real Voltage
  Stand Up? 136

Phase 137

Power Factor 138

AC Safety 140

Grounding 141

Conductor Identification 142

Ground-Fault Devices 143

Transformations 144

Measuring AC 146

Troubleshooting 148

Checking Polarity 150

Boaters are increasingly demanding the convenience of onboard AC power. We are familiar with DC power from Section I. Now we need to know how *alternating current* differs.

In *will the real voltage stand up* we see why 120-volts AC is also called 110, 112, 115, 117, or even 125 volts, but in fact is none of the above!

We'll find that *phase* is as important as voltage and frequency. Some systems have only a single voltage and phase present. Others have three separate voltages and are called three-phase. Because voltage and current in the same conductor may differ in phase, the concept of *power factor* is needed to calculate AC power.

AC safety is largely a function of *grounding*. Because mistaking a hot wire for a ground wire might prove fatal, *conductor identification* is important. Even with proper conductor identification, however, we need *ground-fault devices* to guard against defects in the ground system.

AC is powerful because of the *transformations* we can effect using (what else?) transformers.

As with DC, instruments for *measuring AC* permit *troubleshooting* circuits in order to uncover problems, including *checking polarity* of the incoming conductors.

Alternating-current electricity (AC) is easily understood once you have grasped the fundamentals of direct-current electricity (DC). If you understand the relationships between voltage, current, and resistance in DC circuits, then you are ready for the similar relationships in AC circuits. If you are unfamiliar with Ohm's Law, review the DC concepts presented in Chapters 1 and 2.

ALTERNATING CURRENT

Figure 4.2 in Chapter 4 showed the output of a *rotary-current machine.* Rotation of a magnet between coils of wire induces a sinusoidal current in the wire. Because the current reverses direction, it is known as *alternating current.* If we used a voltmeter to measure the voltage across, instead of current through, the coils, we would see that the voltage is of the same sinusoidal form, as shown in Figure 7.1. All generators and alternators produce this sinusoidal current and voltage prior to rectification.

One full oscillation of voltage or current is known as a cycle. The number of cycles completed in one second is the frequency. The unit of frequency (cycles per second) is the hertz, abbreviated hz. Utility electricity in the U.S. is precisely regulated at 60 hertz and in Europe at 50 hertz. If you plugged a U.S.-built synchronous-motor electric clock into a European outlet, it would advance 50 minutes per hour.

Many people still have not adopted the term hertz, first introduced in the 1960s. They use the colloquial contraction cycles, as in 60 cycles per second, instead of the proper 60 hertz. Little harm is done, though, since everyone knows what they mean.

Figure 7.1 Alternating Voltage/Current

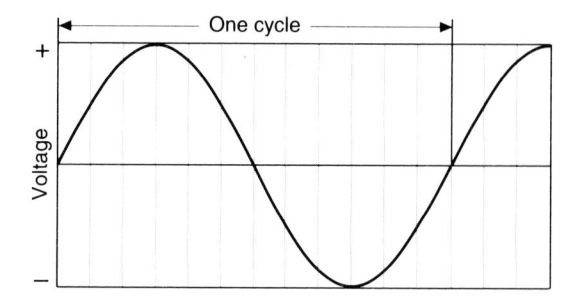

WILL THE REAL VOLTAGE STAND UP?

Read the labels on the undersides of American AC electric appliances, tools and entertainment devices. Which is correct: 110, 112, 115, 117, 120, or 125 volts? There is no universal agreement as to the standard AC voltage. Different utility companies aim at different nominal voltages. In addition, the voltage delivered to your home is likely to vary by a few volts, depending on the other loads in your neighborhood and the total load on the grid.

The first electric service supplied by American utilities was in the form of 120 volts DC. The change to AC power is easily transformed (by transformers) to higher voltage and correspondingly lower current. Since voltage drop is proportional to current, greater voltage results in reduced loss in transmission. The power company distributes power over the grid at extremely high voltages (several hundred thousand), then transforms it down progressive steps to the 120 volts AC that enters your home.

Electric lights, the first electric devices used in the home, work equally well on AC and DC, provided the power dissipated

AC Basics

in the filament is the same. As we learned in Chapter 1, power is the product of voltage and current,

$$P = V \times I$$

where:

P = power consumption in watts

V = volts across the load

I = amps through the load

Using Ohm's Law, which works equally well for DC and AC with purely resistive loads, we can also express power as $P = V^2 / R$. Since the resistance, R, of a lamp filament is resistive, the condition of equal AC and DC power dissipation reduces to:

$$(V_{DC}^2)_{ave} = (V_{AC}^2)_{ave}$$

In other words the average value of the squared AC voltage must equal the average value of the squared DC voltage.

It is easier to think in terms of equivalent DC voltage, so we say,

$$\text{Equiv. } V_{DC} = (V_{AC}^2{}_{ave})^{1/2}$$

The equivalent DC voltage is computed as the square root of the mean value of the squared AC voltage (the root-mean-square value of the AC voltage). In the case of a sinusoidal AC voltage, the peak AC voltage is simply $(2)^{1/2}$, or 1.414, times the equivalent DC voltage. As shown in Figure 7.2, the peak voltage of nominal 120 volts AC is actually 1.414 x 120 volts = 170 volts.

Figure 7.2 AC Voltages

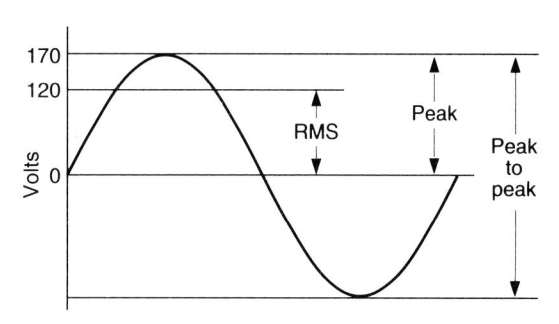

PHASE

The *phase*, Ø, of a sinusoidal wave is its horizontal position along the sinusoidal wave, as shown in Figure 7.3 Consider the waveform starting at the left and labelled A. At Ø = 0°, the voltage is passing through 0 volts and rising. At Ø = 90°, the voltage is at its maximum positive value. At Ø = 180°, the voltage is zero again but decreasing. At Ø = 270°, the voltage is at its most negative value. Finally, at 360° the voltage has come full cycle.

The wave form of Figure 7.2 is called single-phase (abbreviated as 1Ø) because, although changing, there is only one phase present at any time.

Figure 7.3 shows three wave forms, labelled A, B and C. Wave form B lags wave form A by 120°, while wave form C lags A by 240°. Where all three phases are present in the same voltage source (shore-power cable, generator output, distribution panel, etc.), the power is said to be three-phase or 3Ø.

By the same logic, the 120/240 volts AC power coming into your home, as shown in Figure 7.2B, should be termed two-phase. For whatever reason, however, it is also called single-phase.

Figure 7.3 Three-Phase AC

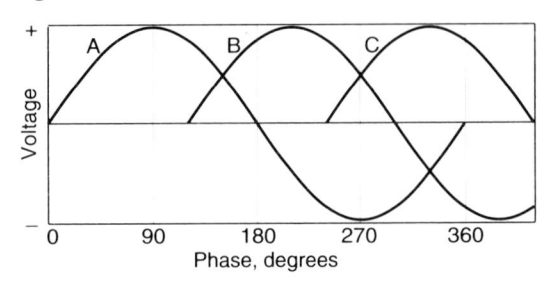

Small boats with minimal AC equipment use only 120 VAC, 1Ø shore power, essentially the same as a heavy duty 120 VAC extension cord. Larger boats often use 120/240 VAC. 1Ø hookups to double the available power and to operate large appliances, such as electric cookers and water heaters. The largest boats may use 120/240 volts AC, 3Ø or 120/208 VAC, 3Ø hookups to increase the power even further, to operate large appliances and to take advantage of the higher efficiencies of 3Ø electric motors.

POWER FACTOR

Figure 7.4 shows a simple AC circuit without the complications of the grounding wire. Until a load is plugged into the socket, the current from the live wire (brown) to the neutral wire (blue) is open. Although a voltage exists between live and neutral, no current flows because the circuit is incomplete.

At bottom we have plugged a load (a motor) into the socket with a two-prong plug. Now a current flows because the circuit has been closed, or completed, by the load.

Note that the load is labelled Z instead of R. Z is the symbol for impedance, the AC equivalent of resistance, or R. Impedance

AC Basics

consists of a combination of the load's DC resistance and its reactance (transient reaction to changing voltage). We won't go into the mathematics, but capacitors show little opposition to changing voltage, while inductors (coils) show large opposition. For this reason, the relationship between voltage and current in an AC circuit is often not one-to-one, as it is in DC circuits.

Figure 7.4 Simple AC Circuit

Figure 7.5 Three-Phase AC

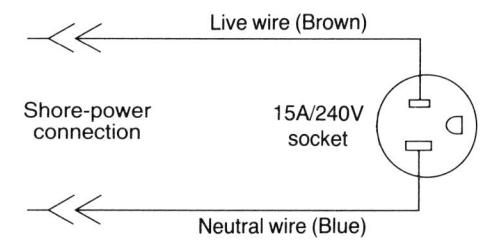

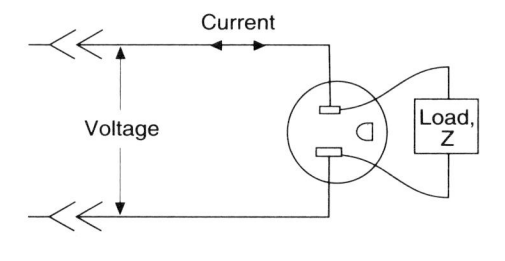

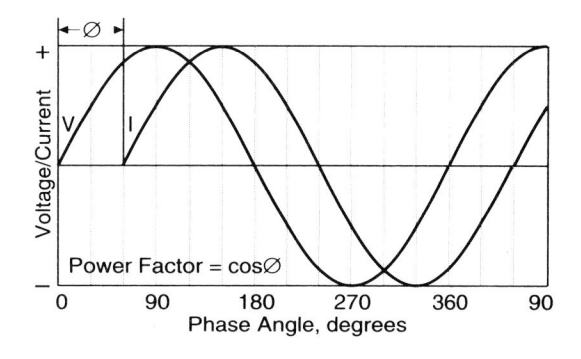

Figure 7.5 shows a plot of both voltage and current in our example AC motor circuit. In this example, the load contains inductance, and the current lags behind the voltage by phase angle Ø. If the load were more capacitive than inductive, voltage would lag current, and Ø would be negative.

The relationship between voltage and current is usefully quantified by the load's power factor.

where PF = Watts ÷ (Volts X Amps)

Watts = true power consumed

Volts = measured volts

Amps = measured amps

If the load were purely resistive, voltage and current would be in phase, watts would equal volts times amps, and the power factor would be 1.0. Since the load has an inductive component, however, voltage and current are never simultaneously at their maximum values, so the true power (instantaneous product of voltage and current) is less than the maximum voltage times the maximum current, and the power factor is less than 1.0.

As shown in Figure 7.5, PF equals cos Ø, the cosine of the phase angle between voltage and current. For purely resistive loads such as incandescent lamps, Ø = 0, so PF = 1.0. In the example shown, current lags behind voltage by 60° (Ø = 60°) so PF = cos 60° = 0.5.

The definition of PF can be rewritten as

$$\text{Amps} = \text{Watts} \div (\text{Volts} \times \text{PF})$$

The above equation indicates the problem with small PF. For the same wattage of useful power, halving PF doubles amps. Greater amps means larger supply conductors, greater voltage drops, greater resistive heating and decreased efficiency.

The power factor of an electric motor can be very small when the rotor is stalled. As a result, locked-rotor and start-up currents can be 3 to 5 times normal running current, a factor which must be considered when fusing motor circuits.

AC SAFETY

We all know that electricity is dangerous. On the other hand, electricity is so useful that it has become indispensable in our daily lives. Understanding electricity and its effects on the body, however, should allow you to understand AC wiring standards.

The basic human body/electricity problem stems from the fact that the body is an electrochemical/mechanical system. At the center of this system is an advanced computer—the brain. External stimulations are converted to electrical signals by transducers, such as the eyes (light to electricity), ears (sound to electricity) and nerves (touch and temperature to electricity). The electrical signals are conducted to the brain through nerve fibers acting much like conducting wires. The brain processes the incoming information and then sends out appropriate electrical signals in response. The most obvious effect of the outgoing signals is the stimulation and resulting contraction of muscles. Herein lies the danger of externally applied electrical current.

Because the fluids in the body have the same approximate composition as salt water, the body has the same electrical conductivity. If your body bridges an electrical circuit, it becomes a part of that circuit, and electric current flows through it. Muscles in the body, including the heart, cannot distinguish between electrical signals from the brain and the electric current we call a shock.

If you are fortunate, the involuntary muscle contraction propels you rapidly and safely away from the source. A less fortunate reaction is contraction of the muscles in the hand and a rigid grip on the source. Worst of all is current flow through the chest and heart muscle, resulting in interruption of the heart beat.

Figure 7.6 compares the dangers of various current paths through the body. The first pattern explains why electricians often work with one hand in ticklish situations. If one hand were to contact a hot wire and the other hand a neutral or ground wire, the resulting current flow would be directly through the chest.

The middle figure illustrates the second dangerous situation: contact with a hot wire while standing on a wet and conductive ground. The current flow is again directly through the chest and heart.

The bottom figure shows a shock that, although painful and possibly causing a burn, is not usually life-threatening. Since both hot and neutral or ground conductors are in the same hand, current flow is limited to the hand muscles. Herein lies the danger of externally applied electrical current.

AC Basics   141

Figure 7.6 AC Safety

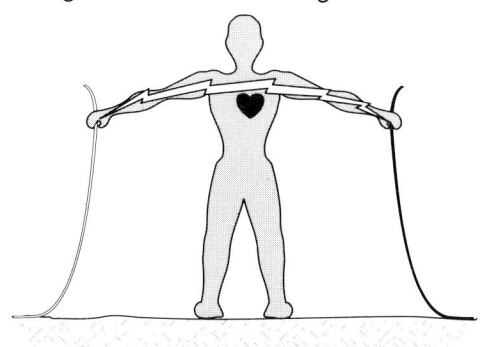

Dangerous: Current Through Chest

Dangerous: Current Through Chest

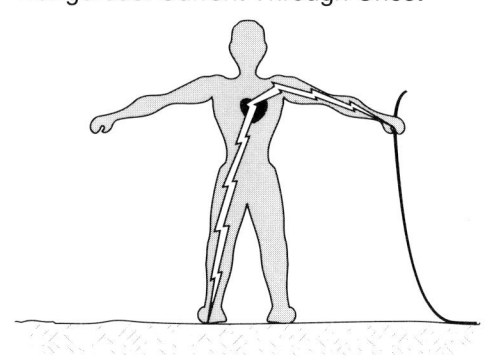

Safer: Current Not Through Chest

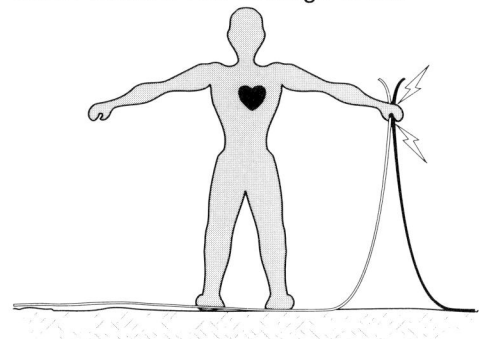

GROUNDING

Figure 7.6 shows what happens when a person contacts a hot (live) wire while standing on a grounded conductive surface. The body serves as a parallel return conductor to ground.

But who would ever grasp a hot wire? Figure 7.7, top, on the following page, shows that it is not always necessary to touch a hot wire to receive a potentially lethal shock. The hot (brown) and neutral (blue) wires of the motor cord are intended to be isolated from each other and from the metal case. Unfortunately, through chafe or overheating of its insulation, the hot wire has shorted to the motor case. Operation of the motor is unaffected, but when the person contacts the case, the result is the same as contacting the hot wire directly.

Figure 7.7, bottom, shows the solution: a green and yellow grounding wire, connected to the blue neutral wire at the power source, runs parallel to the neutral wire throughout the circuit. The green and yellow wire is connected to the exterior metallic case of every electrical device. If the hot wire shorts to the case, the green and yellow grounding wire offers the stray current a low resistance return path to ground, thus preventing significant current through the more resistive human body.

If the short circuit from the hot conductor to the case is of low enough resistance, the short-circuit current will blow the fuse or trip the circuit breaker in the brown conductor. Even if the current is insufficient to trip the breaker, however, the green and yellow wire will provide a low-resistance safety path. It should be obvious that switches, fuses and circuit breakers must never be installed in this green and yellow grounding conductor.

142

AC

Figure 7.7 AC Safety

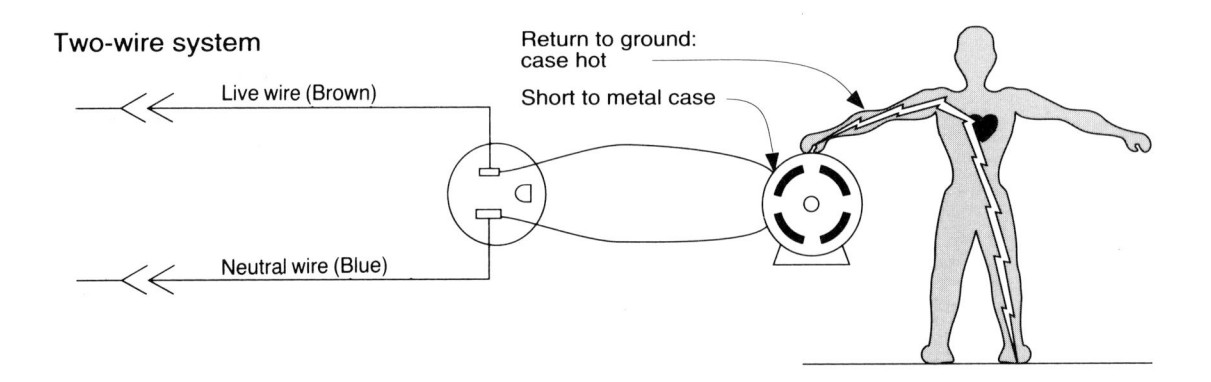

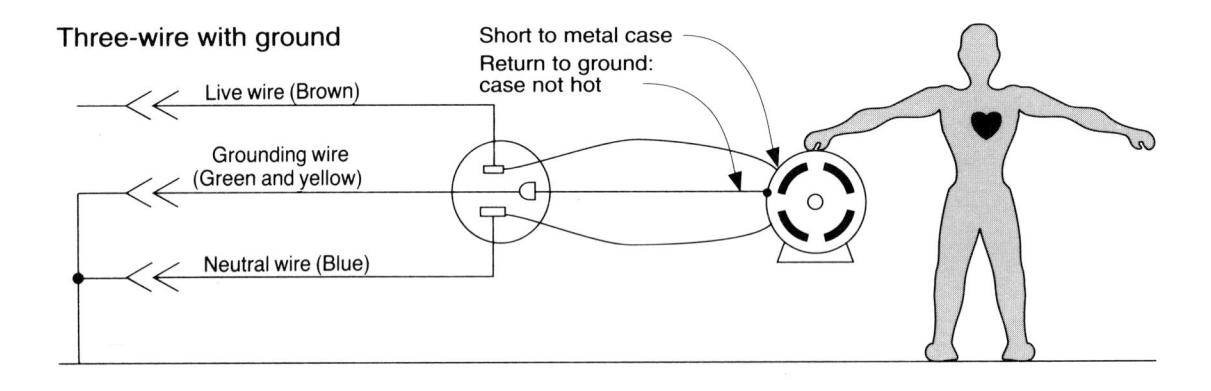

Two-wire system

Live wire (Brown)
Neutral wire (Blue)

Return to ground: case hot
Short to metal case

Three-wire with ground

Live wire (Brown)
Grounding wire (Green and yellow)
Neutral wire (Blue)

Short to metal case
Return to ground: case not hot

AC Basics

AN ADDED LEVEL OF SAFETY: GROUND-FAULT DEVICES

The green grounding conductor of Figure 7.7, bottom, goes a long way toward providing safety from electrocution, but what if the green wire is broken, or what if the device is being used on a two-wire extension cord that contains no grounding conductor? There are numerous ways in which the purpose of the green wire can be circumvented. To protect humans against these accidents, a clever form of circuit breaker is recommended for all AC outlets located in head, galley, machinery space, or on-deck.

Figure 7.9 The RCD

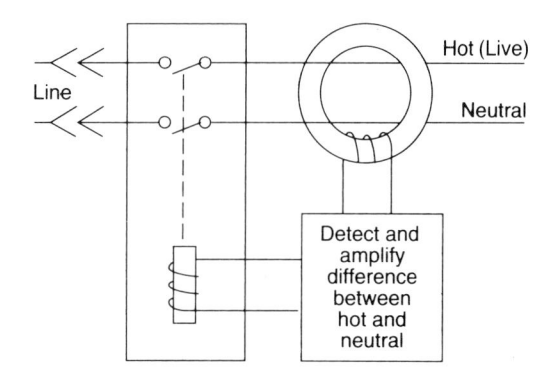

Figure 7.9 demonstrates the operation of the Residual Current Device (RCD). In a normally functioning AC circuit, all current flow is in the hot and neutral conductors. The green and yellow earth conductor is connected to the neutral conductor at the point of origin (distribution panel), but not at individual sockets and devices. Thus, the green wire does not normally carry any current. Every electron flowing in the live (brown) conductor is intended to be returned in the neutral (blue) conductor. Any difference in current

between the two conductors must therefore represent a stray (read potentially dangerous) current.

In the RCD both hot and neutral conductors pass through a circular magnet. Current in the hot conductor induces a magnetic field in the magnet, but the equal and opposite current in the neutral conductor induces an equal and opposite magnetic field. The net magnetic field is thus zero.

Any difference in the two currents, however, produces a net magnetic field, which induces a current in the detecting coil wound around the magnet. The detected current activates a solenoid that opens either the hot conductor (single-pole RCD) or both hot and neutral conductors (double-pole RCD). The Class A RCD recommended for marine use opens on a difference in current of only 5 milliamps—far less than a lethal current to humans. Although the sensitivity of these devices can sometimes be annoying when trying to establish a shore-power connection, remember—it's better to be annoyed than to be dead.

TRANSFORMATIONS
AC to AC
The greatest advantage of AC power over DC power is the possibility of simply increasing and decreasing voltage.

Figure 7.10A shows a simple transformer. It consists of two insulated coils, both wound around the same core of magnetic material. AC current flowing in the input coil at the left induces an alternating magnetic field in the core which, in turn, induces an AC current in the output coil at right. If the number of turns in the input and output coils are identical, output voltage is identical to input voltage.

Figure 7.10A Simple Transformer

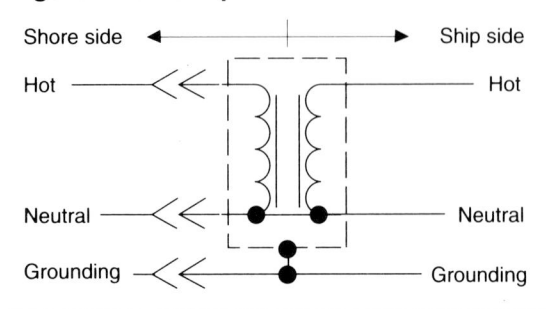

This transformer preserves the identity of the conductors and the phases of the input and output by tying the neutral conductors together. The green grounding wire is similarly uninterrupted and is bonded to the transformer shell or case.

Figure 7.10B shows a step-down transformer. The number of turns in the output coil is less than the number of turns in the input coil. The voltage induced in the output coil is, therefore, less than the voltage in the input coil.

As with Figure 7.10A, the identity of the input and output conductors and phases are preserved in this transformer by tying the neutral conductors together. The green grounding wire is again bonded to the transformer shell or case.

Figure 7.10B Step-Down Transformer

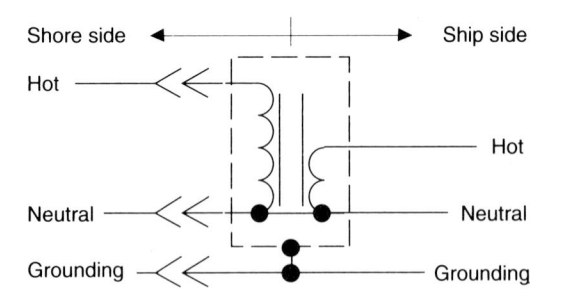

AC Basics

Figure 7.10C shows an isolation transformer. Here neither neutral nor grounding conductors are connected through the transformer. The neutral (blue) and grounding (green) conductors on the output side are connected, however, so that the transformer output acts as an electrical source, which is isolated from shore-ground, just as with an on-board generator.

Note that the green grounding wire from the shore-power side is shown connected to the shield between the input and output coils. Other common configurations include connection of the grounding wire to an inside case or an outside case. In any case, the manufacturer's recommendation should be followed.

Figure 7.10C Isolation Transformer

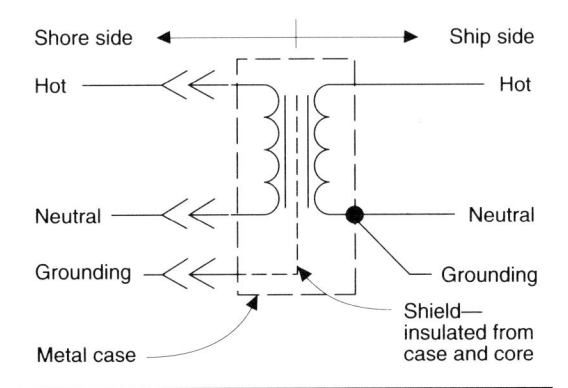

The isolation transformer is ideal for shore-power hookups because it interrupts the green grounding wire from the shore-power circuit, which might otherwise provide a path for stray corrosion currents between boats sharing the same shore-power circuit. Isolation transformers will be discussed further in Chapter 9.

AC to DC

As we saw in Chaper 4, alternating current can be converted to direct current. In Figure 7.11A, a diode in the output allows current to flow only in the direction of the symbolic arrow. As a result, the positive current half-waves are conducted while the negative half-waves are blocked. Although not constant the output current never reverses polarity and is thus direct current.

Figure 7.11A Half-Wave Rectifier

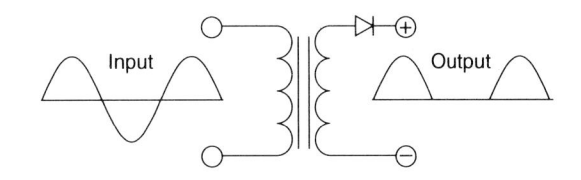

The full-wave rectifier in Figure 7.11B employs a diode bridge of four interconnected diodes to conduct both positive and negative half-waves. During the positive current half-wave, the two diodes at the top conduct. During the negative current half-wave, the bottom two diodes conduct. Since the input and output coils are electrically isolated, both half-waves appear to be positive, when seen at the output.

Figure 7.11B Full-Wave Rectifier

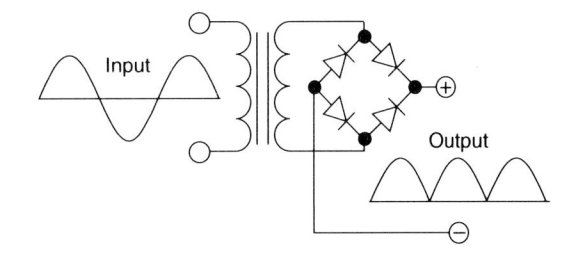

The output voltages of both the half-wave and the full-wave rectifier look to the eye more like alternating current than direct current, due to the extreme amount of ripple. The DC power supply in Figure 7.12A employs a large capacitor across the output to average the pulses for a nearly ripple-free output.

Figure 7.12A DC Power Supply

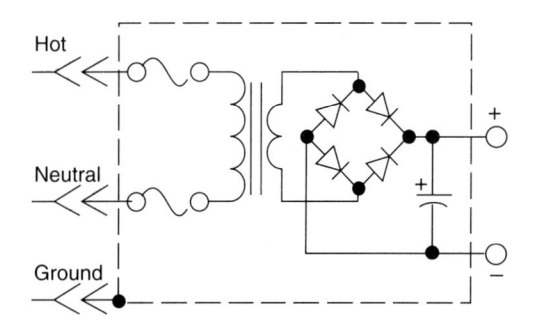

The simple battery charger in Figure 7.12B uses the battery itself to smooth the ripple. As we saw in Chapter 4, the rectified output of an engine alternator is similarly smoothed by the large capacity of the battery it charges.

Figure 7.12B Simple Battery Charger

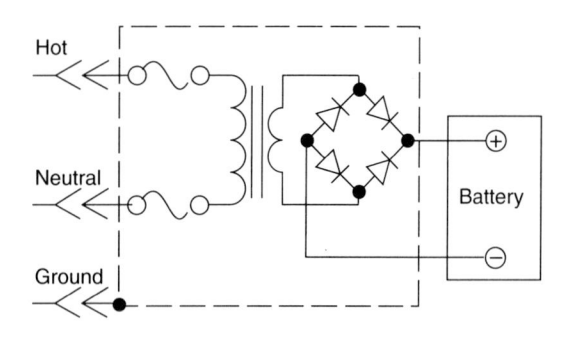

MEASURING AC

The ordinary multimeter can be used in AC as well as DC measurements, although with fewer ranges and with reduced accuracy. Fortunately, accuracy is rarely of importance in AC measurements. While 0.1 VDC represents 10% of the capacity of a 12 volt battery, the normal range of shore-power voltage may be 110 to 125 volts AC.

AC Voltage

Figure 7.13 shows a multimeter measuring AC voltage. The meter employs the same internal circuitry to measure and display both AC and DC voltages, except that the AC voltage is first rectified by a diode bridge. Generally, the positive-test lead must be switched to a separate AC jack that feeds the diode bridge. Attempting to measure AC volts on a DC volts setting will do no harm but will likely result in a reading of 0 volts, corresponding to the average DC value of an AC voltage.

Figure 7.13 Measuring AC Voltage

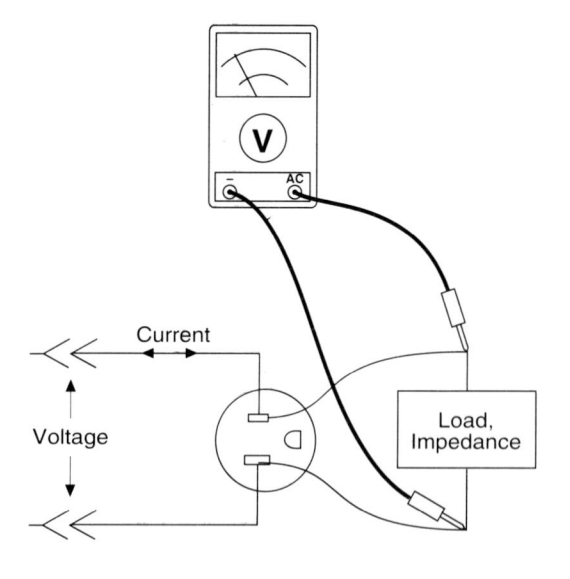

AC Basics

AC Amps

Most multimeters can measure up to 250 milliamps (0.25 amp) of AC current directly, as shown in Figure 7.14, top. To make the measurement, check to make sure the multimeter switches and leads are in the correct positions. Then disconnect the hot conductor from the load and insert the multimeter leads in series with the conductor and the load.

The trick employed in high-current ammeters can be used to measure AC currents greater than 0.25 amp. Figure 7.14, bottom, shows a shunt inserted in the current-carrying conductor. A shunt is a low-ohm precision resistor that generates a voltage drop in accordance with Ohm's Law. Shunts are specified by the ratio of voltage drop across the shunt to the maximum current through the shunt. For example a "50 mV per 100 A" shunt is intended for currents of up to 100 amps and produces 50 millivolts across its terminals at full current. The resistance of such a shunt is

$$R = V/I$$
$$= .050 \text{ volts}/100 \text{ amps}$$
$$= .0005 \text{ ohms}$$

More expensive multimeters contain internal shunts which allow direct measurements of up to 10 amps.

If your multimeter does not have this capability, or if you wish to measure even greater currents, you can purchase a 100 millivolts per 100 amps, 50 millivolts per 200 amps or other shunt for less than the cost of another ammeter. You can then use your multimeter on a millivolts setting to read amps flowing through the shunt.

Figure 7.14 Measuring AC Current

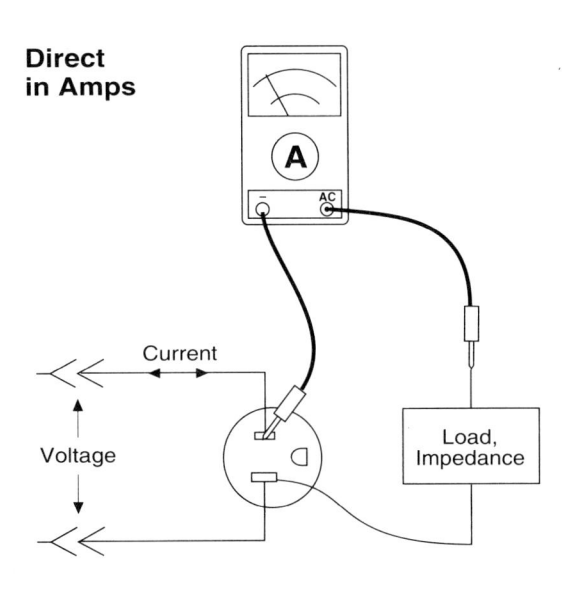

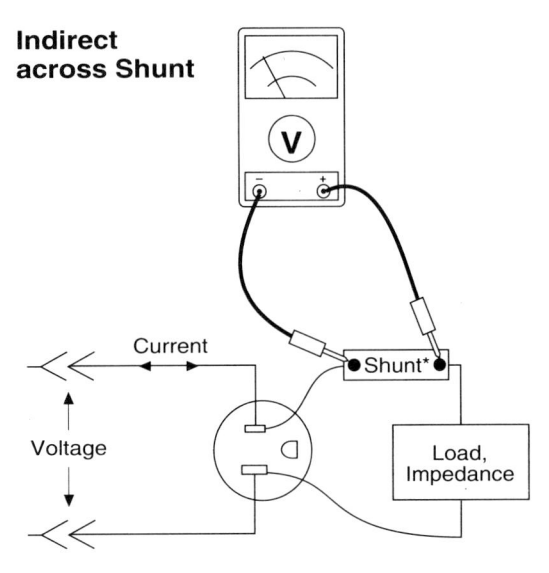

Direct in Amps

Indirect across Shunt

*Shunt may be internal or external to meter

AC

If you have money to spare, a more expensive but less accurate special-purpose AC meter employs a clamp that is placed around the hot conductor. The current in the conductor induces a magnetic field around the conductor which, in turn, induces a current in the clamp. The current is then read as in any other type of test meter.

The advantage of the clamp-on meter is the ability to read current without disconnecting or cutting the conductor. A limitation is the requirement of physically separating the hot and neutral conductors. If both hot and neutral conductors are enclosed by the clamp, the opposing currents will induce cancelling currents so that the meter will read zero.

A second disadvantage of the clamp-on meter is lack of sensitivity. While direct, in-line meters can measure down to microamps, the clamp-on meter is useful down to milliamps.

AC Impedance

As we saw above, impedance varies with frequency and, in the case of AC motors, with the speed of the motor. Such measurements are beyond the scope of this book and the pocketbooks of most boaters. What we can measure, however, is the resistive component of the impedance. To do so, the resistance must be isolated from the rest of the circuit as shown in Figure 7.15. However, one of the leads must be removed to effect electrical isolation.

The resistance component of most AC loads is quite small, so be sure to zero the meter first by touching the test leads together and adjusting the zero-ohms knob. In digital multimeters zeroing is usually automatic.

Figure 7.15 Measuring AC Current

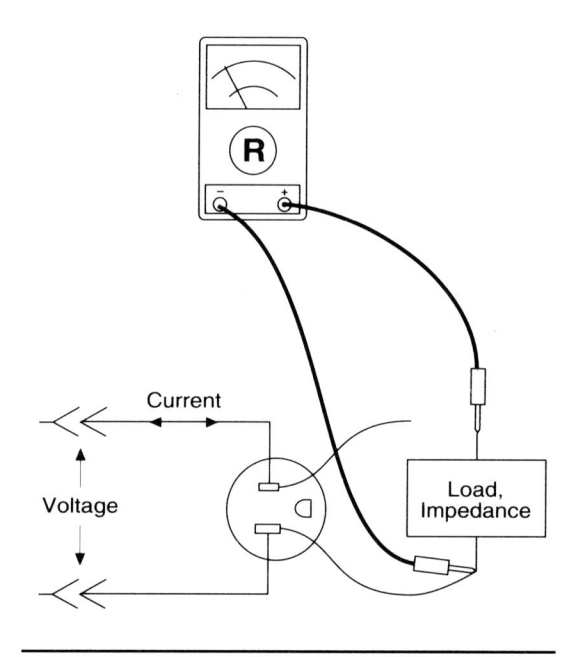

TROUBLESHOOTING

Testing an alternating-current circuit is no more difficult than testing a direct-current circuit, provided you keep in mind the functions of each of the circuit conductors. To review the color code for AC conductors:

- Brown conductors should be hot (live) (240 volts AC)

- Blue conductors should be at 0 volts relative to boat ground

- Green or bare conductors should be at 0 volts relative to boat ground

AC Basics

A 240 volt AC mains circuit is essentially equivalent to a 12 volt DC circuit, with one live (brown) wire supplying the equipment with power and a neutral (blue) wire acting as a return. The third, earth wire (green and yellow) is not part of the circuit unless a fault occurs, so the same kind of voltage tests can be carried out between the live and neutral sides of an AC circuit as between the positive and negative sides of a DC circuit. The important proviso is that you must always take great care with an AC mains supply, bearing in mind its potentially lethal effect.

With the shore-power connected on board, any voltage test between the live wire and the safety earth wire of a cabin supply socket should yield 240 volts, since the earth and neutral wires are connected — not on board but right back at the distribution panel.

Neutral and earth should thus be at the same potential. A voltage test between the neutral wire and the earth wire should always, therefore, yield a result of zero volts. If these effects are reversed, then polarity is reversed, the live and neutral wires are somehow crossed on board, and the situation needs correcting (see the next section on polarity checking).

With AC circuits, just as with DC circuits, open-circuit and short-circuit testing is carried out with an ohmmeter (or the ohmmeter function of a multimeter) *when the shore-power has been completely disconnected from the boat.* An ohmmeter measures electrical resistance and can therefore indicate whether a selected circuit or run of wiring is electrically complete or whether the electrical path is broken.

CHECKING POLARITY

In spite of color-coded conductors and terminals, conductors sometimes get switched. Most often the fault lies in a homemade shore-power cord where the mirror-image male and female plugs and socket patterns are confused.

Reverse polarity is a dangerous situation. The boat's ground is inadvertently raised to 120-volts AC, along with the sea water immediately surrounding the boat via the bonding of underwater metal. A person swimming near the boat can be killed.

Unfortunately, most AC electrical equipment will operate normally with reverse polarity. We, therefore, need some way to test for proper polarity when establishing a shore-power connection.

Figure 7.18 shows how one might perform the test with a 240-volt lamp. The lamp should light whenever one of its leads is in the hot socket and the other in either the neutral or grounding socket. If the lamp lights when the leads are in the large rectangular and U-shaped sockets, then either both the neutral and grounding conductors are hot, or one of them is.

A proper shore-power hookup will have a reverse-polarity warning light in the AC-distribution panel. If yours doesn't, you can install the one described in Chapter 14.

Alternately, you can purchase a plug-in polarity tester at any hardware store for about £5. Plug it into an onboard AC socket every time you establish a shore-power connection. It may save someone's life.

Figure 7.17 Polarity Testing with Lamp

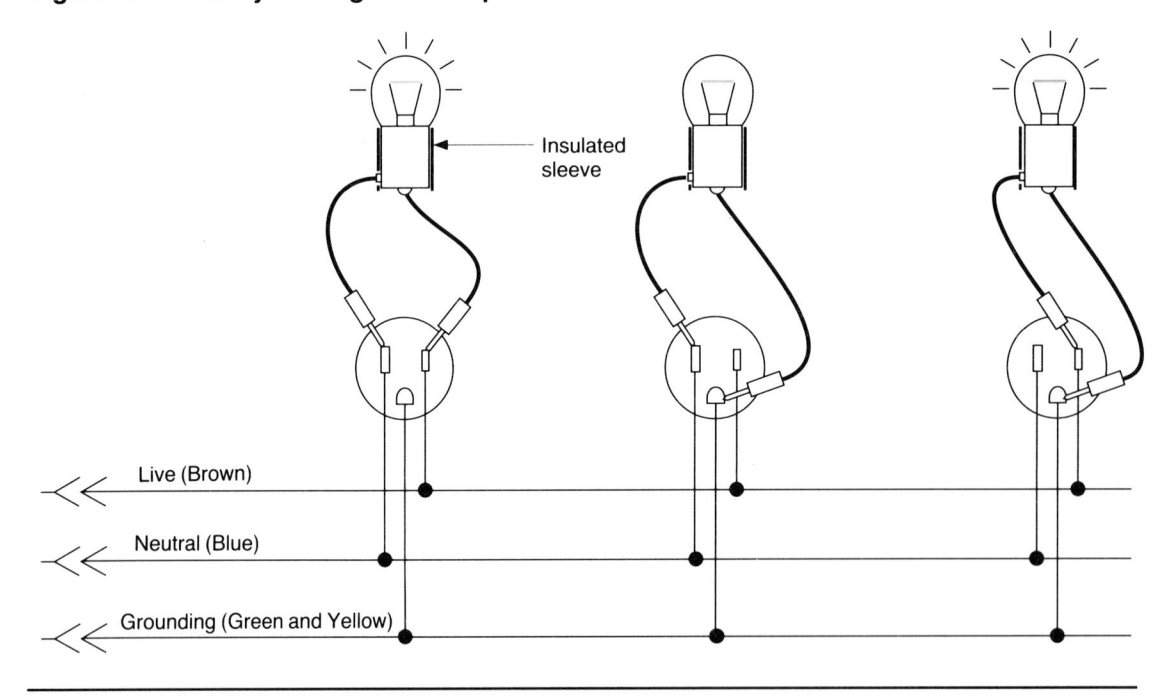

8 INVERTERS AND GENERATORS

Why Have AC Power? 152

AC Options 153

What is Your AC Budget? 153

Modern Inverters 159

Transfer Switching 164

Generators 165

Purchasing Points to Ponder 170

Why have AC power on a boat? Because AC appliances add convenience to shipboard life. *AC options* include shore-power, inverters, and generators.

In order to select an inverter or generator you first need to determine *your AC budget*, or how much AC power you will likely consume.

Modern inverters can supply all the clean, regulated, AC power you wish, along with the conveniences of automatic battery charging and *transfer switching* between shore-power and battery.

Generators can do the same but, before choosing a generator over an inverter, you should consult the *purchasing points to ponder*.

WHY HAVE AC POWER ON A BOAT?

I was cruising the Bahamas a few years ago. There is no significant radio or television programming in the Bahamas so I, like most other cruisers (and Bahamians as well), was idly listening to other boaters' conversations on VHF.

Two women were conversing about the weather, their plans for the afternoon, etc. Suddenly one said, "Whoops, gotta go; my toast is up."

There was a long pause. Then, "You have a toaster?"

"Sure," said the other, "I have toast or an English muffin most mornings."

Another long pause. Then, "I'm going to kill you."

My sentiments exactly. Though there is a certain pristine beauty in adherance to the old ways—reading by oil lamp, navigating by sextant, boiling coffee grounds in a pot—for most boaters the ascetic life wears thin after a season or two. Considering the high performance and low cost of modern inverters, the question should be, "Why not have AC on a boat?"

AC Versus DC

You've probably already tried one or more onboard DC appliances. The notion of trying a DC clone of your land-based kitchen is seductive.

Your first galley appliance may have been the 12-volt DC blender you saw in the mail order catalog. Under the Christmas tree came the 12-volt hair dryer and a 12-volt coffee grinder. Imagine all the comforts of home running on a battery! Within the first season, however, the blender screeched to a halt and the other two appliances disappeared in a cloud of smoke. You quickly learned why the billions of appliances in our homes run on 120-volts AC rather than 12-volts DC.

Several generalizations can be made about DC versus AC appliances:

1. AC appliances cost less than half as much because there are at least 1,000 times as many manufactured.

2. AC appliances last longer because they are expected to survive twenty years of constant use rather than a few seasons.

3. You can only get serious power (saws, toasters, hair dryers) with AC.

The above comparison of AC and DC power is not meant to imply that all household appliances will stand up well in a marine environment, however. Resistance to corrosion, vibration and impact should be considered in purchasing any equipment for a boat. Unfortunately, "marine-grade" is too often a designation assigned by marketing types rather than engineers. Use your boating experience to judge how an appliance is likely to survive aboard your boat.

There are also a few exceptions to the AC/DC rule. Nearly all electronic circuits run on DC. A piece of electronic equipment designed specifically for DC can eliminate the internal AC-to-DC power supply and actually be more efficient than its AC equivalent. The automobile stereo cassette player is the best example. Even with the biggest and best

Inverters and Generators

inverter or generator aboard, your stereo should be powered by DC, just like all of your navigation electronics.

AC OPTIONS
There are three options for getting AC power on your boat:

- Shore power
- Diesel or gasoline generator
- DC to AC inverter

Shore Power
Shore power is the same power you have in your home. Essentially, you plug your boat into the utility via an extension cord. There are significant safeguards, however, which should be installed to protect personnel from dangerous shocks and your boat's underwater metals from stray-current corrosion. These installation safeguards are described in detail in Chapter 9.

Generators
Generators are capable of supplying large currents—enough even to power a full-blown electric range. Unless your boat is a 100-foot yacht with a sound-proofed engine room (room—not compartment), generators are too smelly and noisy to be run 24 hours per day. You may become immune to the noise, but boaters anchored near you in Paradise Lagoon will probably mind it and view you as an inconsiderate jerk.

If you really must have an electric rather than a propane range, electric water heater and air conditioner on the hook, then by all means install a generator, but concentrate the heavy loads for an hour in the morning and an hour in the evening. The smaller loads can be run off your batteries via a silent inverter.

Inverters
Inverters are silent sources of AC that draw battery power stored from the engine alternator, a generator, or wind, water or solar chargers. Many modern inverters are designed specifically for marine or mobile use, are nearly 100% efficient in converting DC to AC, are better regulated in voltage than your local utility, and are capable of more sophisticated battery charging than many stand-alone battery chargers.

If you spend most of the time at a dock, you'll obviously want a substantial shore-power hookup. Even if you spend most of the time anchored or moored, the cost of the most common shore-power system is so small that you should install it for the sake of safety alone.

With an inverter, you'll be able to cast off the dock and shore-power lines and continue to use all of your small AC appliances without interruption.

If you have truly electrically cloned your home with air conditioner, AC refrigerator/freezer and electric range, however, you'll also need a substantial generator in order to continue your opulent life-style afloat.

The first task in selecting the components of an AC installation is to determine your AC budget.

WHAT IS YOUR AC BUDGET?
Table 8.1 lists the typical onboard power consumptions of AC tools and appliances you may consider for your boat. The listed figures are representative and intended to be used for preliminary planning. If you already have the appliances you plan to use, use their actual ratings instead.

Table 8.1
Typical Appliance Power Consumption

Appliance		Typical Watts	Typical Hours Use Per Day
AC, 5,500 BTUH	Air conditioning	750	12
AC, 11,000 BTUH		1500	12
Blender		300	.02
Grill		1,400	.25
Computer		100	2
Drill, 3/8-inch		350	.02
Dryer, hair		1,200	.05
Fan, 6-inch		25	8
Fan, 20-inch		250	8
Electric frying pan		1,200	.25
Heater, space		1,200	12
Heater, water		1,500	1.3
Iron		1,100	.15
Light		25-75	4
Microwave, 0.6 cu.ft.		800	.15
Microwave, 1.5 cu.ft.		1,200	.25
Mixer		240	.05
Percolator		600	.25
Cooker		1,200	1
Refrigerator, 6 cu. ft.		80	10
Refrigerator, 14 cu. ft.		140	10
Soldering Iron		100	.02
TV, 7-inch B&W		20	4
TV, 7-inch color		35	4
TV, 16-inch color		100	4
Toaster		1,100	.15
VCR, play-only		20	2
VCR, play/record		80	2
Vacuum Cleaner		800	.05

Somewhere on every tool and appliance is a nameplate listing either volts and amps or volts and watts. Listed amps and watts are the maximum steady-state values at the specified voltages. Motor-driven tools and appliances often draw start-up currents several times larger than their nameplate ratings. This is usually of small concern with inverters and generators, however, since both are capable of surge currents far in excess of their continuous ratings. As long as your inverter or generator is sized to run well within its steady-state capacity, it should have little trouble starting a motor.

To convert appliance ratings from amps to watts and vice-versa, remember:

Watts = Volts x Amps

Example: the label on the bottom of your toaster lists its power requirements as 115 volt AC, 10 amps. First, ignore the fact that the voltage is listed as 115 (or 110 or 125) instead of 120. Although your toast will brown more quickly on 120 volts than on 115 volts, the toaster will function adequately on any voltage between 110- and 125-volts AC. Don't plug it into 240-volts AC, however, unless you're looking for an excuse to purchase a new toaster.

To convert from amps to watts we use the formula above:

Watts = Volts x Amps

= 115 volts x 10 amps

= 1,150 watts

The voltage of your onboard source may actually be 120-volts AC, in which case the toaster will draw slightly more than 10 amps and 1,150 watts, but we are just estimating our needs at this point.

Inverters and Generators

Column 3 of Table 8.1 lists typical operating times for each appliance. You may not have a listed appliance, or you may have it but rarely use it. The figures in column 3 are suggested operating times in hours per day when applicable. These figures obviously depend on lifestyle. For example, the table lists 1.3 hours per day for a 1,500-watt water heater. A single-handed boater might halve the listed time, but a family with teenagers might quadruple the listed 1.3 hours.

After assembling your list of planned appliances, their rated wattages and estimated hours of use, you are ready to compile your estimated daily electric load.

Table 8.2 provides a blank form you can photocopy and complete to determine your typical daily consumption in watt-hours.

Table 8.2 Daily Electrical Consumption

Appliance	Rated Watts	Typical Hours/Day	Watt-Hours Per Day[1]	Peak Watts Inverter[2]	Peak Watts Generator[3]
_____	____	____	____	____	____
_____	____	____	____	____	____
_____	____	____	____	____	____
_____	____	____	____	____	____
_____	____	____	____	____	____
_____	____	____	____	____	____
_____	____	____	____	____	____
_____	____	____	____	____	____
_____	____	____	____	____	____
_____	____	____	____	____	____
_____	____	____	____	____	____
_____	____	____	____	____	____
_____	____	____	____	____	____
_____	____	____	____	____	____
Totals					

1 Watt-hours supplied by inverter. Total in parenthesis is amp-hours drawn by inverter from battery.
2 Peak watts from inverter while generator is off.
3 Peak watts from generator.

Tables 8.3 to 8.5 show example budgets of minimum (other than zero), medium, and large AC-power use.

The minimum budget shown represents a traditional cruiser with liquid- or gas-fueled cooking, mechanical or 12-volt refrigeration, but 120-volt-AC entertainment.

The minimum budget requires an inverter with a maximum continuous rating of about 500 watts, which draws about 35 Ah per day from the batteries.

Total battery consumption is 33 Ah (35 Ah considering inverter efficiency), plus the sum of the daily DC loads.

Table 8.3 Minimum Power Consumption

Appliance	Rated Watts	Typical Hours/Day	Watt-Hours Per Day[1]	Peak Watts Inverter[2]	Peak Watts Generator[3]
Blender	300	0.02	6	300	—
Computer	100	2.00	200	100	—
Drill, 3/8-inch	350	0.02	7	—	—
Soldering Iron	100	0.02	2	—	—
TV, 7-inch color	35	4.00	140	35	—
VCR, play-only	20	2.00	40	—	—
		Totals	395 (33 Ah)	435	

[1] Watt-hours supplied by inverter. Total in parenthesis is amp-hours drawn by inverter from battery.
[2] Peak watts from inverter while generator is off.
[3] Peak watts from generator.

Inverters and Generators

The medium budget (Table 8.4) adds a small microwave, 120-volt-AC refrigerator and hair dryer to the minimum budget.

This medium budget requires an inverter rated at about 1,300 watts continuous and draws about 125 Ah from the batteries. Since microwave use most often occurs in short bursts, and since inverters can put out much larger currents for short periods, a 1,000-watt continuous inverter would probably suffice.

Total battery drain again consists of the 125-Ah inverter drain plus all DC loads.

Table 8.4 Medium Power Consumption

Appliance	Rated Watts	Typical Hours/Day	Watt-hours per Day[1]	Peak Watts Inverter[2]	Peak Watts Generator[3]
Blender	300	0.02	6	300	—
Computer	100	2.00	200	100	—
Drill, 3/8-inch	350	0.02	7	—	—
Dryer, hair	1,200	0.05	60	—	—
Microwave, 0.6 cu.ft.	800	0.15	120	800	—
Refrigerator, 6 cu.ft.	80	10.00	800	80	—
Soldering Iron	100	0.02	2	—	—
TV, 7-inch color	35	4.00	140	35	—
VCR, play-only	20	2.00	40	—	—
Totals			1,375 (115 Ah)	1,315	

[1] Watt-hours supplied by inverter. Total in parenthesis is amp-hours drawn by inverter from battery.
[2] Peak watts from inverter while generator is off.
[3] Peak watts from generator.

AC

The large budget adds all of the conveniences of the home. Demand in the evening is beyond the capability of standard inverters, so a generator is added to supply the largest loads, which are concentrated for an hour in the morning and an hour in the evening.

The large budget requires a 7.5 kilowatt to 8.0 kilowatt generator during the hours of peak use and an inverter rated at about 2,000-watts continuous. Allowing for the efficiency of the inverter, the inverter alone draws about 280 Ah per day from the batteries.

Table 8.5 Large Power Consumption

Appliance	Rated Watts	Typical Hours/Day	Watt-Hours Per Day[1]	Peak Watts Inverter[2]	Peak Watts Generator[3]
AC, 11,000 BTUH	1,500	12.00	—	—	1,500
Blender	300	0.02	6	300	300
Computer	100	2.00	200	—	100
Drill, 3/8-inch	350	0.02	7	—	—
Dryer, hair	1,200	0.05	60	1,200	1,200
Heater, water	1,500	1.30	—	—	1,500
Lights	50–500	4.00	1,000	250	250
Microwave, 1.5 cu.ft.	1,200	0.25	—	—	1,200
Range/Element	1,200	1.00	—	—	1,200
Refrigerator, 14 cu.ft.	140	10.00	1,400	140	140
Soldering Iron	100	0.02	2	—	—
TV, 16-inch color	100	4.00	400	100	100
VCR, play-only	20	2.00	40	20	20
Vacuum cleaner	800	0.05	40	—	—
Totals			3,155 (263 Ah)	2,110	7,510

[1] Watt-hours supplied by inverter. Total in parenthesis is amp-hours drawn by inverter from battery.
[2] Peak watts from inverter while generator is off.
[3] Peak watts from generator.

Inverters and Generators

MODERN INVERTERS

Figure 8.1 shows, in simplified form, how an inverter transforms direct-current battery power into alternating current. S_1, S_2 and S_3 are all solid-state transistors, which act as switches.

Figure 8.1 Simplified Inverter Schematic

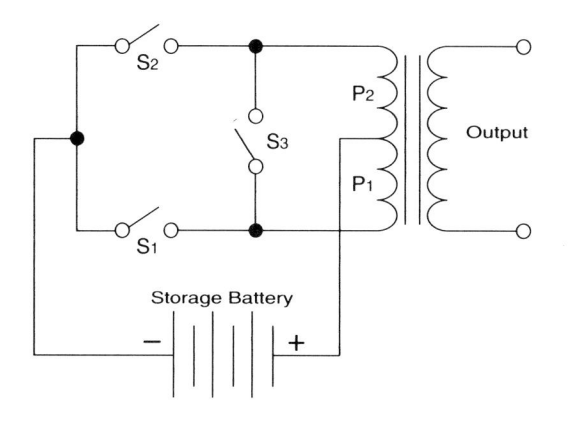

The sequence of electrical events for one AC cycle is shown in Table 8.6. The actual circuitry is far more complex, but the switching sequence demonstrates the principle.

Table 8.6
Transistor Switching In Inverter

S_1	S_2	S_3	Action	Result
closed	open	open	12V applied to primary coil P1	+ output
open	open	closed	primary shorted	0 output
open	closed	open	12V applied to primary coil P2	– output
open	open	closed	primary shorted	0 output

Figure 8.2 compares the output wave forms of utility power (sinusoidal wave), unregulated inverters (square wave) and voltage-regulated inverters (pulse-width-modified sine wave).

Figure 8.2 AC Wave Forms Compared

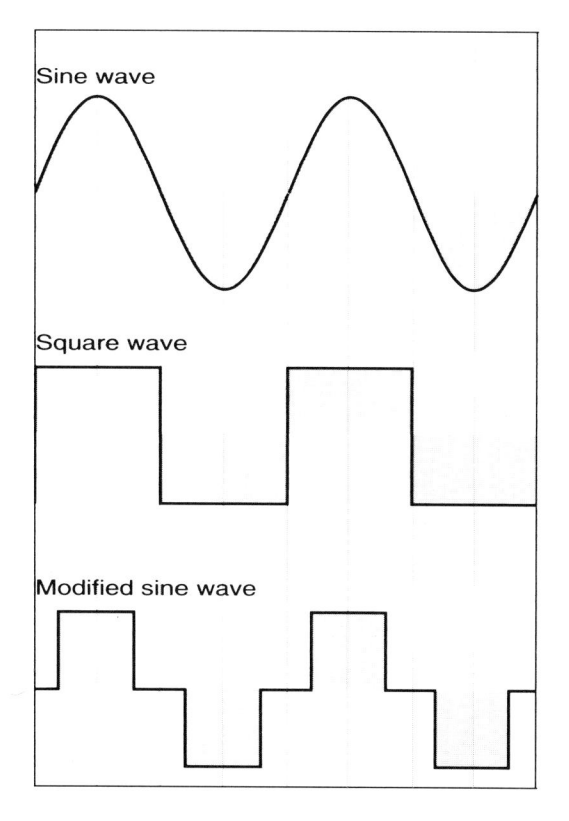

The pulse-width-modified sine wave has two advantages over the square wave. First, it appears slightly more sinusoidal in shape to a load. Second, by varying the width of the output pulse, the average output voltage (area under the voltage curve) can be held constant as the input battery voltage and output peak voltage drop.

Square-wave inverters are notorious for causing 60 hertz hum and interference. To the antenna or input transformer of a piece of sensitive electronic equipment, the square wave appears to be a group of sinusoids at multiples of the fundamental 60 hertz. Whether these higher frequency components interfere depends a great deal on the quality of the equipment's grounding, shielding and power-supply filtering.

High quality pulse-width-modified, sine-wave inverters emit less harmonic power but sometimes still cause difficulty in sensitive equipment. For zero interference and hum, pure sine-wave inverters are available at significantly higher cost.

My experience in operating computers, GPS, loran, VHF, SSB and television receivers concurrently with a Heart pulse-width-modified, sine-wave inverter, is that the computer, GPS and loran seemed unaffected. The television displayed minor interference patterns, and the transmissions of both VHF and SSB contained noticeable hum. I have not found the interference to be serious enough to install line filters.

Chapter 13 contains all the information you need to filter the supply lines of effected equipment If you are still concerned, you can make your purchase of a pulse-width-modified, sine-wave inverter contingent on acceptable interference levels.

Typical Inverter Specifications
Table 8.7 lists the specifications of three popular inverters in a range of sizes.

Input Voltage Range
Most inverters accept a range of input voltage of about 10 to 15 volts DC. To avoid problems, you should make sure the voltage regulators of your engine alternator and solar and wind chargers are set to less than 15 volts, measured on the battery side of any isolation diodes. If you wish to bypass the regulators and equalize your batteries with a voltage greater than 15 volts, first turn the inverter off.

The low voltage cutoff of approximately 10 volts DC is designed to prevent destructive 100% discharge of the batteries. Some inverters sound an audible alarm before cutting off.

Output Voltage
The outputs of all inverters listed in Table 8.7 are pulse-width-modified sine waves, where the duration of the pulses are adjusted to produce a constant rms (root mean square) voltage. The actual peak voltages corresponding to 120-volts AC rms are

- Sine wave   170 volts
- Square wave   120 volts
- Modified sine wave   150 volts

Since the normal range of shore-power voltage is about 110 to 125, or 117 ± 7% volts AC, any regulation of 7% or better is acceptable.

The frequency regulation of most inverters is nearly good enough for celestial navigation. Heart Interface's ±.005% equates to ±4 seconds per day were you to use an old-fashioned electric clock for your chronometer!

Output Power
When sizing an inverter, be careful. Both industry leaders, Heart Interface and Trace Engineering, assign model numbers corresponding to maximum 30-minute output power. For example, maximum continuous output power of the Heart EMS-1800 is not 1,800 watts, but 1,100 watts—roughly 40% less.

Inverters and Generators

The manufacturers reason that many of the larger inverter loads, such as microwaves, hair dryers and clothes irons, are of 30 minute or less duration, so a 30-minute rating is appropriate. It may be appropriate, but it is also misleading.

Figure 8.3 shows how the maximum output of the EMS-1800 varies with duration. The curve reflects the buildup of internal heat, not depletion of the battery, which is assumed to be a constant 13.0 volts DC. The output power versus time curves of all inverters are of similar shape.

Surge current is the momentary current drawn by electric motors at startup. As a rule of thumb, surge currents of inverters are approximately 250% of the continuous-rated currents. In fact, many manufacturers specify surge current in terms of the size motor they will start.

Efficiency and Standby Power

The percentage of battery power converted to AC power depends on two factors:

- Efficiency is the percentage of power converted while the inverter is in its operating mode
- Standby power is the drain on the battery while the inverter is in its standby mode, waiting for a load to be connected

Pulse-width-modified, sine-wave inverters are extremely efficient at mid- to upper-output levels.

Figure 8.4 shows efficiency versus output power for the Heart EMS1800. Most inverters achieve efficiencies in excess of 90% over most of their output ranges. Efficiency drops dramatically, however, at very low power levels. For this reason, most inverters remain in standby mode (on, but not producing power) until they sense a significant load.

For Heart inverters the minimum load required to trigger the on-state is 7 watts. Since the turn-on is instantaneous, the user is usually not aware of the standby mode unless the load is less than the trigger level, as may be the case with a small NiCad battery charger. To overcome the standby mode, I recharge several NiCads at once.

The standby-drain specification is important because it results in a constant drain on the batteries. Heart's .07 amp amounts to 1.7 Ah per day. The PROwatt 800 standby drain of 0.3 amp drains a significant 7.2 Ah per day. With their more complex circuitry, true sine-wave inverters can draw an amp or more on standby, wasting at least 24 Ah per day.

Figure 8.3 Rated Output of the Heart EMS-1800 Inverter

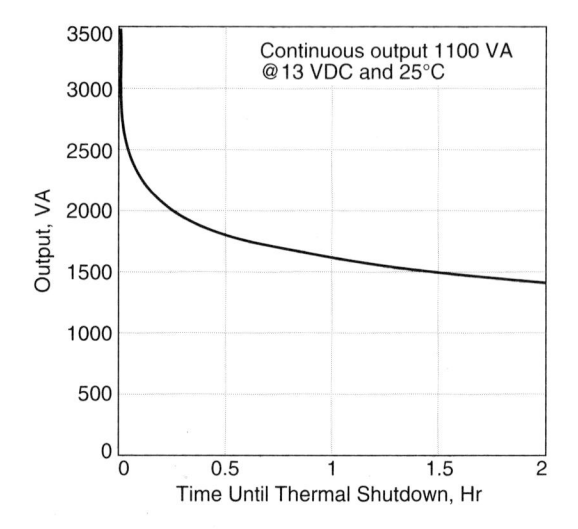

Figure 8.4 Efficiency of the Heart EMS-1800 Inverter

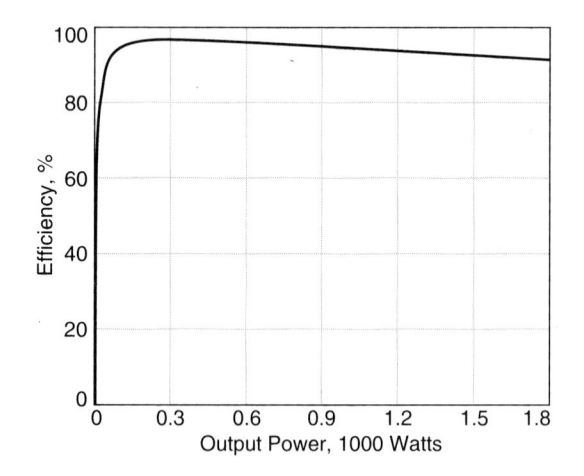

Inverters and Generators

Battery Charging

The most sophisticated inverters offer shore-power battery charging. In effect running backwards, when external AC power is applied from either shore power or an onboard generator, a 30-amp internal - transfer switch connects inverter loads directly to the external AC-power source and, at the same time, begins charging the battery! The battery charging circuitry is as sophisticated as many multicycle stand-alone chargers costing nearly as much as the inverter. The economy is realized through the use of many of the same components for both modes.

Figure 8.5 shows the battery-charging cycles of the Heart EMS inverter series.

Bulk Cycle. Assuming the battery is moderately discharged, the charging current of the EMS1800 starts at 65 amps (100 amps for the EMS2800). Charging current remains constant until the battery voltage reaches 13.0 volts. From 13.0 to 14.3 volts the charging current tapers from 65 amps to about half, or 30 amps.

Absorption Cycle. During the absorption cycle, voltage is held constant at 14.3 volts, while the battery current acceptance drops from 30 amps to 10 amps. Referring to the recommended optimal fast-charging routine for wet lead-acid batteries, shown in Figure 3.16 of Chapter 3, the 10 amp cut-off seems wise, corresponding to a 200 Ah —about the capacity of a size 8D battery.

Float Cycle. Once the current at 14.3 volts drops to 10 amps, the charger reverts to a float state, at a constant 13.3 volts. In the float state, the charger will provide up to its maximum output of 65 amps (100 amps for the EMS2800) while maintaining 13.3 volts. Current demands greater that 65 amps are drawn from the battery.

Figure 8.5 Heart EMS-Series Charging

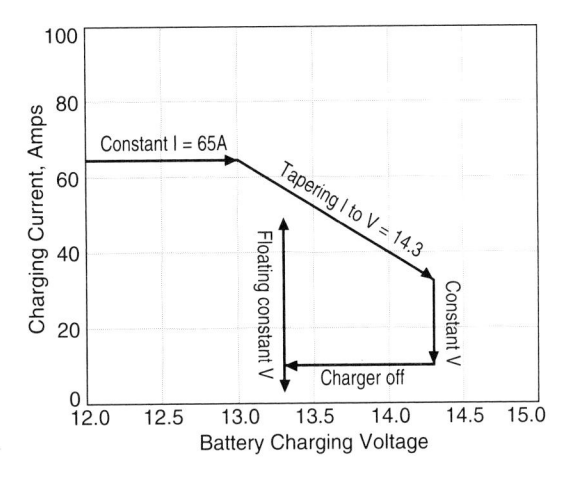

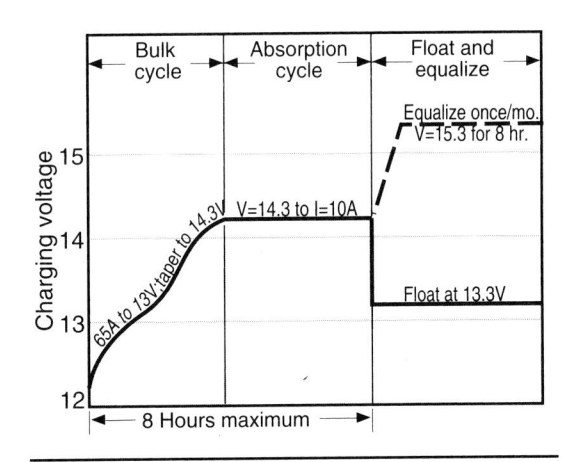

Equalization Cycle. As discussed in Chapter 3, the useful life of a battery is maximized by periodic equalization. Equalization consists of purposefully overcharging the battery, resulting in shedding of hardened lead sulfate from the lead plates. EMS inverters can be manually triggered after reaching the float state to maintain a constant 15.3 volts for 8 hours. They then revert to the float state at 13.3 volts.

TRANSFER SWITCHING

Many inverters offer a transfer switch either as standard equipment or as an option. An inverter transfer-switch automatically switches boat AC loads to shore power or generator output, when available, and back to the inverter output when the external source is removed. This is a great convenience on a boat that goes into and out of slips a great deal.

Boats with onboard generators require an additional transfer switch to select between shore power and generator output.

Figure 8.6 shows the internal configuration of a transfer switch. Input 1 is connected to AC Source 1 (shore power for example). Input 2 is connected to AC Source 2 (internal connection to inverter output). With no AC at the terminals of input 1, power is routed from input 2 (inverter) to the output. When shore power appears at input 1, however, the solenoid pulls the switch up, and power is routed from input 1 to the output.

Operation of a shore power/generator transfer switch can be either manual or similarly automatic.

Figure 8.7 shows the operation of an inverter with both an internal transfer switch and automatic battery charging.

With shore power on, the shore power AC is connected to the AC output and the inverter is turned off. Simultaneously, AC power is applied to the inverter's built-in battery charger, which draws its power from the battery.

The inverter and battery combination thus operates as an "AC battery," supplying AC power when shore power is not available and recharging the batteries when it is.

Figure 8.6 Transfer Switch

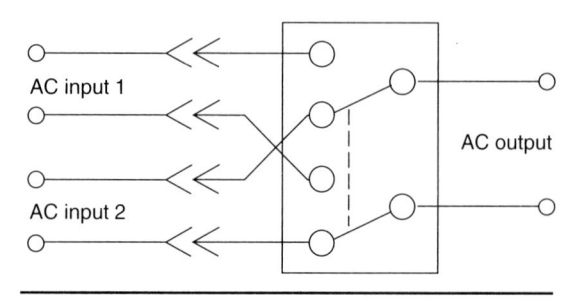

Figure 8.7 Transfer Switch with Automatic Battery Charging

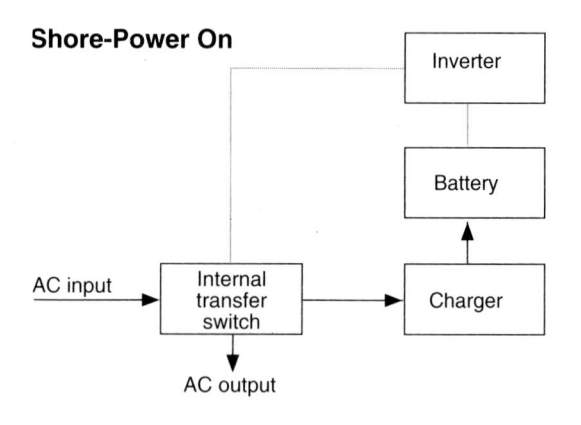

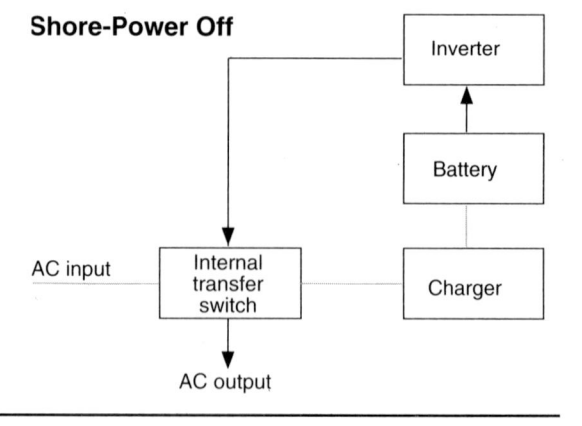

Inverters and Generators

Figure 8.8 shows the operation of a shore-power generator-inverter combination.

When shore power is available, the external transfer switch feeds shore power to both inverter and large-loads panel. The inverter's transfer switch shunts the shore power through to the small-loads panel and simultaneously charges the battery.

When shore power is not available, the external transfer switch selects the generator output, which is fed to both the inverter and the large-loads panel. The inverter's internal transfer switch shunts generator power to the small-loads panel and continues to charge the battery.

When neither shore power nor generator power is available, the inverter stops charging the battery and comes on to supply the small-loads panel. In this mode there is no power at the large-loads panel.

GENERATORS

Prior to the advent of efficient, low-cost, solid-state inverters, the generator was the only source of AC power away from the dock. Now, for loads up to about 2 kw, a combination of large battery and inverter and a means for charging such as engine alternator, solar panel or wind machine will produce AC power at half of the cost of power from the most economical generator. For loads greater than 2,000 watts there is still no substitute for the generator. For boats with large-power budgets a generator-inverter combination is ideal.

Two types of AC generator are:

1. Armature-type, in which the output is generated by the rotor.

2. Alternator-type, in which the output is generated by the stator.

Figure 8.8 Shore-Power Generator-Inverter Switching with Transfer Switches

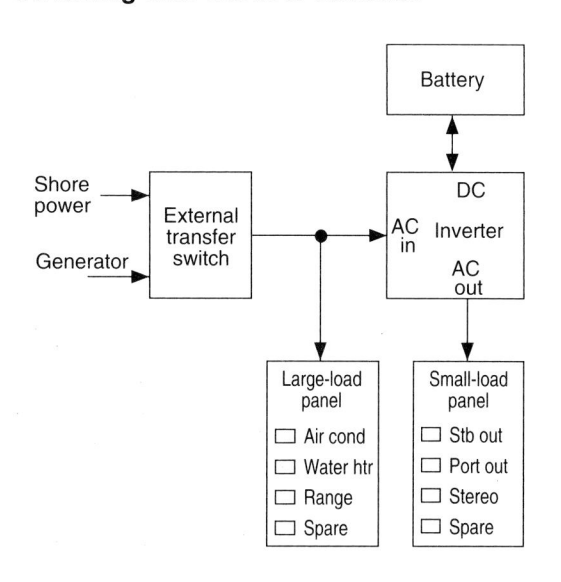

Armature-Type Generators

All generators and alternators rely on the fact that an electric current is induced in either a moving wire in a magnetic field or a stationary wire in a magnetic field that is changing in intensity.

In the armature-type generator, the magnetic field is created by a controlling field current flowing through fixed coils that are placed around the stator (stationary coil). The stator is anchored to the outside case of the generator.

Output current is induced in multiple coils wound on the rotor, which is driven at constant rpm by the generator's engine. Large-capacity slip rings and brushes transfer the large output currents from the moving rotor to the generator-output terminals. The output of the generator is sinusoidal in wave form.

The small DC-field-current is taken from a rectifier bridge that is connected across a pair of output terminals.

Generators with a single 120-volt-AC output generally have two brushes, as shown in Figure 8.9. One brush/terminal is hot (brown conductor); the other brush/terminal is neutral (blue conductor) and is connected to the case of the generator and to ship's ground via the green and yellow grounding conductor.

Generators having both 120-volt-AC output and 240-volt-AC output have either three or four brushes.

Figure 8.10 shows a four-brush generator. Brushes 2 and 3 (neutral) are tied together to the case and to ship's ground. Brushes 1 and 4 are hot. The voltages between brush 1 and neutral and between brush 4 and neutral are both 120 volts AC, but of opposite polarity. The voltage between brushes 1 and 4 is thus 240 volts AC.

Figure 8.9 Two-Brush Armature Generator

Figure 8.10 Four-Brush Armature Generator

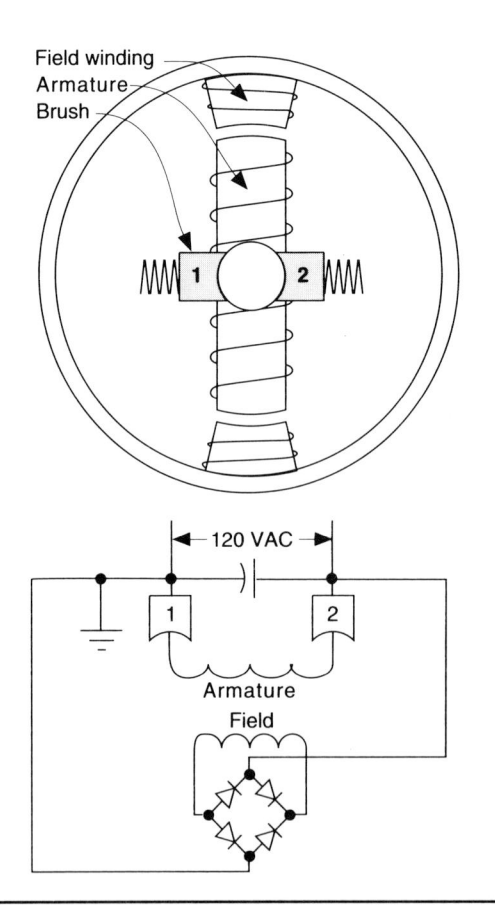

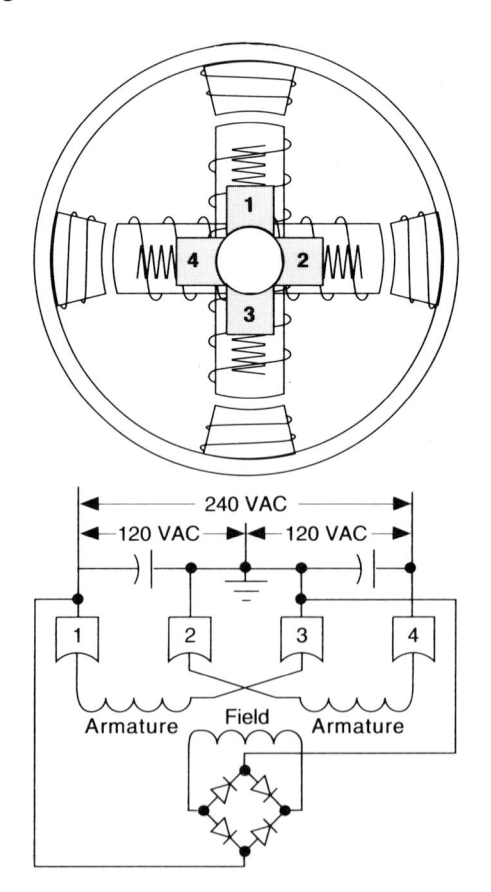

Inverters and Generators

Alternator-Type Generators

In an alternator-type generator the magnetic field is created by magnets and controlling field coils on the rotor. Output current is induced in fixed stator coils located around the inside of the case. In some generators, the field current is generated through rectification of a portion of the AC output and fed to the rotor through brushes—just as in the automotive alternator. Most generators, however, are brushless. An exciter coil in the stator induces AC current in the rotor field coils, which is then rectified by a diode.

Figure 8.11 shows a simplified brushless alternator-type generator. There are two large windings which provide the main generator output. These may be inphase or out of phase. If inphase, there will be two 120-volt-AC outputs. If out of phase, there will be two 120-volt-AC outputs of opposite polarity, which can be combined for 240 volt AC. The small coil to the right provides excitation for the field coils of the rotor. The small coil to the left provides input to a bridge rectifier, which provides 12 volts DC for charging the generator's starting-motor battery.

Figure 8.11 Alternator-Type Generator

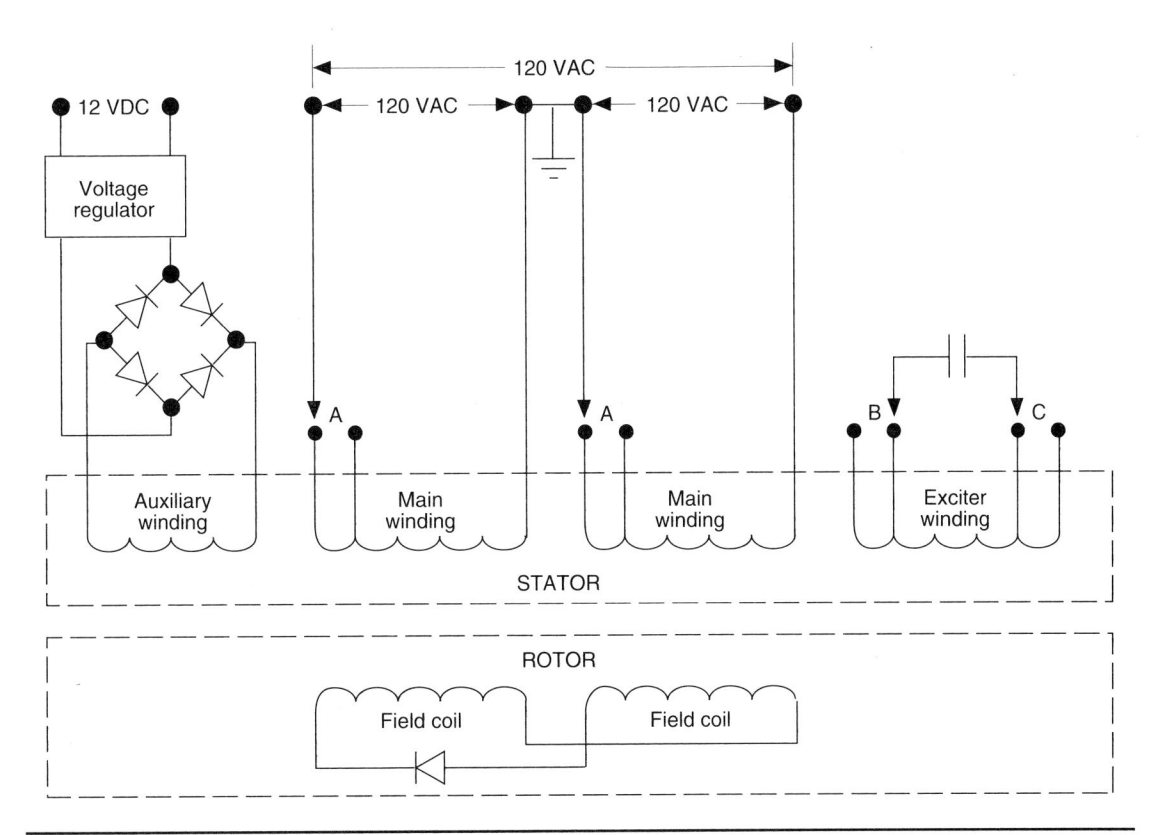

Both main windings and the exciter winding are provided with multiple taps as shown at A, B, and C in Figure 8.11. Output voltage varies slightly with rpm and load, but the nominal voltage is changed by selecting different taps. Output frequency can be controlled *only* by adjusting engine rpm.

Voltage and Frequency Regulation
In both types of generator, the output is taken from the output windings and thus corresponds directly with the rotation of the rotor. Frequency is therefore directly proportional to rpm. This is why fixed-drive generators cannot be driven directly by a boat's propulsion system. Hydraulic drives and variable-speed clutches are available for matching generator and propulsion engine, but they are not as popular as dedicated engines.

Engine rpm is controlled by a mechanical governor on the engine. As the engine slows under increasing load, a centrifugal weight acts to open the throttle. Mechanical governors require an rpm deviation in order to effect a throttle adjustment. The more fuel required, the larger the required deviation in rpm. Thus, generator frequency is necessarily affected by the load. Figure 8.12 shows the typical frequency versus load relationship.

Output voltage is affected by both engine rpm and output load. Since rpm is affected by load, we can think of output voltage as being affected by load. Figure 8.13 shows a typical 110- to 130-volt-AC variation in output voltage from no load to full load. Voltages greater than 130 volts AC shorten the lives of resistive components, such as lamp filaments and heater elements. Low voltages cause motors to draw excessive currents and overheat, or not start at all.

Figure 8.12 Generator Frequency vs. Load

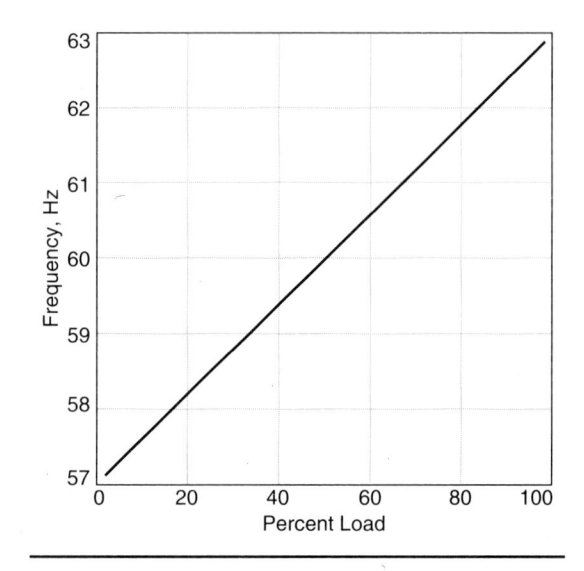

Figure 8.13 Generator Voltage vs. Load

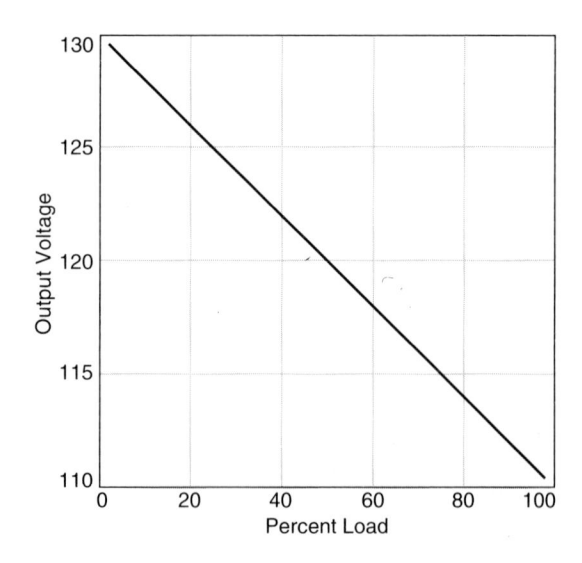

Inverters and Generators

Troubleshooting Generators

The owner's manuals of high-quality generators usually contain extensive maintenance and troubleshooting guides for the specific model. If yours doesn't, purchase a copy of the shop manual, which will have the guides.

The troubleshooting guide below is general and not intended to replace a manufacturer's guide.

Most generators have sealed bearings, which require no lubrication. This does not include the generator engine, which must be maintained to the same degree as the boat's propulsion engine. Crankcase oil should be changed every 100 hours of operation and just prior to any extended lay-up.

If the boat is in the north and the generator is not removed from the boat, the engine will require winterization, as well. If the engine is gasoline-fueled, the spark plugs should be replaced every year.

If the generator contains brushes, check the brushes for excessive wear (more than 50%) and the slip rings for burning and pitting. Replace worn brushes with exact replacements from the manufacturer and follow the directions for seating the new brushes.

Below is a general troubleshooting guide that applies to both armature- and alternator-type generators. You will need to measure output AC volts, AC amps and frequency. A proper generator installation should include AC volts, AC amps and frequency panel meters in the AC distribution panel. For smaller generators use a multimeter to measure volts and amps. If you don't have a frequency meter, you can build the one described in Chapter 13.

1. Erratic Voltage
   - Check brushes for wear.
   - Check slip rings for burning and/or pitting (requires machine shop).

2. High Voltage
   - Check frequency for normal range (57 to 63 hertz).
   - Adjust voltage regulator if possible.
   - Have voltage regulator checked. Consult manual for terminal changes.

3. Low Voltage
   - Check voltage at generator terminals. If O.K. problem is voltage drop in connectors or conductors.
   - If voltage is O.K. initially, then drops, check voltage regulator temperature. Should be cool enough to touch.
   - Adjust voltage regulator if possible.
   - Consult manual for terminal change.

4. Erratic Frequency
   - Check for cycling loads.
   - If erratic with no load connected, check engine governor.

5. High (over 63 hertz) Frequency
   - Adjust engine governor, clean and lubricate linkage.
   - Consult engine manual.

6. Frequency Low (below 57 hertz)
   - Reduce load. If frequency increases to normal range, generator is overloaded.
   - Adjust engine governor, clean and lubricate linkage, consult manual.

PURCHASING POINTS TO PONDER
When sizing and purchasing a generator keep the following in mind:

1. Diesel generators are rated for continuous operation. Petrol generators are usually rated for surge capability, and their continuous ratings are often 50% smaller than the listed surge ratings.

2. Generators with dual outputs may be limited to 50% of their rating on each output. For example, a 2 kilowatt generator with dual outputs may only be able to supply 1 kilowatt to any one load.

3. Petrol generators are generally not ignition protected. They are thus subject to all of the ignition isolation recommendations described in Chapter 6.

4. If you think you can solve problem three by keeping a small petrol generator on deck, consider that it is built to the same standard and will survive about as well as a petrol lawn mower from the same manufacturer.

5. A high rpm (3,600 rpm) petrol generator is built to last about 1,000 hours. Over ten years it can be used about two hours per week. At £1,500 it will have cost £1.50 per hour for amortization alone.

The same capacity (say 5 kilowatt) 1,800 rpm diesel generator can be expected to last about 10,000 hours. Over ten years it can be used 20 hours per week. At £6,000 it amortizes at £0.60 per hour.

9 AC STANDARDS AND PRACTICES

Shore Power   172

Generator and Inverter
   Sources   175

Main Panelboard   177

Grounding   177

Load Calculations   178

Over-current Protection   184

Ground Fault Protection   184

Approved Wire and
   Cable   186

Receptacles   193

Conductor Installation   194

Ignition Protection   195

Galvanic Protection   201

Typical Shore-Power
   Circuits   206

As with Chapter 6, the DC equivalent, this chapter is essentially an amplification of the best industry standards for AC power aboard boats.

We start with sources of AC power: *shore power, generators and inverters*, all of which feed the AC *main panelboard.*

Two primary AC-safety considerations are *grounding* (including *ground-faults*) and over-current protection.

Load calculations allow us to size the *over-current protection* and to select both the *approved wire and cable* and *receptacles* for the application.

The probability of moisture, salt, and vibration, as well as the possibility of gasoline vapors, mandate standards for *conductor installation* and *ignition protection.*

As with DC wiring, the issue of *galvanic protection* and grounding must be addressed. The two solutions— isolating diodes and isolation transformers— are incorporated into approved shore-power circuits.

As with domestic wiring standards adopted by house builders, standards for AC electrical systems on boats are designed to prevent electrical fires and shock to personnel. One should not assume that familiarity with residential wiring qualifies one to do marine wiring, however. Wiring standards for boats are more stringent than those for homes for three major reasons:

1. Boats sit in a conductive medium.

2. Metal parts of boats, including electrical wiring and connections, are exposed to a corrosive environment.

3. Boats are subject to fatiguing vibration and impact.

AC power may come from a shore-power connection, an onboard generator, a DC-to-AC inverter or a combination of the above. The nature and operation of generators and inverters were covered in Chapter 8. Specifics of shore-power, generator and inverter installations will be covered here.

SHORE POWER
Sooner or later someone will use the shore-power cable from the dock to the boat as a dockline. It may be from grasping at the nearest object while headed for the water, or it may be that someone forgot to unplug the power when getting underway. In addition, plugs and sockets are subject not only to vertical rain, but to horizontal spray from washdown hoses, both fresh and salt. For these reasons standards for shore-power cables and inlets are rigorous.

Cable
Standards for shore-power cable are far above those for the garden variety extension cords one finds in building supply outlets. The cable must be designated as heavy-duty flexible cord as shown in Table 9.1

Table 9.1 Shore-Power Cable

Type	Description	Temperature Rating
SO	Hard-service cord, oil resistant compound	140°F (60°C)
ST	Hard-service cord, thermoplastic	140°F (60°C)
STO	Hard-service cord, oil resistant thermoplastic	140°F (60°C)

Current-carrying conductors (hot and neutral) must be sized for the capacity of the shore-power circuit, as shown in Table 9.2.

Table 9.2 Ampacity of AC Conductors

Conductor Size, AWG	2 Conductors[1] Maximum Amps	3 Conductors[2] Maximum Amps
14	18	15
12	25	20
10	30	25
8	40	35
6	55	45
4	70	60
2	95	80

[1] Not including the green grounding wire, which is considered non-conducting.
[2] For four to six conductors, reduce current rating to 80%.

A green grounding wire is required in all shore-power cables, but since the grounding wire is considered normally not current-carrying, it may be of smaller size than the current-carrying conductors. Commonly, it is one size smaller.

The shore end of the cable must have a locking and grounding cap with the proper male (plug) connector that matches the female shore receptacle. The boat

AC Standards and Practices 173

end of the cable must have a locking and grounding cap with the proper female (receptacle) connector to match the boat's male-power inlet.

Figure 9.1 shows the boat end (top) and shore end (bottom) of a 30 A/120 VAC, 1Ø shore-power cable. The weatherproofing sleeves slide over the connectors.

Figure 9.1 30 A/120 VAC Shore-Power Cable

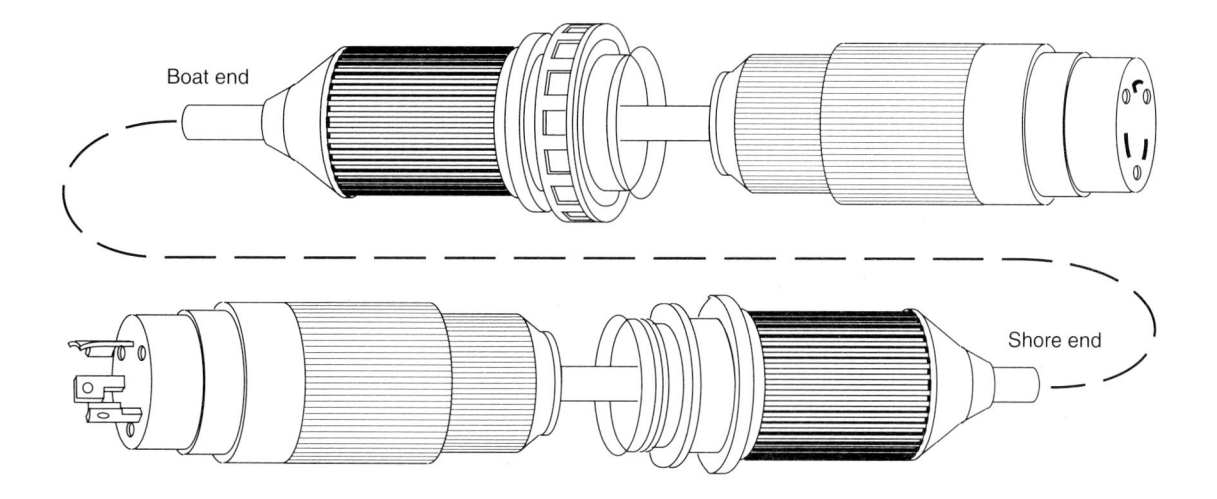

Boat Inlet

The inlet on the boat end (Figure 9.2) must be a male (plug) type connector. If the inlet is in a location subject to rain, splash or spray, it must be weatherproof, regardless of whether the cable is connected. If the location is subject to submersion, no matter how brief, the inlet must be watertight; again, whether the cord is connected or not.

If the boat's AC system includes either an isolation transformer or a galvanic isolator, metal components of the inlet must be isolated from a metal hull or any metal parts that are connected to the boat's ground.

Both boat- and shore-end connector configurations must match the type (amps, volts and phases) of service, as shown in Figure 9.3.

Figure 9.2 Boat Inlet

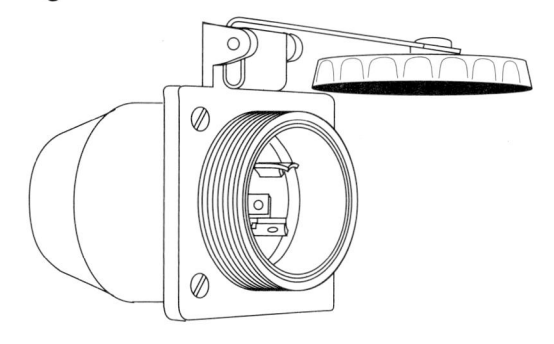

174   AC

Figure 9.3 Matching AC Connectors

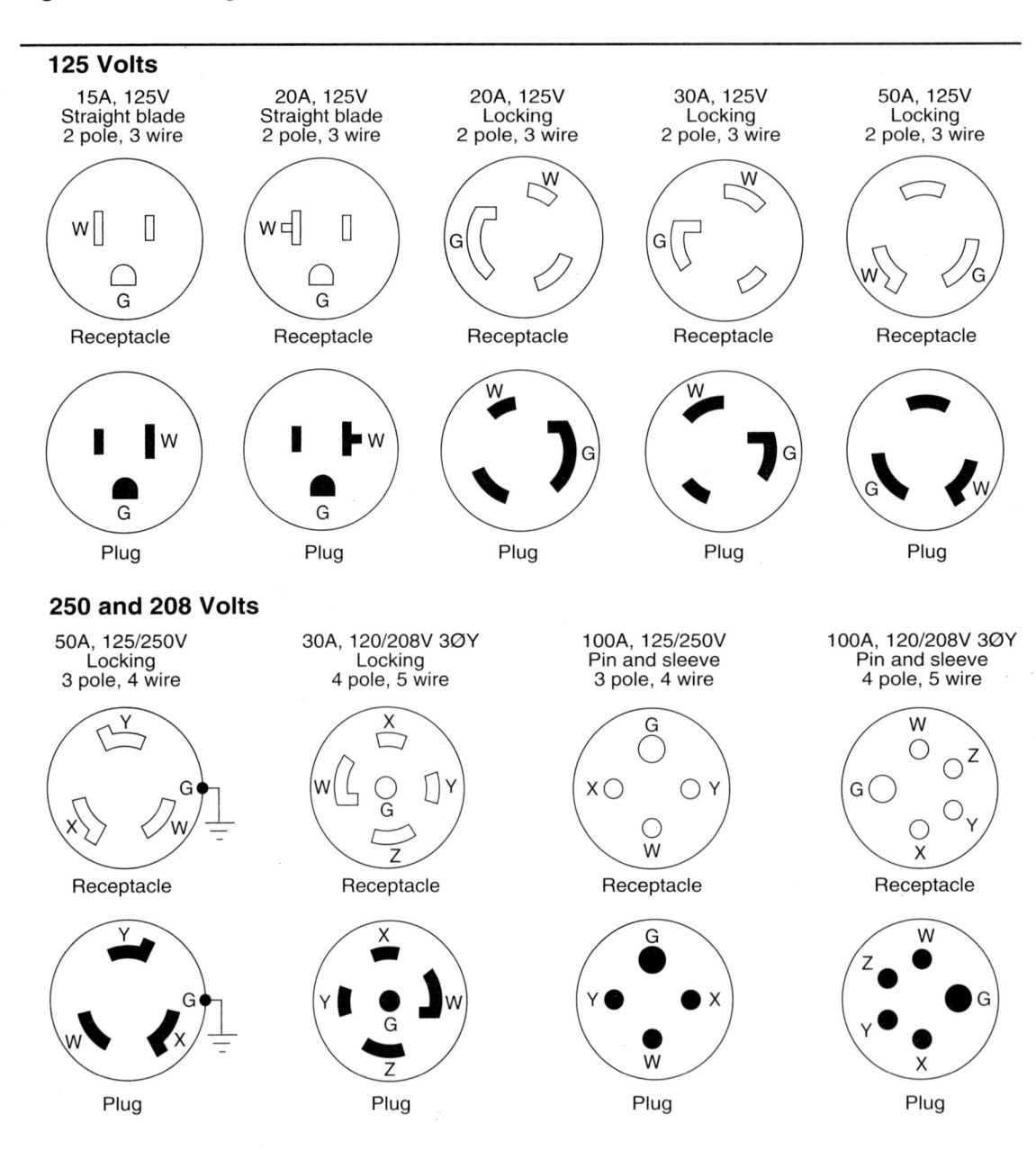

125 Volts

15A, 125V Straight blade 2 pole, 3 wire	20A, 125V Straight blade 2 pole, 3 wire	20A, 125V Locking 2 pole, 3 wire	30A, 125V Locking 2 pole, 3 wire	50A, 125V Locking 2 pole, 3 wire
Receptacle	Receptacle	Receptacle	Receptacle	Receptacle
Plug	Plug	Plug	Plug	Plug

250 and 208 Volts

50A, 125/250V Locking 3 pole, 4 wire	30A, 120/208V 3ØY Locking 4 pole, 5 wire	100A, 125/250V Pin and sleeve 3 pole, 4 wire	100A, 120/208V 3ØY Pin and sleeve 4 pole, 5 wire
Receptacle	Receptacle	Receptacle	Receptacle
Plug	Plug	Plug	Plug

AC Standards and Practices

A permanent waterproof warning placard or notice must be displayed prominently at all shore-power inlets. Figure 9.4 illustrates suggested wording. Photocopy and laminate Figure 9.4 if you wish.

GENERATOR AND INVERTER SOURCES
Transfer Switch
The connection(s) to shore power, onboard generators and inverters must be such that not more than one source can be connected to a circuit simultaneously. Transfer between power sources must be made with a device that prevents arc-over between the contacts of the different sources. Such a device is called a transfer switch.

Grounded Neutral
The AC system on a boat uses a grounded neutral, as do residential systems. Where the neutral (blue conductor) and grounding (green and yellow) are connected is critical. *The neutral must be grounded only at the source of power,* that is, at a generator, at an inverter, at the secondary of an isolation or polarization transformer, or through the shore-power cable to shore.

Figure 9.4 Suggested Wording for Shore-Power Connection

WARNING
To minimize shock and fire hazards:

1. Turn off the boat's shore-connection switch before connecting or disconnecting shore cable.

2. **Connect** shore-power cable at the boat first.

3. If polarity warning indicator is activated, immediately disconnect cable.

4. **Disconnect** shore-power cable at shore outlet first.

5. Close shore-power inlet cover tightly.

DO NOT ALTER SHORE-POWER CABLE CONNECTORS

Figure 9.5 shows a system consisting of shore power, onboard generator and inverter. A two-pole transfer switch selects the power source. Note that the neutral (blue) and grounding (green and yellow) wires are connected at the generator, at the inverter, and (not shown) at the shore-end source.

A galvanic isolator serves to block stray current in the shore-power grounding wire. Thus, whichever source is selected, the neutral is grounded only at the source of power in use. Furthermore, the neutral and grounding conductors are maintained at boat ground, which is critical for the safety of onboard personnel.

Ampacity

An onboard generator or inverter must be rated to supply the entire load, as calculated below, unless the system is designed to isolate certain loads from connection to the generator.

In either case, the feed conductors from the generator or inverter must be of sufficient ampacity to carry the maximum rated output. In addition, the generator or inverter output must be protected at the output with an over-current device, rated at no more than 120% of the rated output, unless the generator or inverter is self-limiting to the same degree.

Figure 9.5 Typical Use of Transfer Switch

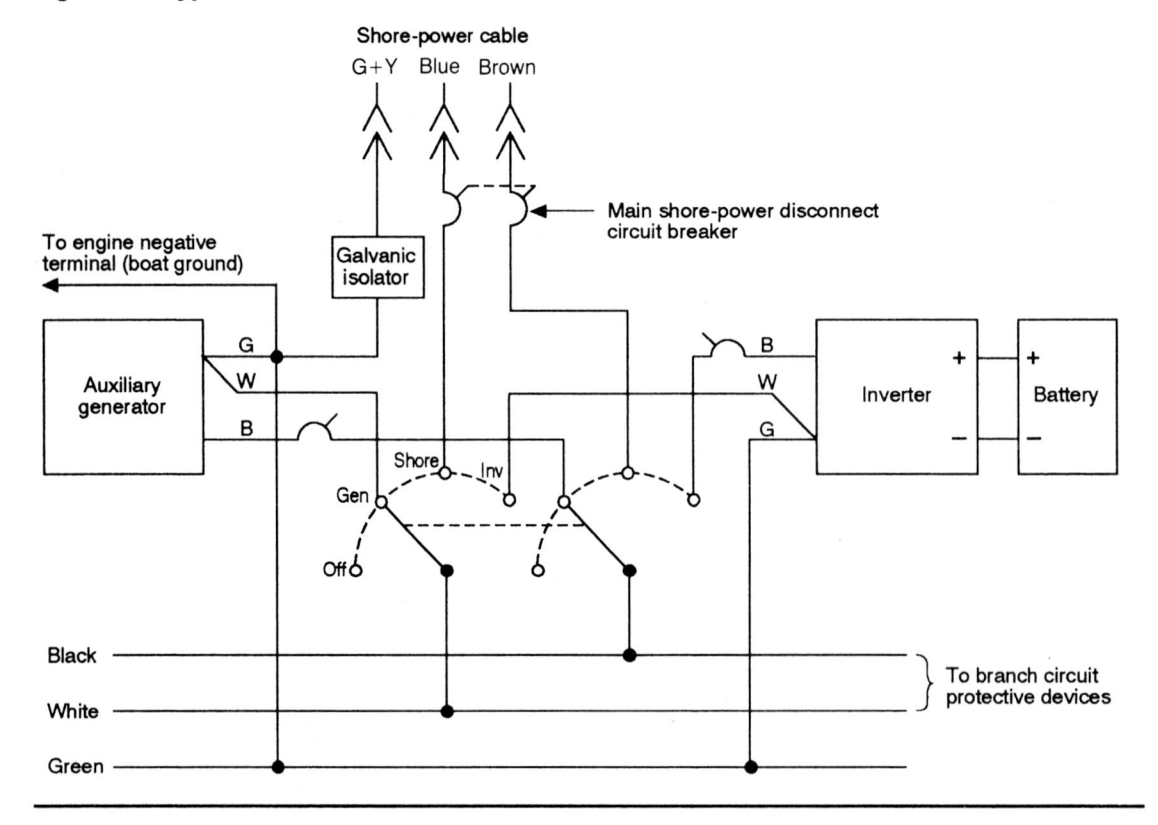

AC Standards and Practices

MAIN PANELBOARD

All boat AC systems must have a main panelboard, which may (it usually does) also serve as the AC-distribution panel. The panelboard must be easily accessible and either weatherproof or in a location protected from the weather.

The panelboard must be clearly and permanently marked with the system voltage and frequency. Two common markings are "120 VAC" and "120V—60Hz." If there are either AC motors or an AC generator aboard, the panelboard should include an AC voltmeter. It is recommended that this voltmeter display upper and lower AC-voltage limits.

The main panelboard should also contain a shore-power polarity indicator, that warns of reversed polarity in the shore-power connection, with either a continuous sound or a continuous light.

A polarity indicator *must* be installed if:

1. any of the boat's branch circuits have overcurrent protection in the ungrounded conductor only, or

2. polarity is critical to the operation of any of the AC devices on the boat.

A polarity indicator is not needed, however, if the shore power feeds through an isolation transformer, since the transformer acts as a separate source of power on the boat, and its output conductors are permanently wired.

In order to limit current on the normally noncurrent-carrying green-grounding wire, the impedance of polarity indication devices must be at least 25,000 ohms.

Figure 9.6 shows a simple polarity-indicating circuit that satisfies the 25,000 ohm criterion. A green light indicates the correct polarity (voltage between the hot and neutral conductors). A red light indicates an incorrect polarity where either the neutral or grounding conductor is hot.

Figure 9.6 Polarity Indicating Circuit

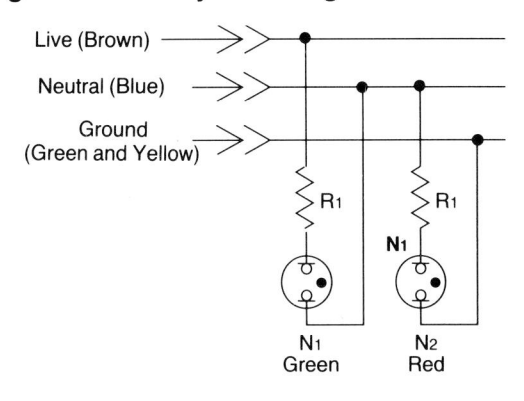

Plug-in polarity indicators, no larger than a three-prong adapter, are available at electrical stores for around £10. If your AC panel doesn't have a built-in polarity indicator, one of these devices can be used to quickly check for damaging reverse polarity when establishing a shore-power connection.

GROUNDING

All AC appliances and fixed electrical equipment on a boat must be designed so that exposed parts, such as the case, are electrically insulated from the current-carrying conductors. Exposed parts should be connected to the green grounding conductor. Since the neutral- and green-grounding conductors are to be connected only at the power source, any bonding strap or wire between the neutral and grounding terminals of the device should be removed.

All AC-outlet receptacles on a boat must have a green terminal for connection to the green-grounding conductor.

LOAD CALCULATIONS
Sources
The ABYC suggests a method for determining the minimum sizes of AC panelboards, supply conductors and AC-power sources. The total load may be supplied by:

1. A single shore-power cable of the required ampacity.

2. Multiple shore-power cables, provided each inlet is marked with volts, amps, phase (if 3Ø), and load it serves.

3. One or more onboard generators of continuous rating equal to the load.

4. Shore power plus generator of combined capacity equal to the load, provided the loads connected to each are isolated.

Instructions
Table 9.3, on pages 180 and 181, is a form that follows the ABYC-recommended procedure for calculating AC loads. As you read the instructions below, you might also find it helpful to refer to the completed example on pages 182 and 183.

Lighting and Small Appliances
Lighting includes all AC-powered lights on the boat. Small appliances are those used in the galley and dining areas that have power cords and plugs, such as blenders, mixers and toasters.

Step 1. Calculate the total square feet of all of the living areas on the boat. Do not count storage and engine spaces. Multiply this area by two to find the total watts for line 1.

Step 2. Count the number of 20-amp circuits used for small appliances in the galley and dining areas. Multiply by 1,500 to find the total watts for line 2.

Step 3. Add lines 1 and 2 and enter in line 3.

Step 4. Enter line 3 in line 4. Subtract 2,000 from line 3, multiply by 0.35, and enter in line 5 (do not enter if negative). Add lines 4 and 5 and enter in line 6.

Step 5. If you have a 240-volt-AC system that splits into two onboard 120-volt-AC systems, enter half of line 6 on each of lines 7A and 7B. From this point on, you will have to distinguish between columns A and B in making your entries.

If your shore power inlet is 120-volt AC, enter line 6 on line 7B. From this point on, use only the right-hand (column B) lines.

Motors and Heaters
For steps 6 to 25, you will need the amps listed on the nameplates of each piece of equipment. The nameplate is usually found on the backside of the equipment.

Step 6. Add and enter the total amps for all fans on line 8.

Step 7. Add the amps for all air conditioners. If there are three or more units, multiply the total amps by 75% and enter on line 9. If the total is less than line 8, leave line 9 blank.

Step 8. Add the amps for electric, gas and oil heaters. If the total is less than the number calculated in Step 7 (not line 9), leave line 10 blank.

Step 9. Take 25% of the nameplate amps for the largest motor in any of the appliances listed in Steps 6 to 8.

Step 10. Add lines 8 to 11; enter in line 12.

Fixed Appliances
Steps 11 to 25. For each of the appliances listed, multiply the amps listed on the nameplates by the use factors shown in parentheses after the appliance name, then enter the result on the right-hand line. If the unit is a

AC Standards and Practices

240-volt appliance, enter the amps on both lines A and B.

Step 26. Add lines 13 to 27 and enter in line 28.

Step 27. If there are four or more appliances listed in lines 13 to 27, multiply line 28 by 60% and enter result in line 29.

Free-Standing Range
Step 28. A free-standing range is one which contains surface burners and an oven. First, read the watts listed on the range nameplate. Next, consult the table at the bottom of the form to find the corresponding "load watts." Enter load watts on line 30.

Step 29. Enter the appliance voltage (found on the nameplate) and enter in line 31.

Step 30. Divide line 30 by line 31 and enter result in both lines 32A and 32B.

Total AC Load
Step 31. Enter line 7 in line 33.

Step 32. Enter line 12 in line 34.

Step 33. Enter line 29 in line 35.

Step 34. Enter line 32 in line 36.

Step 35. Add lines 33 to 36 and enter both totals in lines 37A and 37B.

Step 36. Your total AC load in amps is the larger of line 37A and 37B. Enter in line 39.

Example
Use Table 9.4 to calculate the 120 VAC load for a boat with 240 square feet of space, one 20-amp small appliance circuit, and:

- 50-watt (0.4 amps) ventilation fan
- 1,500-watt (12-amps) water heater
- 85-watt (0.7 amps) refrigerator
- 120-watt (1 amp) air compressor
- 420-watt (3.5 amps) battery charger

Lighting and Small Appliances
The lighting load is 2 x 240 square feet = 480 watts, which we enter on line 1.

The small appliance load for one 20-amp circuit is 1 x 1,500 watts = 1,500 watts, which we enter on line 2.

The sum of lines 1 and 2 is 1,980 watts, which is less than 2,000 watts, so we enter 1,980 watts on line 4 and 0 watts on line 5.

We divide 1,980 watts by 120 volts to get 16.5 amps. Since 120-volt shore power only has one leg, we enter the 16.5 amps on line 7A.

Motors and Heaters
We have only one motor—the 0.4-amp fan, which we enter on line 8. Adding 25% (step 9), we get 0.5 amps, which we enter on line 12A.

Fixed Appliances
Our fixed appliances include the 12-amp water heater, 0.7-amp refrigerator, 3.5-amp battery charger and 1-amp air compresser. The first three have a duty factor of 1.00, so we enter their amps directly. The compresser has a duty factor of only 0.10, so we enter 0.10 x 1.0 amp = 0.1 amp in line 24A.

Adding lines 13 – 27 we get 16.3 amps. Since there are more than three fixed appliances, we multiply the sum by the factor 0.60 and enter the result, 9.8, on line 29.

Total AC Load
Adding line 7 (16.5 amps), line 12 (0.5 amps), line 29 (9.8 amps) and line 32 (0.0 amps), we get a total of 26.8 amps.

Since our system has only a single phase and, thus, a single leg, our total AC load for sizing the main AC panel board is 26.8 amps. Rounding up, we'll call it *30 amps*.

Table 9.3 ABYC AC Load Calculation Method

Step	Loads		A	B	Line
	LIGHTING AND SMALL APPLIANCES				
1.	Lighting and receptacles Multiply area of enclosed living spaces by 2 watts: area	sq. ft. x 2 watts =		_____	1
2.	Small appliances (galley and dinette) Multiply number of 20-amp circuits by 1,500 watts:	circuits x 1,500 watts =		_____	2
3.	Add lines 1 and 2			_____	3
4.	Load Factor: 1.00 x line 3 =			_____	4
	0.35 x (line 3 – 2,000) =			_____	5
	Add lines 4 and 5			_____	6
5.	Split Load: If shore power is 240 VAC, split line 6's load onto 7A and 7B. If shore power is 120 VAC, use only line 7A.		_____	_____	7
	MOTORS AND HEATERS Enter total nameplate amps for all motors and heaters				
6.	Exhaust and supply fans		_____	_____	8
7.	Air conditioners (If 3 or more ACs, multiply by 75%; omit if smaller than Step 8)		_____	_____	9
8.	Electric, gas or oil heaters (Omit if smaller than Step 7)		_____	_____	10
9.	25% of largest motor in Steps 6 – 8		_____	_____	11
10.	Total of lines 8 – 11		_____	_____	12
	FIXED APPLIANCES Enter indicated factor times nameplate amps of fixed appliances				
11.	Disposal (x 0.10)		_____	_____	13
12.	Water heater (x 1.00)		_____	_____	14
13.	Wall-mounted oven (x 0.75)		_____	_____	15
14.	Stove-top cooking unit (x 0.75)		_____	_____	16
15.	Refrigerator (x 1.00)		_____	_____	17
16.	Freezer (x 1.00)		_____	_____	18
17.	Ice maker (x 0.50)		_____	_____	19
18.	Dishwasher (x 0.25)		_____	_____	20

AC Standards and Practices 181

ABYC AC Load Calculation Method (continued)

Step	Loads	A	B	Line
19.	Clothes washer (x 0.25)	_____	_____	21
20.	Clothes dryer (x 0.25)	_____	_____	22
21.	Trash compactor (x 0.10)	_____	_____	23
22.	Air compressor (x 0.10)	_____	_____	24
23.	Battery charger (x 1.00)	_____	_____	25
24.	Vacuum system (x 0.10)	_____	_____	26
25.	Other fixed appliances (x 1.00)	_____	_____	27
26.	Subtotal lines 13 to 27	_____	_____	28
27.	If there are more than three (3) entries in lines 13 to 27, multiply line 28 by 0.60	_____	_____	29
28.	**FREE STANDING RANGE** (burners and oven in same unit) Enter load watts from Table 9.5	_____	_____	30
29.	Enter nameplate volts (either 120 or 240)	_____	_____	31
30.	Divide line 30 by line 31 for amps	_____	_____	32
31.	**TOTAL AC LOAD** Enter Lighting and Small Appliances total from line 7	_____	_____	33
32.	Enter Motors total from line 12	_____	_____	34
33.	Enter Fixed Appliances total from line 29	_____	_____	35
34.	Enter Freestanding Range load from line 32	_____	_____	36
35.	Add lines 33 to 36: TOTALS =	_____	_____	37
36.	Use the larger of Total A or Total B to determine total amps	_____	_____	39

Table 9-5 Load Watts for Free-Standing Ranges

Nameplate Watts	Load Watts
0 – 10,000	80%
10.001 – 12,500	8,000
12,501 – 13,500	8,400
13,501 – 14,500	8,800
14,501 – 15,500	9,200
15,501 – 16,500	9,600

Table 9.4 Sample of Completed ABYC AC Load Calculation Method

Step	Loads	A	B	Line
	LIGHTING AND SMALL APPLIANCES			
1.	Lighting and receptacles Multiply area of enclosed living spaces by 2 watts ft.: area 240 sq. ft. x 2 watts =		480	1
2.	Small appliances (galley and dinette) Multiply number of 20-amp circuits by 1,500 watts: 1 circuits x 1,500 watts =		1,500	2
3.	Add lines 1 and 2		1,980	3
4.	Load Factor: 1.00 x line 3 =		1,980	4
	0.35 x (line 3 – 2,000) =		0	5
	Add lines 4 and 5 and divide by 120 V		16.5	6
5.	Split Load: If shore power is 240 VAC, split line 6's load onto 7A and 7B. If shore power is 120 VAC, use only line 7A.	16.5		7
	MOTORS AND HEATERS Enter total nameplate amps for all motors and heaters			
6.	Exhaust and supply fans	0.4		8
7.	Air conditioners (If 3 or more ACs, multiply by 75%; omit if smaller than Step 8)			9
8.	Electric, gas or oil heaters (Omit if smaller than Step 7)			10
9.	25% of largest motor in Steps 6 – 8	0.1		11
10.	Total of lines 8 – 11	0.5		12
	FIXED APPLIANCES Enter indicated factor times nameplate amps of fixed appliances			
11.	Disposal (x 0.10)			13
12.	Water heater (x 1.00)	12.0		14
13.	Wall-mounted oven (x 0.75)			15
14.	Stove-top cooking unit (x 0.75)			16
15.	Refrigerator (x 1.00)	0.7		17
16.	Freezer (x 1.00)			18
17.	Ice maker (x 0.50)			19
18.	Dishwasher (x 0.25)			20

AC Standards and Practices   183

ABYC AC Load Calculation Method (continued)

Step	Loads	A	B	Line
19.	Clothes washer (x 0.25)			21
20.	Clothes dryer (x 0.25)			22
21.	Trash compactor (x 0.10)			23
22.	Air compresser (x 0.10)	0.1		24
23.	Battery charger (x 1.00)	3.5		25
24.	Vacuum system (x 0.10)			26
25.	Other fixed appliances (x 1.00)			27
26.	Subtotal lines 13 – 27	16.3		28
27.	If there are more than three (3) entries in lines 13 – 27, multiply line 28 by 0.60	9.8		29
28.	**FREE STANDING RANGE** (burners and oven in same unit) Enter load watts from Table 9.5			30
29.	Enter nameplate volts (either 120 or 240)			31
30.	Divide line 30 by line 31 for amps			32
31.	**TOTAL AC LOAD** Enter Lighting and Small Appliances total from line 7	16.5		33
32.	Enter Motors total from line 12	0.5		34
33.	Enter Fixed Appliances total from line 29	9.8		35
34.	Enter Freestanding Range load from line 32			36
35.	Add lines 33 – 36: TOTALS =	26.8		37
36.	Use the larger of Total A or Total B to determine total amps	26.8		39

Table 9.5 Load Watts for Free-Standing Ranges

Nameplate Watts	Load Watts
0 – 10,000	80%
10.001 – 12,500	8,000
12,501 – 13,500	8,400
13,501 – 14,500	8,800
14,501 – 15,500	9,200
15,501 – 16,500	9,600

OVER-CURRENT PROTECTION
Amp Ratings
All fuses and circuit breakers must be rated at or less than the ampacity of the conductors of the circuit being protected.

Circuit Breaker Specifications
All circuit breakers should be of the manual-reset type (except if integral to a piece of equipment) and be of the trip-free type (cannot be held closed while the over-current condition persists).

Main Supply Protection
Figure 9.7 illustrates the requirements for over-current protection of the main supply:

1. The shore-power feeder conductors should be protected by multipole breakers. In a 120-VAC system, the breakers should protect both the ungrounded (brown) and the neutral (blue) conductors. In any system containing either 240 VAC or 208 VAC, there should be breakers in *all* ungrounded conductors. Note that the green grounding conductor is *never* interrupted.

2. If there are isolation or polarization transformers in the shore-power feed, primaries should be protected by a separate fuse or circuit breaker rated at no more than 125% of the primary rating.

3. The maximum unprotected conductor length from shore-power inlet to circuit breaker must not exceed 10 feet. If the length is greater than 10 feet, additional slow-blow fuses should be added within 10 feet of the inlet.

4. The maximum unprotected conductor length from an AC generator must be less than 7 inches. However, up to 40 inches is allowed if the conductor is protected by a sheath or enclosure.

Branch-Circuit Protection
Circuit breakers and fuses should be rated at less than the ampacity of the smallest current-carrying conductor in the circuit.

The ungrounded conductor alone may be protected, provided:

1. The entire system is polarized, including lighting fixtures, and there is a polarity indicator between the shore power inlet and the main circuit breakers, or

2. The neutral and grounding conductors are connected at the secondary of an isolation or polarization transformer.

All motors must be protected by either an overcurrent or a thermal device unless they do not overheat, even when the rotor is locked.

GROUND-FAULT PROTECTION
Residual Current Devices were described in Chapter 7 (Figure 7.9).

RCD Breakers
RCD breakers must meet the same requirements as circuit breakers of the same rating. They may be used to protect individual branch circuits, or they may protect a group of associated circuits. Like other circuit breakers they may interrupt only the ungrounded conductor, if the system is polarized and has a polarity indicator, the system has an isolation or polarization transformer, or if the system is 120/240 VAC.

RCD Sockets
RCD socket units must be two-pole and meet all of the requirements of US standards UL943 and UL498. They may protect either a single socket or multiple sockets in the same circuit.

AC Standards and Practices 185

Figure 9.7 Main Supply Over-Current Protection Requirements

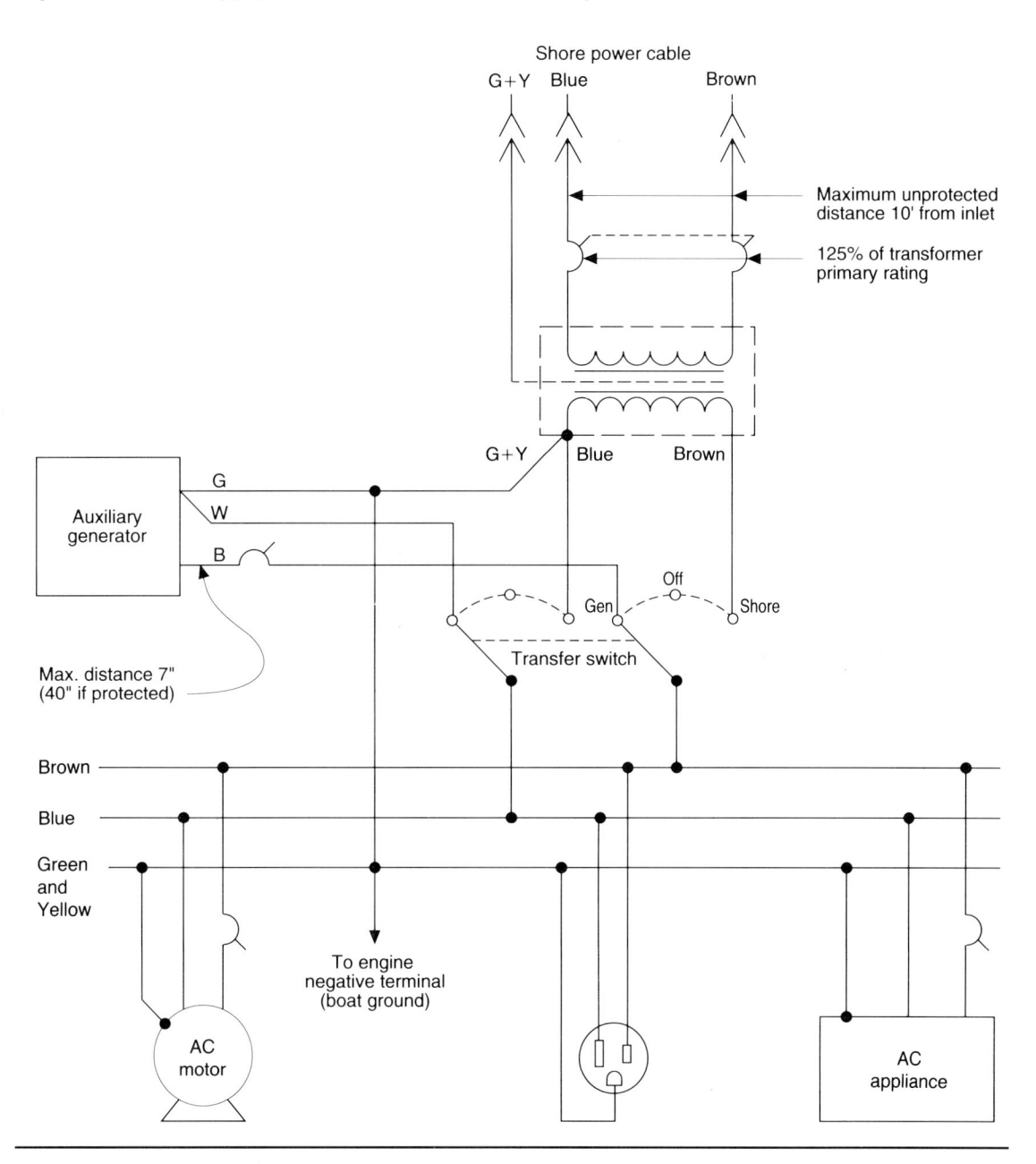

APPROVED WIRE AND CABLE

All conductors must meet and display the recommended standard. No conductor should be less than 16 AWG except those internal to panelboards. The temperature ratings of all conductors and flexible cords should be at least 140°F (60°C), except 167°F (75°C) in engine spaces. Individual conductor insulations must be rated at 600 volts minimum. Flexible cords may be rated at a minimum of 300 volts.

Conductors must be one of the types listed in Table 9.6. Flexible cords must be one of the types listed in Table 9.7 Conductors and flexible cords must be of the stranding as shown in Table 9.8.

Table 9.6 Acceptable Insulation Types

Type	Description
THW	Moisture and Heat Resistant, Thermoplastic
TW	Moisture Resistant, Thermoplastic
HWN	Moisture and Heat Resistant, Thermoplastic
XHHW	Moisture and Heat Resistant, Cross-Linked Synthetic Polymer
MTW	Moisture, Heat and Oil Resistant, Thermoplastic
AWM*	Moisture, Heat and Oil Resistant, Thermoplastic, Thermosetting
UL1426	Boat Cable

Table 9.7 Acceptable Flexible Cord Types

Type	Description
SO	Hard-Service Cord, Oil Resistant
ST	Hard-Service Cord, Thermoplastic
STO	Hard-Service Cord, Oil Resistant, Thermoplastic
SEO	Hard-Service Cord, Oil Resistant, Thermoplastic
SJO	Junior Hard-Service Cord, Oil Resistant
SJT	Hard-Service Cord, Thermoplastic
SJTO	Hard-Service Cord, Oil Resistant, Thermoplastic

Table 9.8 Minimum AC Conductor Stranding

Size AWG	Dia., in.	Minimum Type 1[1]	Number of Strands Type 2[2]	Type 3[3]
18	.044	7	16	–
16	.055	7	19	26
14	.069	7	19	41
12	.086	7	19	65
10	.109	7	19	105
8	.137	7	19	168
6	.182	–	37	266
4	.218	–	49	420
2	.282	–	127	665
1	.315	–	127	836
0	.355	–	127	1064
2/0	.399	–	127	1323
3/0	.449	–	259	1666
4/0	.512	–	418	2107

[1] Conductors with Type 1 stranding to be used only where firmly attached to a rigid structure and not subject to movement or vibration.

[2] Conductors with Type 2 stranding to be used where conductor is subject to motion from vibration or minor flexing. If four or more conductors are run in a cable, Type 2 stranding may be used for frequent-flexing applications.

[3] Conductors with Type 3 stranding to be used where frequent flexing is expected.

The minimum ampacities of current carrying conductors are shown in Tables 9.9 to 9.14. Noncurrent carrying conductors (green and yellow grounding and blue neutral conductors in 240 VAC systems) are exempt but must be at least 16 AWG. As a rule, they are the same or one size smaller than the accompanying current-carrying conductors.

AC Standards and Practices

Table 9.9 Amperage of No More than Two Bundled Conductors

Conductor Size, AWG	60°C (140°F)	75°C (167°F)	80°C (176°F)	90°C (194°F)	105°C (221°F)	125°C (257°F)	200°C (392°F)
\multicolumn{8}{c}{**Outside Engine Spaces**}
18	10	10	15	20	20	25	25
16	15	15	20	25	25	30	35
14	20	20	25	30	35	40	45
12	25	25	35	40	45	50	55
10	40	40	50	55	60	70	70
8	55	65	70	70	80	90	100
6	80	95	100	100	120	125	135
4	105	125	130	135	160	170	180
2	140	170	175	180	210	225	240
1	165	195	210	210	245	265	280
1/0	195	230	245	245	285	305	325
2/0	225	265	285	285	330	355	370
3/0	260	310	330	330	385	410	430
4/0	300	360	385	385	445	475	510
\multicolumn{8}{c}{**Inside Engine Spaces**}
18	5	7	11	16	17	22	25
16	8	11	15	20	21	26	35
14	11	15	19	24	29	35	45
12	14	18	27	32	38	44	55
10	23	30	39	45	51	62	70
8	31	48	54	57	68	80	100
6	46	71	78	82	102	111	135
4	60	93	101	110	136	151	180
2	81	127	136	147	178	200	240
1	95	146	163	172	208	235	280
1/0	113	172	191	200	242	271	325
2/0	130	198	222	233	280	316	370
3/0	150	232	257	270	327	364	430
4/0	174	270	300	315	378	422	510

Temperature Rating of Conductor Insulation

Table 9.10 Amperage of Three Bundled Conductors

Conductor Size, AWG	60°C (140°F)	75°C (167°F)	80°C (176°F)	90°C (194°F)	105°C (221°F)	125°C (257°F)	200°C (392°F)
\multicolumn{8}{c}{Outside Engine Spaces}
18	7	7	10	14	14	17	17
16	10	10	14	17	17	21	24
14	14	14	17	21	24	28	31
12	17	17	24	28	31	35	38
10	28	28	35	38	42	49	49
8	38	45	49	49	56	63	70
6	56	66	70	70	84	87	94
4	73	87	91	94	112	119	126
2	98	119	122	126	147	157	168
1	115	136	147	147	171	185	196
1/0	136	161	171	171	199	213	227
2/0	157	185	199	199	231	248	259
3/0	182	217	231	231	269	287	301
4/0	210	252	269	269	311	332	357
\multicolumn{8}{c}{Inside Engine Spaces}
18	4	5	8	11	11	15	17
16	6	7	10	14	14	18	24
14	8	10	13	17	20	24	31
12	10	13	19	23	26	31	38
10	16	21	27	31	35	43	49
8	22	34	38	40	47	56	70
6	32	49	54	57	71	77	94
4	42	65	71	77	95	105	126
2	56	89	95	103	125	140	168
1	67	102	114	120	145	165	196
1/0	79	120	133	140	169	190	227
2/0	91	139	155	163	196	221	259
3/0	105	162	180	189	229	255	301
4/0	121	189	210	221	264	295	357

AC Standards and Practices

Table 9.11 Amperage of Four to Six Bundled Conductors

Conductor Size, AWG	60°C (140°F)	75°C (167°F)	80°C (176°F)	90°C (194°F)	105°C (221°F)	125°C (257°F)	200°C (392°F)
\multicolumn{8}{c}{Temperature Rating of Conductor Insulation}
Outside Engine Spaces							
18	6	6	9	12	12	15	15
16	9	9	12	15	15	18	21
14	12	12	15	18	21	24	27
12	15	15	21	24	27	30	33
10	24	24	30	33	36	42	42
8	33	39	42	42	48	54	60
6	48	57	60	60	72	75	81
4	63	75	78	81	96	102	108
2	84	102	105	108	126	135	144
1	99	117	126	126	147	159	168
1/0	117	138	147	147	171	183	195
2/0	135	159	171	171	198	213	222
3/0	156	186	198	198	231	246	258
4/0	180	216	231	231	267	285	306
Inside Engine Spaces							
18	3	4	7	9	10	13	15
16	5	6	9	12	12	16	21
14	7	9	11	14	17	21	27
12	8	11	16	19	23	26	33
10	13	18	23	27	30	37	42
8	19	29	32	34	40	48	60
6	27	42	46	49	61	66	81
4	36	56	60	66	81	90	108
2	48	76	81	88	107	120	144
1	57	87	98	103	125	141	168
1/0	67	103	114	120	145	162	195
2/0	78	119	133	140	168	189	222
3/0	90	139	154	162	196	218	258
4/0	104	162	180	189	227	253	306

Table 9.12 Amperage of Seven to 24 Bundled Conductors

Conductor Size, AWG	60°C (140°F)	75°C (167°F)	80°C (176°F)	90°C (194°F)	105°C (221°F)	125°C (257°F)	200°C (392°F)
			Outside Engine Spaces				
18	5	5	7	10	10	12	12
16	7	7	10	12	12	15	17
14	10	10	12	15	17	20	22
12	12	12	17	20	22	25	27
10	20	20	25	27	30	35	35
8	27	32	35	35	40	45	50
6	40	47	50	50	60	62	67
4	52	62	65	67	80	85	90
2	70	85	87	90	105	112	120
1	82	97	105	105	122	132	140
1/0	97	115	122	122	142	152	162
2/0	112	132	142	142	165	177	185
3/0	130	155	165	165	192	205	215
4/0	150	180	192	192	222	237	255
			Inside Engine Spaces				
18	2	3	5	8	8	11	12
16	4	5	7	10	10	13	17
14	5	7	9	12	14	17	22
12	7	9	13	16	19	22	27
10	11	15	19	22	25	31	35
8	16	24	27	28	34	40	50
6	23	35	39	41	51	55	67
4	30	46	50	55	68	75	90
2	40	63	68	73	89	100	120
1	47	73	81	86	104	117	140
1/0	56	86	95	100	121	135	162
2/0	65	99	111	116	140	158	185
3/0	75	116	128	135	163	182	215
4/0	87	135	150	157	189	211	255

AC Standards and Practices

Table 9.13 Amperage of More than 24 Bundled Conductors

Conductor Size, AWG	60°C (140°F)	75°C (167°F)	80°C (176°F)	90°C (194°F)	105°C (221°F)	125°C (257°F)	200°C (392°F)
\multicolumn{8}{c}{Outside Engine Spaces}							
18	4	4	6	8	8	10	10
16	6	6	8	10	10	12	14
14	8	8	10	12	14	16	18
12	10	10	14	16	18	20	22
10	16	16	20	22	24	28	28
8	22	26	28	28	32	36	40
6	32	38	40	40	48	50	54
4	42	50	52	54	64	68	72
2	56	68	70	72	84	90	96
1	66	78	84	84	98	106	112
1/0	78	92	98	98	114	122	130
2/0	90	106	114	114	132	142	148
3/0	104	124	132	132	154	164	172
4/0	120	144	154	154	178	190	204
\multicolumn{8}{c}{Inside Engine Spaces}							
18	2	3	4	6	6	8	10
16	3	4	6	8	8	10	14
14	4	6	7	9	11	14	18
12	5	7	10	13	15	17	22
10	9	12	15	18	20	24	28
8	12	19	21	23	27	32	40
6	18	28	31	32	40	44	54
4	24	37	40	44	54	60	72
2	32	51	54	59	71	80	96
1	38	58	65	68	83	94	112
1/0	45	69	76	80	96	108	130
2/0	52	79	88	93	112	126	148
3/0	60	93	103	108	130	146	172
4/0	69	108	120	126	151	169	204

Table 9.14 Amperage of Flexible Cords [2,3]

Conductor Size, AWG	Nominal CM Area[1]	30°C (86°F) Ambient 3 Conductor	2 Conductor	50°C (104°F) Ambient 3 Conductor	2 Conductor
16	2,580	10	13	6	8
14	4,110	15	18	9	11
12	6,530	20	25	12	15
10	10,380	25	30	15	20
8	16,510	35	40	20	25
6	26,240	45	55	30	35
4	41,740	60	70	35	40
2	66,360	80	95	50	55

1. Actual nominal circular mil (CM) area may differ from specified CM area by no more than 7%.
2. Current ratings are for flexible cords containing no more than three conductors. For four to six conductors, reduce ampacity to 80%.
3. Shore-power cables rated at 86°F (30°C).

Figure 9.8 Approved and Disapproved Connectors for Marine Use

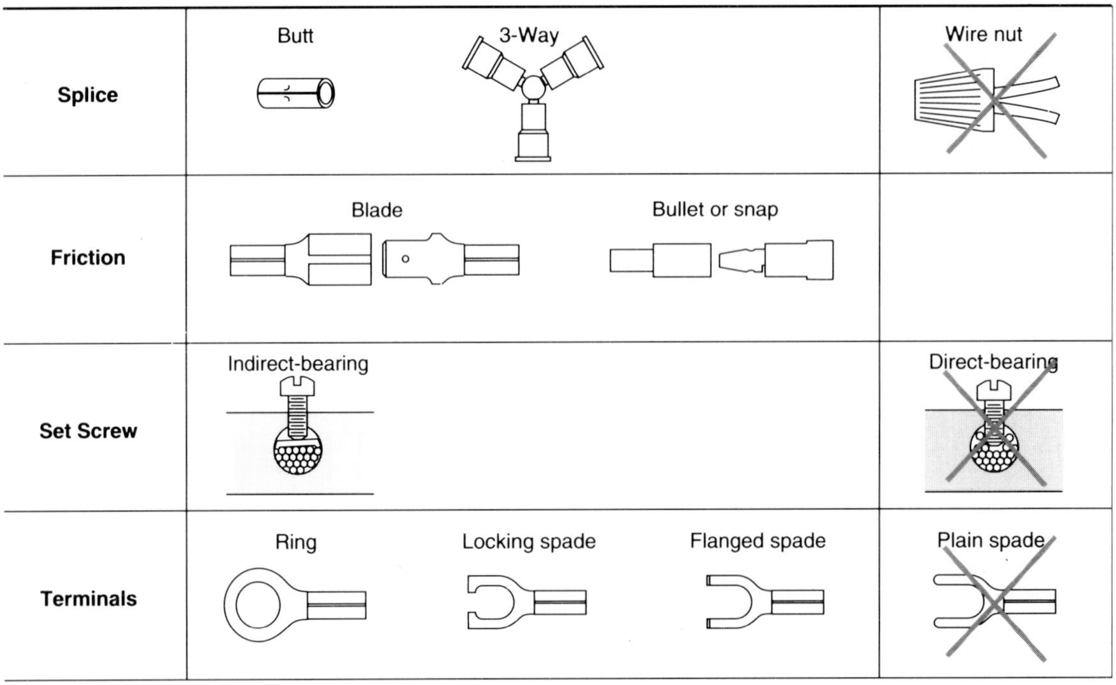

Splice	Butt	3-Way	Wire nut
Friction	Blade	Bullet or snap	
Set Screw	Indirect-bearing		Direct-bearing
Terminals	Ring	Locking spade	Flanged spade	Plain spade

AC Standards and Practices 193

SOCKETS
Polarity
AC sockets on a boat are usually the same type of 13 amp sockets used at home. They must be of the grounding type with one terminal connected to the green grounding wire. In order not to reverse the polarity of the conductors, all plugs and sockets must match and must not be interchangeable with plugs and sockets of the DC system. In addition, plug and socket terminals must be identified either by letter or by the following wiring colour scheme:

- Ungrounded conductors (brown)

- Grounded conductor (blue)

- Grounding conductor (green and yellow)

Loads
Fixed loads on circuits which serve both fixed and socket loads must not exceed the combined totals of:

- 600 watts for a 15-amp circuit

- 1,000 watts for a 20-amp circuit

Location
Galley sockets should be placed so that appliance cords do not cross a stove, sink or traffic area, as shown in Figure 9.10.

Sockets in the head, galley, machine space or deck should be protected by a Type-A (trip on fault-current of 5 milliamps) GFCI.

Sockets normally should be installed in locations that are protected from weather, spray, and flooding. If not they should be protected whenever not in use by a spring-loaded cover. Sockets subject to submersion must be watertight.

Figure 9.10 Galley Socket Layout

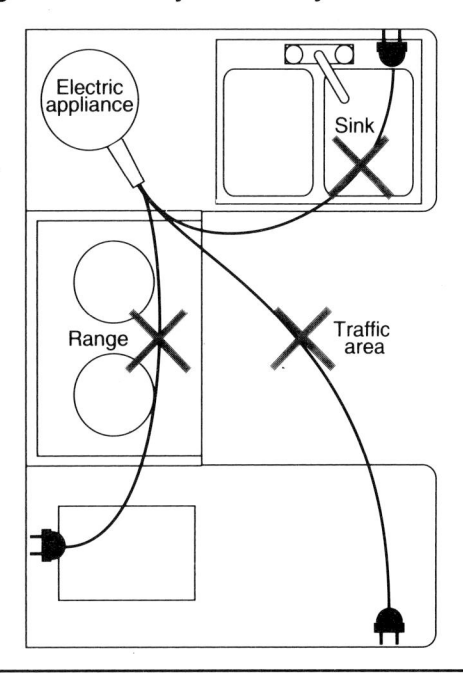

CONDUCTOR INSTALLATION
Securing Wire and Cable Runs
Conductors should be either supported continuously or secured at a maximum spacing of 18 inches with clamps or straps.

Plastic clamps can be used anywhere except over an engine, a shaft, machinery, or passageway, where clamp failure could result in danger.

Metal clamps must have smooth, rounded edges, and the cable must be protected from the metal by tape or other wrapping (around either the cable or the clamp) to protect the conductors.

Conductors should be clamped close to connections in order to remove all strain from the connections.

Conductor Routing
Conductors should be routed well above the bilge or any other area where water might accumulate. If passage through such an area cannot be avoided, both the conductors and connections should be watertight. (I have serious reservations about the watertightness of most "watertight" junction boxes found in chandleries.)

Conductors should also be kept clear of exhaust pipes and other heat sources. Minimum clearances should be 2 inches for wet exhaust and 4 inches for dry exhaust, unless equivalent heat barriers are provided.

Connections
Fabrication and installation of wiring connections should not damage the conductors. Special tools (see Figure 6.10 and discussion in Chapter 6) are available for making approved crimp-on connections.

All connection components (conductors, terminals, studs, washers and nuts) should be galvanically compatible and corrosion resistant. Specifically, aluminum and unplated steel are not appropriate for studs, nuts and washers. The cadmium-plated terminal strips found in non-marine electrical and electronic supply stores quickly rust in the marine environment. There is no substitute for marine-type plated brass and stainless steel terminal strips.

Marine connectors also differ from the more common electronic-type connectors, in that they must withstand vibration and tensile stresses. Figure 9.11 shows the types of connectors approved for marine use, along with several types specifically disapproved.

Friction connectors (the blade and bullet variety in Figure 9.11) are allowed, provided they resist a six-pound pull. The other approved connectors of Figure 9.11 must resist the pulls shown in Table 9.15 for at least one minute.

Table 9.15 Tensile Test Values for Connections

Conductor Size, AWG	Force, Lb.	Conductor Size, AWG	Force Lb.
18	10	4	70
16	15	3	80
14	30	2	90
12	35	1	100
10	40	0	125
8	45	2/0	150
6	50	3/0	175
5	60	4/0	225

AC Standards and Practices

Although not always used on board boats, pre-tinned conductors are preferred in marine use. The reason why will be apparent, as soon as you attempt to repair a conductor that has been on a boat for a few years. Chances are, if it is untinned, it will be corroded far into the insulating sleeve, due to capillary wicking of moisture into the stranded conductor. Soldering corroded copper wire is not very effective and definitely not recommended.

Although solder makes a strong connection, it is not recommended that solder provides the sole means of mechanical connection in any circuit. One reason is that the solder may melt if the terminal heats, due to either an over-current condition or high resistance in the connection. If the solder melts, without any other means of attachment, the terminal may separate from the conductor. If you want to use solder (and many professionals do), crimp the connector to the conductor and then flow solder into the crimped joint.

As an alternative to solder, adhesive-lined, heat-shrink tubing is available. It seals out moisture, mechanically strengthens the connection, and electrically insulates the terminal shank at the same time. Figure 9.11 shows how to make a terminal connection using adhesive-lined, heat-shrink tubing.

Other Considerations

Figure 9.12, on the following page, demonstrates further recommendations for AC connections. You may have noticed that the conductor specifications and wiring techniques for DC and AC systems are nearly identical. Some of the illustrations are repeated to save the reader from having to flip between Chapters 6 and 9.

Figure 9.11 Adhesive-Lined, Heat-Shrink Connectors

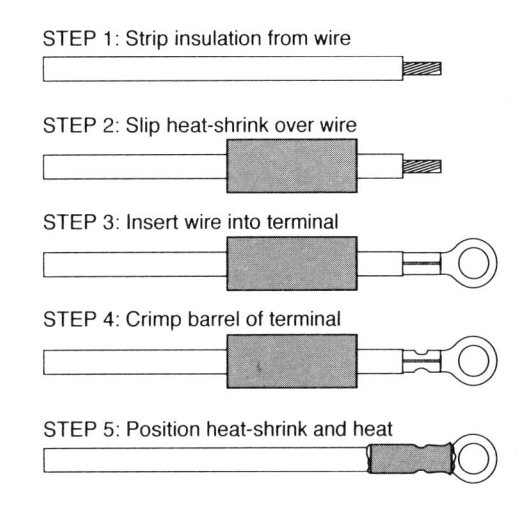

STEP 1: Strip insulation from wire

STEP 2: Slip heat-shrink over wire

STEP 3: Insert wire into terminal

STEP 4: Crimp barrel of terminal

STEP 5: Position heat-shrink and heat

IGNITION PROTECTION
Recommended Standards for Ignition Protection

Fuels

1. Gas tank connections and regulators are outside of the hull or are located in an enclosure which is vapor-tight to the interior of the boat and vented overboard, and

2. The gas supply can be shut off at the tank by a control that is part of or located near the appliance. Manual controls must provide a warning when the supply valve at the tank is open.

Boats using petrol as a fuel for either propulsion or auxiliary generator should always adopt these standards.

Figure 9.12 Proper Terminations

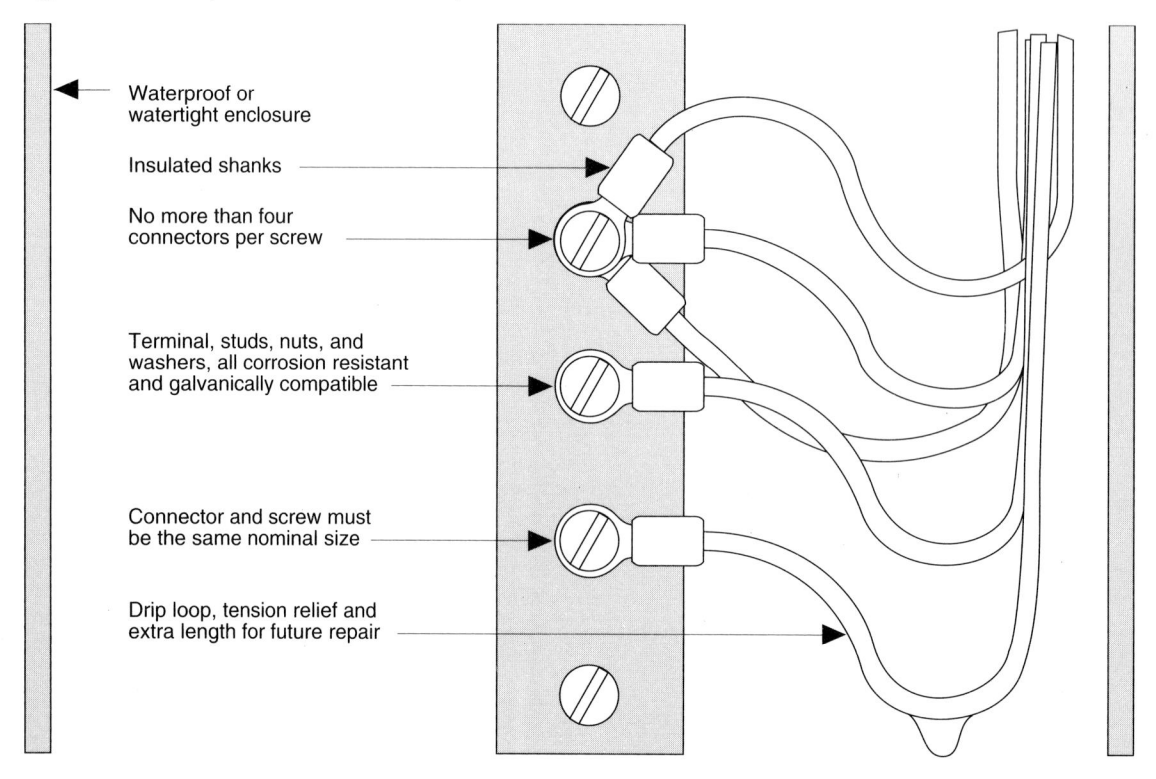

- Waterproof or watertight enclosure
- Insulated shanks
- No more than four connectors per screw
- Terminal, studs, nuts, and washers, all corrosion resistant and galvanically compatible
- Connector and screw must be the same nominal size
- Drip loop, tension relief and extra length for future repair

Ignition sources located in the same spaces as gasoline engines, gasoline tanks, and gasoline fuel joints and fittings must be ignition protected unless the components are isolated from the fuel sources. An electrical component is considered isolated from a fuel source if:

1. It is separated by a bulkhead of full width and height that leaks no more than 1/4 oz. of water per hour with a water height of 12" or one-third the bulkhead height (whichever is less), and has no higher opening with greater than 1/4" gap around its perimeter.

2. The electrical component is separated by a floor, deck, or other enclosure.

3. The distance between the electrical component and the fuel source is at least 24 inches, and the space between is open to the atmosphere. "Open" means 15 square inches of open area per cubic foot of compartment volume.

Figure 9.13 delineates the requirements for an acceptable bulkhead.

Figures 9.14 through 9.17 illustrate application of the requirements for a variety of installations.

AC Standards and Practices

Figure 9.13 Requirements for Isolation Bulkheads

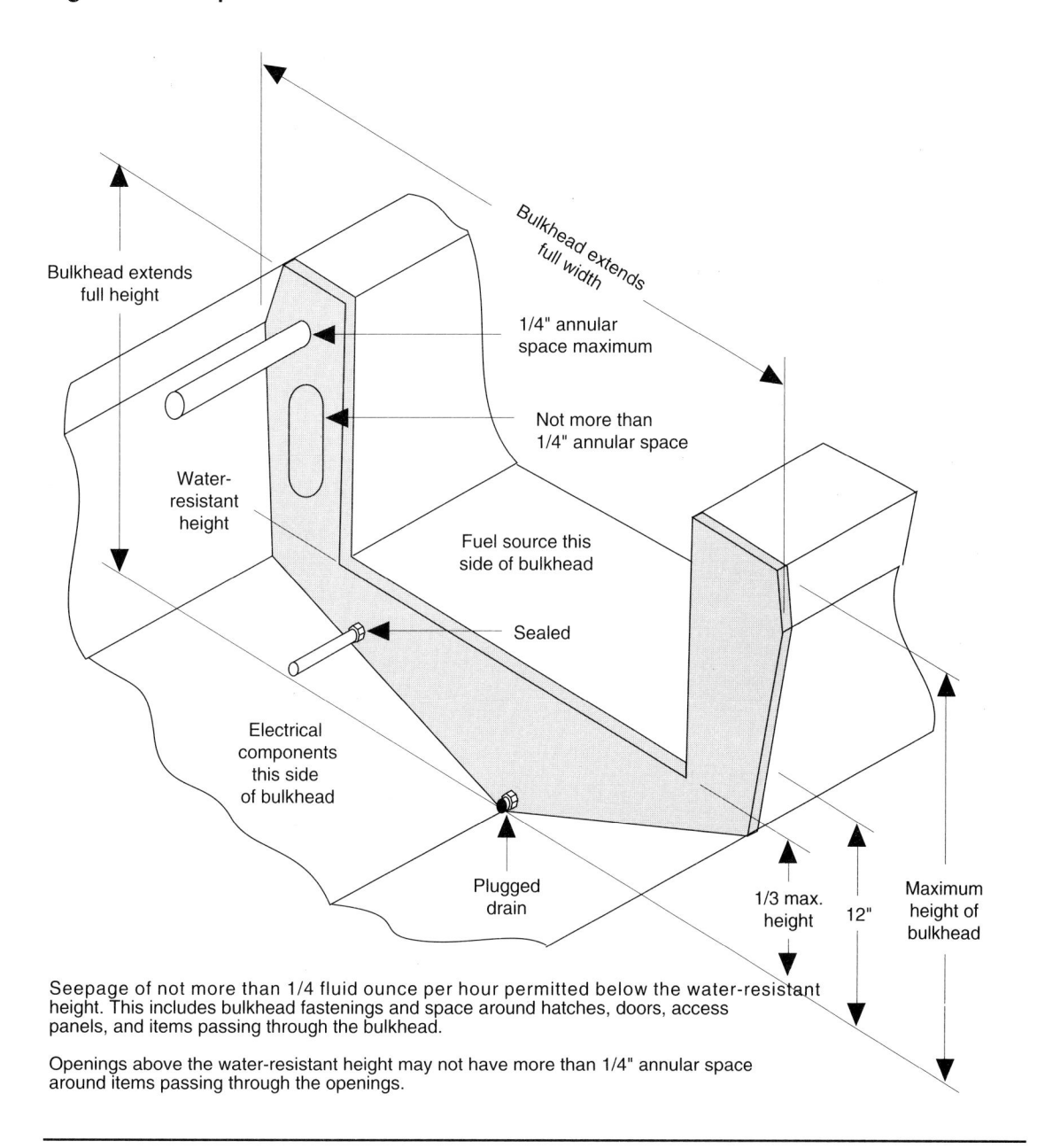

- Bulkhead extends full height
- Bulkhead extends full width
- 1/4" annular space maximum
- Not more than 1/4" annular space
- Water-resistant height
- Fuel source this side of bulkhead
- Sealed
- Electrical components this side of bulkhead
- Plugged drain
- 1/3 max. height
- 12"
- Maximum height of bulkhead

Seepage of not more than 1/4 fluid ounce per hour permitted below the water-resistant height. This includes bulkhead fastenings and space around hatches, doors, access panels, and items passing through the bulkhead.

Openings above the water-resistant height may not have more than 1/4" annular space around items passing through the openings.

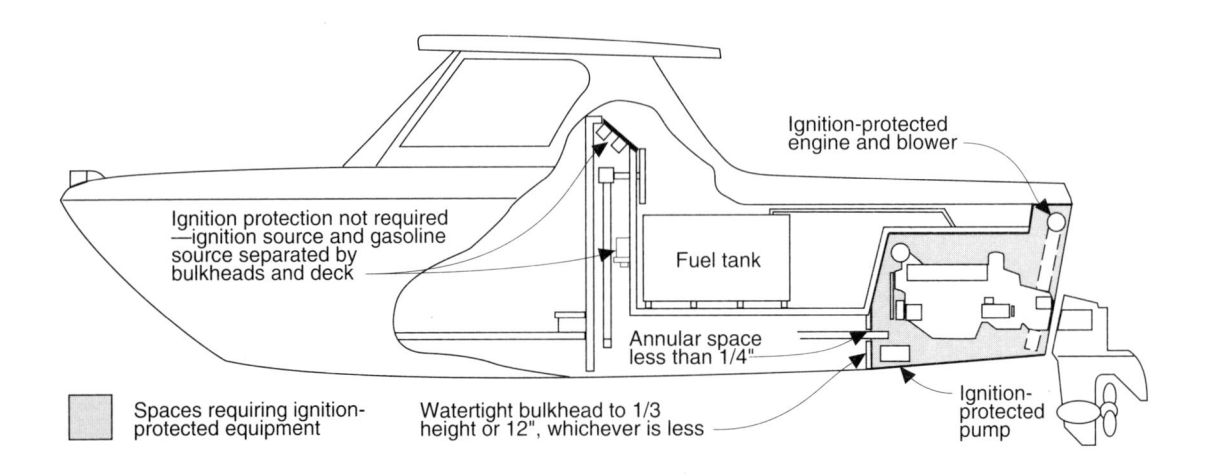

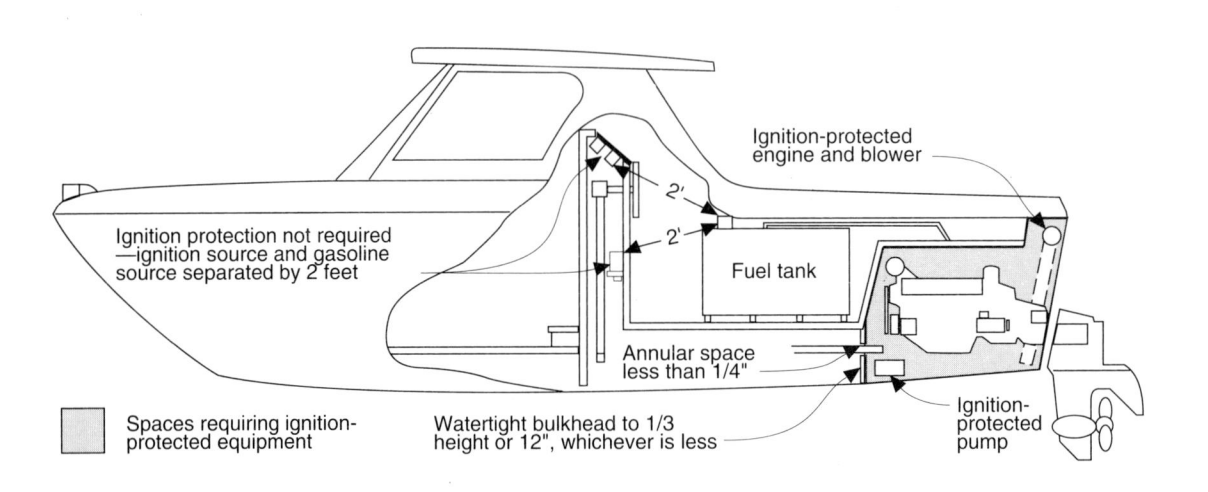

Figure 9.14 Isolation of Electrical Components

AC Standards and Practices

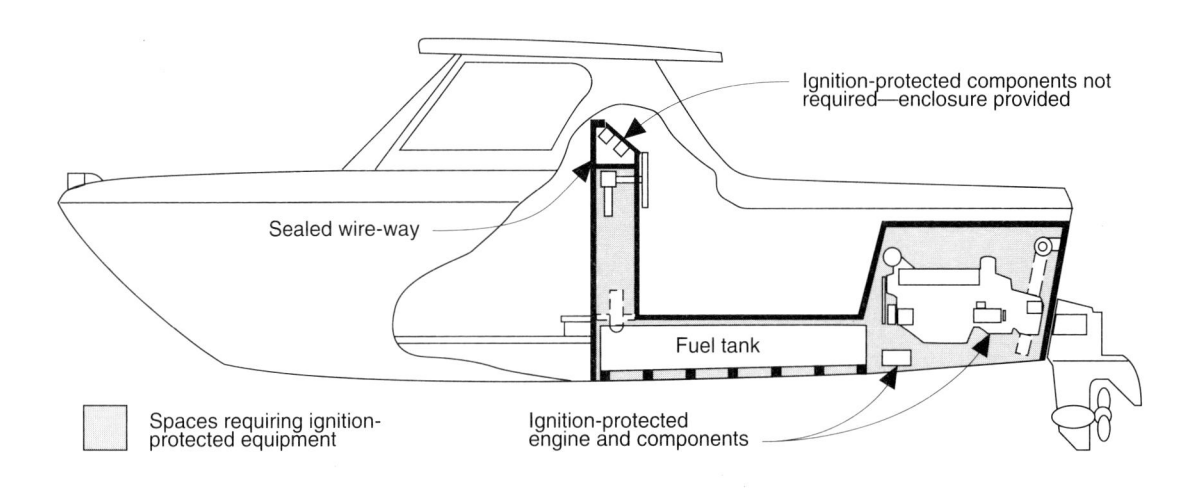

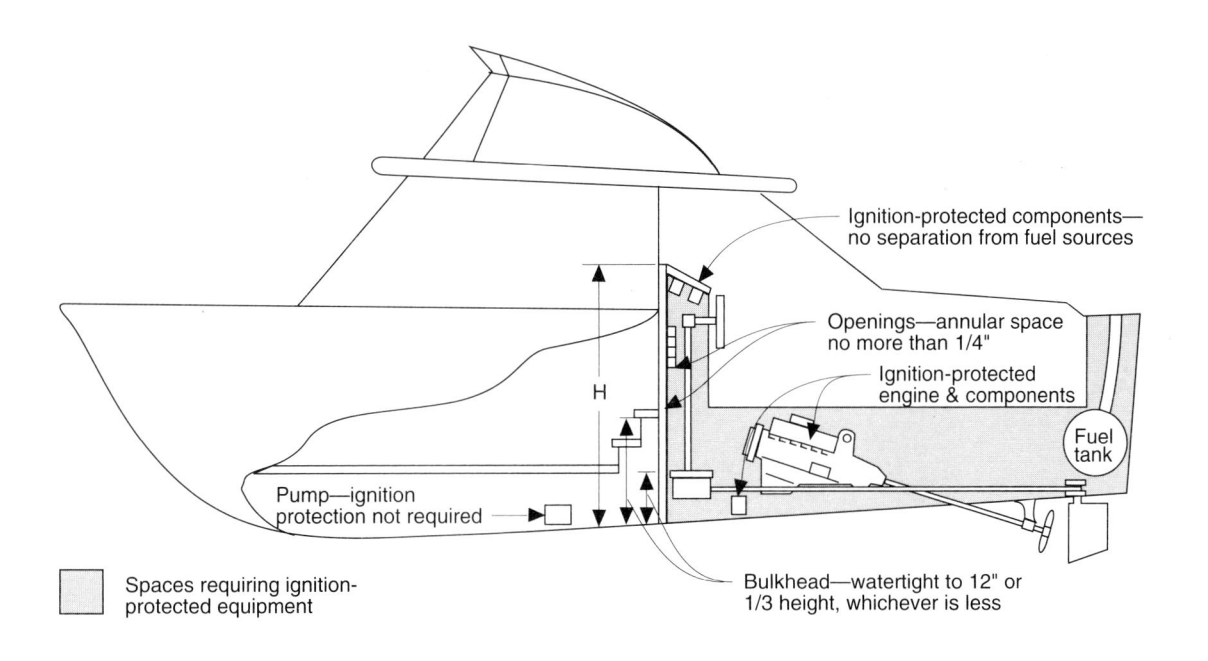

Figure 9.15 Isolation of Electrical Components

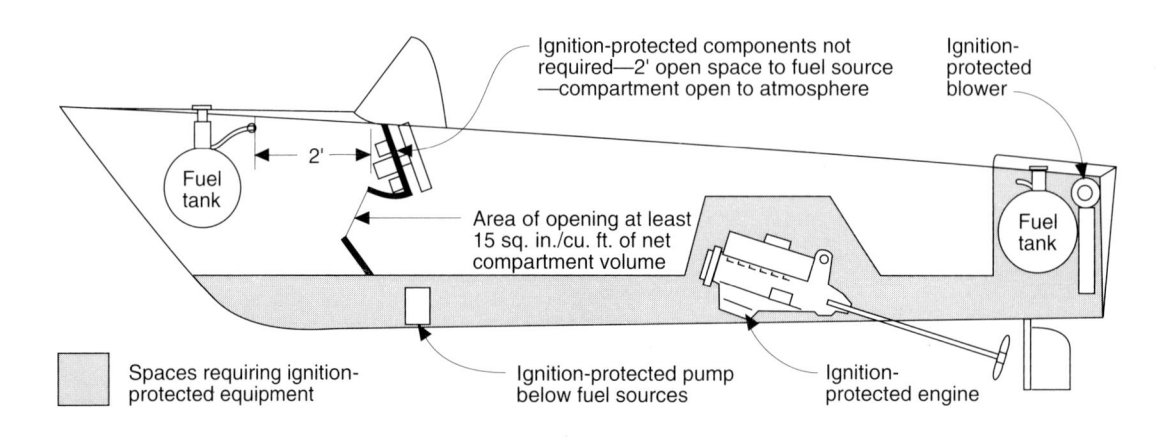

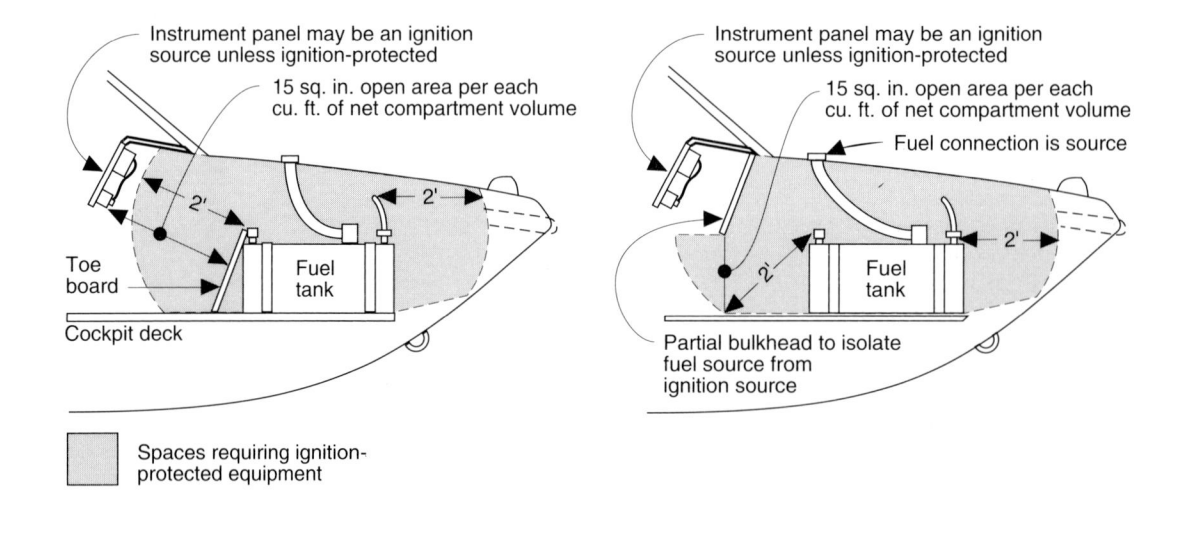

Figure 9.16 Isolation of Electrical Components

AC Standards and Practices   201

Figure 9.17 Isolation of Electrical Components

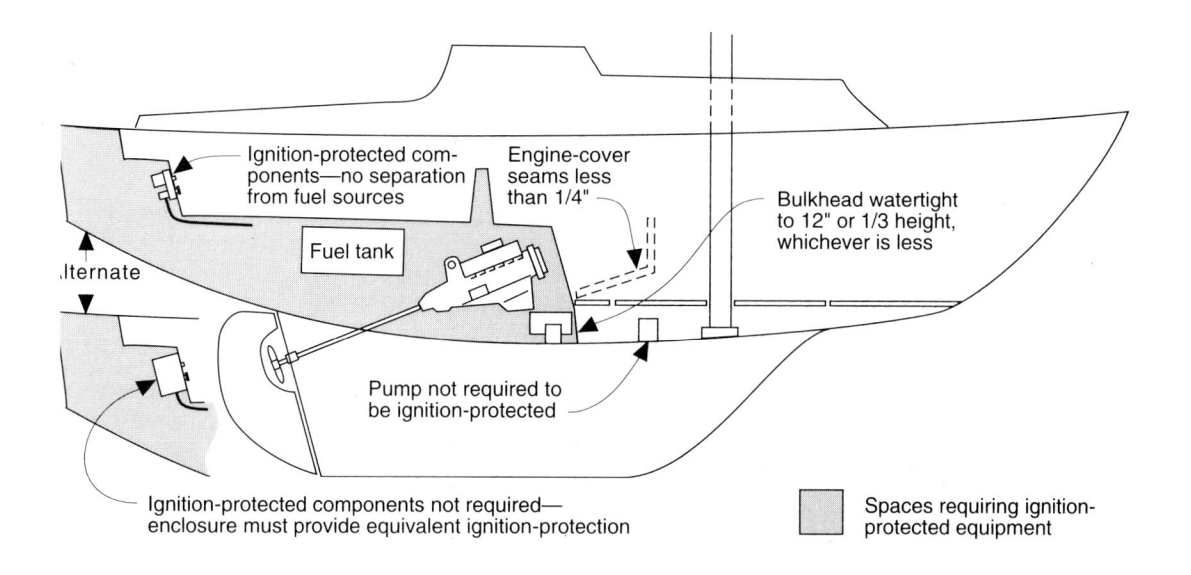

- Ignition-protected components—no separation from fuel sources
- Engine-cover seams less than 1/4"
- Bulkhead watertight to 12" or 1/3 height, whichever is less
- Alternate
- Fuel tank
- Pump not required to be ignition-protected
- Ignition-protected components not required—enclosure must provide equivalent ignition-protection
- Spaces requiring ignition-protected equipment

GALVANIC PROTECTION
The Green Wire

As we saw in Chapter 7, the green wire required in all AC circuits provides a potentially life-saving return path for stray electric currents.

Figure 9.18 illustrates the type of danger the green wire is designed to protect against. The engine, through the transmission, shaft, and water surrounding the boat, is at earth potential. One of the ungrounded conductors serving a piece of electrical equipment (a hot-water heater) has shorted to the metal case. With one hand on the grounded engine and the other hand on the hot metal case of the water heater, the person serves as a return-to-ground path for the AC current. A green grounding wire connected to the water-heater case and the engine would

Figure 9.18 Stray Current – Potentially a Lethal Experience

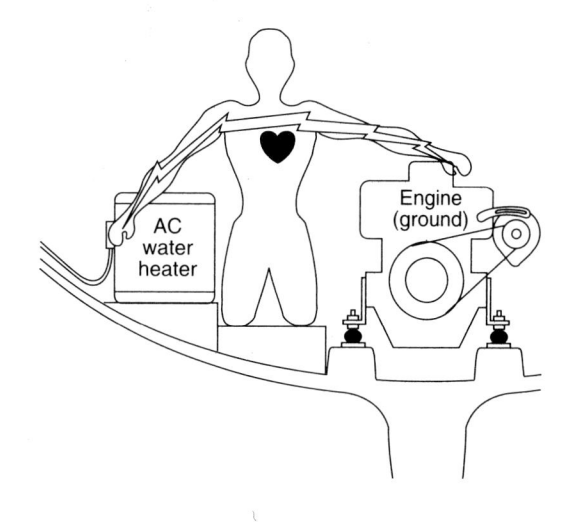

- AC water heater
- Engine (ground)

provide a lower-resistance return path and force the water heater and the engine to be at the same potential. With no potential difference, there would be no reason for current to flow through the person.

A Boat is Not a House
Boaters who are familiar with residential wiring often assume erroneously that a boat is just like a house. On that assumption, they connect the neutral (blue) and grounding (green) shore-power conductors at the onboard AC main panel.

Figure 9.19 shows what happens in that case. All of the current flowing in the hot (brown) conductor must ultimately find its way back to the shore-power ground — a metal rod driven into the ground. In a proper system, the sole return path would be the neutral conductor. In the improper system shown, the return current flows through three parallel paths: the neutral conductor, the green grounding conductor and — via the boat's grounded underwater-metal-hardware — the seawater.

If trouble develops in the blue and green conductors, most or all of the return current could be through the water. You can imagine what would happen to a swimmer near the boat.

Principle: The green and blue shore-power conductors must never be directly connected on the boat, but at the shore-power source.

Figure 9.19 What Can Happen When Blue and Green Wires are Connected on the Boat

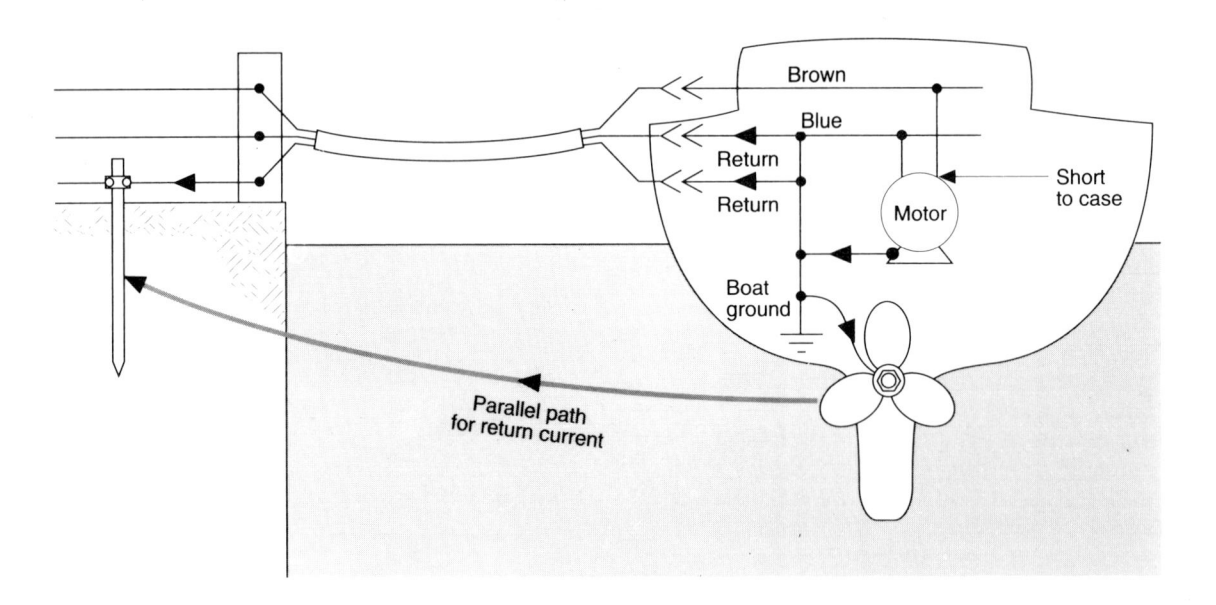

AC Standards and Practices

Figure 9.20 shows a second common mistake. This time the blue and green wires are properly separated on the boat, but, in order to prevent corrosion due to stray current flowing through the boat's underwater hardware, the unwitting boat owner has cut the green wire to the boat's ground (engine and metallic underwater hardware). A short develops in a piece of electrical equipment, so that the green wire is called upon to return the current. If there is enough resistance in the green wire and its connections, the metal case may be, not at ground, but considerably above ground potential. A person contacting the metal equipment case and any piece of metal underwater hardware would be shocked to find that he was serving as a parallel return path.

Principle: the green wire must be connected to the boat's ground.

The Properly-Wired Green Wire Problem

We have found that, from a safety standpoint, the green and blue wires must be kept separate on a boat, and the green wire must be connected to all metal equipment cases and metal underwater hardware (the boat's ground).

Unfortunately, we still may have a problem. We may have unwittingly created a galvanic cell, which, as we saw in Chapter 5, leads to corrosion of underwater metals.

Figure 9.21 shows two boats in a marina, hooked up to shore power. Both of their green wires are properly connected to their respective boat grounds. Unfortunately, the green wires of the two boats are also directly connected to each other through the shore power connection.

Thus, we have created a galvanic cell with one boat serving as the anode and the other

Figure 9.20 What Can Happen When Blue and Green Wires are Connected on the Boat

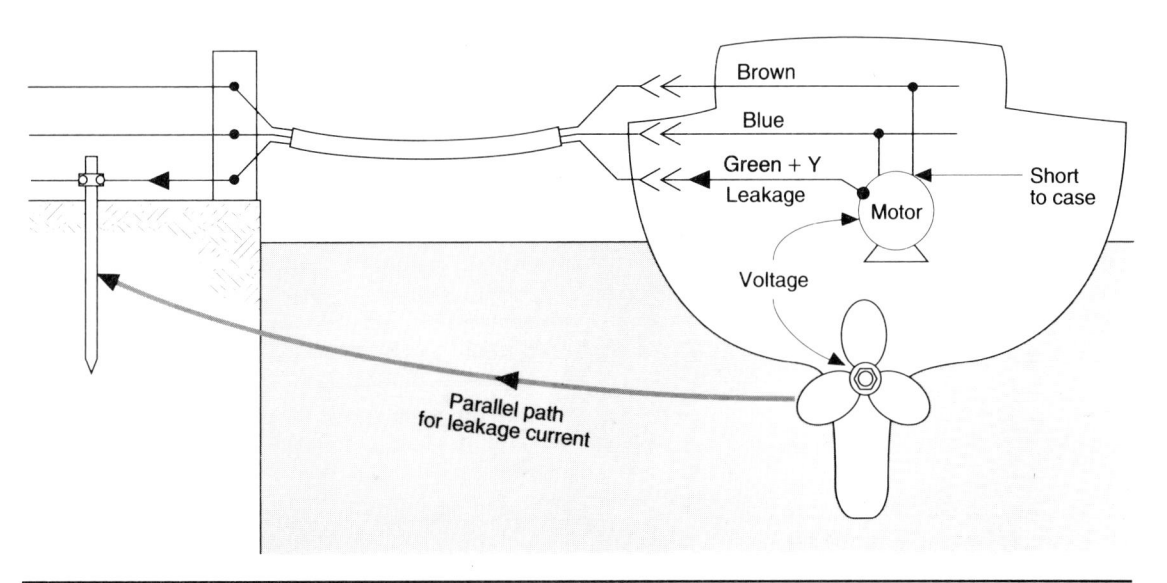

Figure 9.21 A Shore-Power Galvanic Cell

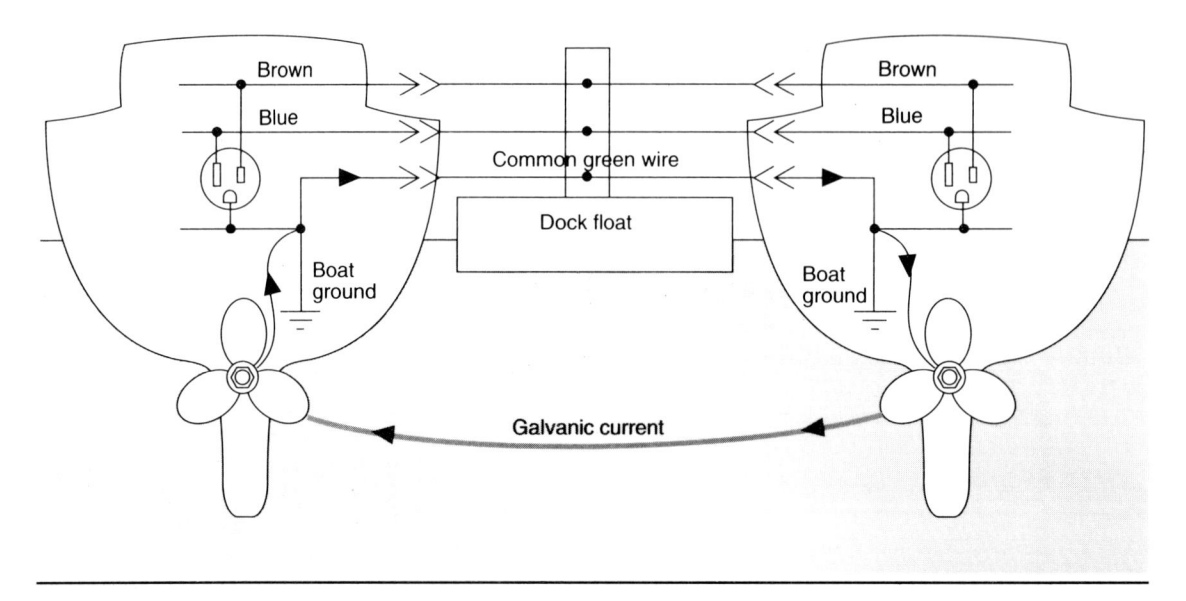

boat as the cathode. Even if the underwater metals of the two boats were of identical composition, they could suffer from impressed-current corrosion due to the presence of a voltage field in the water.

Woe is us; what can we do?

Solution 1: The Galvanic Isolator
The problem we face is the need for a green wire that conducts stray current to ground, but does not conduct galvanic DC currents. A galvanic isolator, inserted into the green wire, does just that.

Figure 9.22 on the following page shows three variations on the isolator theme. At top is a simple pair of parallel and opposite diodes. As you will recall, a diode passes current in the direction of its arrow but blocks current in the opposite direction. In the forward direction, a small voltage drop (0.6 volt for a silicon diode) occurs. Thus the pair of diodes will pass mains AC but will block up to 0.6 volt DC in both directions.

Adding diodes in series doubles the DC voltage blocked. The galvanic isolator in the middle will block galvanic currents of ±1.2 volts.

At bottom is a simple and inexpensive way to create a galvanic isolator from two full-wave diode bridges—common components in battery chargers and AC-to-DC power supplies. By tapping the DC–out and DC+out terminals, we have a galvanic isolator, which will block ±1.2 volts DC and pass twice as much AC current.

Warning. Isolators must be capable of passing short-circuit currents of 5,000 amps long enough to trip a circuit breaker.

AC Standards and Practices 205

Figure 9.22 Galvanic Isolators

Single Diodes Block 0.6 VDC

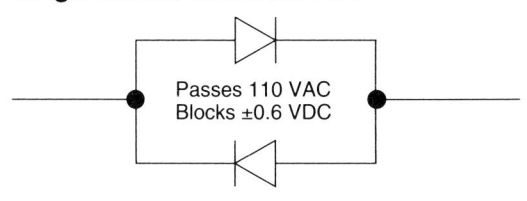

Passes 110 VAC
Blocks ±0.6 VDC

Double Diodes Block 1.2 VDC

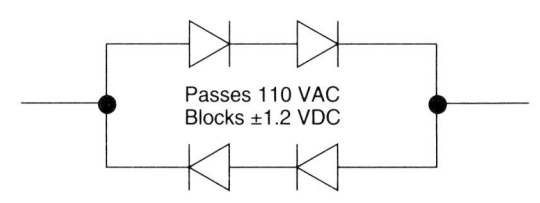

Passes 110 VAC
Blocks ±1.2 VDC

Two Full-wave Bridges Block 1.2 VDC and Conduct Doubled Current

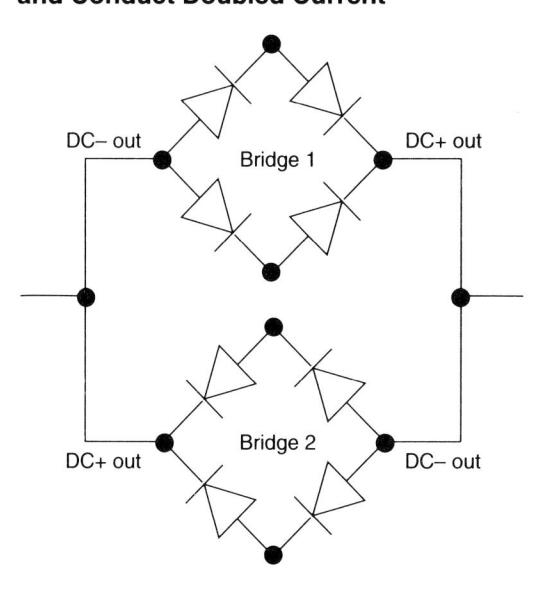

Bridge 1
DC− out   DC+ out

Bridge 2
DC+ out   DC− out

Solution 2: The Isolation Transformer

If we could create a new "source" of electricity that acted like an onboard generator, there would be no need for the green wire to run back to the shore-power ground, and we could break the galvanic connection to other marina-bound boats. An isolation transformer is the answer. It creates onboard power with no electrical connection to the shore-power conductors.

Figure 9.23 shows how an isolation transformer works. The transformer primary coil is connected to the hot and neutral shore-power conductors. The transformer secondary coil is connected to the hot and neutral ship's-power conductors. A metal shield is placed between the primary and secondary with no electrical connection to either coil. A lead, however, is brought out from the shield. The ship's neutral and grounding (green) conductors are connected at the transformer, since the transformer secondary is now truly a new source of electricity. As you will see on the following pages, connections between shield, conductor, transformer case, shore-power ground and ship's ground vary with the transformer. Follow the manufacturer's directions.

Figure 9.23 Isolation Transformer

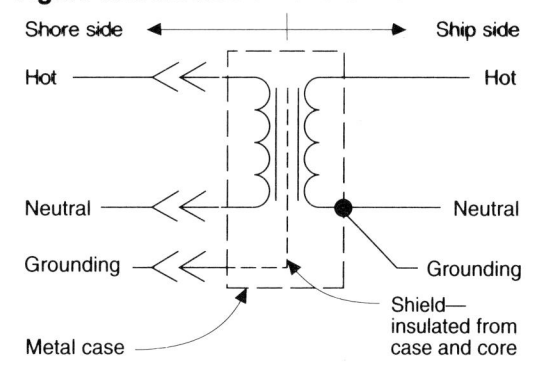

Shore side ◄──────► Ship side

Hot ────── ──────── Hot
Neutral ──── ──────── Neutral
Grounding ── ──────── Grounding

Metal case
Shield—insulated from case and core

TYPICAL SHORE-POWER CIRCUITS

Table 9.16 lists a variety of approved shore-power circuits. They range from the simplest and most common 120-volt AC, 30-amp circuit to 120/240-volt AC, three-phase systems found on the largest power yachts. Each circuit incorporates galvanic protection in the form of either a galvanic isolator or an isolation transformer.

Table 9.16 ABYC-Approved Shore-Power Systems

Figure	Voltage	Phase	Galvanic Protection
9.24	120 volt AC	1Ø	Galvanic isolator
9.25	120/240 volt AC	1Ø	Galvanic isolator
9.26	120/240 volt AC	3Ø∆	Galvanic isolator
9.27	120/208 volt AC	3Ø Y	Galvanic isolator
9.28	120 volt AC	1Ø	Isolation transformer—shield and case grounded to shore
9.29	120 volt AC	1Ø	Isolation transformer—shield to shore; case to boat
9.30	120-volt AC	1Ø	Isolation transformer—no shield; frame grounded to shore
9.31	120 volt AC	1Ø	Isolation transformer—shield and case grounded to boat
9.32	240 volt AC	1Ø	Isolation transformer—shield and case grounded to shore
9.33	240 volt AC	1Ø	Isolation transformer—shield to shore; case to boat
9.34	240 volt AC	1Ø	Isolation transformer—shield and case grounded to boat

AC Standards and Practices

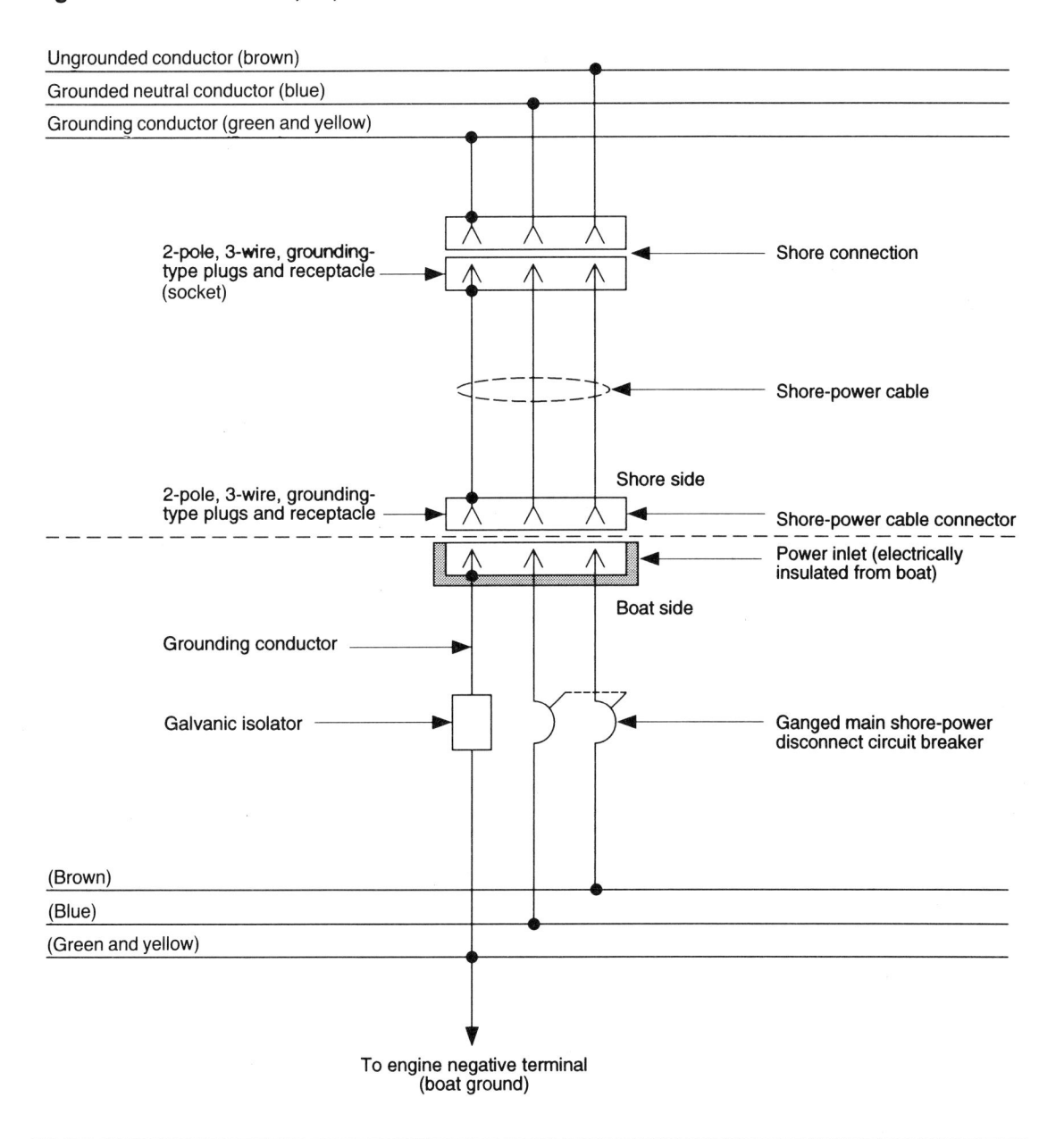

Figure 9.24 120-Volt-AC, 1Ø, Galvanic Isolator

208   AC

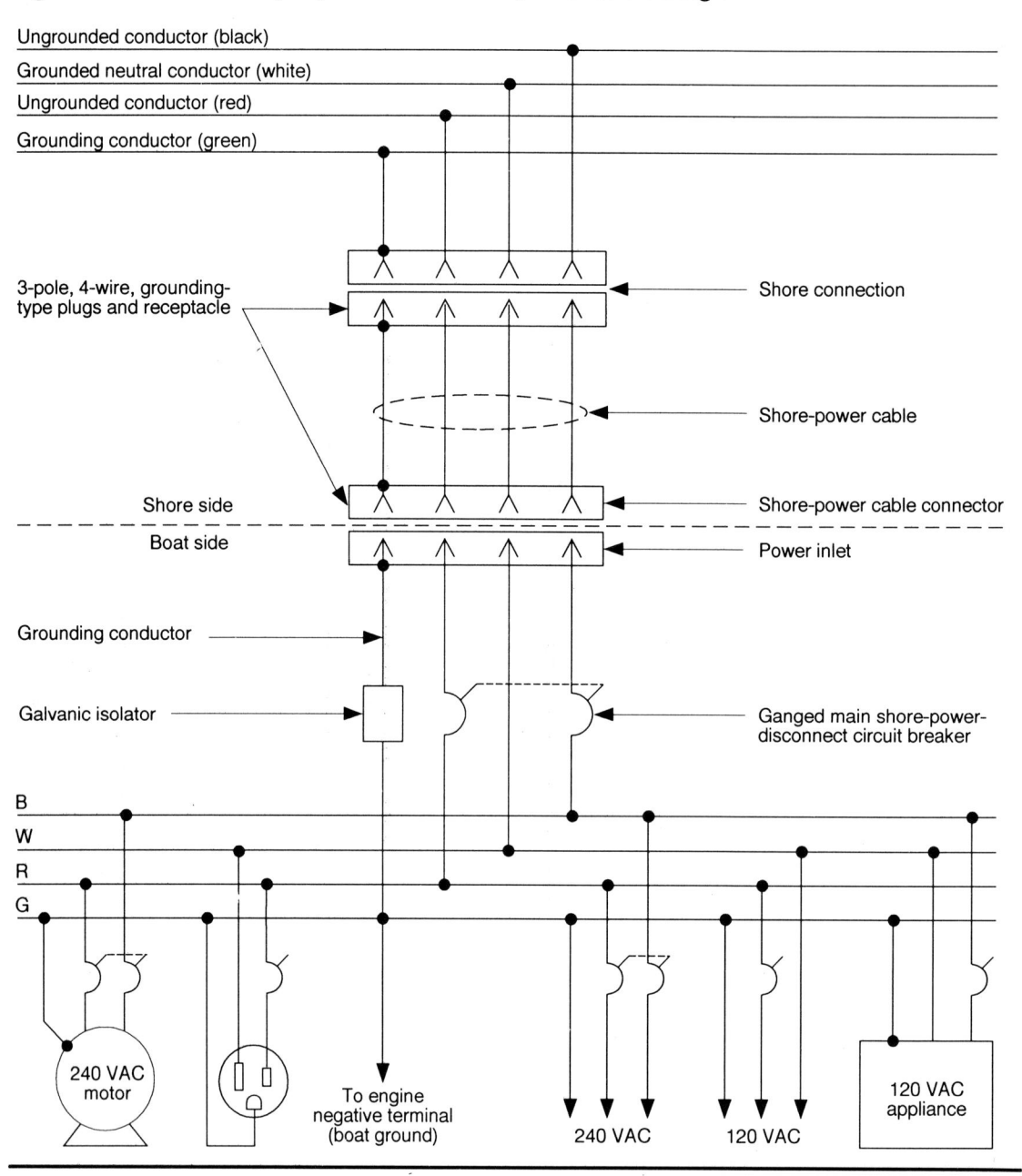

Figure 9.25 120/240-Volt, 1Ø, Galvanic Isolator, American Wiring

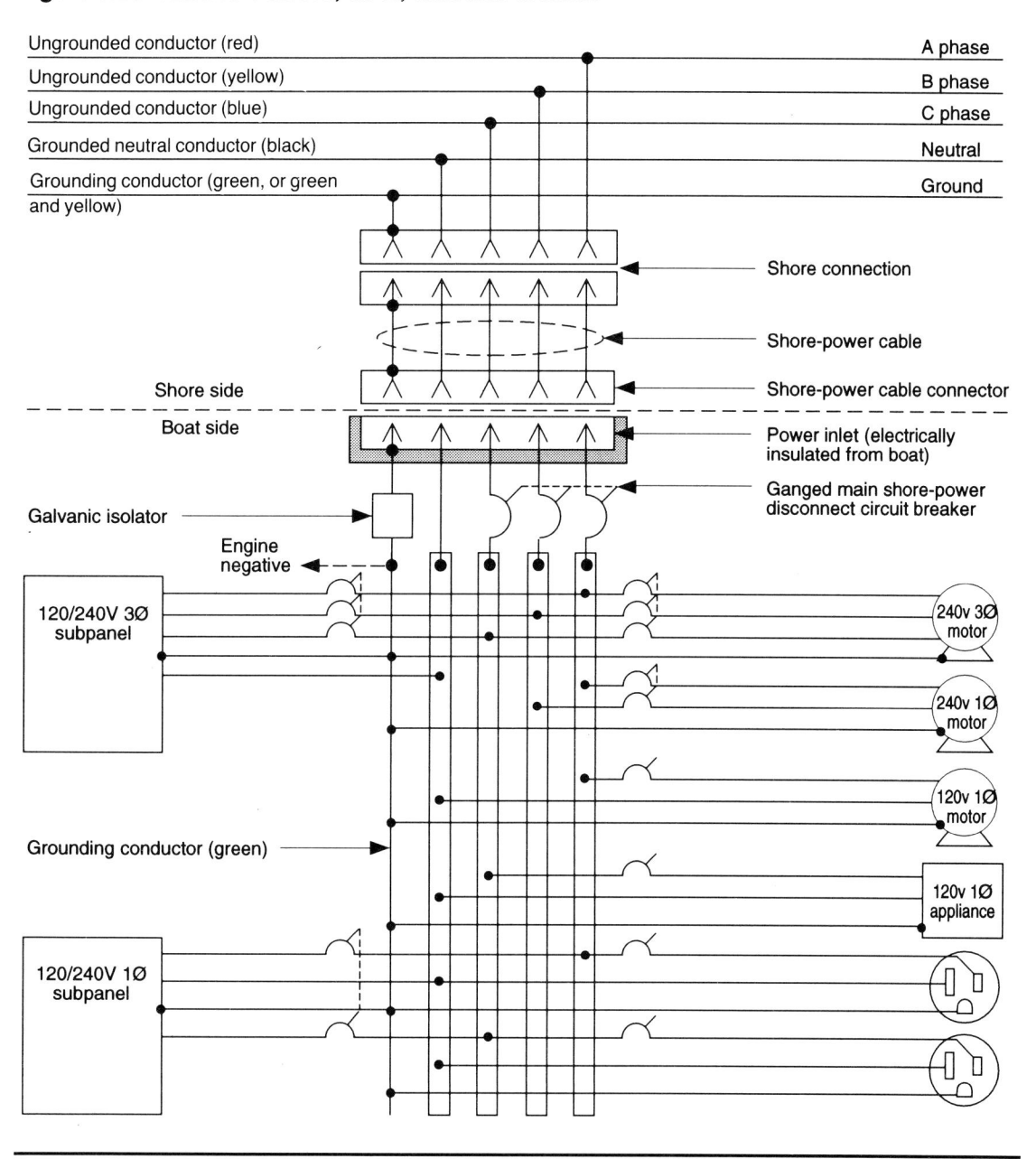

AC Standards and Practices 209

Figure 9.26 120/240-Volt-AC, 3Ø Δ, Galvanic Isolator

Ungrounded conductor (red) — A phase
Ungrounded conductor (yellow) — B phase
Ungrounded conductor (blue) — C phase
Grounded neutral conductor (black) — Neutral
Grounding conductor (green, or green and yellow) — Ground

Shore connection
Shore-power cable
Shore-power cable connector

Shore side
Boat side

Power inlet (electrically insulated from boat)
Ganged main shore-power disconnect circuit breaker

Galvanic isolator
Engine negative

120/240V 3Ø subpanel

240v 3Ø motor
240v 1Ø motor
120v 1Ø motor
120v 1Ø appliance

Grounding conductor (green)

120/240V 1Ø subpanel

Figure 9.27 120/208-Volt-AC, 3Ø Y, Galvanic Isolator, American Wiring

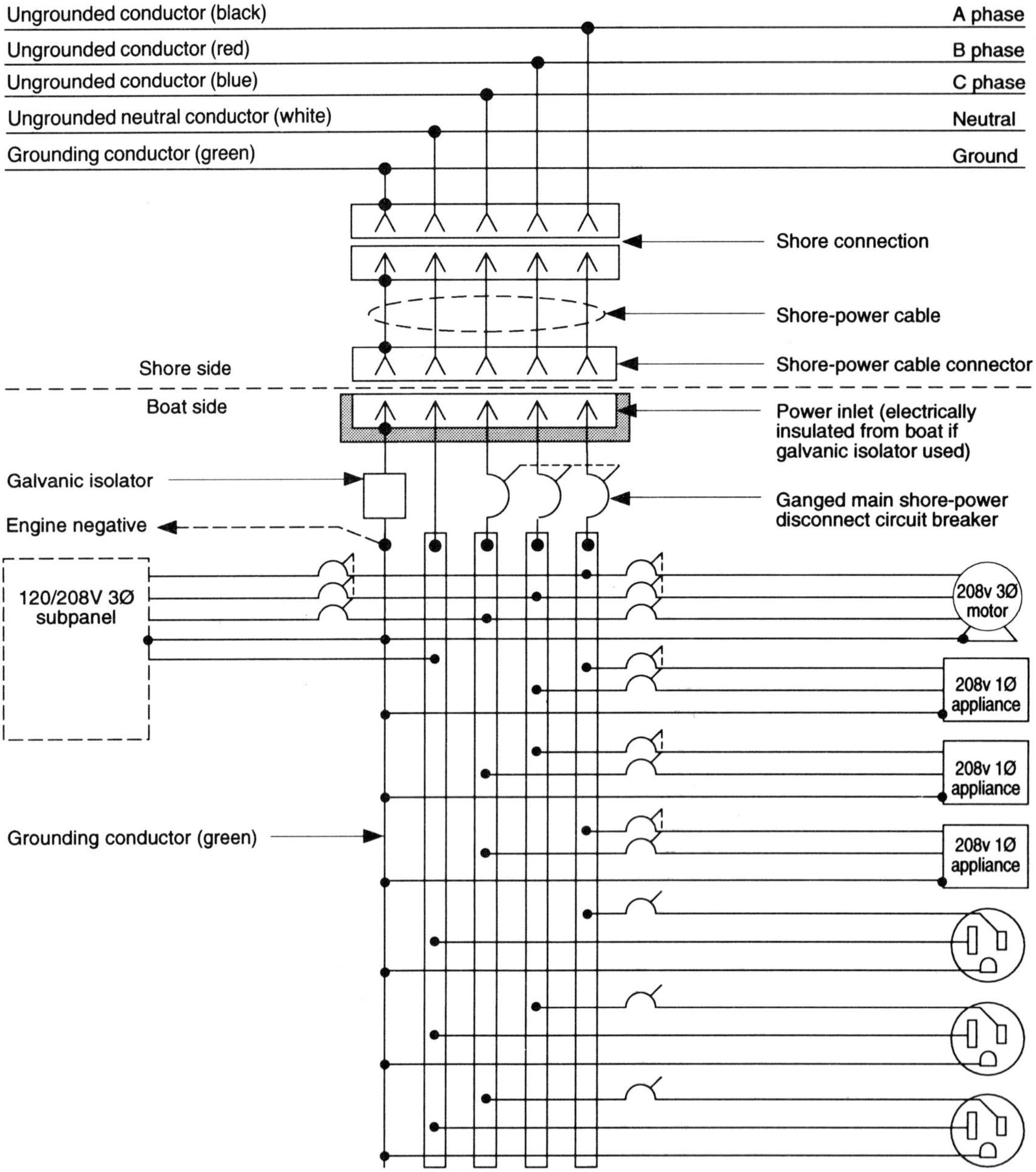

AC Standards and Practices   211

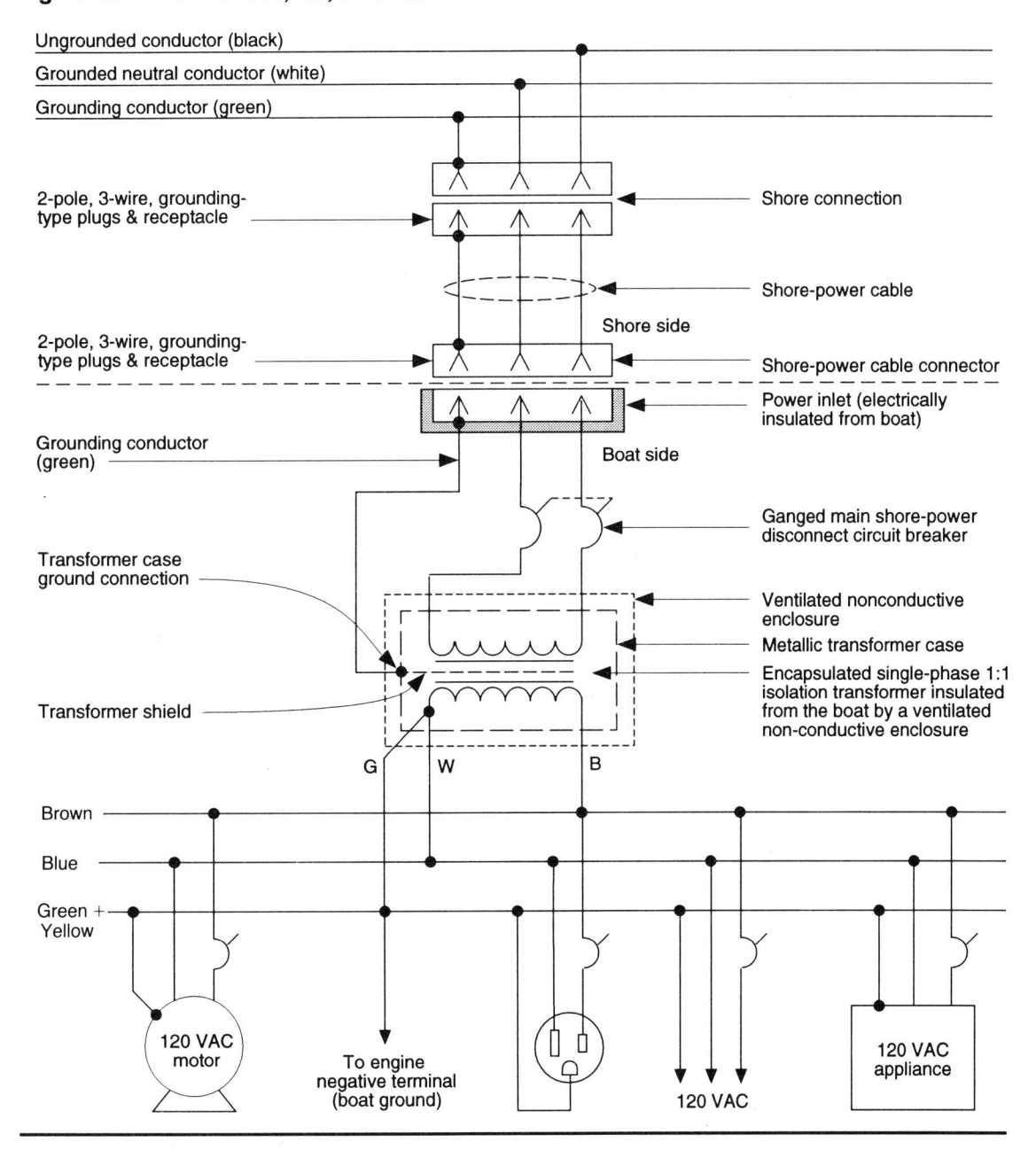

Figure 9.28 120-Volt-AC, 1Ø, Isolation Transformer—Shield and Case Grounded to Shore

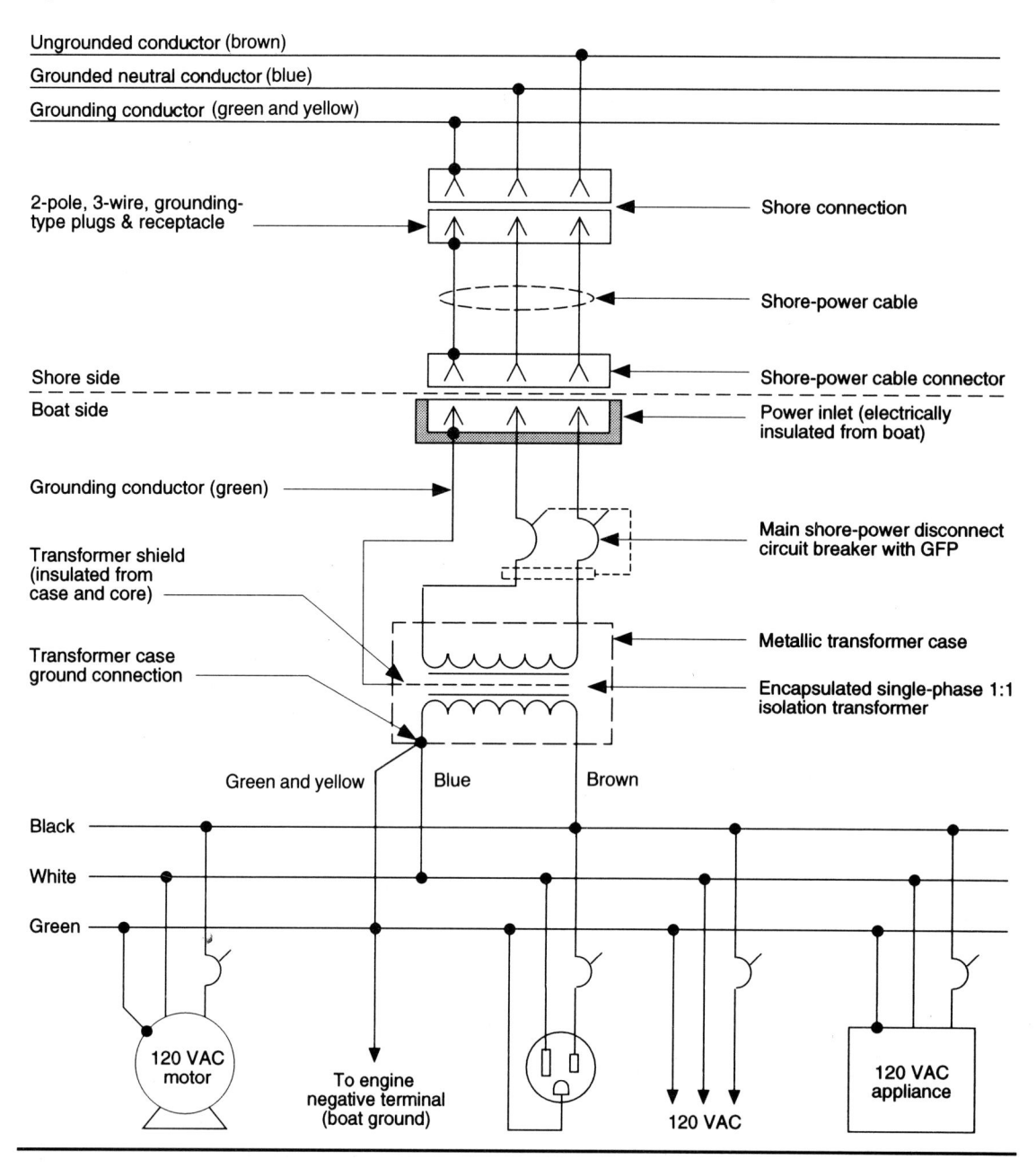

Figure 9.29 120-Volt-AC, 1Ø, Isolation Transformer—Shield to Shore; Case to Boat

AC Standards and Practices 213

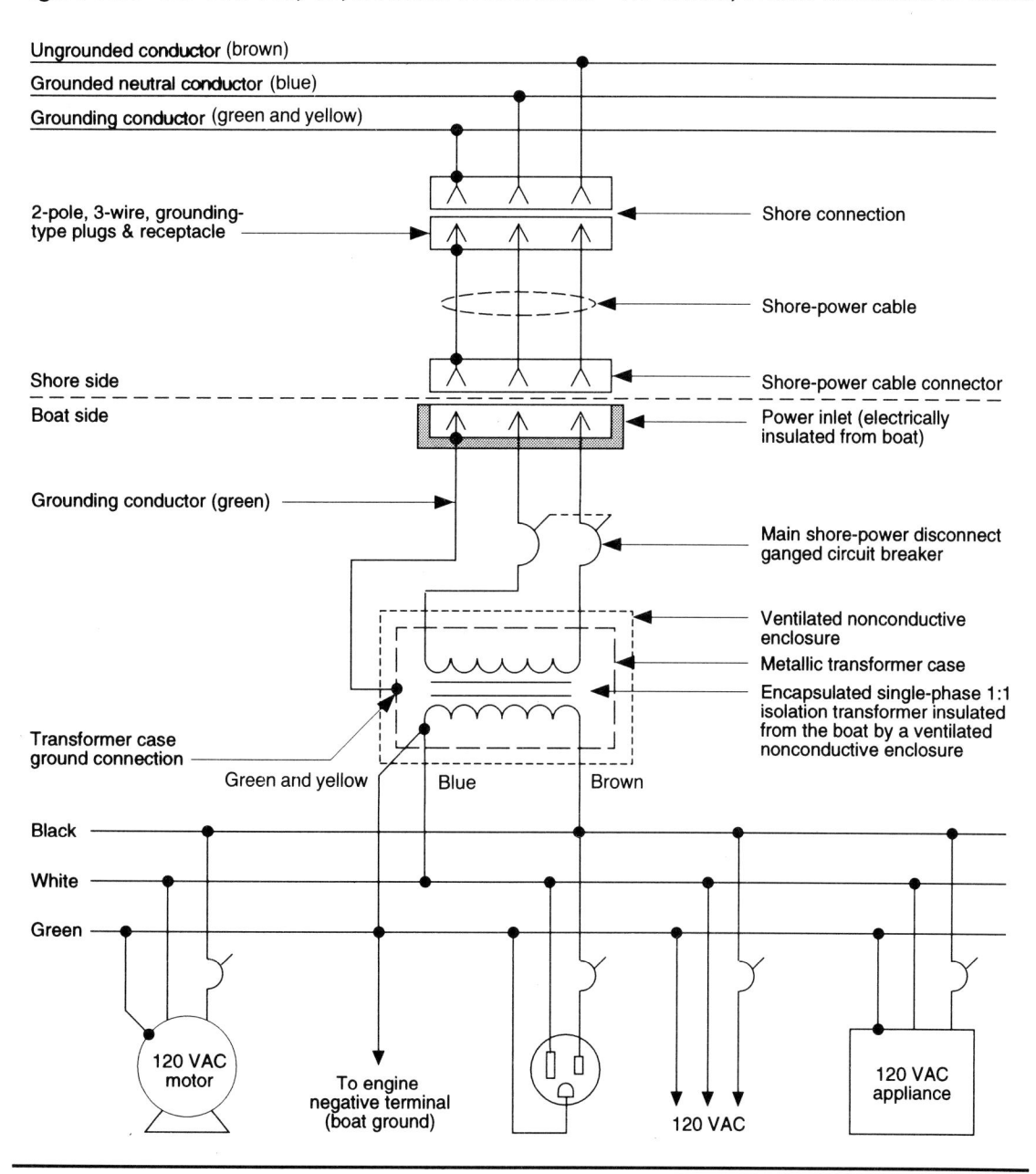

Figure 9.30 120-Volt- AC, 1Ø, Isolation Transformer—No Shield; Frame Grounded to Shore

214 AC

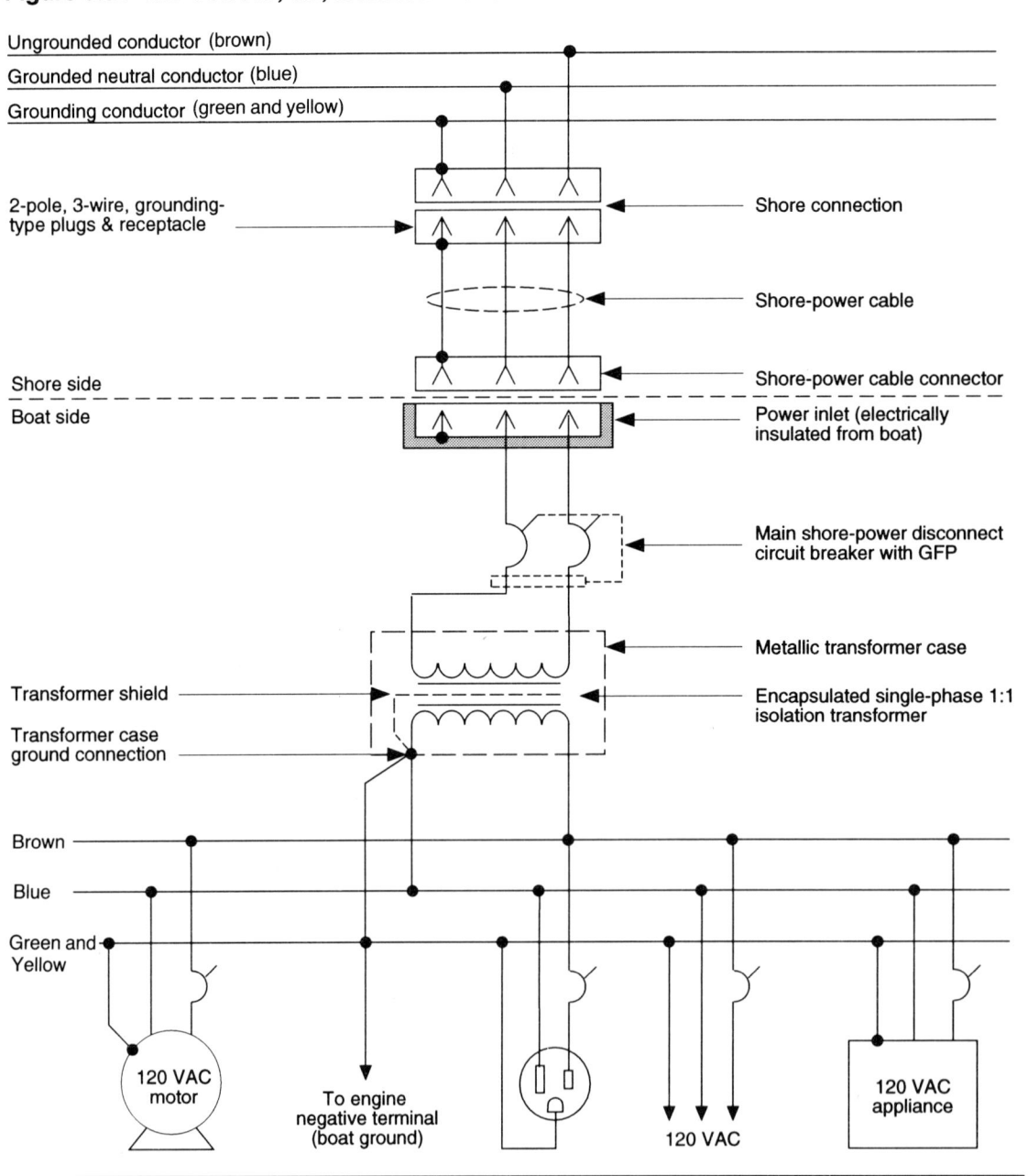

Figure 9.31 120-Volt-AC, 1Ø, Isolation Transformer—Shield and Case Grounded to Boat

Ungrounded conductor (brown)
Grounded neutral conductor (blue)
Grounding conductor (green and yellow)

2-pole, 3-wire, grounding-type plugs & receptacle

Shore connection

Shore-power cable

Shore side
Boat side

Shore-power cable connector

Power inlet (electrically insulated from boat)

Main shore-power disconnect circuit breaker with GFP

Metallic transformer case

Transformer shield

Encapsulated single-phase 1:1 isolation transformer

Transformer case ground connection

Brown
Blue
Green and Yellow

120 VAC motor

To engine negative terminal (boat ground)

120 VAC

120 VAC appliance

AC Standards and Practices 215

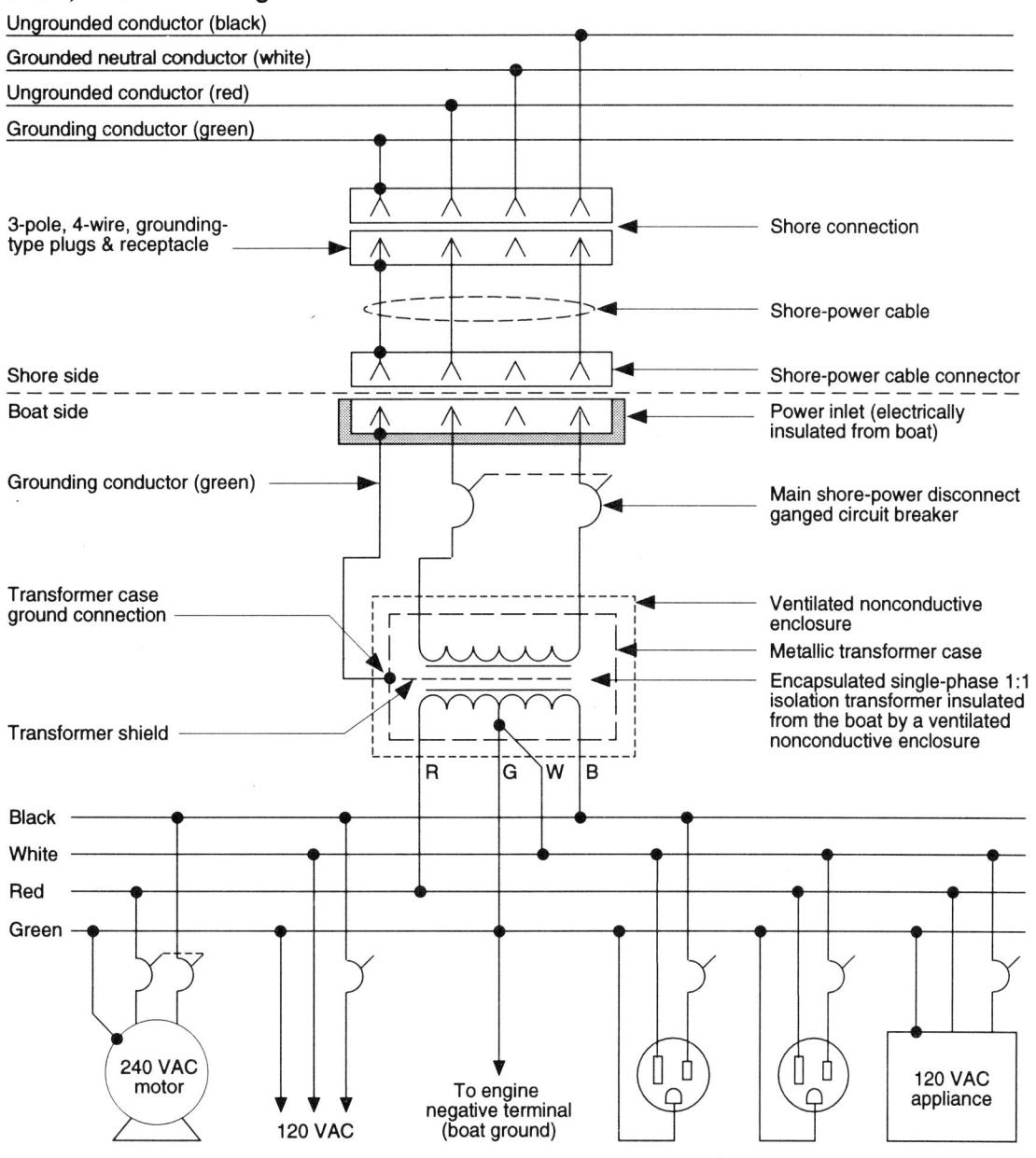

Figure 9.32 240-Volt-AC, 1Ø, Isolation Transformer—Shield and Case Grounded to Shore, American Wiring

Ungrounded conductor (black)
Grounded neutral conductor (white)
Ungrounded conductor (red)
Grounding conductor (green)

3-pole, 4-wire, grounding-type plugs & receptacle

Shore connection

Shore-power cable

Shore side
Boat side

Shore-power cable connector

Power inlet (electrically insulated from boat)

Grounding conductor (green)

Main shore-power disconnect ganged circuit breaker

Transformer case ground connection

Ventilated nonconductive enclosure
Metallic transformer case
Encapsulated single-phase 1:1 isolation transformer insulated from the boat by a ventilated nonconductive enclosure

Transformer shield

R G W B

Black
White
Red
Green

240 VAC motor

120 VAC

To engine negative terminal (boat ground)

120 VAC appliance

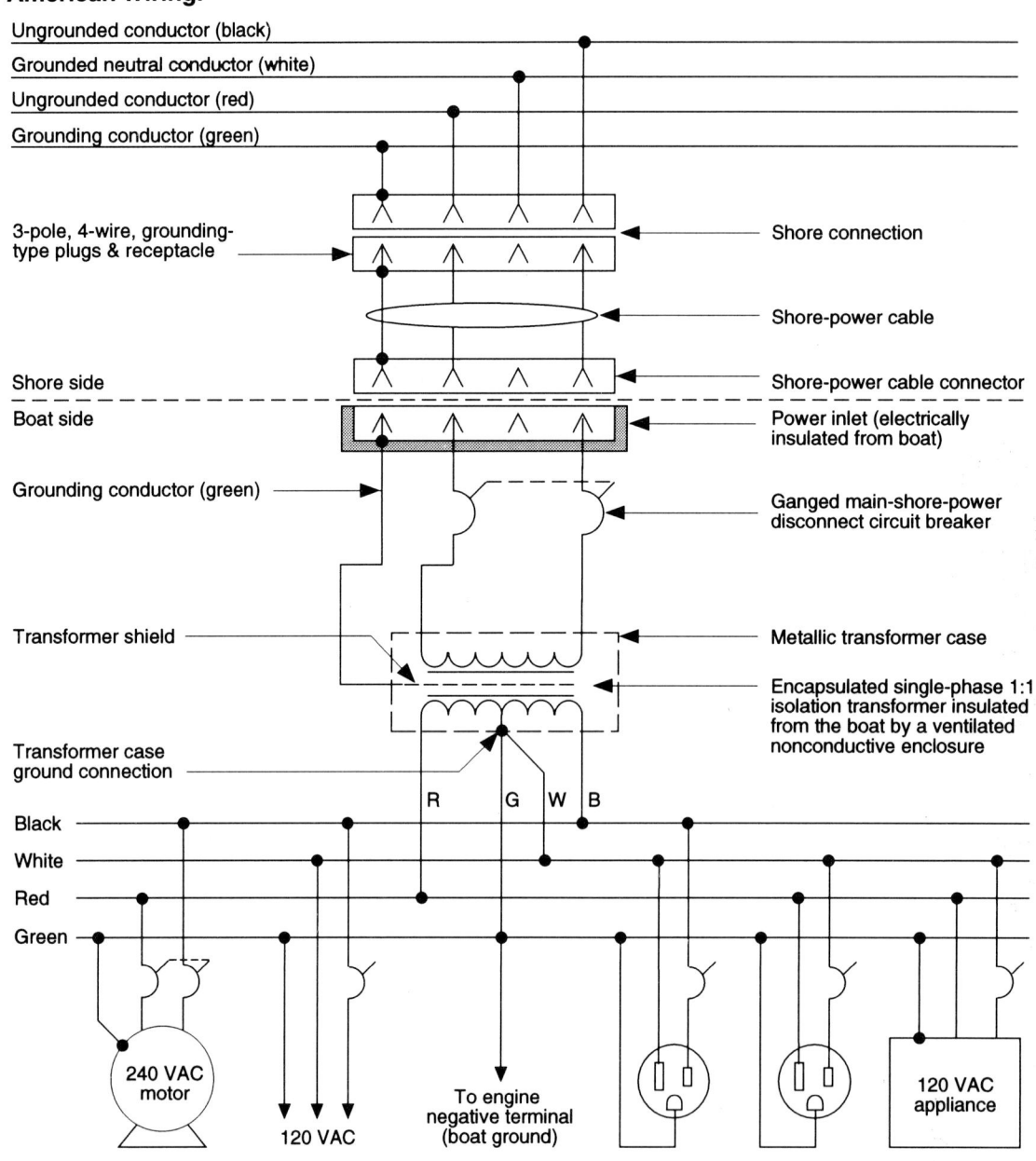

Figure 9.33 240-Volt-AC, 1Ø, Isolation Transformer—Shield to Shore; Case to Boat, American Wiring.

AC Standards and Practices

Figure 9.34 240-Volt-AC, 1Ø, Isolation Transformer—Shield and Case Grounded to Boat, American Wiring.

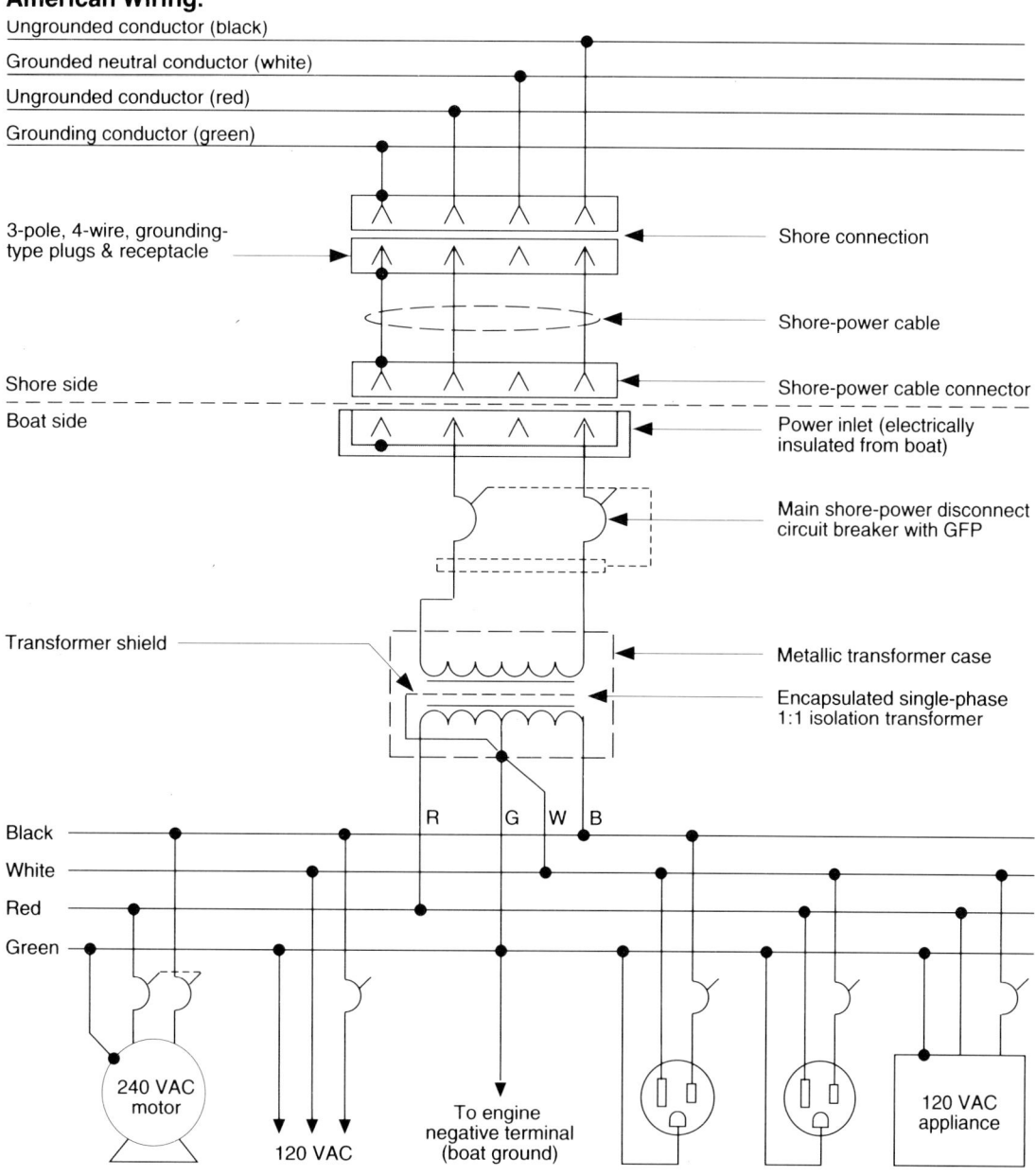

PART III
ALTERNATE ENERGIES

10 CONSERVATION FOR LIVEABOARDS

Costs per Kilowatt-Hour 222

Lighting Savings 225

Refrigeration Savings 225

Other Savings 229

The Bottom Line 229

The *cost per kilowatt-hour* of shipboard power is high, whether computed in money or in aggravation. It is easily shown that the monetary cost of a saved kilowatt-hour is far less than that of a generated kilowatt-hour.

This chapter shows you how to reduce your electrical appetite through *lighting savings, refrigeration savings*, and miscellaneous *other savings*.

The bottom line is that most boaters can cut their on-board power consumption by half with little or no reduction in lifestyle.

Note: On the following pages, the dollar cost is roughly equivalent to the same sterling figure, thus £10 can be substituted for $10.

ALTERNATE ENERGIES

Before considering solar and wind power, the liveaboard boater should consider an alternate form of energy—*conservation*.

Put yourself to the following test. Your boat suddenly begins leaking more water. What solution first comes to your mind? If it is to buy a larger bilge pump, then forget conservation, solar, and wind, and get yourself to a dock where you can tap into shore power. If fixing the leak seems more logical to you, however, then read on.

If we have learned anything in the past twenty years, it is that, with modest investment, increased awareness and attention to detail, we can save a lot of expensive energy in our homes and offices. The same is true of boats.

If your boat is typical, this chapter will show you how to reduce the drain on your batteries by half with virtually no effect on your lifestyle. By cutting consumption in half, you will also reduce the required sizes and costs of the solar and wind systems you may be considering adding to your boat.

In fact, you may reduce your consumption to the point where you never need run your engine again just to charge your batteries!

COST PER KILOWATT-HOUR

The old saying, "a penny saved is a penny earned," has its analog in energy conservation:

"A kilowatt saved is a kilowatt made."

If we can save energy without materially altering our lifestyle, then we can compare the cost of saving a kilowatt-hour to the cost of producing or purchasing a kilowatt-hour in order to see which is the better deal.

Costs of Producing Electricity

Figure 10.1 shows the costs per kilowatt-hour of electricity produced by:

- 220-amp alternator on a 20-hp diesel
- 110-amp alternator on a 20-hp diesel
- 55-amp alternator on a 20-hp diesel
- Solar panel at $10 per peak watt
- 5-foot wind machine at $1,500

The assumptions used include:

Diesel Power:

- Used at anchor
- Fuel consumption—0.5 gallon/hour
- Fuel price—$1.30/gallon
- Price including controls—$6,000
- Life—10,000 hours
- Maintenance—$0.10/hour

Solar Power:

- Used all year
- Size—50 watts peak output
- Price including controls—$500
- Life—10 years
- Average daily sunshine—5.2 hours
- Maintenance—$0

Wind Power:

- Used all year
- Size (blade diameter)—5 feet
- Price including controls—$1,500
- Life—10 years
- Average wind speed—10 knots
- Maintenance—$25/year

Conservation for Liveaboards

Figure 10.1 Costs per Kilowatt-Hour of Generated Power

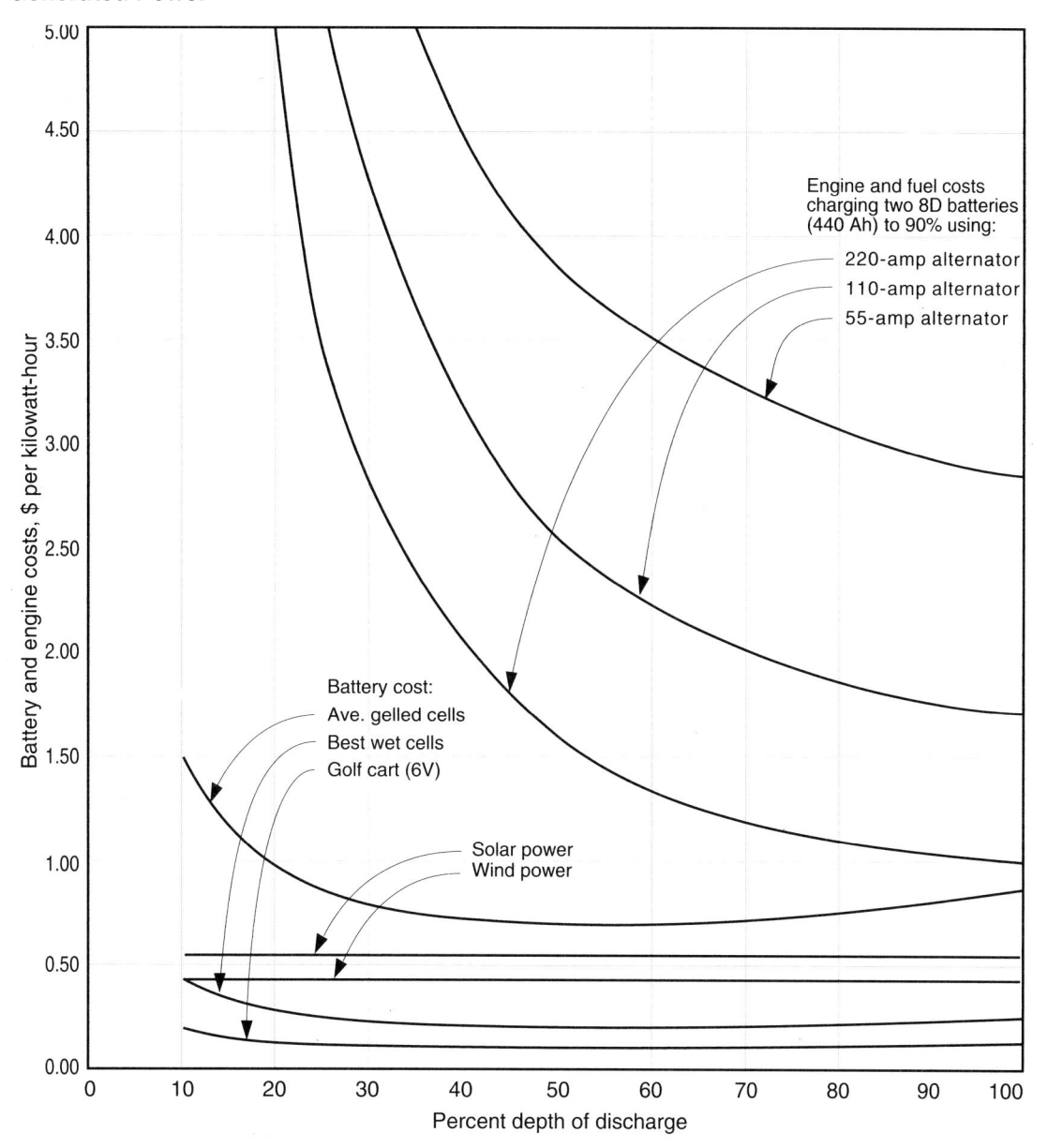

Engine and fuel costs charging two 8D batteries (440 Ah) to 90% using:
- 220-amp alternator
- 110-amp alternator
- 55-amp alternator

Battery cost:
- Ave. gelled cells
- Best wet cells
- Golf cart (6V)

Solar power
Wind power

Assuming the alternators cycle the battery between the charge states of 50% and 90%, the relative costs per kilowatt-hour shown in Figure 10.1 of electricity are:

- 220-amp alternator—$3.80
- 110-amp alternator—$2.50
- 55-amp alternator—$1.60
- Solar panel—$0.53
- 5-foot wind machine—$0.48

The Cost of Conserving Electricity
Now let's compare the costs per kilowatt-hour of electricity saved by two simple changes: switching from incandescent to fluorescent lighting, and halving the heat loss of our DC-powered refrigerator.

Fluorescent Conversion
An 8-watt fluorescent fixture puts out as much light as a 25-watt incandescent lamp. The replacement fluorescent fixture costs $30. Fluorescent bulbs cost four times as much as incandescent bulbs, but they last proportionally longer, so the cost of bulb replacement is the same.

Assuming a 10-year fixture life, and that the lamp is operated an average of two hours per day throughout the year, the lifetime savings of the fluorescent replacement fixture is 124 kilowatt-hours. The cost per kilowatt-hour saved is $0.24—half of the cost of electricity produced by the cheapest alternative means, and one-tenth of the cost of the 110-amp alternator power.

Refrigerator Heat Loss
Assume that a 6-cubic-foot refrigerator with 2-inch wall insulation draws 5.5 amps at 12 volts DC and has a 40 percent duty cycle. Its daily consumption would be: 5.5 amps x 24 hours x 0.40 = 52.8 Ah, or 0.63 kilowatt-hour.

If we were to double the insulation of the refrigerator walls to 4 inches, install a better door gasket and install a trap in the drain, we would probably reduce the refrigerator's total heat loss by half, or 0.315 kilowatt-hour/day. Over ten years of continuous use, the savings would amount to 1,186 kilowatt-hours.

The most effective way to double the refrigerator insulation would be to line the inside of the box with 2-inch polyurethane foam board and then glass over the foam. If accessible, cavities between the box and the hull and cabinetry can be filled with expanding foam.

The first method has the advantage of certainty, but reduces the volume of the box. The second method retains the box dimensions, but is uncertain in effectiveness without disassembly of the cabinetry.

Method one could be accomplished for about $50 in materials and $200 in labor by a reasonably competent fiberglass technician. Cost per kilowatt-hour saved is thus $250 ÷ 1,186 kilowatt-hours = $0.21/kilowatt-hour.

Both of our retrofits are at least twice as cost effective as adding solar and wind power, and ten times cheaper than diesel production.

Caveat. The above calculations assume year-round use of your boat for 10 years. If you use your boat only 10% of the year, then conservation, solar, and wind costs per kilowatt-hour should be multiplied by a factor of 10. Alternator costs should remain about the same since the primary use of the engine is propulsion and not power generation. That is why this chapter is titled *Conservation for Liveaboards.*

LIGHTING SAVINGS

Most boats arrive from the factory equipped with incandescent lighting. Both the bulbs and the fixtures are inexpensive, but it is a false economy for the owner. You can reduce your lighting load by a full two-thirds through two simple retrofits, including the one described above.

Fluorescent Fixtures

The galley requires bright lighting, but 8-watt fluorescent slim-line fixtures cast as much light as common 25-watt incandescent fixtures. The head is another good location for fluorescent lighting.

If you have 120-volt-AC light fixtures aboard, you can convert them with fluorescent screw-in replacement bulbs and then run these fixtures from a DC-to-AC inverter for similar savings.

Fluorescent fixtures have a reputation for driving loran sets crazy. I have never experienced the problem, though I operate two 8-watt fixtures within 4 feet of my loran. If fluorescent fixtures affect your loran or other electronics, install the filters described in Chapter 13.

Halogen Spot Fixtures

Many of the lights below deck are for reading. The most common incandescent fixtures spread the light from 15-watt bulbs over an area ten times that of a page. These lamps can be directly replaced with 5-watt halogen spot-task lamps, which achieve the same light intensity by concentrating the beam from a high-efficiency halogen bulb onto a page or task.

You can save further lighting energy by installing the solid-state dimmer circuit described in Chapter 14. You can then dim the lights for a warmer ambience, save electricity and double the lifetime of the lamps, all at the same time.

Anchor Lights

International navigation law requires boats of less than 20-meter length to display an anchor light which is visible at least two nm. The required luminance is equivalent to that produced by a 10-watt incandescent lamp.

The battery-powered "marker lights" many use do not meet the two-mile specification. Other than converting to a slightly more efficient halogen bulb, to simply reduce lamp wattage is to put one's boat in jeopardy—at least from a liability standpoint. To run the light from sunrise to when you rise is wasteful, however. The automatic anchor light switch in Chapter 14 turns the anchor light on and off precisely at sunset and sunrise, thus saving about 2 Ah per day. If you leave your boat unattended it will save an average of about 10 Ah per day.

REFRIGERATION SAVINGS

To understand all of the things you can do to make your electric refrigeration system more efficient you have to understand how a refrigerator works.

How Refrigerators Work

If you remember the sensation of stepping from the water into a breeze, you already half understand refrigeration. That day at the beach the wind was evaporating the liquid on your skin into a vapor. The process of evaporation was removing heat from your skin at the rate of 970 BTUs per pound of water.

Since the BTU is defined as the amount of heat required to change the temperature of 1 pound of water 1°F, 1 pound of evaporated water could cool a 100-pound person by 9.7 °F!

This is marvelous! What if we could build a closed system (so we wouldn't have to add water) in which water was evaporated on one side, the vapor transported to the other side, the vapor condensed, and the condensed water sent back to evaporate again? We could call the device a "refrigerator" ("Frigidair" might be even snappier). We could patent it and make a million !

Figure 10.2 shows the basic idea of the refrigerator and its implementation with a few minor changes.

Figure 10.2 How Refrigerators Work

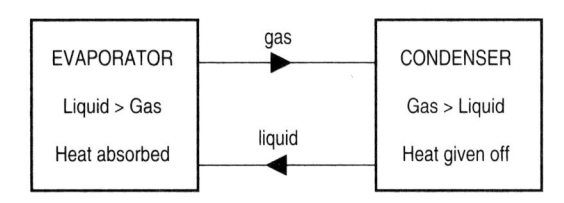

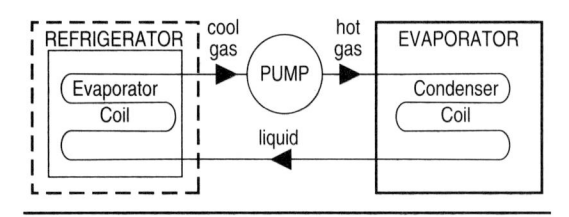

First, water won't do because the temperature at which it most rapidly vaporizes, or boils, is 212°F, far too warm to keep chicken from spoiling. We therefore use a specially-formulated refrigerant whose boiling point is 20 to 30° F below zero.

Second, we add a compressor pump to force the condensed refrigerant back into a liquid, and a thermostat to control the pump, so that we can control the average temperature at which the refrigerator runs.

The Cooling Load
First, two definitions:

- BTU = heat that changes the temperature of 1 pound of water by 1°F.
- Heat of Fusion of Water (heat absorbed by 1 pound of ice in melting) = 144 BTU.

Next, Figure 10.3 shows the basic equation of conductive heat loss:

$$H = A \times \Delta T \div R$$

Where:

H = heat loss through A, in BTU/hour

A = area of surface in square feet

ΔT = temperature difference, $T_1 - T_2$, °F

R = R/inch x inches of thickness

Figure 10.3 Conductive Heat Loss

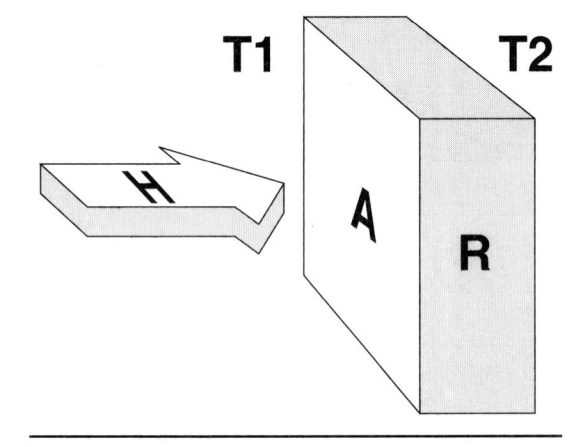

To this conductive heat loss through the walls of the refrigerator we have to add the losses of infiltration (air leakage through the lid and drain) and cool-down (heat that must be removed from warm objects we add to the box).

Conservation for Liveaboards

A Typical Refrigerator Box

Figure 10.4 shows the dimensions of a typical 6-cubic-foot refrigerator. The walls are constructed of 2-inch urethane foam, lined with fiberglass. Plugging the numbers into the heat-loss equation above:

   A = 28 square feet

   ΔT = 75°F outside - 40°F inside = 35F°

   R = 2 inches x R-6/inch = 12

   H = 28 x 35 ÷ 12 = 81.7 BTU/hour

If this box had a perfect lid and we never opened it, it would melt 35.7 BTU/hour ÷ 144 BTU/pound = 0.5 pounds/hour of ice, or 12 pounds of ice per day. Of course we do open the lid and we do put warm things into it that must be cooled down, so it might melt 16 pound of ice per day.

How much electricity will it take to replace the ice? The answer is—it all depends. It depends primarily on the efficiency of the refrigeration system—the refrigerator's Coefficient of Performance (COP), defined as:

   COP = watts removed ÷ watts used.

We'll also need a conversion factor:

   Ah/day = 0.586 x BTU/hour

The COP of a refrigerator depends on how hard it has to work pumping heat from the evaporator (cold) side to the condenser (hot) side. When the temperatures of evaporator and condenser are the same, the refrigerator can remove about 3 BTUs of heat energy, using the equivalent of 1 BTU of electrical energy, giving it a COP of 3.0.

At the opposite extreme, the typical refrigerator is capable of moving heat across a maximum difference of about 150°F, at which point its COP becomes zero.

Figure 10.4 Refrigerator Box Dimensions Before and After Retrofit

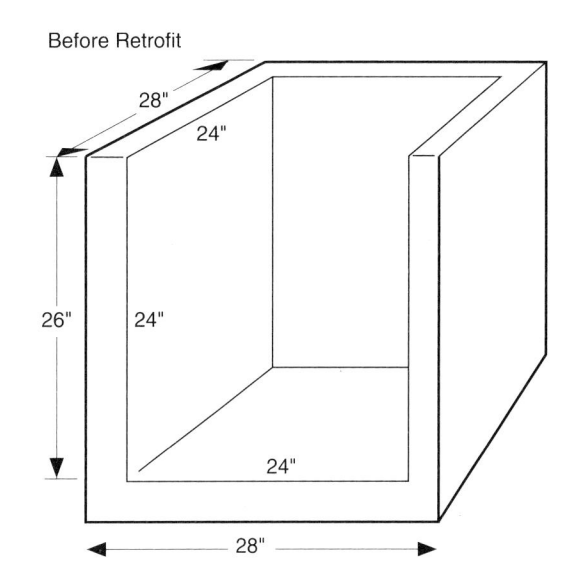

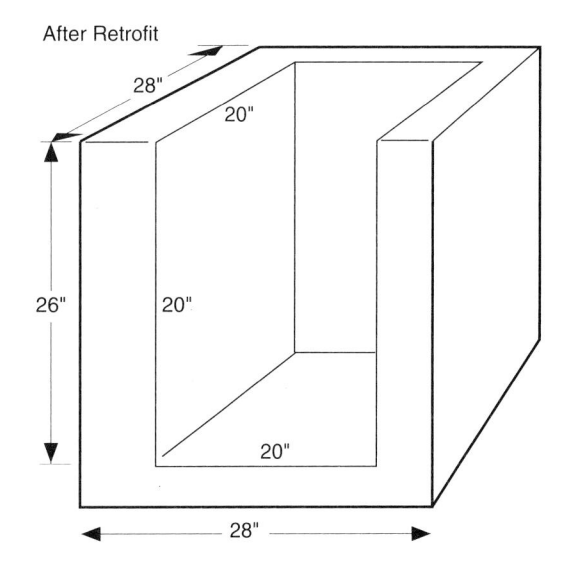

ALTERNATE ENERGIES

Figure 10.5 shows the relationship between COP and condenser temperature for a typical small refrigerator, assuming the evaporator is at 20°F.

Figure 10.5 COP versus Temperature

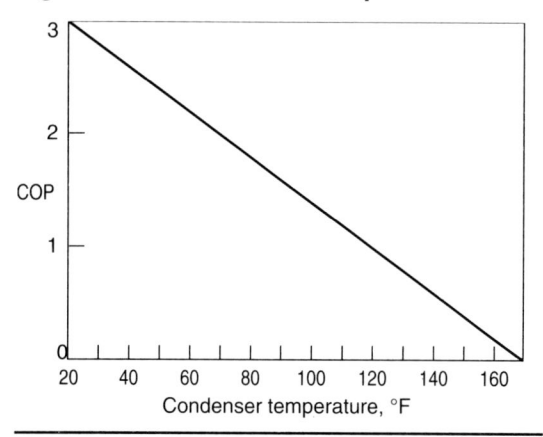

The temperature of the condenser depends on its type and location. Table 10.1 shows typical condenser operating temperatures and resulting COPs for different condenser types and locations in the boat.

Table 10.1. Refrigerator COP versus Location

Condenser/Location	Condenser Temp., °F	COP
Air-cooled in 110°F engine compartment with no fan	140	0.6
Air-cooled in 110°F engine compartment with fan	120	1.0
Air-cooled in 75°F free air with no fan	105	1.3
Air-cooled in 75°F free air with fan	85	1.7
Water-cooled, intake water 60°F	70	2.0
Water-cooled, intake water 75°F	85	1.7

Assume the condenser is located in free air at 75°F but has no fan. According to Table 10.1, its COP will be about 1.3. Our example refrigerator will then draw about 81.7 BTU/hr x 0.586 ÷ 1.3 = 36.8 Ah/day for conductive heat loss alone. If we add another third, (13.2 Ah/day) for combined infiltration and cool-down loads, the total refrigerator electrical load becomes 50 Ah/day.

A Typical Refrigerator Retrofit
To reduce the refrigeration load we can take three steps:

    1. Increase wall insulation

    2. Increase condenser COP with a fan on the condenser

    3. Decrease infiltration with a better lid gasket and a drain trap.

WALL INSULATION
At the cost of 1.4 cubic feet of interior space, we can double the insulation of all surfaces and double their R-value to R-24. Because we also have decreased the heat loss area (measured at the midpoint of the insulation), conductive heat loss is decreased to 29.5 BTU/hour.

CONDENSER COP
By installing a thermostatically controlled 12-volt-DC fan to move air through the condenser coils, we increase the condenser COP from about 1.3 to 1.7 at the cost of about 2 Ah per day of fan power.

INFILTRATION
By installing a better lid gasket and a better melt-water drain trap, we might decrease the losses due to air leaks by 50%.

With all of the above improvements, our refrigeration load drops by more than 50% to 21.9 Ah/day.

Conservation for Liveaboards

OTHER SAVINGS
Cabin Fans

The most efficient way to cool a hot cabin is with a cloth wind chute attached to a hatch, but its use requires that there be a breeze and that the boat be free to swing into it.

On hot, still nights, small fans directed at your body can make the difference between sleeping and not. The typical 6-inch cabin fan draws about 1 amp, but the most efficient fan draws only 0.3 amp. In 8 hours the accumulated difference is more than 5 Ah per fan.

Electronics

It's difficult to identify the power consumption of auto AM/FM cassette players because the label lists the maximum power consumption when they are playing full blast. Ask an auto sound shop to measure the draw with an ammeter when the unit is playing at normal volume into speakers similar to your own. Better yet, purchase low-wattage speakers at the same time.

Color television sets consume twice as much power as their black and white counterparts, and wattage is roughly proportional to the area of the screen (diameter squared). I promised energy conservation with no degradation of lifestyle, so we'll drop the black and white set from consideration.

Typical power consumptions for color television sets are: 19-inch—80 watts, 10-inch—36 watts, 6-inch—20 watts. From the largest to the smallest set there is a 60-watt, or 5-amp, difference. If you are an average five hour-per-day boob-tube watcher, the difference over five hours is greater than the drain of the anchor light.

VCRs are becoming very popular on boats. In fact, trading video tapes is nearly as common as trading paperback books. The typical 120-volt-AC remote/record/play video cassette recorder draws about 30 watts. Portable 12-volt-DC play-only models draw 10 watts.

THE BOTTOM LINE

Table 10.2 shows, as promised, how the daily power consumption of a typical cruising boat can be reduced by half with no significant degradation of lifestyle.

So what are you waiting for?

ALTERNATE ENERGIES

Table 10.2 Power Consumption of a Typical versus an Efficient Liveaboard Boat

Area	Device	Watts	÷ 12 = Amps	Ave. Hours per Day	Typical Amp-Hour	Efficient Amp-Hour
Galley	Microwave (9 minutes/day)	550	45.8	0.15	6.9	6.9
	Toaster (5 minutes/day)	800	66.7	0.04		
	Blender (30 seconds/day)	175	14.6	0.01	0.1	0.1
	Coffee grinder (15 seconds/day)	160	13.3	0.01		
	Refrigerator—2-inch insulation	60	5.0	10.00	50.0	
	—4-inch insulation	60	5.0	5.00		21.9
Head	Hair dryer (2 minutes /day)	1,200	100.00	0.03		
Lighting	Reading —2 incandescent, 15-watt	30	2.5	2.00	5.0	
	—2 halogen spots, 5-watt	10	0.8	2.00		1.6
	Galley —2 incandescent, 25-watt	50	4.2	2.00	8.4	
	—2 fluorescent, 8-watt	16	1.4	2.00		2.8
	Anchor — manual,10-watt	10	0.8	14.00	11.2	
	—automatic,10-watt	10	0.8	11.00		8.8
Fans	Typical 6-inch, 100 cfm	12	1.0	5.00	5.0	
	Most efficient, 100 cfm	4	0.3	5.00		1.5
Electronics	Stereo—20 watts/channel	60	5.0	1.00	5.0	
	—7 watts/channel	35	3.0	1.00		3.0
	Television— 19-inch color	80	6.7	4.00		
	—10-inch color	36	3.0	2.00	6.0	
	—6-inch color	20	1.7	2.00		3.4
	VCR— 120-volt-AC	28	2.3	1.00	2.3	
	—12-volt- DC play-only	10	0.8	1.00		0.8
				Totals	100.0	50.8

11 SOLAR POWER

Is Solar for You?   232

Commercially Available Panels   233

How Photovoltaic Panels Work   234

Interpreting Specifications   235

Panel Orientation   236

Estimating Average Daily Output   241

Mechanical Installation   241

Electrical Installation   243

Rules for a Successful Solar Installation   244

Is solar for you? Would the power produced by solar panels pay back their cost?

There is quite a collection of *commercially-available panels*. To *interpret specifications* we first need to understand *how photovoltaic panels work*. We also need to consider *panel orientation* before we can *estimate average daily output*.

Once the decision has been made, *mechanical installation* is quite simple. *Electrical installation* integrates the panels into the existing 12-volt-DC alternator/battery system.

Following the *rules for a successful solar installation* virtually guarantees your solar satisfaction.

IS SOLAR FOR YOU?

A solar, or photovoltaic, installation is a one-time investment with a fuel- and maintenance-free lifetime of ten years or longer. Whether a photovoltaic system would prove cost effective on your boat, depends on how much you use the boat. If you live aboard and are away from the dock at least half the time, the answer is a definite "yes." If you cruise one month each summer, the answer is probably "no."

Figure 11.1 shows the percentage of daily electrical load supplied by photovoltaic panels among 71 liveaboard cruisers surveyed in Florida and the Bahamas. The average installation was far smaller than optimum, yet the average percentage of power supplied was a significant 40 percent. Had the array sizes been optimum, I am sure the power supplied would have been in the 80 to 100 percent range.

Also note from Figure 11.1 that cruisers who had both solar and wind systems garnered over 90% of their power from the combination. Those having wind power, but no solar, generated 60% from the wind.

Figure 10.1 compared the costs per kilowatt-hour of electricity produced by photovoltaic panels, wind machines, and engine-driven alternators. The photovoltaic cost of $0.53/kilowatt-hour assumed:

- System used year-round
- Panel size—50 watts peak output
- Price including controls—$500
- Life—10 years
- Average daily sunshine—5.2 hours
- Maintenance—$0

Figure 11.1 Solar Energy Production among Cruisers

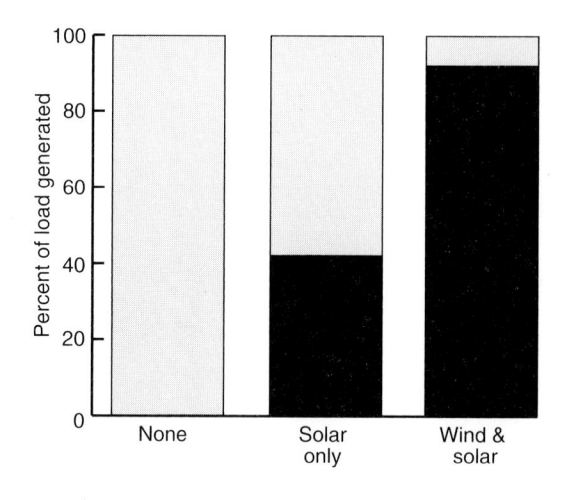

Such a panel would produce on average 5.2 hours x 50 watts = 0.26 kilowatt-hours per day, or 95 kilowatt-hours per year. An alternative source of power would be a high-output, 110-amp alternator, charging batteries on a 50 to 90 percent-of-charge cycle. This, according to Figure 10.1, would produce power at a cost of $2.53 per kilowatt-hour.

Compared to the cost of alternator power, solar savings would be $2.53 – $0.53 = $2.00 per kilowatt-hour. At 95 kilowatt-hours per year, annual savings would be $190, and the photovoltaic system would pay for itself in 500 ÷ 190 = 2.6 years. That is the same as receiving a tax-free return on investment of 38 percent. Just try to match that at your local bank!

On the other hand, if the boat were used but one month out of the year, the payback would be 31 years and the interest on the investment only 3.2 percent.

ALTERNATE ENERGIES

HOW PHOTOVOLTAIC PANELS WORK

Figure 11.2 shows how a photovoltaic panel works. Solar energy in the form of photons penetrates the photovoltaic material. Each photon transfers enough energy to the photovoltaic atoms to release an electron. If we connect the grid on the sun-lit side to the conducting base on the backside, the free electrons will flow through the external conductor and load to rejoin atoms with missing electrons.

Each free electron has a potential of about 0.6 volt. A panel typically consists of from 30 to 36 cells, connected in series to produce an open-circuit voltage of from 18 to 22-volts DC.

Photovoltaic collector materials take three common forms: single-crystal silicon, polycrystalline silicon and amorphous silicon. Crystalline silicon is grown as large crystals, which are sliced into thin wafers to form the cells. Single-crystal cells consist of single, large crystals; polycrystalline cells consist of multiple smaller crystals. The conversion efficiency of both forms of crystalline silicon averages about 13 percent and does not decrease noticeably with age. Most crystalline photovoltaic panels are warranted for ten years, but there is no reason, barring physical damage, that they would not last 30 years or longer.

Amorphous silicon is produced by the less expensive process of depositing vaporized silicon onto a glass or metal substrate. In addition to being less expensive to produce, amorphous silicon can be fabricated into flexible panels, which can be stepped on and attached to boat canvas. Unfortunately, amorphous silicon is only half as efficient (six percent) as crystalline silicon (13 percent), so twice as much col-

Figure 11.2 How Photovoltaics Work

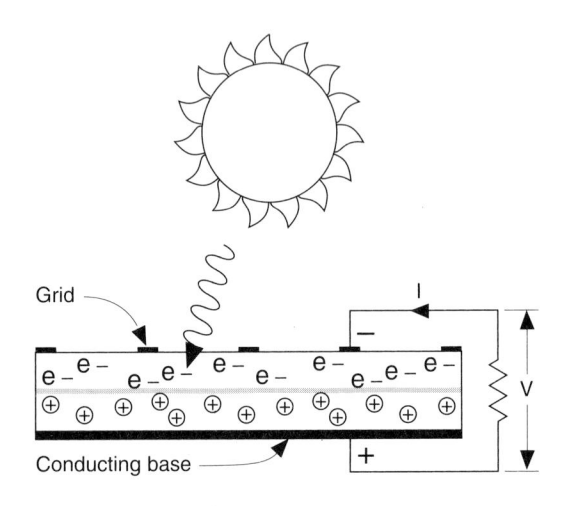

lector area is required for the same output. Since boats have limited suitable areas for solar collection, the more efficient crystalline-silicon collectors are preferred in most cases.

Figure 11.3 Photovoltaic Panel Output Curve and Specifications

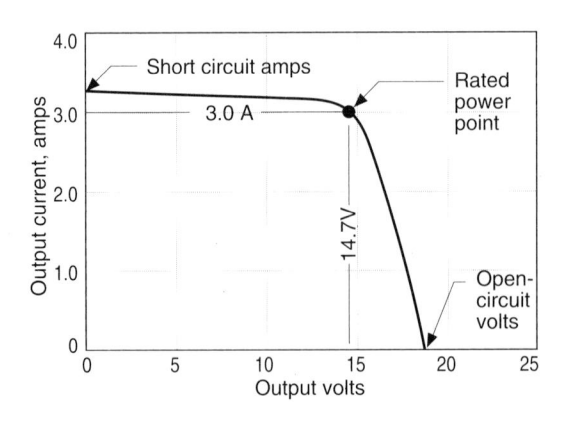

Solar Power

INTERPRETING SPECIFICATIONS

Figure 11.3 shows the voltage-current curve for a typical 30-cell photovoltaic panel in full sunlight. ("Full sunlight" is defined by government test procedure specifications as roughly equivalent to the strength of the noon sun directly overhead at sea level.) With its output terminals shorted, the panel puts out its *short-circuit current* (3.3 amps for the panel shown). With its output terminals not connected, current is zero, but output voltage is its maximum *open-circuit voltage* (18.0 volts for this panel). Maximum power is achieved at the knee of the curve where the *rated current* (3.0 amp) times the *rated voltage* (14.7 volts) equals the *rated power* (44 watts).

Figure 11.4 shows how output voltage-current curves vary both with number of cells and with panel temperature. Panel specifications are given for a panel (not air) operating temperature of 25°C (86°F). Both output voltage and current decrease at higher temperatures. For this reason, panels should be mounted with free air flow beneath to minimize operating temperature. Panels that will spend a high percentage of time in the tropics should have higher voltage ratings as well.

The effect of shading is not shown in manufacturers' voltage-current curves. A typical shadow on the panel will not effect open-circuit voltage, but will reduce power under load at least in proportion to the percentage of shaded area.

Finally, unless built in, you should install a Schottky blocking diode to prevent reverse-current flow from the batteries at night. Better yet, install a regulator that opens the circuit whenever the panel voltage is less than the battery voltage.

Figure 11.4 Photovoltaic Output versus Number of Cells and Temperature

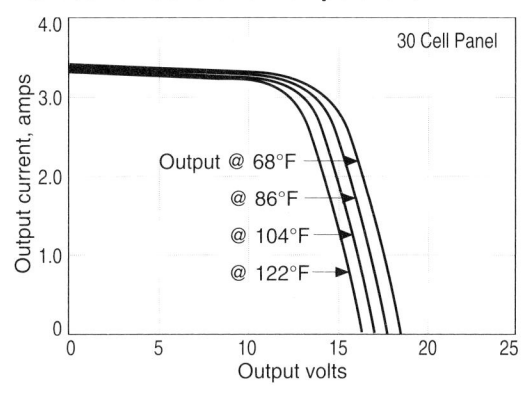

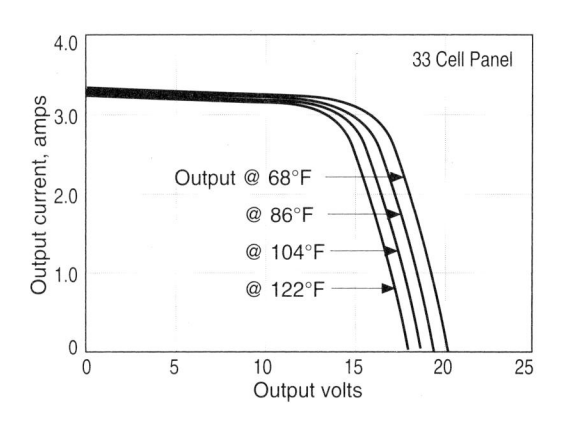

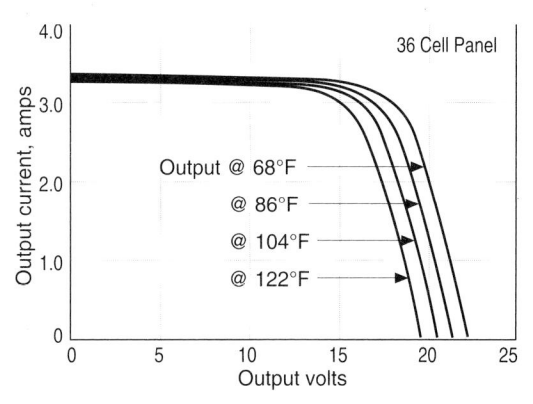

The most common mistake in selecting solar panels is failure to account for all of the voltage drops in real applications. Be sure to select a panel whose rated voltage *at your expected operating temperature* is at least 14.8 volts, since 14.8 volts − 0.4 volt (blocking diode drop) = 14.4 volts, the voltage required for fully charging lead-acid batteries. To equalize the batteries, the blocking diode can be temporarily shorted with clip leads.

PANEL ORIENTATION

To understand how panel orientation affects the output of a photovoltaic system, we must consider how the sun moves through the sky, both through the day and with the seasons.

Figure 11.5 shows the track of the sun over a boat located at latitude 24°N (Southern Florida) at the spring and fall equinoxes (March 21 and September 21), and the summer and winter solstices (June 21 and December 21). On June 21, the sun reaches its highest noon elevation, 90°. On December 21, the sun reaches its lowest noon elevation, 43°. Further, the sun is above the horizon approximately 16 hours in June but only eight hours in December. We would, therefore, expect a lot less solar input in December than in June.

Figure 11.5 Track of the Sun through the Day and the Seasons

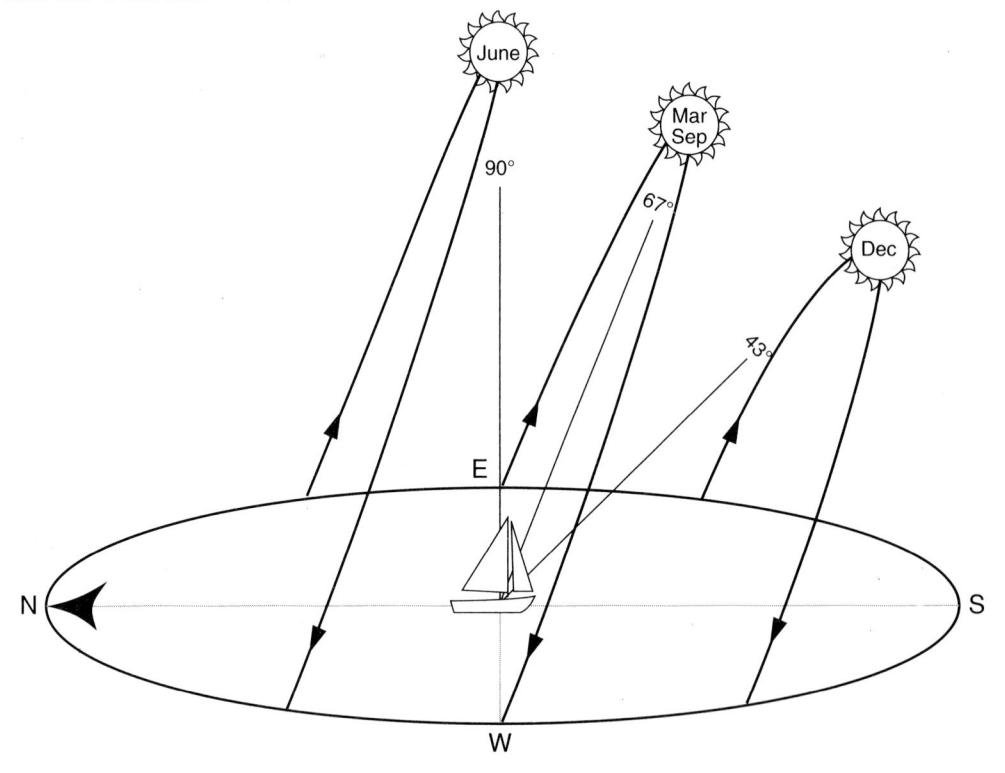

Solar Power

Panel output ratings assume full sunlight with the sun's rays normal (perpendicular) to the panel surface. Panels in large utility "solar farms" are mounted on frames that continuously track the sun's orbit for maximum output.

What can we do about orientation on a boat? You're obviously not going to install a tracking mechanism, and most people would get tired of adjusting panel orientation three or four times a day. So the question is: what fixed tilt is best?

Figure 11.6 Radiation on Horizontal and Tilted Surfaces

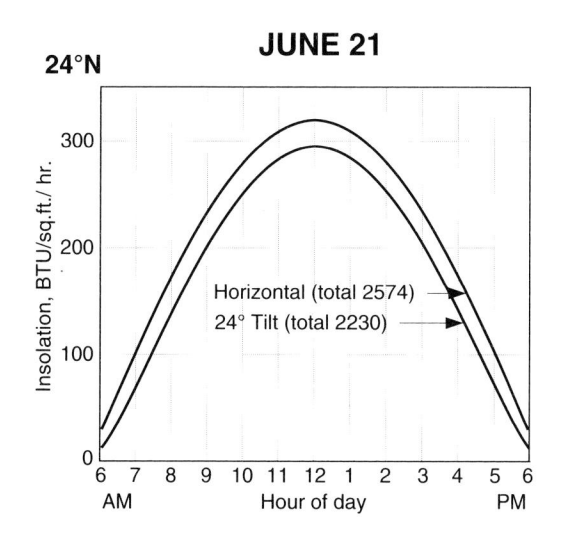

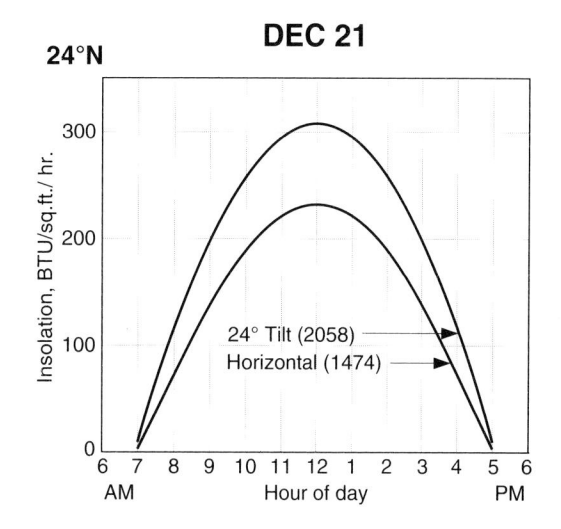

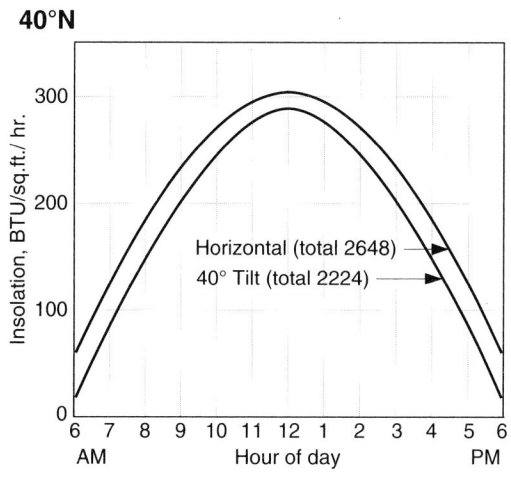

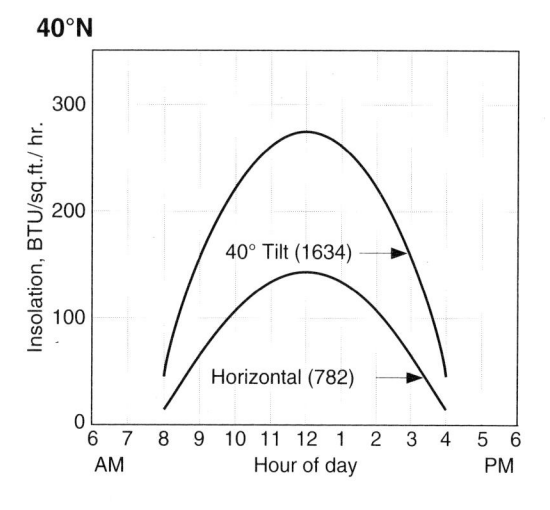

JUNE 21

24°N
- Horizontal (total 2574)
- 24° Tilt (total 2230)

40°N
- Horizontal (total 2648)
- 40° Tilt (total 2224)

DEC 21

24°N
- 24° Tilt (2058)
- Horizontal (1474)

40°N
- 40° Tilt (1634)
- Horizontal (782)

ALTERNATE ENERGIES

Figure 11.6 (previous page) compares the solar radiation on a horizontal surface (tilt = 0°) and surfaces tilted to the south at the latitude angle, for latitudes 24°N (Miami) and 40°N (New York), on both the longest (June 21) and shortest (December 21) days. On June 21, if we are both smart and mobile, we will be at, or around, latitude 40°N. Figure 11.6 shows that a horizontal panel will collect 119 percent of the radiation collected by a fixed panel tilted south at 40 degrees.

Figure 11.7 Radiation on Horizontal and Vertical Surfaces

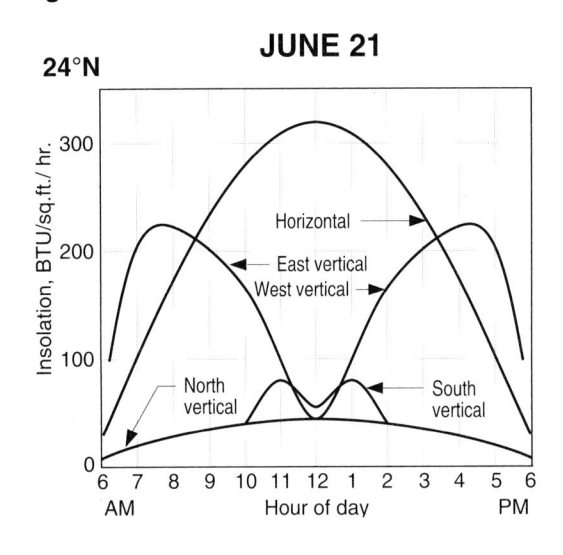

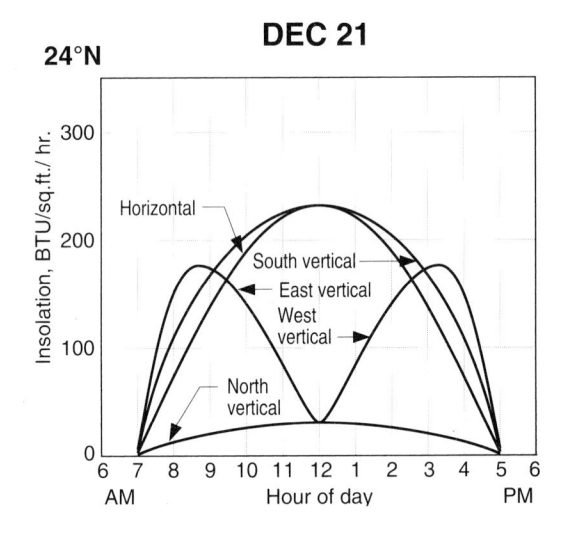

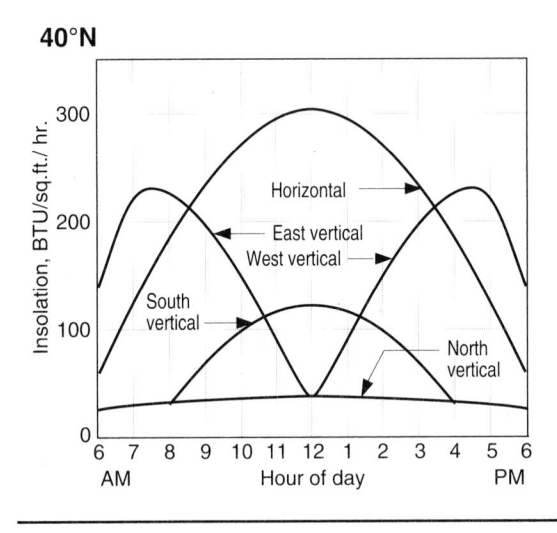

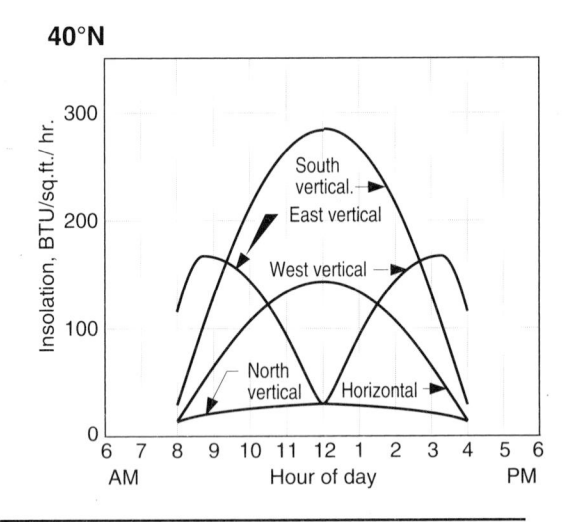

Solar Power

On December 21 we hope to be in the neighborhood of Miami, where our horizontal panel will collect 78 percent as much radiation as a fixed panel tilted south at 24 degrees.

Conclusion: over the year a horizontal panel will perform as well as a fixed, south-tilted panel.

"But," you say, "if I were at a dock, I could tilt my panels toward the noon sun." But if you were at a dock, you wouldn't need photovoltaic panels.

Further, if you were on a mooring or anchor, your boat would swing with little or no correlation to the position of the sun. Any fixed orientation you selected might be perfectly right at one moment but perfectly wrong an hour later. There is only one orientation that doesn't change as the boat swings—horizontal, or facing straight overhead.

To show the effect of compass direction, Figure 11.7 on the previous page compares the solar radiation on horizontal (facing straight up) panels and vertical panels facing north, east, south and west. Although vertical east and west panels collect significant amounts of radiation in morning and afternoon, both collect for only half a day, so their total collection is small. Again, fixed north, east, south or west orientation is impossible on a boat that swings.

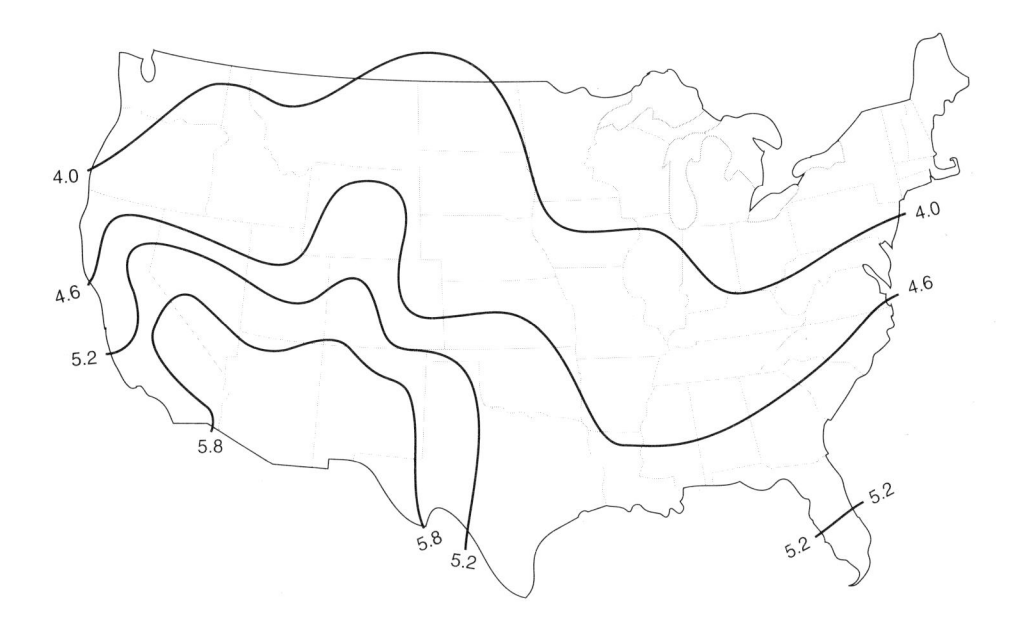

Figure 11.8 Annual Average of Daily Radiation on a Horizontal Surface

ALTERNATE ENERGIES

Figure 11.9 December Average of Daily Radiation on a Horizontal Surface

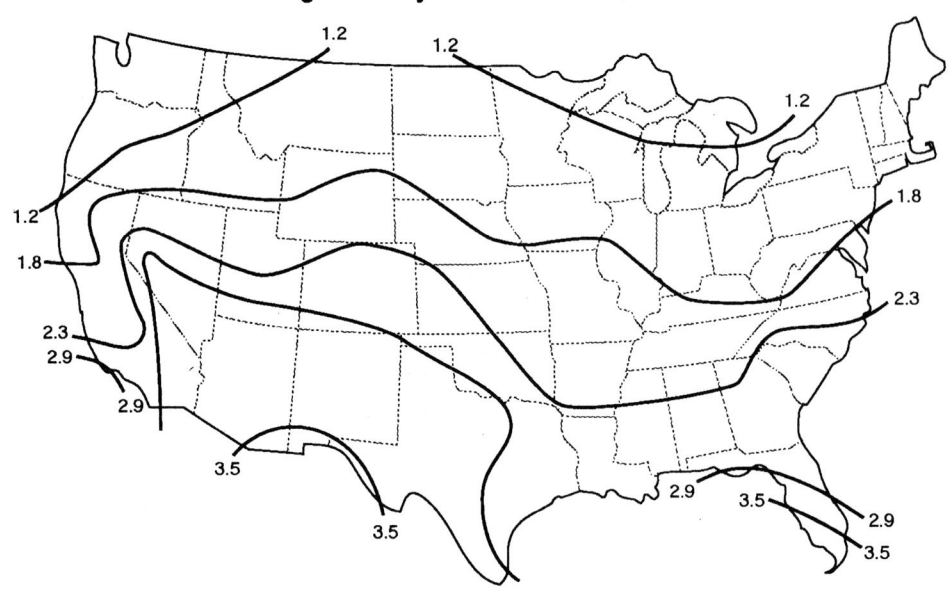

Figure 11.10 June Average of Daily Radiation on a Horizontal Surface

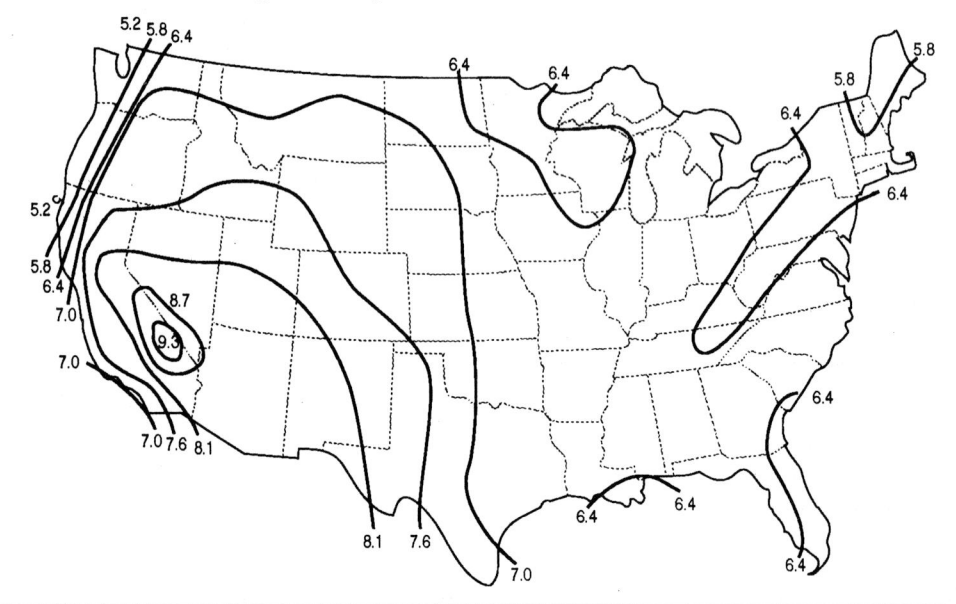

Solar Power

ESTIMATING AVERAGE DAILY OUTPUT

Because the fixed horizontal orientation is the most practical, solar-availability maps most often show total radiation received on a horizontal surface. Figures 11.8 to 11.10 show the average daily solar radiation falling on horizontal surfaces in units of hours of full, direct sunlight. Such maps allow estimation of solar panel performance.

Average daily output is simply the rated panel output in watts times the number of hours of sunlight shown on the map. For example, on an annual basis in Miami, we can expect a 44-watt panel to produce an average of 44 watts X 5.2 hours = 229 watt-hours per day. Over the entire year, we would expect 365 x 229 watt-hours = 83.5 kilowatt-hours.

I have included Figures 11.9 and 11.10 for those who cruise only in the summer or only in the winter. To calculate seasonal kilowatt-hours, multiply the figure from the appropriate map by the number of days you are on the boat.

We can also use the figures in the maps to calculate the daily average of Ah added to our batteries. Our example 44-watt panel had a rated current of 3.0 amps, so, on an annual basis, 3.0 amps x 5.2 hours = 15.6 Ah per day.

In Chapter 10, we retrofitted a boat to reduce its electrical load to 50.8 Ah per day. A solar array consisting of three 44-watt panels could be expected to provide an average of 3 x 15.6 Ah/day =- 46.8 Ah/day, or about 90 percent of the load. With a net-average deficit of only 5 to 10 Ah per day, the average cruiser would rarely have to use his engine for the sole purpose of charging the batteries.

MECHANICAL INSTALLATION
Fastening

Solar panels are extremely lightweight and strong. Their extruded aluminum frames make mechanical fastening a snap. Multiple panels can be fastened together loosely using stainless machine screws, lock-nuts and rubber grommets as shown in Figure 11.11 top. The assembly of panels can then be fastened to the stainless or aluminum frame of a dodger or bimini, as shown in Figure 11.11 bottom.

Alternately, each panel can be fastened individually, or multiple panels can be fastened within a frame, and the frame fastened to the deck like any other deck hardware.

Figure 11.11 Clamping Solar Panels to Bimini or Dodger Frame

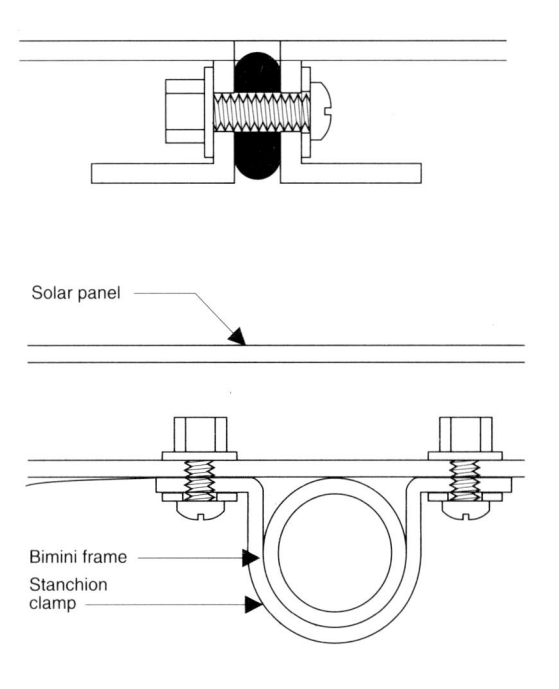

Solar panel

Bimini frame
Stanchion clamp

ALTERNATE ENERGIES

Panel Location

The critical part of panel installation is choosing the location. Figure 11.12 shows five locations for a system of four panels.

Location A is my least favorite spot. It is shaded by both mast and boom, is in the way during mainsail operations, and is a target for objects dropped from the mast.

Location B is a better location than A because it is out of the way and farther from the drop zone. To avoid shading, the boom can be held to the side using a preventer.

Location C is often seen because solar suppliers offer the mounting hardware and because it allows tilting of the panels. I rejected it because I didn't want the hassle of constant tilt adjustment, and because the panels extend beyond the rail, where they are subject to damage during docking.

Location D, on top of a permanent bimini frame, is the one I use and is my favorite. It is out of the way and free from shade. I've now had three 51-watt panels fastened to my bimini for four years. The panels are so inconspicuous that most people don't realize they are there.

The set of three panels is fastened to the stainless frame with two of the U-clamps shown in Figure 11.11. I've removed the panels twice in anticipation of hurricanes. Removal and storage below requires about ten minutes. Once I was caught with panels up in a tornado-spawning squall on Chesapeake Bay. Because the panels are horizontal, they offer little wind resistance and survived the squall's 70-knot winds with no damage.

Location E, in a horizontal frame fastened to dinghy davits, is as good as Location D. It is shade-free, out of the way, and very secure.

Figure 11.12 Solar Panel Locations

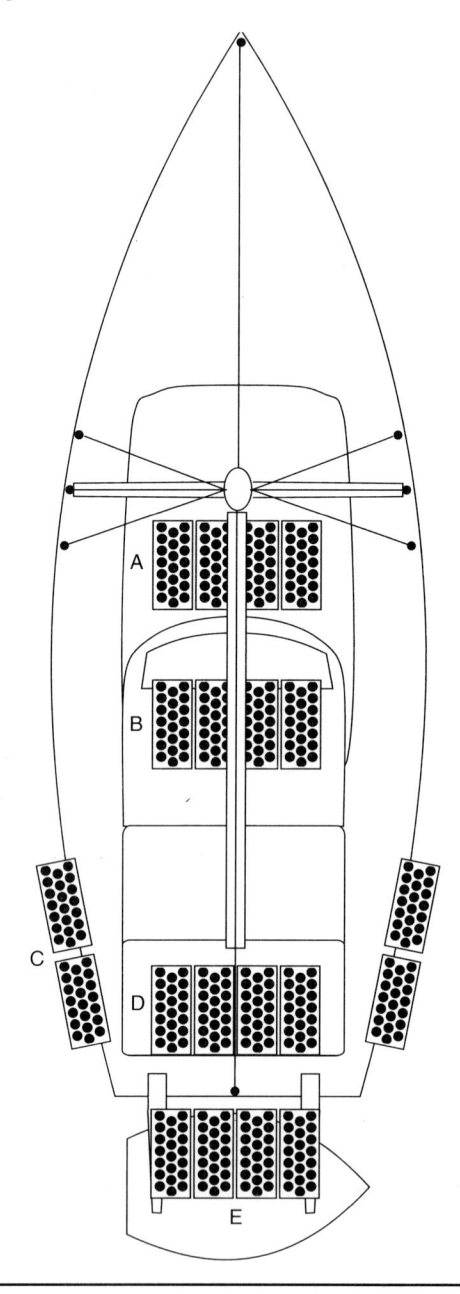

Solar Power

ELECTRICAL INSTALLATION

Figure 11.13 shows a typical proper photovoltaic installation. The important elements are:

1. *Fuse or circuit breaker.* The positive leads from all charging sources except the alternator should be over-current protected by fuse or circuit breaker, as close to the battery as possible. The reason is that unprotected leads might short, melting the conductor insulation, damaging the batteries, and possibly starting a fire.

2. *Blocking diode.* There should be blocking diodes between the battery and panel positive terminals to prevent reverse flow at night (unless the charge controller opens the circuit when panel voltage is too low). The diodes should connect to the battery side of any isolation diodes from the alternator to avoid adding the diode's voltage drops.

3. *Charge controller.* Unless the total panel-rated current is less than 0.5 percent of total battery capacity (2 amps for a 400-Ah battery bank),

Figure 11.13 Proper Photovoltaic Installation

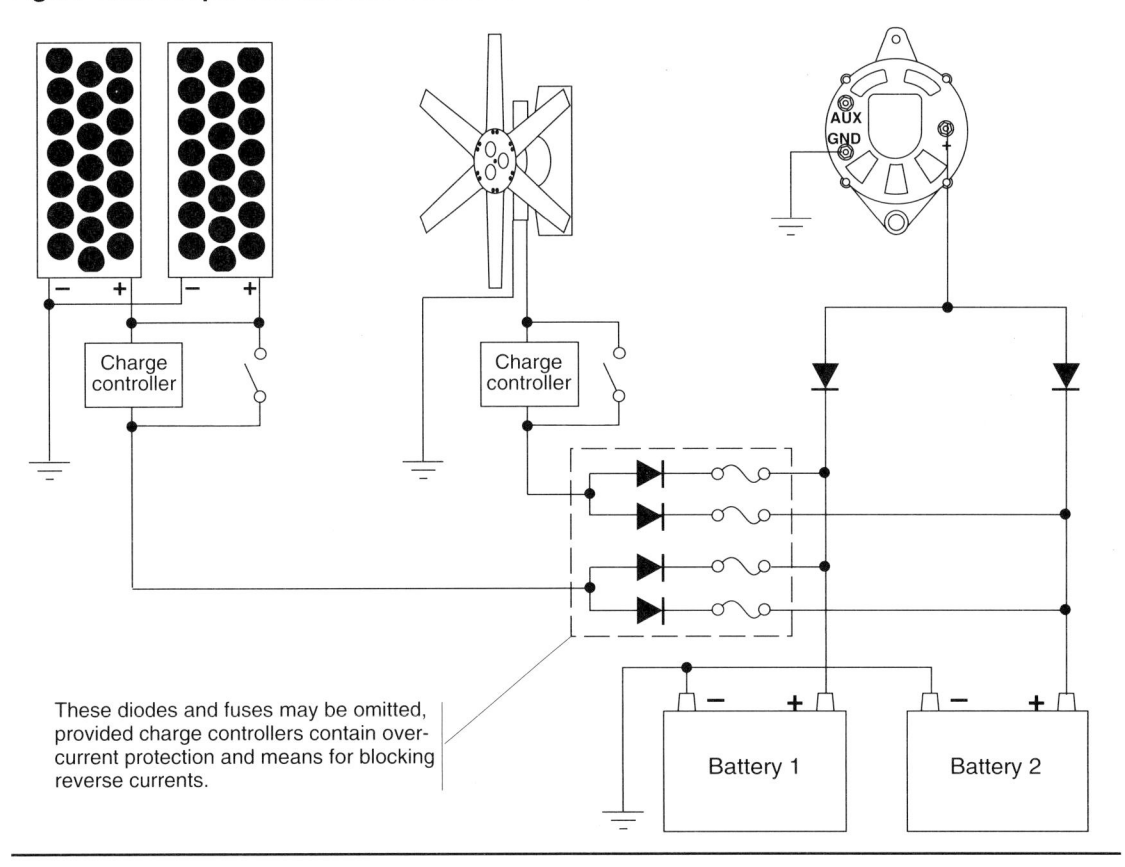

These diodes and fuses may be omitted, provided charge controllers contain over-current protection and means for blocking reverse currents.

a charge controller is required to prevent overcharging of the batteries. A switch should be provided to bypass the controller, however, so that a battery equalization charge can be applied occasionally. If panel voltage is marginal, you might install a switch to temporarily bypass the blocking diodes as well.

The simplest way to satisfy all three requirements is to purchase a charge controller that contains all three features. The best controllers allow full-current up to about 14.4 volts, then taper to a floating charge. Some controllers automatically switch excess panel output to a resistance load, such as a 12-volt-DC water-heater element.

Naturally, all DC wiring standards, such as conductor ampacity, stranding, insulation and fastening, apply as well to solar installations.

RULES FOR A SUCCESSFUL SOLAR INSTALLATION

If you want a photovoltaic system to supply all or nearly all of your electrical energy needs, you must obey the following rules:

1. Reduce your average daily electrical consumption to 60 Ah or less. See Chapter 10 for suggestions.

2. Install sufficient panel area. Use Figures 11.8 to 11.10 to calculate the required panel wattage for the areas you plan to cruise.

3. Install the panels in a permanent, horizontal, shade-free location.

4. Do not depend on tilting of the panels, removing shading objects or controlling boat orientation to increase panel output.

5. Select panels with sufficient rated voltage to overcome the voltage drops due to blocking diodes (if present), operating temperature, and anticipated shading.

6. Install a charge controller that does not require blocking diodes.

7. Make solid, corrosion-free electrical connections and protect with corrosion inhibitor.

8. Clean the panel surfaces of dust and salt spray regularly.

12 WIND AND WATER POWER

Is Wind Power for You? 246

Economics 246

Getting Power from the Wind 247

How Much Wind is There? 251

Estimating Average Daily Output 252

Specifications 253

Mechanical Installation 254

Electrical Installation 257

Water Generators 258

If not solar power, then *is wind power for you*? Again, calculating the *economics* will tell.

Getting power from the wind explains how the kinetic energy of moving air can be converted to electrical energy.

In order to estimate the *average daily output* of a wind machine, we need to know *how much wind* there is where we will be cruising and the *specifications* of our wind machine.

The most difficult part of *mechanical installation* is simply selecting the best location on the boat. As in the case of solar panels, the *electrical installation* of a wind machine requires integration with the existing alternator/battery system.

Many popular wind machines can be converted into *water generators*—a feature long-distance cruisers may wish to consider.

ALTERNATE ENERGIES

IS WIND POWER FOR YOU?

The variables determining the viability of wind power on a boat are more complicated than those for photovoltaics, but the general criteria remain the same—if you live aboard and are away from the dock at least six months out of the year, the answer is *yes*; if you use your boat only one month per year, the answer is *no*.

Before delving into the economics of wind power production, you should note several non-economic factors that are unique to wind:

    1. *Maintenance*—wind machines are essentially electric motors running backward. All have bearings and most have brushes. Ask the manufacturer how often each must be replaced.

    2. *Noise*—all wind machines make sounds, ranging from the barely-perceptible whisper of a small, 6-bladed Ampair, to the "woof, woof, woof" of a large, 2-bladed, mizzen-mounted machine.

    3. *Safety*—some large-diameter machines must be shut down in winds in excess of 30 knots to prevent burnout or damage to the blades. Look for a machine having automatic speed control or shutdown, since stopping blades in a high wind is dangerous.

ECONOMICS

Figure 12.1 shows the percentage of daily electrical load supplied by wind among 71 liveaboard boats surveyed in Florida and the Bahamas. Most of the wind machines were of the large (60-inch blade diameter) variety. The fact that 40% of the average daily load still had to be supplied by running the engine shows that wind is not constant. Decreasing the daily load through conservation (see Chapter 10) and increasing battery capacity could increase the wind contribution to 80% or more.

An interesting alternative is the combination of wind and solar which, as shown in Figure 12.1, supplied an average of 96% of the daily load.

Figure 12.1 Wind Power Production on Cruising Boats

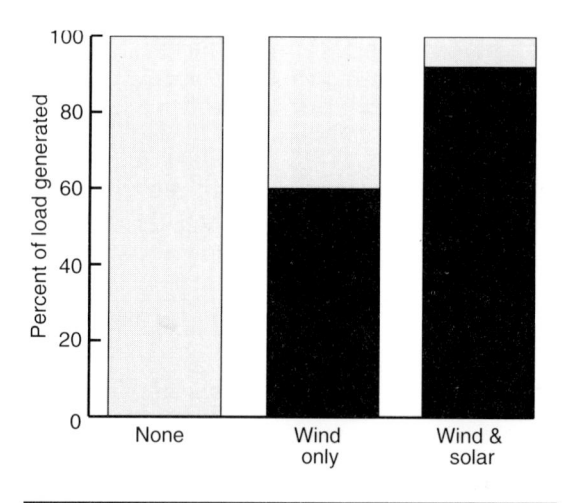

Figure 10.1 compared the costs of power generated by wind, solar, and alternators of various sizes. The $0.44/kilowatt-hour cost of wind power assumed:

- Wind machine lifetime—10 years
- Installed cost—$1,500
- Annual maintenance—$25
- Blade diameter—60 inches
- Conversion efficiency—30 percent
- Average wind speed—10 knots

Wind and Water Power

Such a wind machine would produce 45.6 watts, or 400 kilowatt-hours per year in a steady 10-knot wind. One of the conventional alternatives, also shown in Figure 10.1, is a 110-amp engine alternator charging the batteries on a 50 to 90% cycle at a cost of $2.53 per kilowatt-hour.

The example wind machine savings would thus be $2.53 − $0.44 = $2.09 per kilowatt-hour, or $836 per year. The wind machine would pay for itself in less than two years. Of course, if the wind machine were used only one month per year, the savings would fall to $70 per year, and the payback period would increase to over 20 years.

GETTING POWER FROM THE WIND

The electrical power that a wind machine can extract from the wind is:

$$P = K \times E \times D^2 \times V^3$$

where: P = power in watts

K = 0.0653

E = mechanical efficiency in %

D = blade diameter in meters

V = wind speed in knots

Example: Calculate the power output of a wind machine having a blade diameter of five feet (1.52 meters) and efficiency of 30% in a steady 10-knot wind.

$$P = 0.0653 \times 0.30 \times 1.52^2 \times 10^3$$
$$= 45 \text{ watts}$$

The equation highlights the important factors in selecting and sizing a wind machine to satisfy a boat's electrical demand:

Efficiency, E, can never be 100%. If it were, the blades would extract 100% of the kinetic energy of the wind, bringing the wind to a complete halt. Aeronautical theoreticians have proved that the maximum possible efficiency of a wind machine is 59.3%. Because there are losses in the generating coils, rotor bearings, and transmission gearing, the average efficiency of commercial wind machines is around 30%.

Diameter, D, enters the equation squared. Doubling blade diameter thus quadruples power output. Machines with small blades produce less noise at the cost of greatly reduced output. Most popular wind machines have blade diameters of either one meter (36 inches) or five feet (1.52 meters). Squaring the ratio of diameters shows that the theoretical maximum output of the one-meter machines is only 43% that of the five-foot machines.

Wind Speed, V, is the most important factor of all because it enters the equation cubed. The difference between eight knots and 10 knots is barely noticeable when sailing, but theoretically results in a 100% difference in the output of a wind machine. Every attempt must, therefore, be made to use true average wind speed when making the purchase decision.

Figure 12.2 plots wind machine output, in amps versus knots of wind speed. The two theoretical curves (dashed) assume efficiencies of 30% and output at 14 volts.

The curves for the commercially available machines were drawn to fit data points in the manufacturers' literature. The three 5-foot machines (Fourwinds II, Neptune Supreme and Wind Baron NEO) loosely conform to the theoretical curve with two exceptions:

ALTERNATE ENERGIES

Figure 12.2 Theoretical and Claimed Output of Wind Machines

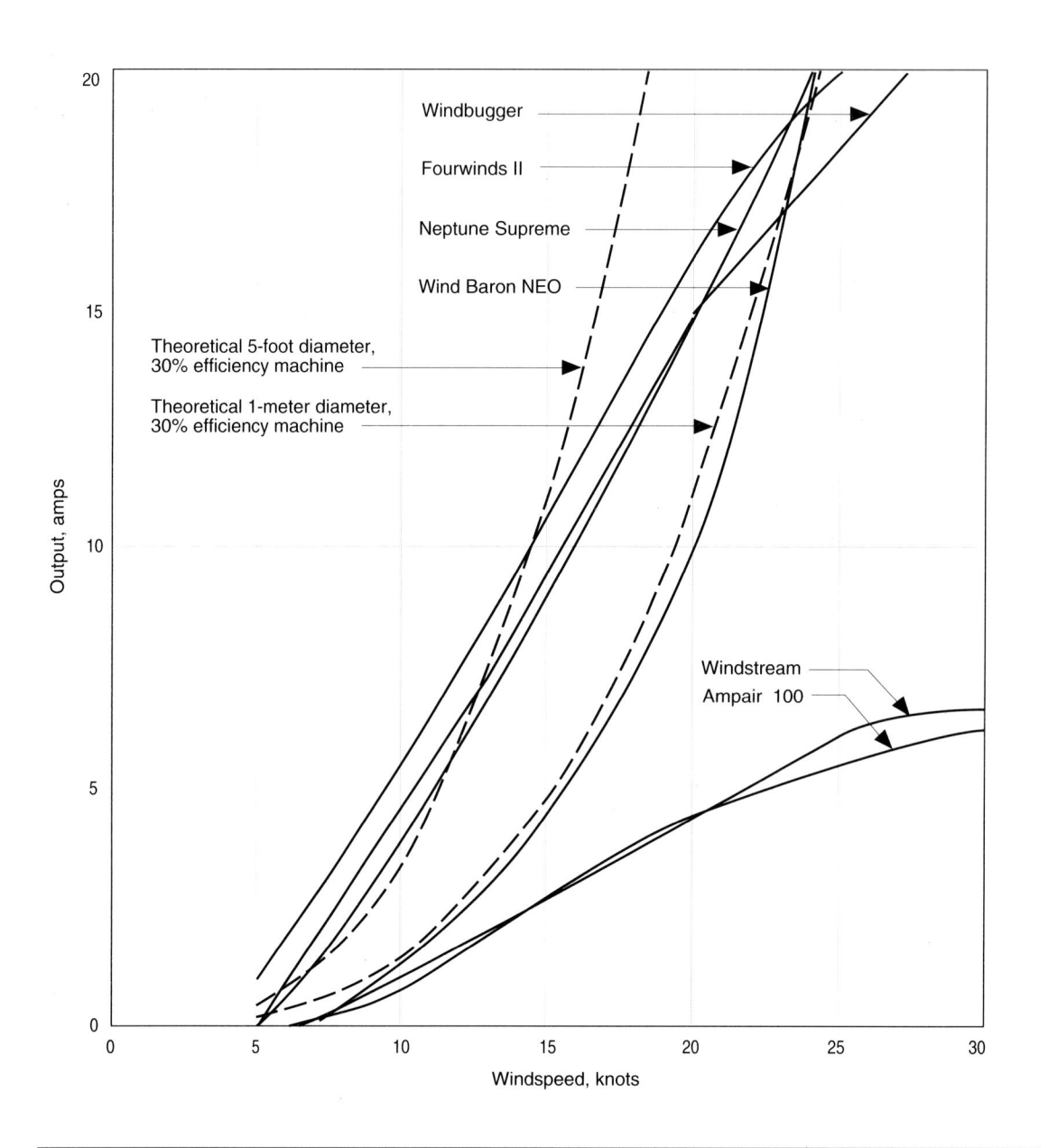

Wind and Water Power

1. All claim more than 30% efficiency at 5 to 10 knots. The Fourwinds claims nearly 50% at 10 knots.

2. All fall off the V^3 curve at high wind speeds, due to self-limiting.

The Windbugger, with a 54-inch blade diameter, competed well with the slightly larger machines.

The only output curve that conformed to the theoretical V^3 form was that of the Wind Baron NEO. Since the graph from which the data was obtained was labeled "projected power curve," you should confirm actual output before purchasing.

The two smaller machines, Windstream and Ampair 100, demonstrate the same characteristics but proportional to their smaller squared diameters.

You would be wise to question the output figures claimed by the wind machine manufacturers. The important specification is *continuous rated output*, not *maximum output*. I have attempted to obtain and list such figures in Table 8.1. Verify output figures before putting down money.

Since average wind speeds are rarely above 15 knots, claimed outputs at wind speeds in excess of 15 knots are not very important in the choice of a wind machine. My further advice is to use the theoretical formula and the 30% efficiency curves in predicting output, rather than the manufacturers' claims.

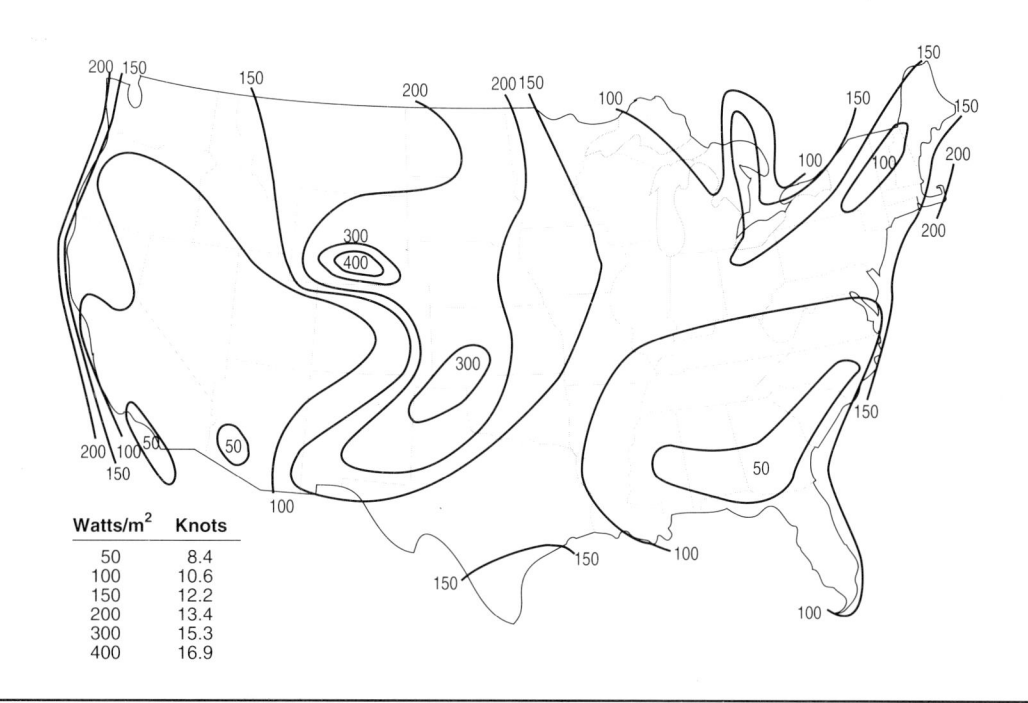

Figure 12.3 Annual Average Power in the Wind, Watts per Square Meter

Watts/m²	Knots
50	8.4
100	10.6
150	12.2
200	13.4
300	15.3
400	16.9

Figure 12.4 Winter Average Power in the Wind, Watts per Square Meter

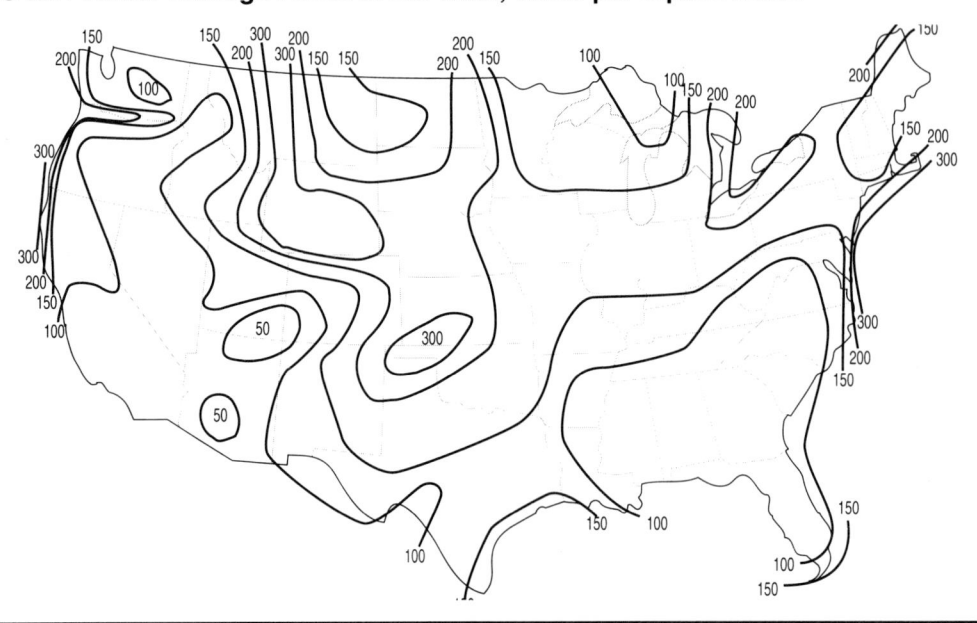

Figure 12.5 Summer Average Power in the Wind, Watts per Square Meter

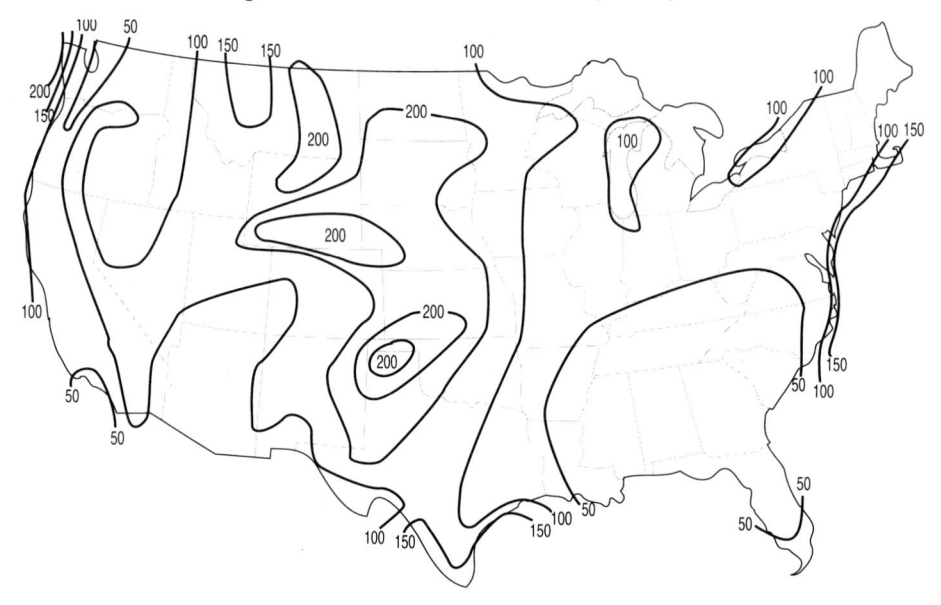

Wind and Water Power

HOW MUCH WIND IS THERE?

When you want the wind to blow, it always seems to drop to nothing. On the other hand, when you are crossing the ocean, it seems to blow a gale half of the time. Since power output depends on wind speed cubed, wind is the most important variable.

Figures 12.3 through 12.5 show average wind power, in units of watts per square meter, computed from hundreds of exposed locations across the U.S. The figures shown are the power contained in the wind and must be multiplied by wind machine efficiency to predict electrical output. Figure 12.3 also lists the equivalent wind speeds in knots.

What is striking about the maps is the low average wind speeds. While we all know of places where the wind blows much harder, you would be well advised to ignore such places. In reality, it is human nature to seek anchorages that offer protection from the wind. Considering the fact that most boaters seek shelter when on the hook, the wind speeds shown on the map may, in reality, be a little too high.

The wind speeds shown in the figures were observed in exposed locations, such as airports, and at an average height above ground of about 30 feet. Figure 12.6 shows how wind speed and power are likely to vary with actual height in both open-water and harbor locations.

Over open water a wind machine at a height of 10 feet will be exposed to 90% of the 30-foot wind speed and produce about 72% as much power. In a protected harbor, the same ten-foot height will result in about 80% of the 30-foot wind speed and 50% of the 30-foot power.

Figure 12.6 Variation of Windspeed with Height over Terrain

Over Open Water

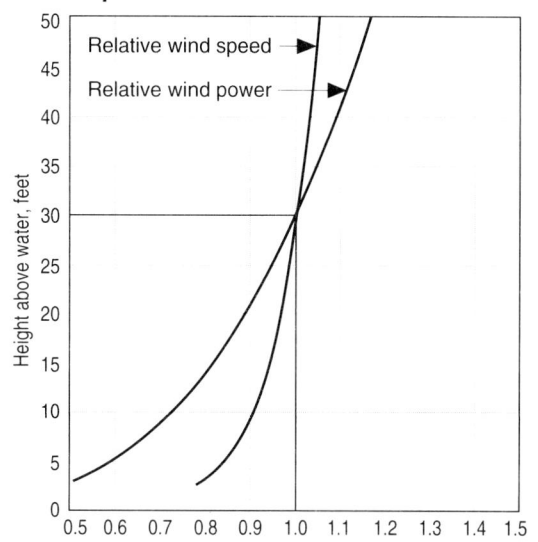

Harbor With Trees and Boats

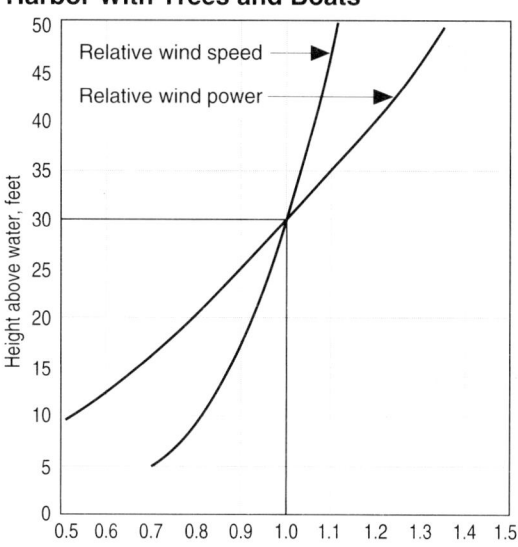

ALTERNATE ENERGIES

ESTIMATING AVERAGE DAILY OUTPUT

Selecting the right-size wind machine for your boat is not quite the same as designing a solar system. While we have a variety of solar panel sizes to select from, there are really only two sizes of wind machine—1-meter, and 5-foot. So selecting a wind machine comes down to deciding whether one of the two available sizes is worth the investment.

Start by determining your average daily load in Ah, just as in Chapter 11. Next, determine the available power in the wind for the areas you plan to cruise, using either the annual map (Figure 12.3) or the seasonal maps (Figures 12.4 and 12.5).

Calculating the expected average electrical power from a wind machine is then a simple matter of plugging the numbers into the equations below.

$$\text{Watts} = \pi \times D^2 \times E \times P \div 4$$

where:

$\pi = 3.14$

D = blade diameter in meters

E = wind machine efficiency in %

P = annual wind power in W/m^2

Assuming E = 30%:

Watts = 0.24 D^2 x P

kWhr/yr = 2.10 D^2 x P

Ah/day = 0.44 D^2 x P

Example: How much average power can you expect from a wind machine of 5-foot (1.52 m) blade diameter, 30% efficiency, and 12-foot mounting height on a boat located in protected harbors in New England in the summer and the Florida Keys in the winter?

Answer: The New England coast in summer and the Florida Keys in winter both have average wind power of about 100 watts per meter^2 at 30-foot height. Assuming harbor locations, at 12-foot height (Figure 12.6) the available power is 60% of the power at 30 feet. Therefore,

Watts = 0.24 D^2 x P
= 0.24 x 1.52^2 x 0.6 x 100
= 33 watts

kWhr/yr = 2.10 D^2 x P
= 2.10 x 1.52^2 x 0.6 x 100
= 292 kilowatt-hours

Ah/day = 0.44 D^2 x P
= 0.44 x 1.52^2 x 0.6 x 100
= 61 Ah

This wind machine would be well matched to the load of the energy-efficient boat discussed in Chapter 10.

Note that the output of this wind machine could be increased by either of two steps:

1. Changing to a 30-foot mizzen mount would theoretically increase output by a factor of 100% ÷ 60% = 1.67.

2. With the same 12-foot mount, anchoring in unprotected locations would theoretically increase output by a factor of 75% ÷ 60% = 1.25.

Example: For the same conditions as in the previous example, how much power would a 1-meter wind machine produce?

Answer: The ratio of blade diameters is 1m ÷ 1.52m = 0.66. The ratio of outputs is the ratio of diameters, squared, or 0.43. Outputs are, therefore, 14 watts, 126 kilowatt-hours per year and 26 Ah per day.

Wind and Water Power 253

Table 12.1 Wind Machine Specifications

Specification	Four-winds	Neptune Supreme	Wind Baron	Wind-bugger	Ampair 100	Wind-stream
Blade diameter	60"	60"	60"	54"	36"	41"
Number of blades	2	2	2	2 & 3	6	2
Weight, pounds	22	25	20	38	28	20
Voltage	14.35[1]	12–16	14.8	16.0	14.0	13.8
Adjustable?	Y	N	Y	N	N	N
Regulated?	Y	Option	Y	N	Y	Y
Amps at 15 knots	10	10	5	9	3	3
Amps continuous	20	20	15	?	8	8
Brushes?	Y	Y	N	Y	N	Y
Slip rings?	Y	N	Y	Y	Y	Y
Shutdown required?	Y[2] (25 Kn)	Y (25 kn)	N	Y (35 kn)	N	N
For information	(305)968-7358	(508)881-4602	(602)526-6400	(305)451-4495	(203)961-8133	(802)658-1098

[1] Voltage is factory-set at 14.35 volts for wet-acid batteries and 14.15 for gelled-electrolyte batteries.
[2] Shutdown is automatic with optional airbrake, which is guaranteed to 50 knots steady wind.

SPECIFICATIONS

Table 12.1 lists the specifications for the wind machines included in figure 12.2. As the manufacturers say, "specifications subject to change without notice," so call the numbers listed to get the latest information before making your purchase.

Blade Diameter. As already discussed, power output varies with diameter squared, so a large diameter is necessary for large output. On the other hand, weight, noise, and potential danger all increase with diameter as well.

Number of Blades. Theoretically, the efficiency of a wind machine is unrelated to the number of blades. A two-bladed machine can be as efficient as a six-bladed machine. However, noise level decreases with increased number of blades, and blade diameter. The six-bladed Ampair 100 is the quietest machine of all, and the three-bladed Windbugger is quieter than the otherwise identical two-bladed version.

Weight. Weight is a two-edged sword. Lighter weight makes the machine easier to handle—particularly in the case of a halyard mount. On the other hand, light weight may equate to a flimsier construction and smaller continuous-rated output.

Voltage. Some machines are regulated, much like an automobile alternator, to produce a constant voltage. If so, select a regulator which can be adjusted for your type of batteries. Gelled-electrolyte batteries can be ruined by charging at over 14.1 volts DC.

ALTERNATE ENERGIES

When a manufacturer claims his machine is "battery regulated," watch out! While the current acceptance rate of the battery does determine the voltage, once the battery is fully charged, the voltage can climb to 16 volts and cook the battery! Such machines must be monitored while charging and cannot be left unattended for long periods.

Amps at 15-knots. Again, watch out! This may be the output when the machine is cold, before self-regulation kicks in. Make sure the rating for maximum continuous output is at least as large as the claimed 15-knot output.

Brushes. If a machine is used continuously, it may require new brushes every year. If this sort of maintenance doesn't appeal to you, check with the manufacturer, or go with a brushless machine.

Slip rings. Slip rings pass current from a swiveling wind machine to the power cables leading to the battery. While slip rings also have brushes, the brushes are subject to less wear and don't require much attention. Without slip rings a fully-swivelling wind machine cannot make more than a few revolutions before fouling its output cable.

Rigidly-mounted machines don't swivel and thus don't require slip rings. In not swivelling, however, they miss a lot of wind. A ±180° swivel-mount has no slip rings but tracks the wind 99% of the time.

Shutdown. This is the most important safety factor. A machine that must be manually secured in high winds is at best inconvenient and at worst dangerous. Even if the machine has an automatic governor or brake, make sure the braking device is guaranteed to at least 50-knot winds. Otherwise, you are likely to have a broken or burned out machine within the year.

MECHANICAL INSTALLATION

Figure 12.6 shows a common large wind machine (the 5' Fourwinds) mounted in all of its possible configurations on a 35-foot ketch. Most wind machines can be mounted in several configurations with mounting accessories. Check with dealers for the possibilities.

Figure 12.7 shows one of the 1-meter machines, the Ampair-100, mounted in its three configurations on the same 35-foot boat. Both figures have been drawn to scale to give an idea of what the machines look like when installed.

Pole Mount

Of the three mounting options, the stern pole is the most common. The pole is usually of 2-inch schedule-40 or -80 pipe. Bracing is provided either by two lengths of rigid stainless tubing to the deck or by one rigid standoff to the backstay plus two guywires to the deck. Pole height should be such that the blade clears the head of the tallest crew, but can be secured without standing on a pulpit rail.

The advantages of the pole mount are that it is accessible from the deck and that it allows use while under sail. Disadvantages include smaller output due to low height, relatively high noise level, and potential danger to unwary crew.

Mizzen Mount

Mizzen mounts, for boats with a second mast, raise the wind machine for greater output and decreased danger. In spite of the height, if an unbalanced machine is mounted near the midpoint of the mast, noise levels may be even greater than those for the pole mount. Blade distance from the mast is also important in reducing noise levels. Note that Fourwinds offers four different mizzen mounts.

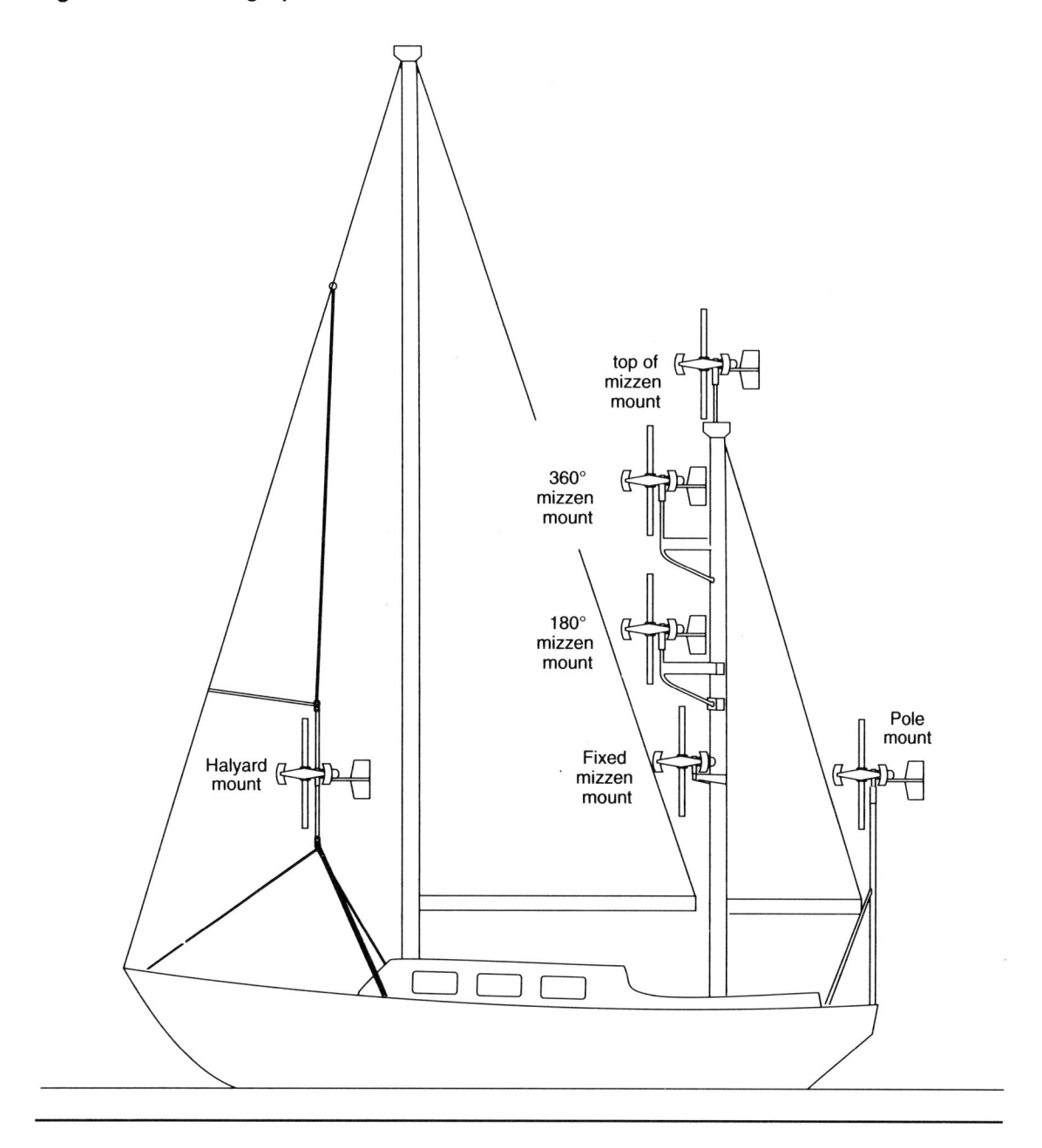

Wind and Water Power

Figure 12.6 Mounting Options for Wind Generators

ALTERNATE ENERGIES

Figure 12.7. Ampair 100 Mounting Options

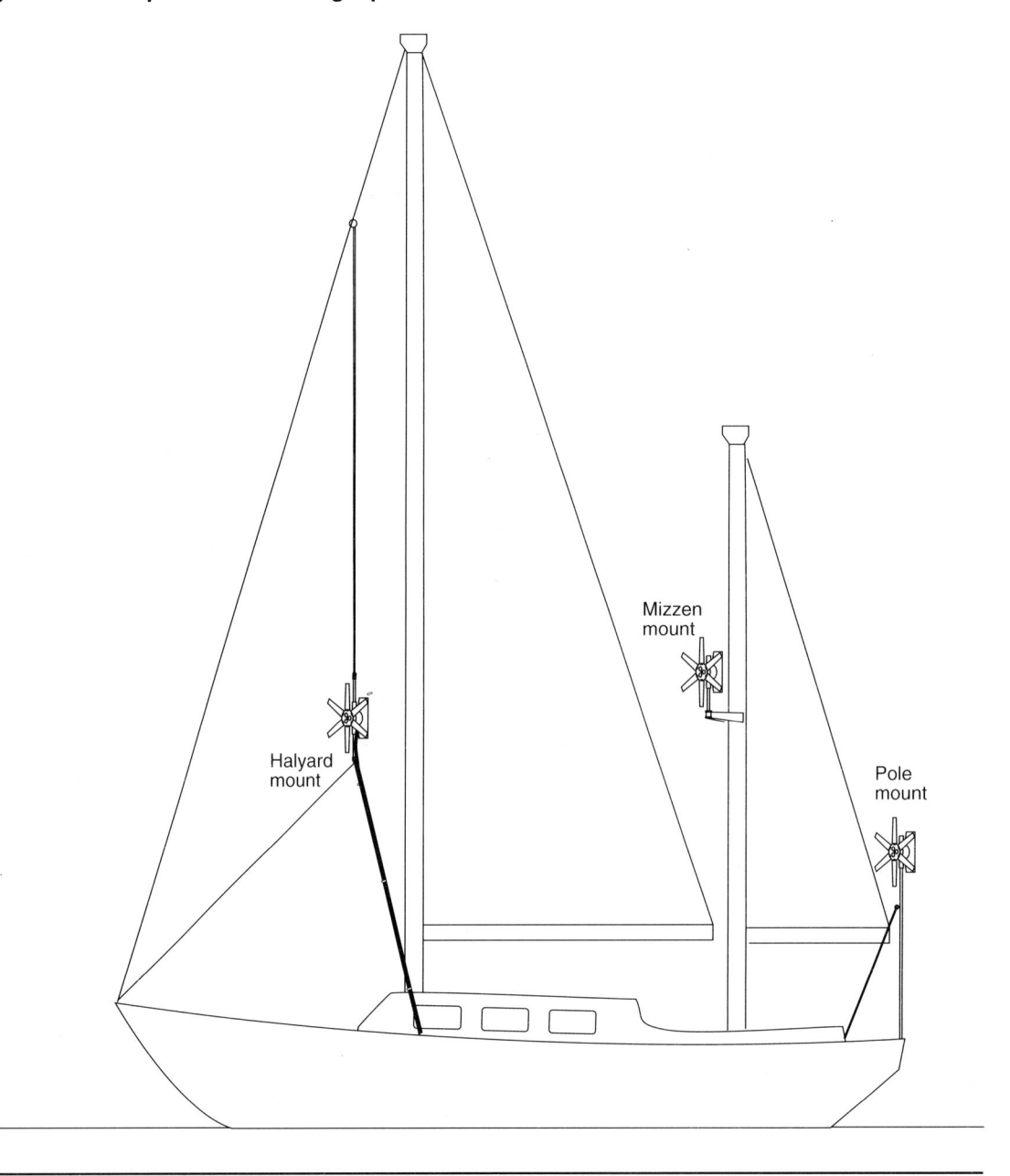

Wind and Water Power

Halyard Mount

While the ability to raise a wind machine to great height would seem to promise the highest output, least noise, and greatest safety, a halyard-mounted machine should not be raised beyond the reach of a person standing on deck. Shutdown or recovery of a halyard-mounted machine in a high wind can be exceedingly dangerous. In addition, the hassle of deployment, recovery, and storage at every anchoring makes them less popular.

In spite of these negatives, some owners swear by the halyard-mount, claiming deployment and recovery in less than three minutes, as well as lowest initial cost.

Large halyard-mount machines are always two-bladed because they are most conveniently stored in the V-berth and handled through a forward hatch.

ELECTRICAL INSTALLATION

Figure 12.8 shows a wind machine electrical installation. Voltage and current meters are not shown but are often supplied with wind machines. If they are, simply follow the manufacturer's directions for installation.

A solar system is also shown in the figure because wind and solar are often combined. The installation is designed so that the wind and solar systems are completely independent, though complementary. Deleting the solar system has no effect on the wind system hookup.

Elements of the installation include:

> **1.** *Fuses or circuit breakers.* Because a short circuit in one of the battery positive leads could lead to fire or explosion of the battery, all positive battery leads except those from the alternator are required to be over-current protected, as close to the battery terminals as possible.

> **2.** *Blocking Diodes.* Most wind machines are little more than DC motors. The blocking diodes prevent current from the batteries from spinning the wind machine backward in the absence of wind. The pair also act as isolation diodes, preventing the battery with greater charge from discharging into the battery with lesser charge. Note that the blocking diodes are installed downstream (down current) of the alternator isolating diodes so that the voltage drops are not additive.

> **3.** *Charge controller.* Unless the wind machine contains a voltage regulator, a charge controller should be inserted in the output to prevent overcharging of the batteries. The bypass switch shown is provided to allow periodic equalization of the batteries.

Some charge controllers dump excess current into heat-sinked transistors. Others divert current to an external load, such as a 12-volt water heater element. In any case make sure the controller can handle the *maximum* output current.

All of the DC-wiring standards and practices discussed in Chapter 6 apply to wind machine installations as well. Make sure the ampacity of the output conductors exceeds the wind machine's *maximum* output. Sizing the conductors for a 3% maximum voltage drop is not as important with wind machines as with solar panels, however, since the open-circuit voltage in winds over 10 knots is at least 20 volts and the voltage regulator is clamped at less than 15 volts. I'd use a 10% drop.

Figure 12.8. A Proper Wind Machine Installation

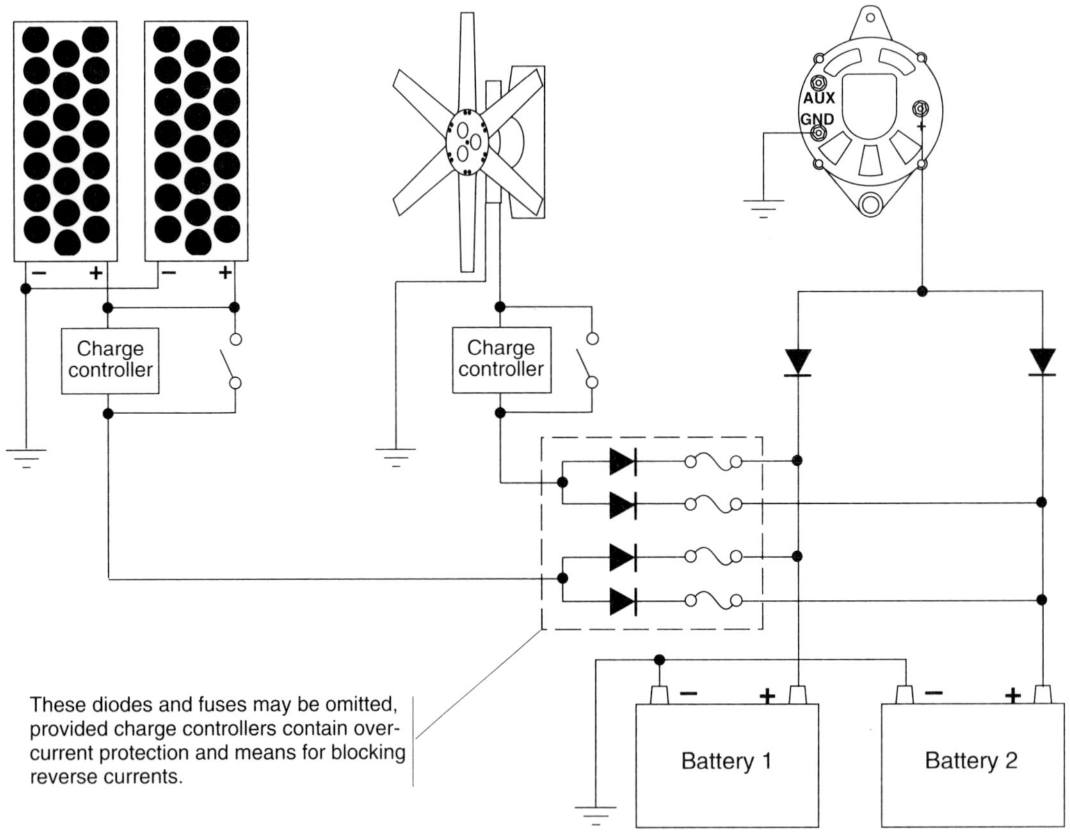
AUX
GND
Charge controller
Charge controller
These diodes and fuses may be omitted, provided charge controllers contain over-current protection and means for blocking reverse currents.
Battery 1
Battery 2

WATER GENERATORS

Three of the wind machines discussed above can be converted to water generators. Figure 12.9 shows the outputs of four water generators, versus water speed. All are sized to carry the electrical load of a typical cruising boat at less than hull speed. The drag typically slows a boat by a knot or less, and they are usually deployed only as needed to recharge the batteries.

They are popular with down-wind passage-makers who are already equipped with wind machines, since relative airspeed downwind is low, but water speed is high. Some water generators place the generator in the water. Others mount the generator on the stern rail and trail a line with the propeller. The former have the advantage of greater weight holding the propeller down at high speeds. The disadvantage, however, is the chance that a large fish will mistake it for a very expensive lunch.

The electrical installation remains the same for both wind and water operation.

Wind and Water Power

Figure 12.9. Water Generator Output versus Boat Speed

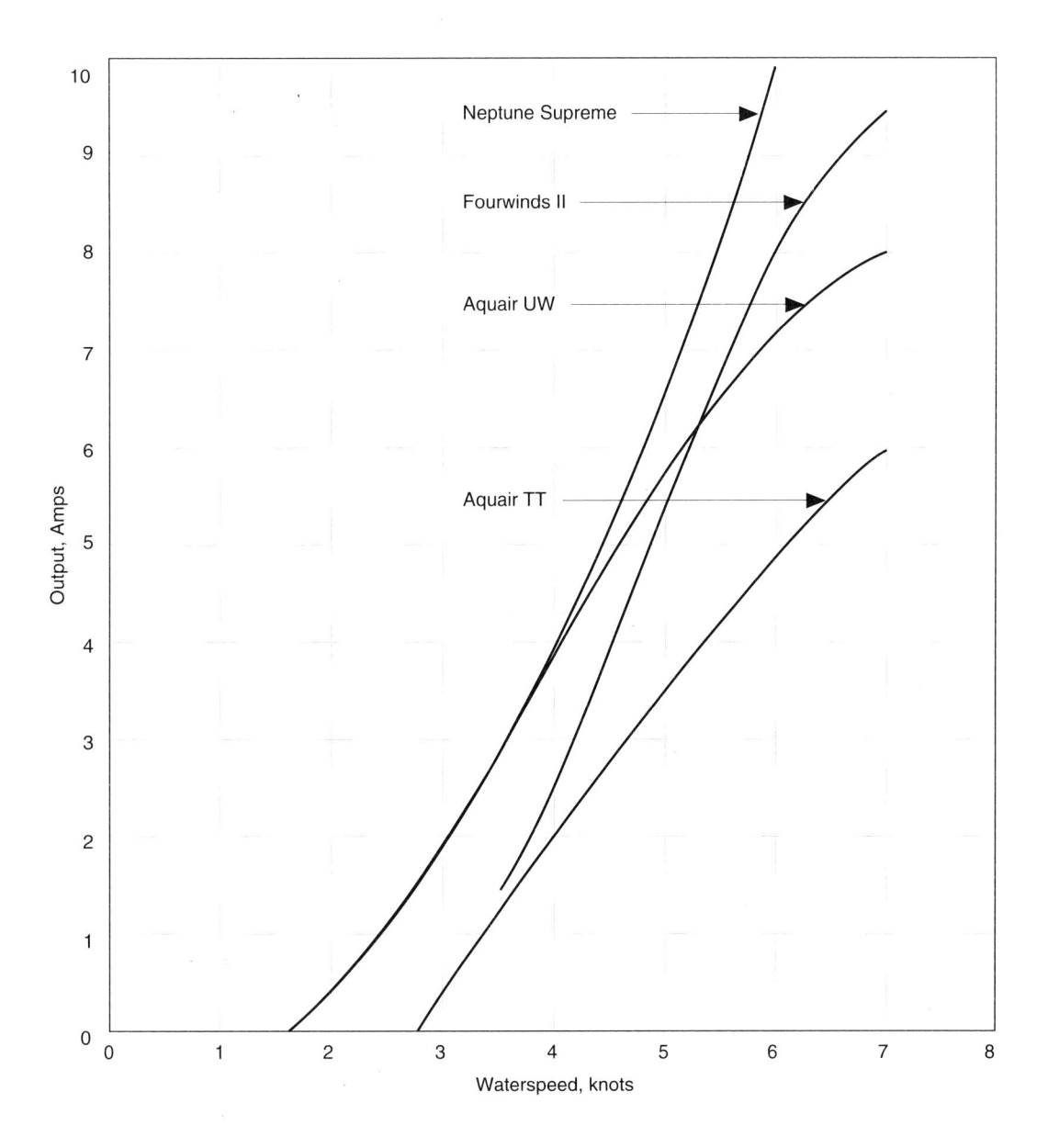

PART IV
PROJECTS

13 INSTALLING ELECTRONICS

Antennas 264

Receivers/Transmitters 273

Electrical Noise 274

If you can install a towel rack, you can install an electronic cabinet or case. But there is often more to a successful electronic installation than meets the eye.

This chapter focuses on communication and navigation electronics—that is, electronics that use antennas.

Antennas are intended to receive signals. The problem is they also receive electrical noise. *Receivers and transmitters* also pick up noise, most often through their incoming power leads.

Step-by-step procedures are given for first identifying the sources of *electrical noise*, and then for reducing the levels.

Few things are as satisfying aboard a boat as installing your own electronics. While the design and repair of today's digital electronic circuitry are beyond the abilities of most, installation is not.

The requirements are no more than an understanding of the *DC Wiring Standards and Practices* of Chapter 6, materials available through most chandleries and mail-order catalogs, and the principles outlined in this chapter.

With these in hand, you should be able to install any piece of marine electronic equipment within a weekend, and as well as any professional. The obvious benefits are a significant cost saving and satisfaction at accomplishing a professional job. The less obvious benefit occurs when something goes wrong, and you find that you are now able to retrace your steps and often locate the problem.

The equipment covered in this chapter includes VHF and SSB radios, loran, GPS and radar. From an installation standpoint, all marine electronics are similar. You'll find that the principles and techniques apply to stereos, televisions, depth sounders, and wind indicators, as well.

ANTENNAS
Types
You can find books on antenna design and specific antenna designs in electronics and ham radio magazines. My advice, however, is to start with the antenna recommended or supplied by the manufacturer of the equipment. Many antennas are designed to work only with the specific brand and model of equipment. After you have the equipment up and running, you may decide to experiment with a different antenna. The original antenna will then serve as a reference.

Location
Figure 13.1 shows a variety of antenna locations that will be referenced in the discussions of particular equipment types.

VHF and radar signals travel in straight lines, so their antennas should be mounted high.

GPS and satnav signals travel line-of-sight from outer space and, except for the requirement for a clear view of the sky, are independent of height.

SSB and ham signals arrive from space, having bounced one or more times off the ionosphere. While their antennas are independent of height, their great lengths (23 to 60 feet) often result in height.

Loran and omega signals are of very low frequency and long wavelength. As a result these "ground-wave" signals follow the surface of the earth, so antenna height is not important. Their great wavelengths are also immune to obstructions.

Radar, GPS, and satnav have wavelengths of the same order, or smaller than, objects on the boat. Large objects between the antenna and the source of the signal may block the signal in the same way that sunlight is blocked by a mast. Thus, an unobstructed view of the horizon may be important.

Finally, signals are absorbed by grounded rigging. Antennas placed too close to metal standing rigging may suffer loss of signal strength. The exception that proves the rule is the use of an insulated backstay as a long SSB or ham antenna. To avoid interference, antennas that are used to transmit as well as receive should be spaced from other antennas.

Installing Electronics

Figure 13.1 Antenna Locations

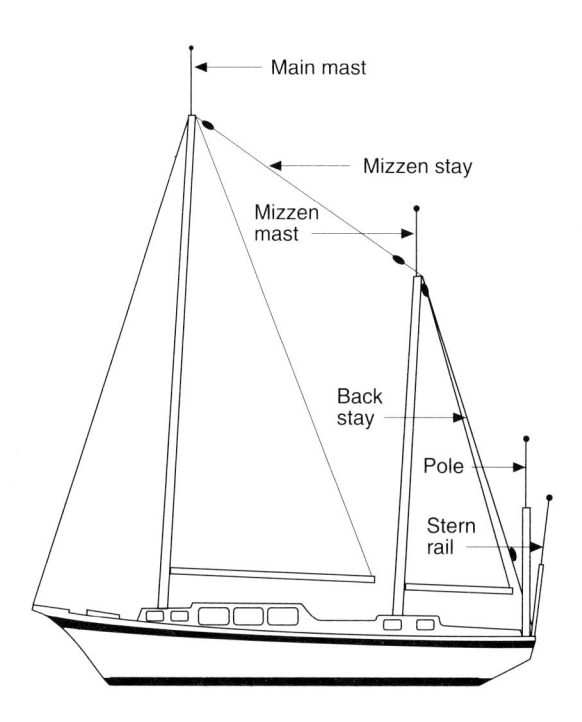

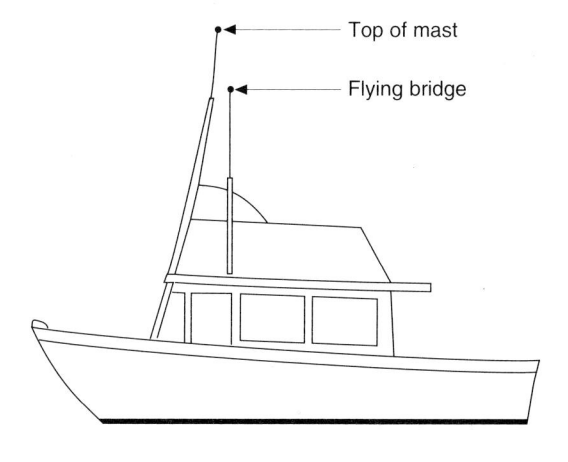

Antenna Cable

To minimize interference from shipboard noise generators, all antennas aboard a boat are, or should be, connected to their respective receivers with coaxial cable. Table 13.1 lists the most common coaxial cable types and their specifications.

Table 13.1 Coaxial Cables

Specification	RG58U	RG8X	RG8U	RG213
Nominal O.D.	3/16"	1/4"	13/32"	13/32"
Conductor AWG	#20	#16	#13	#13
Impedance	50	50	52	50
Attenuation per 100 Feet				
@ 50 MHz	3.3 db	2.5 db	1.3 db	1.3 db
@ 100 MHz	4.9 db	3.7 db	1.9 db	1.9 db
@ 1000 MHz	21.5 db	13.5 db	8.0 db	8.0 db

Conductor size (AWG) is important in transmitters where large currents may result in resistive loss of power in the cable.

Impedance should match the output impedance of the transmitter/receiver and the impedance of the antenna to maximize signal strengths.

Attenuation is the loss of transmitted power in the cable between transmitter and antenna. Each 3 decibels (db) of loss is equivalent to a reduction in power at the antenna of 50 percent.

Coax cables may have identical specifications, yet vary greatly in quality. Cables aboard boats are exposed to salt spray, sunlight, oil, and sometimes battery acid mist. Use only the highest quality cable, consisting of tinned center conductor and braid, solid polyethylene dielectric, and UV-resistant non-contaminating outer jacket.

PROJECTS

Figure 13.2 demonstrates the four-step process for the large diameter RG8U and RG213 cables. Although there are solderless versions of the PL-259 connector, they are not recommended in marine applications due to the moist environment and the likelihood of corrosion, which solder excludes. After assembly the connector and cable should be sealed with adhesive-lined, heat-shrink tubing, as shown in Figure 13.6, to exclude moisture.

Figure 13.3 shows the slightly more complex assembly with the smaller-diameter RG58U, RG59U, and RG8X cables.

Figure 13.2 Installation of Coaxial Connector on RG8U and RG213 Cable

STEP 1: Strip to center conductor back 3/4"

STEP 2: Strip outer jacket additional 5/16"

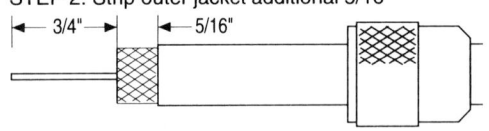

STEP 3: Slip on body; solder tip and shield through hole

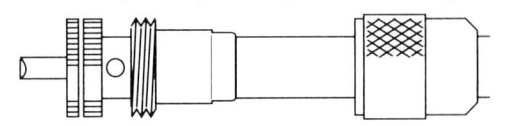

STEP 4: Screw shell onto body

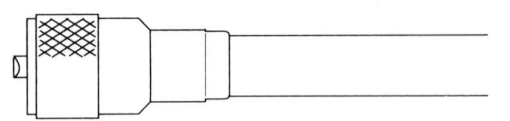

Figure 13.3 Installing Coaxial Connector on RG58U, RG59U and RG8X Cable

STEP 1: Slip on shell and adapter: strip outer jacket back 21/32"

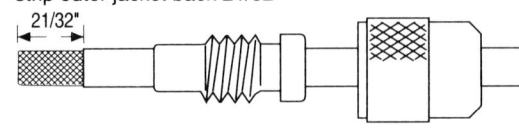

STEP 2: Bend back braided shield

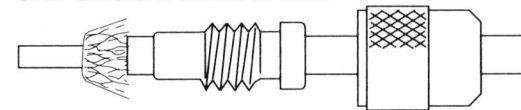

STEP 3: Slip adapter under braided shield

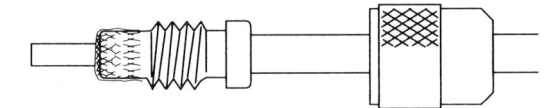

STEP 4: Strip center conductor 1/2" and tin

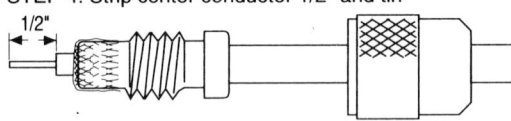

STEP 5: Screw on body and solder tip and braid through holes in body

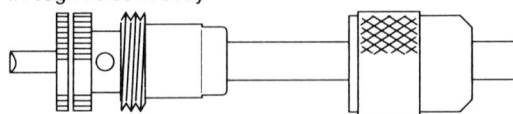

STEP 6: Screw shell onto body

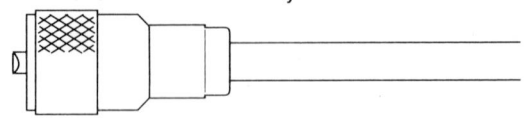

Installing Electronics

Cable Connectors

The majority of marine coaxial connectors are of the "UHF" type. Figure 13.4 shows the most useful types. The inserts used to adapt the connectors to RG-58 and RG-8X cable are not shown.

The "BNC" coaxial connector, shown in Figure 13.4 only as an adapter, is often used in low-frequency digital data transmission. The UHF female/BNC male adapter shown allows connection of a handheld VHF to the masthead antenna in an emergency.

Chandleries usually stock the most common type of connector, but TV and radio shops often carry an even broader line, as well as a complete line of audio and video connectors and adapters.

Thru-Deck and Bulkhead Connectors

Coaxial cables are often required to pass through bulkheads and the deck. How to pass a cable, with a large-diameter UHF connector intact, is an age-old problem. Several solutions are shown in Figure 13.5.

The *panel socket* is used where the cable terminates at a metal case.

The *bulkhead/jack-jack* is a versatile adapter for connecting cables at either bulkheads or the deck.

The *Cable through-deck with split insert* allows installation and removal of a single cable and connector intact.

The *Drill through-deck* can be drilled for multiple cables, but requires removal of connectors or all cables at the same time.

Figure 13.4 UHF-Type Connectors

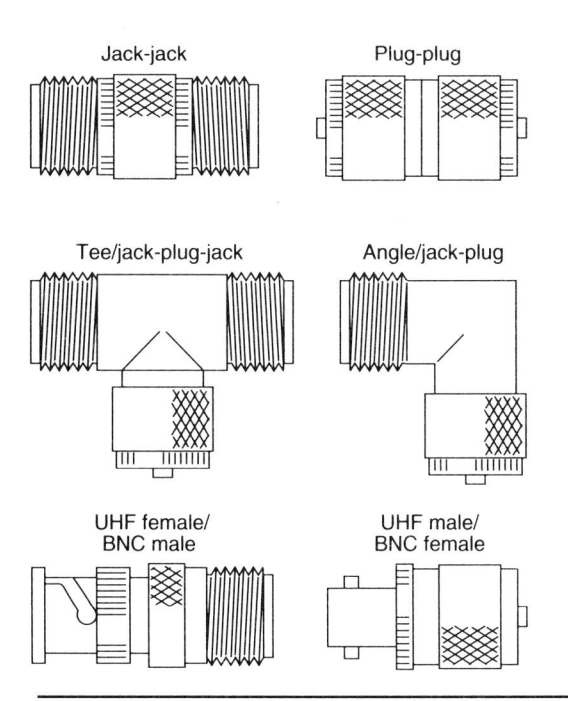

Jack-jack

Plug-plug

Tee/jack-plug-jack

Angle/jack-plug

UHF female/BNC male

UHF male/BNC female

Figure 13.5 Through-Deck Hardware

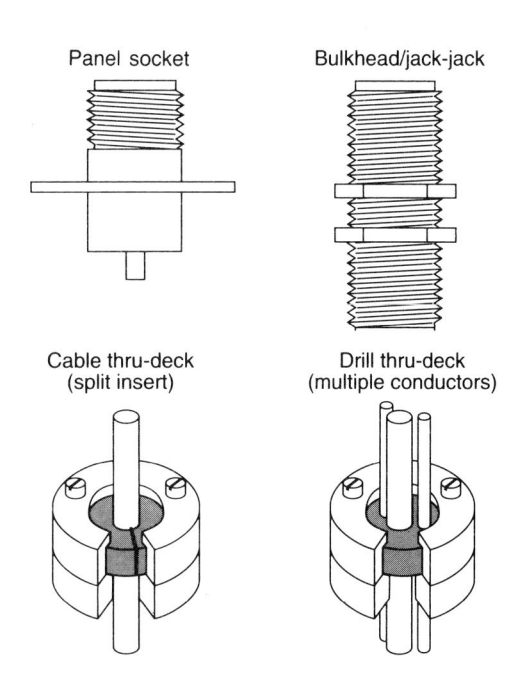

Panel socket

Bulkhead/jack-jack

Cable thru-deck (split insert)

Drill thru-deck (multiple conductors)

PROJECTS

Protecting Connections Against Moisture

Moisture is the enemy of the marine connector. Probably more than 90% of all marine electronics problems are due to corrosion in connectors and conductors. Water that penetrates the connector wicks into the fine-stranded center conductor and shield and travels far into the cable. The resulting copper oxide is an insulator, so resistance goes up and signal strength goes down.

Figure 13.6 shows two lines of defense against moisture in exposed locations:

1. *Drip loops* near the connector force water running along the conductor to drop before reaching the conductor. The loops cannot prevent incursion of water falling on the connector, but they minimize guttering. A single drip loop at the top of a vertical cable/connector diverts water running down the mast.

2. *Adhesive-lined, heat-shrink tubing* seals the connector to the cable, preventing water leaks. The heated tubing shrinks (up to 85%), and the adhesive flows, sealing the connection.

Figure 13.6 Moisture Protection

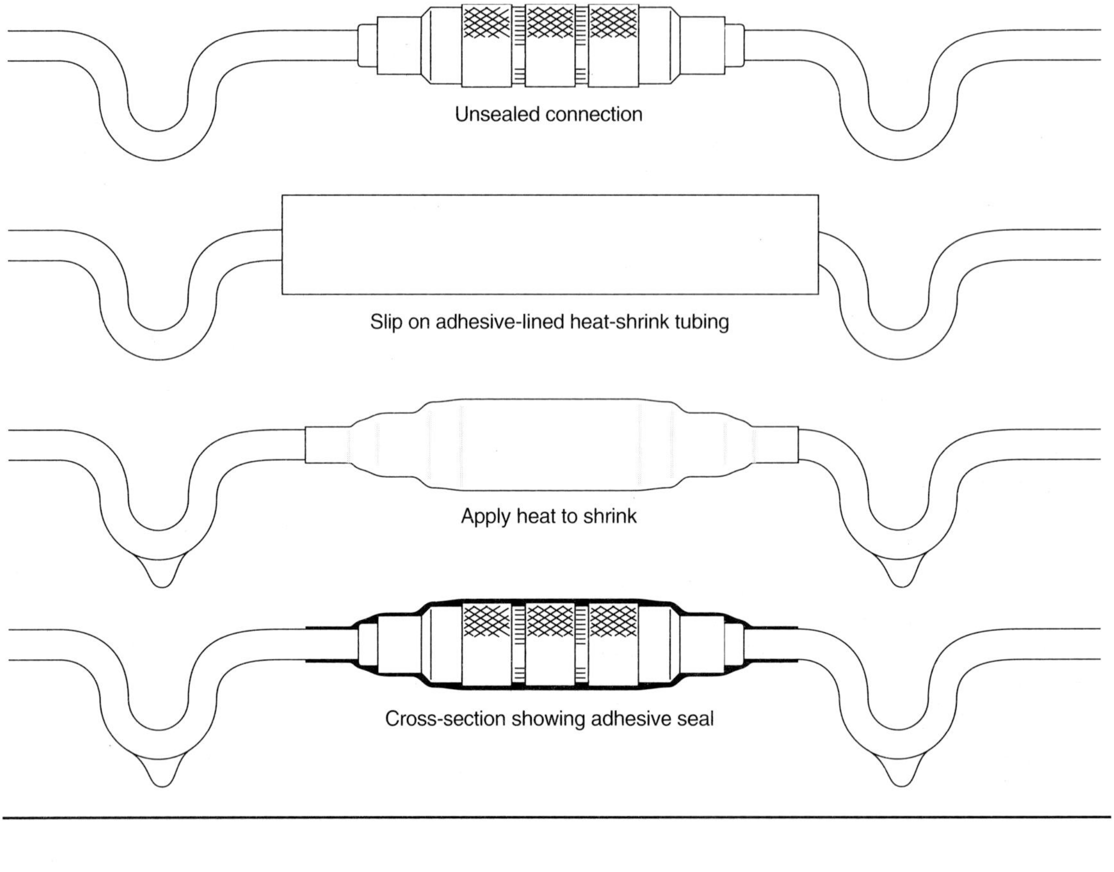

Unsealed connection

Slip on adhesive-lined heat-shrink tubing

Apply heat to shrink

Cross-section showing adhesive seal

Installing Electronics

Specific Equipment
VHF Radio

Three factors affect how far a properly-working VHF radio can be heard:

1. *Cable transmission loss.* At the VHF frequency of 157 megahertz, the lengths of coaxial cable for a three-db (50%) power loss are RG-58—49 feet; RG-8X—66 feet; and RG-8U—111 feet. A sailboat with a 50-foot mast and a 16-foot run to the mast will thus suffer a loss of half its VHF transmitting power if it uses RG-8X (most do). The loss will be reduced by half by switching to RG-8U or RG-213.

2. *Antenna gain.* As shown in Figure 13.7, antennas can radiate equally in all directions, or they can be designed to concentrate the radiation in a flatter pattern toward the horizon. The concentration is expressed as gain in db. Generally, the longer the antenna, the greater the gain. Popular models and their lengths are three db—38 inches; six db—eight feet; and nine db—19 feet. A masthead, three-db, 38-inch whip antenna is most appropriate for a sailboat because the mast height compensates for the lack of gain, and the less concentrated pattern allows heeling. Bridge-mounted, six- or nine-db antennas are best for powerboats, because they are low and do not heel.

3. *Antenna height.* VHF transmission is line-of-sight. The distance two antennas can communicate is the same as the distance two observers at their heights can see each other. Figure 13.8 demonstrates the principle. Table 13.2 lists the distances, versus the heights, of the two antennas.

Figure 13.7 VHF-Antenna Gain

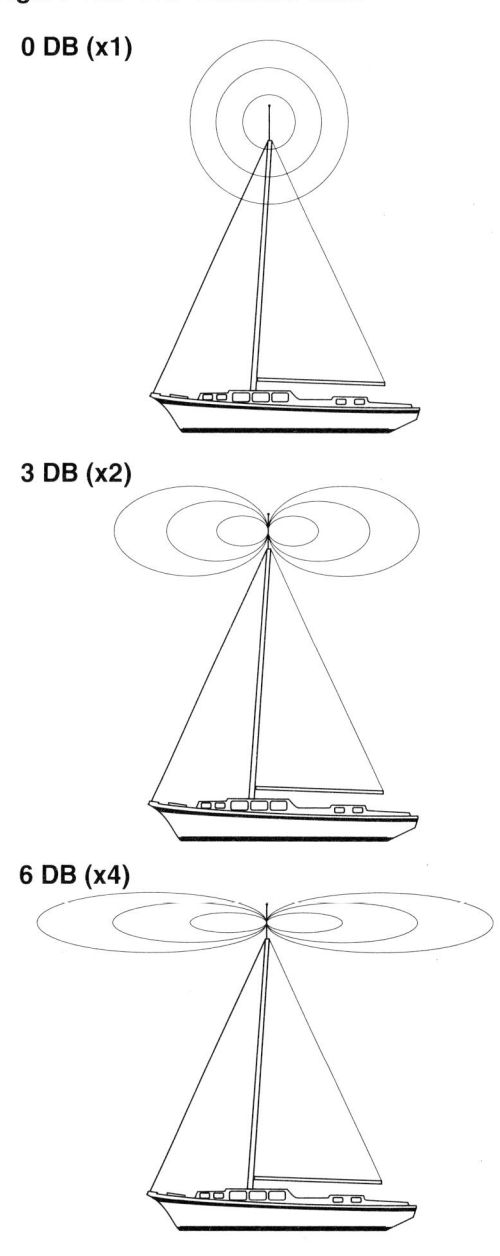

0 DB (x1)

3 DB (x2)

6 DB (x4)

PROJECTS

Figure 13.8 VHF Line-of-Sight Range

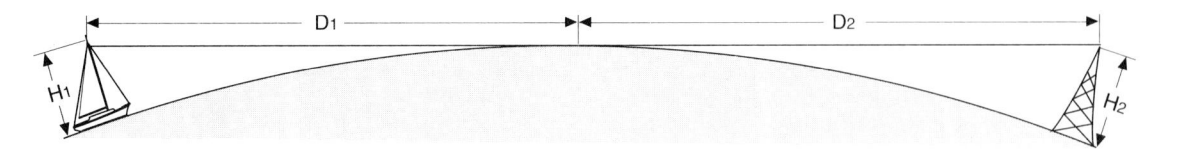

Table 13.2 Line-of-Sight Transmission Distance, $D_1 + D_2$, for VHF Radios

Receiver Height, feet	\multicolumn{10}{c	}{Transmitter Height, feet}
	5	10	20	40	60	80	100	200	400	1000
0	3	4	7	8	10	11	12	17	25	39
5	6	7	10	11	12	14	15	20	27	42
10	7	8	11	12	13	15	16	21	28	43
20	10	11	14	15	16	18	19	24	31	46
40	11	12	15	16	17	19	20	25	32	47
60	12	13	16	17	19	21	22	27	34	48
80	14	15	18	19	21	22	23	28	36	50
100	15	16	19	20	22	23	25	30	37	51

The theoretical distances in Table 13.2 are based on the formulae:

$$D = 1.23\sqrt{H}$$
$$D_1 + D_2 = 1.23(\sqrt{H_1} + \sqrt{H_2})$$

where D is in nm and H is in feet.

Actual transmission distances are observed to be about $1.4\sqrt{H}$, about 15% greater than the table values under average conditions. Thus, two powerboats with 10-foot antenna heights and two sailboats with 60-foot masts can be expected to communicate about eight nm and 19 nm respectively.

Powerboaters sometimes make the mistake of raking a high-gain VHF antenna back to make the boat look more streamlined. This leads to a radiation pattern that will be into space in the forward direction and into the water aft.

If your VHF transmitting range decreases, the first thing to suspect is corrosion in the cable and connectors. You can check the antenna by substituting a handheld VHF for the high-power unit and asking for a radio check. On five watts you should be heard at least five nm.

Installing Electronics

SSB or Ham

Both marine single-sideband and ham HF transceivers operate in the same approximate frequency bands. SSB transmissions are restricted to designated SSB bands, and ham radio transmissions are restricted to FCC-designated ham bands. The two transceiver types, however, are otherwise functionally identical. Although it is illegal to operate a ham transmitter as an SSB transmitter (except in an emergency), removal of a single diode allows the ham radio to transmit on all frequencies, from 300 kilohertz to 30 megahertz.

There are two types of SSB antenna. A 23-foot whip antenna works well down to four megahertz on both power and sailboats. The antenna should be mounted vertically and located out of easy reach, since touching it may result in radiation burns.

A second option, available on sailboats, is the insulated backstay. The backstay, insulated with special fittings at upper and lower ends, acts as a simple "long-wire" antenna. To protect crew from radiation burns, either the bottom insulator and electrical connection should be placed beyond reach, or a length of hose should be slid over the exposed lower portion.

Both antennas require tuners to achieve resonance and maximum output. The tuners can be an option built into the radio chassis or a separate unit installed between the radio and the antenna. Most hams feel the separate units work better in the relatively low frequency SSB bands.

Both antenna types work well. The advantages of the 23-foot whip include smaller size, lower cost, and a vertical orientation for omnidirectional transmission. The insulated backstay results in a cleaner deck and captures more incoming signal.

Use either RG-8 or RG-213 coax to connect transceiver, tuner, and antenna. Attenuation is less important in the 2- to 12-megahertz SSB bands than in the 157-megahertz VHF band. But output currents are much greater for the 150-watt SSB than the 25-watt VHF, so we need a larger center conductor. Use RG-8 or RG-213 coax between transceiver, tuner, and antenna.

Loran

Loran receivers come supplied with antenna coupler bases. A whip antenna with a 3/8" x 24 threaded male base screws into the coupler, which tunes the whip and amplifies the loran signals. Since the 100-kilohertz loran signals follow the ground, antenna height is relatively unimportant. Most sailors mount the antenna on the stern rail.

A range of antenna lengths is available. For maximum signal strength in fringe areas, choose the eight-foot fiberglass whip. For a lower profile but normally adequate performance, choose from stainless steel whips ranging down to 39 inches.

Since loran signals are of both low power and low frequency, the small-diameter RG-58 coaxial cable is acceptable. However, protection against cable and connector corrosion is still critical.

GPS and Satnav

GPS and satnav receivers are supplied with matched antennas. With signal frequencies of about 1,500 megahertz, the wavelengths are about eight inches, and the antennas are tiny. The only location requirements are that the antennas have clear views of the sky and that they be located outside the radar beam and a few meters away from VHF and SSB antennas. Frequency and power between antenna and display are low, so RG-58 cable is acceptable.

Radar

As with GPS and satnav, radar units include matching antennas. The transmission frequency of around 9,500 megahertz corresponds to a wavelength of about one inch. The radar waves are therefore easily blocked by metallic objects of greater than one inch in diameter.

A second location requirement is that the antenna, essentially a microwave generator, be located at least two feet from humans. Just ahead of the steering station on a flying bridge is *not* a good position!

The third location criterion is height. Since radar transmission is line-of-sight and limited in distance by the curvature of the earth, the higher the antenna, the farther one can see. On the other hand, the radiation has a vertical beam width of about 40 degrees, so objects more than 20 degrees below the horizontal will not be seen either.

Figure 13.9 shows both far ($D_1 + D_2$) and near (N_1) distances. Table 13.2 can be used to get the far distance by substituting target height for tower height. For example, a ship with a 60-foot superstructure can be seen by a radar with a 20-foot antenna at a distance of 16 nm.

The near distance can be calculated from the relationship,

$$N_1 = H_1 \div \tan 20°$$
$$= 2.75 \times H_1$$

For example, a 40-foot-high antenna can not see surface objects closer than 110 feet. Reducing the antenna height to 20 feet reduces the blind zone radius to 55 feet.

Note that it is the difference in height between the antenna and the target that determines the blind zone. A 40-foot high antenna can see a 20-foot high target, such as another boat, at a distance of 55 feet.

The cable between the radar scanner (antenna assembly) and the display unit typically contains a dozen conductors. Use only the type of cable supplied with the unit.

Assuming you are skilled at soldering multipin connectors, you can shorten the supplied cable by any degree. A longer cable can generally be ordered as well. A third option is to purchase an extension cable with matching connectors.

The extension cable is very useful in the case of mast-mounted antennas in sailboats. Provided the original cable and the extension cables join at the mast step, stepping and unstepping the mast requires only connecting and disconnecting the cable. In any case, never locate connectors in the bilge, where they are subject to corrosion.

Leaving extra cable at the display end allows cockpit use when desired.

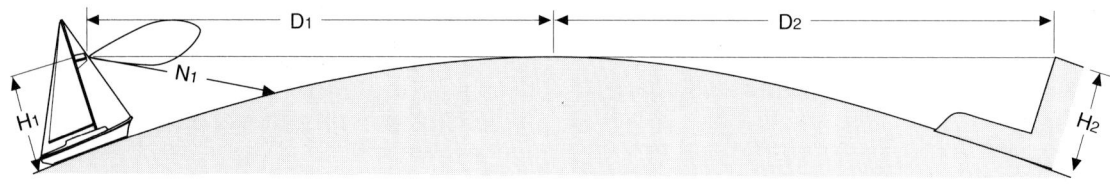

Figure 13.9 Radar Near and Far Ranges

Installing Electronics

RECEIVER/TRANSMITTER INSTALLATION
Location

1. *Install in a dry location.* As we saw in Chapter 3, moisture serves as an electrolyte and promotes corrosion. Salt spray has a way of infiltrating anything located on deck or in the cockpit. A thin film of salt on a circuit board may have much lower resistance than many of the circuit components, effectively shorting them out and altering, if not disrupting, performance.

2. *Prevent overheating.* Electronics are designed to operate in any temperature a person can tolerate. They are designed to dissipate internally generated heat either by conduction through the case, by natural convection through vents, or by fan-forced convection. The most common mistake is to restrict ventilation.

3. *Do not strain cables.* Install the equipment so that both antenna and power cables are secure but not taut. Excessive tension on the conductors can pull the connectors apart.

4. *Keep away from magnetic compasses.* Direct current produces a magnetic field around a conductor. The fields can be reduced but not eliminated if the power leads are either coaxial or twisted. Even stronger magnetic fields are caused by radio-speaker magnets and ferrite-rod radio antennas.

5. *Secure firmly at a good viewing/listening angle.* Equipment cases are usually supplied with convenient mounting brackets that allow either vertical or horizontal mounting. Secure the mounting bracket to a bulkhead or overhead with panhead self-tapping stainless screws.

12-Volt DC Power Hookup

1. Do not install more than one radio on any one circuit. If you do, CB, VHF and SSB radios may interfere with each other through their power leads.

2. Loran, GPS and satnav receivers contain memories that retain coordinates and reduce settling time considerably. Turning off the power switch does not disconnect the power to the memory, but a drop in voltage may erase the memory. Powering navigation electronics from the house battery rather than the engine-starting battery will prevent memory loss.

Grounding

If there is a separate chassis, or case, ground (usually a wing nut labeled "Gnd"), then:

1. Run a #10 AWG minimum green or bare copper grounding wire to ground.

2. Run a separate ground from each piece of equipment.

3. On a steel boat, ground as close as possible to the equipment. On a wood or fiberglass boat, make the common ground point either the engine negative terminal or an external ground plate.

4. SSB/ham transmitters require special grounds. Grounding conductors should be of two-inch minimum width copper strap, connected to a large sintered-copper external ground plate, an external or internal metal keel, or a large area of bronze screening epoxied to the inside of the hull. If all underwater metals are bonded, then the boat's ground might prove sufficient. Remember, however, that bonding all underwater metals may increase corrosion.

ELECTRICAL NOISE
Conducting a Noise Audit
Most loran sets will display the signal-to-noise ratio (SNR) of their received 100-kilohertz loran signals. In this mode, they are a marvelous tool for detecting the presence of radio frequency noise aboard your boat. Here's how:

1. Disconnect shore power.

2. Turn off all electrical equipment, including lights, refrigeration, receivers and transmitters, inverter, generator, and engine.

3. Turn on the loran and let it settle.

4. Call up the SNR display. If any of the SNRs (one master and three slave stations should be available for display) is greater than 50, proceed to the next step. If all SNRs are less than 50, select another loran chain with greater SNR or get your loran set fixed.

5. Note the SNR values of one of the stations for a few minutes and average to obtain the clean-boat reference SNR.

6. Start the engine and bring it up to normal cruising rpm. Compare the SNR with the engine running to the reference SNR. If the SNR has dropped by more than 20% (from 50 down to 40, for example), your engine alternator or generator is a source of noise.

7. Repeat step six for each additional piece of equipment, one at a time; i.e., turn off the engine before testing the next item. Any item causing a greater than 20% drop in SNR is a source of noise which should be corrected. Between tests recheck the reference SNR, with all equipment off, to make sure it hasn't changed.

Curing Noise
The first step in curing a noise problem is recognizing how noise is generated and how it gets into electronic equipment. Figure 13.10 shows that electrical equipment can be divided into *noise generators* (alternators, generators, ignitions, regulators, DC motors, fluorescent fixtures, and some types of digital electronics) and *noise receivers* (radios and electronic navigation devices).

Sometimes a single piece of equipment falls into both categories. I am reminded of my autopilot, whose DC motor causes noise in my radios, but whose electronics control goes crazy when I transmit on my hand-held VHF nearby.

Cures fall into two categories: *shielding* and *filtering*.

Shielding consists of enclosing electronics in a metal case and connecting the case to ground, thereby shunting radiated noise to ground. By enclosing power and signal leads in shielded cable and connecting the cable shield to the metal case, we shunt noise induced in the leads to ground.

Filters are little more than capacitors and inductors. Capacitors conduct AC but block DC. Inductors conduct DC but block AC. The ideal 12-volt source is pure DC. Noise is AC, either generated by the power source itself (alternator or generator), or picked up by power leads acting like antennas. To reduce the AC in a DC supply, we place capacitors across the + and − leads and inductors in series with the leads.

Capacitors for 12-volt DC applications should be rated at 50-working volts (50 WVDC) minimum. Large capacitors are generally polarized electrolytics, so make sure you observe proper polarity.

Installing Electronics 275

Figure 13.10 RFI Generators and Receivers

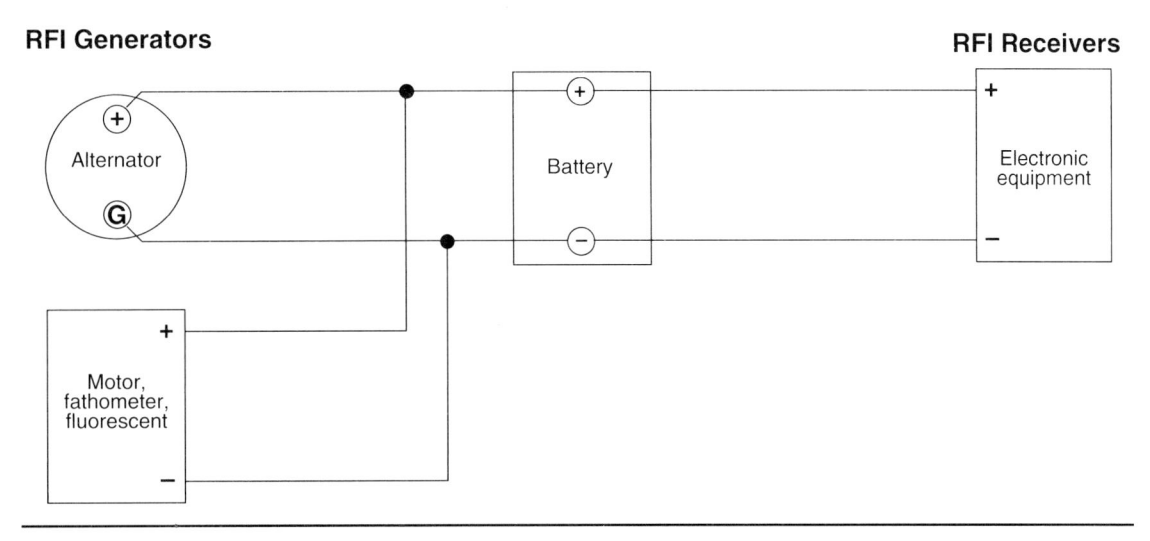

RFI Generators

Alternator

Motor, fathometer, fluorescent

Battery

RFI Receivers

Electronic equipment

Inductors are rated by the maximum continuous DC current they can carry, as well as the value of inductance. For electronic navigation equipment, a five-amp rating is generally sufficient. For DC motors (pumps and autopilots), a 10-amp rating is common. Alternators and generators require ratings that match or exceed their peak output ratings. Inductors with 50-, 70-, and 100-amp ratings are common. You may have to search for inductors large enough to serve some high-output alternators.

In the case of radiated and induced noise on power leads, it is the unprotected length of lead that serves as an antenna, picking up the noise. Thus, it is important to install the filtering component as close as possible to the noise generator or receiver. Even capacitor leads should be clipped to minimum length.

Figure 13.11 Typical RFI Filter

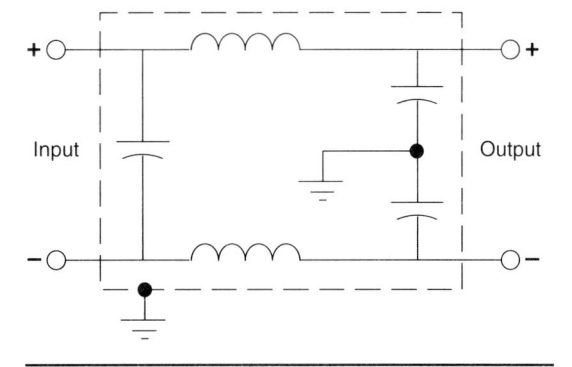

Input

Output

Sometimes a single capacitor or inductor will reduce the noise to an acceptable level. More powerful solutions are provided by a variety of special filters, combining capacitors and inductors, as shown in Figure 13.11.

Figure 13.12 lays out a staged attack against electronic noise. The first six steps attack noise sources, since killing a single source may reduce the noise on all receivers. The last four steps treat the receivers, with each affected receiver being treated individually.

The plan also proceeds roughly in order of increasing cost. It is assumed that, as each step is implemented, all previous cures are left in place.

1. Run separate grounding conductors from the alternator (or generator) case and affected equipment cases to boat ground.

2. Install a 10,000-μF, 50-WVDC electrolytic capacitor across the alternator + output and ground terminals.

3. Install a 1-μF, 50-WVDC capacitor from the voltage regulator battery terminal to ground.

4. Install 1-μF, 50-WVDC capacitors across the + and − power input leads of all motors, fluorescent fixtures, and the depth sounder.

5. Install an "alternator filter" across the alternator + output and ground terminals. The filter rating must exceed the peak output rating of the alternator.

6. Install 10-amp filters across the + and − power input leads of all motors and 10-amp filters across the + and − power input leads of fluorescent fixtures and the depth sounder.

7. Install 1-μF, 50-WVDC capacitors across the + and − power input leads of all affected electronics.

8. Install 1-μF, 50-WVDC non-polarized capacitors from the + power lead to chassis ground and the − power lead to chassis ground.

9. Install five-amp line filters across the + and − power input leads of each piece of affected electronics.

10. Enclose affected electronic equipment in screened-metal enclosures, or wrap in foil tape and connect the enclosure, or tape, to boat ground.

In case grounding, shielding, and filtering prove insufficient, the only remaining option is relocation of antenna, cables, or the equipment itself.

Remove both antenna and equipment chasses from their mounts and connect temporary power and antenna leads. Experiment with the location of the antenna and chassis and routing of supply and antenna cables until the best results are obtained.

Installing Electronics 277

Figure 13.12 Electronic Noise Filters

Step 1. Ground all Cases

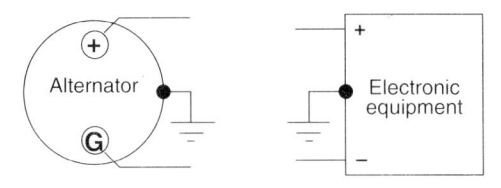

Step 2. Capacitor across Alt. Output

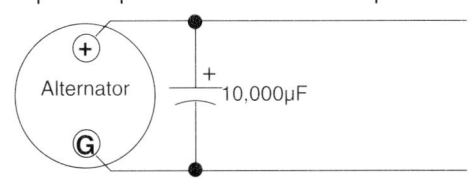

Step 3. Capacitor on Regulator Input

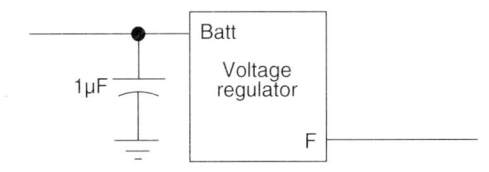

Step 4. Capacitor on Accessory Supply

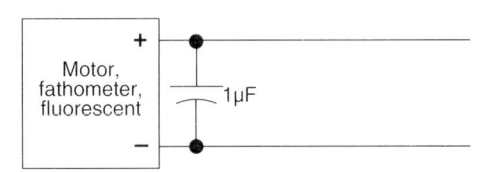

Step 5. Alternator Filter

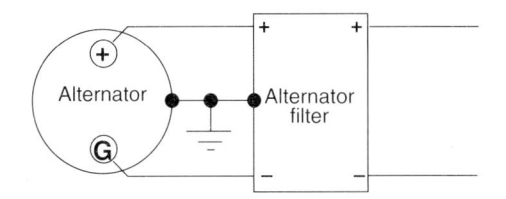

Step 6. Filter on Accessory Supply

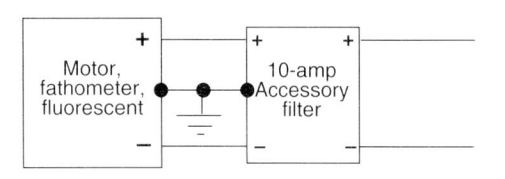

Step 7. Capacitor on Equipment Supply

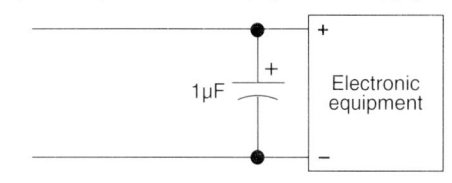

Step 8. Capacitors from Supply to Gnd

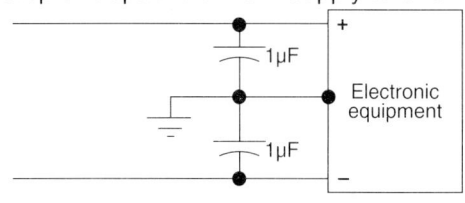

Step 9. Filter on Equipment Supply

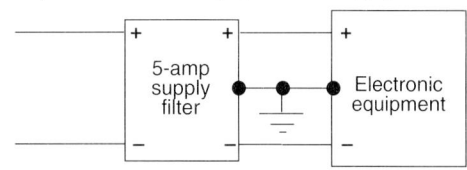

Step 10. Grounded Equipment Screen

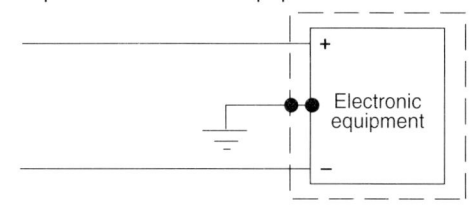

14 FUN WEEKEND PROJECTS

Circuit Components   280

AC Polarity Indicator   288

LED Panel Indicators   289

AC-Frequency Meter   290

Small Battery Eliminator   291

Low-Voltage Alarm   292

Battery Monitor   293

Automatic Anchor Light   294

Cabin-Light Dimmer   295

Bilge Water Alarm   296

Water-Tank Indicator   297

Boat-Burglar Alarm   298

Electronic Ship's Horn   299

Fan Control for Refrigeration Compresser   300

This chapter describes 13 do-it-yourself projects that are fun, can be completed in an afternoon, will add to the comfort and convenience of your boat, and will further your electrical education.

All of the *circuit components* are simple to use and can be purchased at good TV and electronics shops, or through specialist electronics magazines. The 13 *projects* are listed in the contents at left.

PROJECTS

This is a fun chapter. By doing these projects, you can increase your understanding of electricity and electronics, upgrade your boat's electrical system, and save money—all at the same time.

Each project can be completed in a Sunday afternoon and typically costs less than £10. With few exceptions all components are available at radio shops or through electronics magazines.

CIRCUIT COMPONENTS

Projects are always more fun and generally more successful when you understand how they work. To understand the behavior of a circuit, you first have to understand how each of its components work. A few of the integrated circuits listed are actually complex circuits containing, in a single small package, hundreds of components. For these we will have to settle for an action/reaction, or input/output understanding. Each of the discrete components is described in a thumbnail sketch below.

Conductors
No Connection

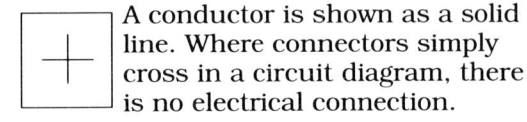

A conductor is shown as a solid line. Where connectors simply cross in a circuit diagram, there is no electrical connection.

Connected Conductors

When two or more conductors are electrically connected, the connection is indicated by a dot at the intersection. Think of the dot as a small blob of solder on the connection.

Connector

Connectors are used to mate conductors when assembling or installing equipment. Connectors may mate single conductors, as in AC and DC distribution circuits; a shielded pair, as in coaxial antenna connections; or dozens of conductors as in computer applications.

Resistors
Fixed Resistor

A zig-zag symbol indicates a fixed-value resistor. The resistance in ohms is constant regardless of current, temperature, or any other variable. The ability of a resistor to dissipate heat (calculated as $W = I^2 \times R$ where W = watts, I = amps, and R = ohms) is determined largely by the size of the resistor. The value (ohms and precision) of a resistor is shown by a series of colored bands, as shown in Appendix D.

Variable Resistor

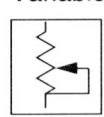

A zig-zag with an arrow indicates a resistor whose resistance can be changed. Externally there are three terminals: one at each end of the full resistance, and a third connected to a wiper, which slides along the resistance wire or film. The wiper is generally moved by turning a screw or knob.

The value of the variable resistor is its maximum value, which can be read with an ohmmeter across the two end terminals. By connecting to the wiper terminal and the appropriate end terminal, we can have a resistance that either increases or decreases with clockwise rotation of the screw. Using all three terminals one has, in effect, two resistors which form a voltage divider.

Fun Weekend Projects

Low-power variable resistors are known as trimmers or trimpots; high-power variable resistors are generally called potentiometers.

Thermistor

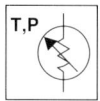

In reality a semiconductor, the thermistor (symbol T) is a component whose resistance changes with temperature. Thermistors are specified by their resistance value at 25°C, for example 10K (10,000 ohms) at 25°C.

If the variation of resistance with temperature were linear, measuring temperature with an ohmmeter would be a simple matter. Thermistors are more often used to control temperature, however, using their deviation in resistance from a set point as an error signal.

Capacitors
Non-polarized Capacitor

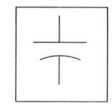

If electricity is like water, then capacitors are like pressurized water tanks: the higher the voltage you place across them, the more electric charge they store. Electric charge is measured in coulombs, which equal 6.24×10^{18} electrons. A 1-farad capacitor will store 1 coulomb of charge at a potential of 1 volt; 10 coulombs at 10 volts; etc.

Electronic circuits require much smaller charge storage, however, so the more common units of capacitance are the microfarad, or µF (10^{-6} farad), and the picofarad, or pF (10^{-12} farad).

Capacitors are made of extremely thin, interleaved or wound, films of insulation (the dielectric) and aluminum. At high potentials the insulation can break down, so capacitors are also rated by their maximum working voltage.

Polarized Capacitor

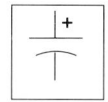

A device which is halfway between a capacitor and a battery is the electrolytic capacitor, which stores charge in a chemical electrolyte. The advantage is large capacitance in a small size. The disadvantage is that, as with a battery, reversing the voltage will damage the capacitor. Such polarized capacitors can be used only where the applied voltage is always of the same sign.

You can identify polarized capacitors by the + and − markings next to their leads.

Batteries
Single Cell

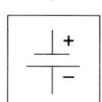

A single electrochemical cell is generally used to supply power at low voltage. Nominal voltages for common cells are:

- Alkaline   1.50
- Carbon zinc   1.50
- Lead acid   2.10
- Lithium manganese   3.00
- Mercury oxide   1.35
- Nickel cadmium   1.20
- Zinc air   1.45
- Zinc chloride   1.50

Battery

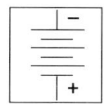

The word *battery* actually means a group of cells. By packaging cells in series, manufacturers create batteries of nearly any voltage, the most common being 6, 9, and 12 volts. You can create a battery of nearly any voltage yourself by connecting cells in *battery holders*, which are designed to hold multiples of AAA, AA, C, and D-size cells.

Switches

SPDT Switch

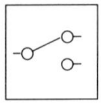

The Single-Pole, Double-Throw is the simplest form of switch, allowing a single conductor (pole) to be routed to either of two routes (throws).

Think of the SPDT switch as a switch in a railroad track, shunting the track to either of two destinations. Of course, one of the destinations can lead nowhere, in which case the switch acts like a simple On-Off light switch. A SPDT switch used in the simple On-Off mode can be wired to be Normally Open (NO) or Normally Closed (NC).

DPDT Switch

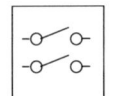

Going back to the railroad analogy, if you consider the two rails to be two conductors, then the railroad switch is analogous to the DPDT switch. Two poles are switched simultaneously to either of two destinations. You can also think of the DPDT switch as being two SPDT switches ganged, or locked together.

Given enough contacts, rotary switches can switch any number of poles to any number of destinations. They are specified as X-pole, Y-position. Examples include: 1-pole, 12-position; 3-pole, 4-position; 2-pole, 8-position.

PB Switch

Push-Button switches are of two types: push-on, push-off; and momentary contact. The first is often used to control power on-off and to activate options. The second is to activate a circuit or function briefly, such as a battery indicator or a microphone transmit switch.

Relay

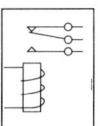

The relay is an electrically activated switch. Current through its coil pulls on a magnetic slug, which triggers a switch. The automotive solenoid is a high-current relay where a few amps from the ignition switch activate the high-current (several-hundred amps) switch to the starter motor. Electronic relays are rated by:

1. Input coil characteristics

2. Output switch maximum voltage and current

Sometimes the input coil voltage and resistance is specified, allowing you to calculate the current using Ohm's law.

Example specifications are:

Coil: 12-volts-DC, 43 milliamps

Contacts: 2 amps, 120-volts-DC

or,

Coil: 12-volts-DC, 320 Ω

Contacts: 2 amps, 120-volts-DC

Relays can also have multiple poles. Except for now-outdated stepping relays, however, they are always either single- or double-throw.

Over-current Devices

Fuse

A fuse (short for fusible link) protects a circuit from excessive current and damage by melting and breaking the circuit. The fuse is obviously a one-shot deal! In spite of the hassle of having to carry replacements, the fuse is still popular, due to low cost and high reliability.

Fun Weekend Projects

Circuit Breaker

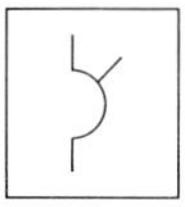

You can think of the circuit breaker as a relay whose input current is routed through its output switch. The rated current of the circuit breaker is also the current required to activate the relay. Upon reaching its rated current, the circuit breaker disconnects itself, interrupting current flow to everything downstream of its output. Most circuit breakers operate on the same magnetic principle as coil relays. Some, however, contain a thermally activated bimetallic switch that opens at high temperature and won't close again until the temperature drops. Such thermal breakers are common in motors.

Lamps

Incandescent

The incandescent lamp is simply a miniature version of the ubiquitous household light bulb. Its tungsten filament acts like a high-temperature resistor, glowing white-hot at normal operating voltage. Incandescent bulbs are rated by volts, either amps or watts, and type of base.

By filling lamps with noble gases (inert gases which will not react with the filament), lamp manufacturers have been able to increase filament operating temperatures, which results in both greater light output and higher efficiency. The halogen lamps recommended in Chapter 10 are an example.

Neon

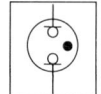

The neon bulb contains no heated filament which can burn out. Instead, light is given off by neon gas, which is stimulated by an electric current. Neon bulbs require at least 60 volts to operate and give off little light, but they consume very little power and last indefinitely. They are often used as indicator lights in 120- and 240-volt AC circuits.

Meters

Ammeter

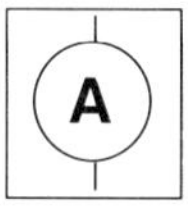

The principles of both ammeters and voltmeters were discussed in Chapter 2, DC Measurements.

The ideal ammeter passes current with no voltage drop. In other words, it appears to a circuit as a resistor of near-zero resistance. Real ammeters come very close to the ideal with resistances of the order 0.001 ohms.

There are two fundamentally different ammeter styles: analog and digital. The difference between analog and digital presentation is best exemplified by analog (sweep hands) and digital (LCD digits) watches. For quick recognition analog is best; for accuracy you need digital.

Beware of cheap analog meters. They do not stand up well to the marine environment. On the other hand, the differences between high- and low-cost digital meters are often more in styling and name than in performance. The integrated circuitry inside the case may be identical.

Voltmeter

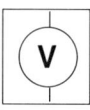

Voltmeters are ammeters with a high resistance in-series with the input. The ideal voltmeter would appear to a circuit as an infinite resistance. Real voltmeters range from 5,000 to 50,000 ohms per volt for analog meters and 1 to 10 megohms for digital meters.

Keep in mind that neither ammeters nor voltmeters need always be dedicated to a single purpose. A single panel meter can monitor an unlimited number of voltages or amperages by routing its input through a rotary switch. I use a convenient and light pocket-digital volt-ohm meter strapped to my electrical panel, with its leads plugged into test jacks. When I need it for troubleshooting elsewhere, I simply unstrap it and substitute whatever test leads are appropriate to the job.

Motors
Motor
The most common motor on a boat is that driving the bilge pump. All small-boat bilge-pump motors run on DC and consume from 2 to 20 amps. Startup and locked-rotor currents can be three to four times as great, however, so contact ratings of switches and relays are important.

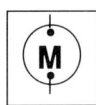

Fans
Most of the fans in a boat run on DC. A useful fan for the do-it-yourselfer is the "muffin" fan—a zero-maintenance, brushless and nearly noiseless fan originally developed for cooling electronic equipment. Sizes range from about 2 to 6 inches square. Drawing little current, they are ideal for circulating air through the condenser coils of small marine refrigerators under thermostatic control. A very convenient feature of these fans is that both their speed and resulting noise level can be reduced by simply reducing their input voltage.

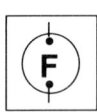

Acoustic devices
Speaker
The purpose of speakers is to reproduce a range of frequencies, i.e. voice or music. They may also be used to emit very loud fixed-frequency sounds, as in burglar alarms and ship's horns. Speakers are rated by maximum power consumption in watts, frequency range and input impedance, which is nearly always 8 ohms.

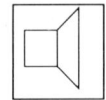

A buzzer is an acoustic transducer, which produces, most often, a single-frequency sound. Its primary use is as an alarm, indicating such things as:

- Voltage too high
- Voltage too low
- Temperature too high
- Water in the bilge

They are available in fixed frequencies from about 1 to 5 khz. Current consumption depends on sound level and ranges from about 10 milliamps, which can be driven directly by integrated circuits, to 100 milliamps, which requires a driver transistor or relay.

Diodes
Rectifier Diode
The most common diode passes current in the direction of the arrow but blocks current in the reverse direction. Actually, a minimum voltage of about 0.6 volts must be exceeded in the silicon diode (0.25 volt in germanium diodes) before current begins to flow in the forward direction. In the forward direction, the diode looks, to a circuit, like nearly zero resistance and a voltage drop of 0.6 volt. In the reverse direction, it looks like infinite resistance.

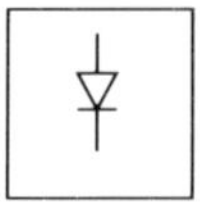

With too high a forward current, diodes will overheat and be destroyed; at excessive reverse voltage, they will break down.

Fun Weekend Projects

Diode specifications, therefore, include maximum forward current and peak reverse voltage. For example, a 1N4001 diode is rated at 1-amp continuous-forward current and 50 volts peak-reverse voltage.

Rectifier diodes are used in high-current applications, such as power supplies and battery chargers. Signal diodes handle a few milliamps and are used in signal processing. An example is the 1N914, rated at 10-milliamps continuous-forward current and 75 volts peak-inverse voltage.

Zener Diode

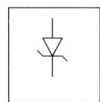

All diodes breakdown and pass current in the reverse direction, when the voltage exceeds their rating. Zener diodes are carefully manufactured to breakdown without destruction at precise voltages, ranging from 2 to 200 volts. The characteristic of switching from nonconducting to conducting at a precise voltage is used to regulate voltage in a circuit.

Light-Emitting Diode (LED)

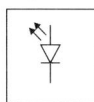

When free electrons flow across a diode junction, some electrons fall back into their normal, lower-energy state, releasing the extra energy in the form of radiation. In the rectifier and zener diode, the frequency of the radiated energy is outside the range of visible light. In the LED gallium, arsenic and phosphorus replace silicon, and the released radiation falls within the visible range. LEDs are available in red, green and yellow.

Threshold voltages (voltage at which the LED begins to emit light) are typically 1.5 volts, rather than 0.6 volt. LEDs are rated, in addition to color, by maximum-forward current and maximum-reverse voltage. In practice, a resistor is placed in series with the LED to limit the forward current to the nominal value. Light output, however, is nearly linear with forward current, so the LED can run usefully at lower current and light levels simply by increasing the series resistance.

Since LEDs can be destroyed by reversing the leads, it is important to distinguish the anode (+ voltage lead) from the cathode (- voltage lead). If a specification sheet with a drawing is not available, polarity can be checked by connecting to a battery of 1.5 volts, which is sufficient to cause light output but generally less than the peak inverse voltage.

Active Solid-State Devices

NPN Transistor

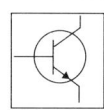

Transistors are usually explained in terms of electrons and holes. I prefer a water analogy, which will serve our purposes well enough.

Figure 14.1 shows the names of the three terminals of the NPN transistor: base, collector, and emitter. The small arrows show the direction of current flow in the leads: I_B, I_C and I_E. Note that the arrow in the emitter lead serves the same purposes and distinguishes the NPN from the PNP transistor.

The transistor is constructed like a pair of back-to-back diodes. Current I_B will flow from the base to the emitter, in the direction shown, whenever the base is at a higher voltage than the emitter.

Now the analogy—the base acts like a valve in the collector-to-emitter waterline. A small change in I_B results in a large change in I_C and I_E. The ratio of current changes is called the forward current gain:

$$h_{FE} = \Delta I_C / \Delta I_B$$

Typical values of h_{FE} range from 20 to 100.

Figure 14.1 NPN Transistor

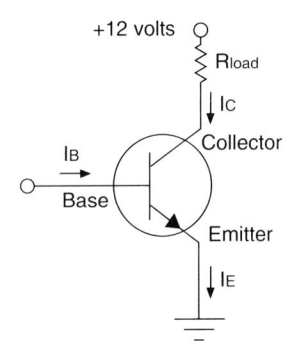

Figure 14.2 PNP Transistor

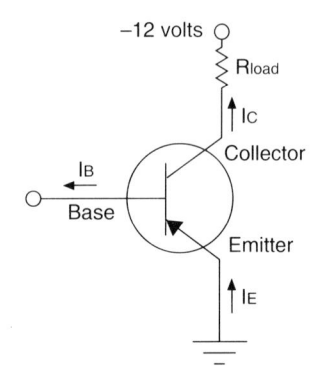

The most common use of the transistor is to multiply current and, thus, increase the power of a signal.

PNP Transistor

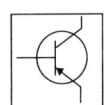

The PNP transistor functions in exactly the same way as an NPN transistor, except that its diodes are reversed. Figure 14.2 shows the lead definitions and current directions in the PNP transistor. Due to the reversal of diodes, current I_B will now flow whenever the base is negative relative to the emitter. Current gain is defined as:

$$h_{FE} = \Delta I_C / \Delta I_B$$

The choice between PNP and NPN transistors depends on the supply voltage configuration of the circuit.

MOSFET

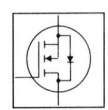

Both the field-effect transistor (FET) and the metal-oxide semiconductor field-effect transistor (MOSFET) act like transistors, except that the controlling input signal is a voltage rather than a current. Since almost no current flows into the input lead (the gate), the input resistance of the MOSFET is virtually infinite. FETs and MOSFETs are therefore primarily used where high input resistance is required. A perfect application is the input of a voltmeter.

Operational Amplifier

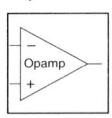

The single integrated circuit I'll describe is the opamp. If one were to describe the perfect amplifier, it's specification would read:

- Voltage gain = ∞
- Input resistance = ∞Ω
- Input offset voltage = 0 volts

A real opamp, the LM353, costs less than $1.00 in single quantity and has the following specifications:

- Voltage gain $> 10^6$
- Input resistance = $10^{12} \Omega$
- Input offset voltage < 0.002 volts

The utility of the opamp derives from its essentially infinite voltage gain and input resistance. Figure 14.3A shows the basic opamp. Since the output voltage is limited by the supply voltage (usually ± 15-volts-

Fun Weekend Projects

Figure 14.3 Operational Amplifier Applications

(A.) Basic Operational Amplifier

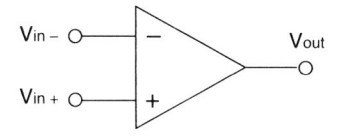

(B.) Unity-Gain Voltage Follower
$V_{out} = V_{in}$

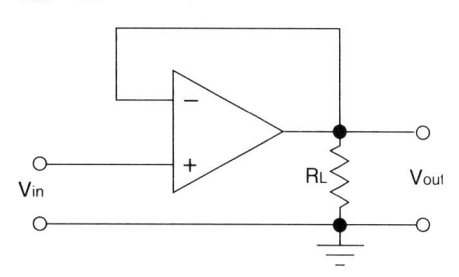

(C.) Inverting Amplifier
$V_{out} = -V_{in}$

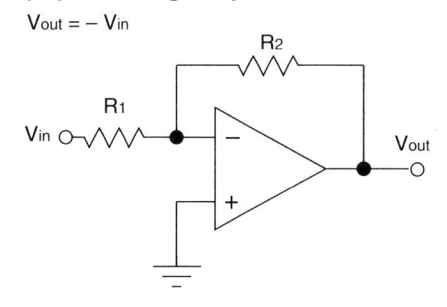

(D.) Non-Inverting Amplifier
$V_{out} = V_{in}(R_2/R_1)$

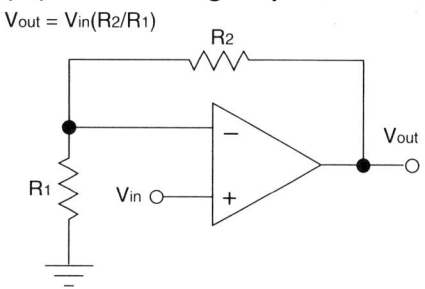

(E.) Summing Amplifier
$V_{out} = -(R_f/R_1 \times V_1 + R_f/R_2 \times V_2 + ...)$

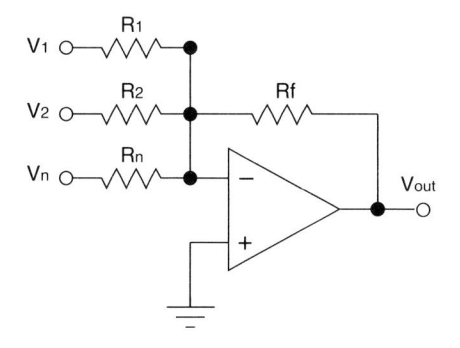

(F.) Difference Amplifier
$V_{out} = -(V_1 - V_2)R_2/R_1$

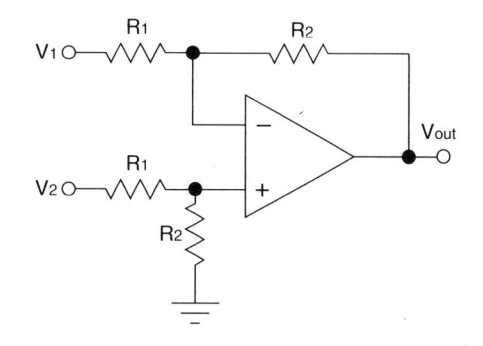

DC, although single-voltage operation is possible too), infinite voltage gain implies zero volts between the positive (V_{in+}) and negative (V_{in-}) inputs. Further, since the input resistance is infinite, no current flows into either input.

Figure 14.3B shows the opamp connected as a unity-gain voltage follower. Zero difference voltage means that $V_{in+} = V_{in-}$, and since $V_{out} = V_{in-}$, then $V_{out} = V_{in}$. The voltage follower is used to match a high-resistance source to a low-resistance load, i.e., to boost current while maintaining voltage.

Figure 14.3C shows an inverting amplifier with voltage gain. Since no current flows into the – input, and since the – input is at the same potential as the + input (ground), then the input current flowing through R_1 must cancel the feedback current through R_2: $I_1 = -I_2$.

Using Ohm's Law, $I = V/R$,
$$V_1/R_1 = -V_2/R_2$$
$$V_2 = -V_1(R_2/R_1)$$

Figure 14.3 shows a variety of other useful opamp configurations (D, E F). To understand how they work, you need remember only that $V_{in+} = V_{in-}$.

The equation relating V_{out} to V_{in} can then be derived from the cancelling input and feedback currents flowing into each input.

PROJECT 1
AC Polarity Indicator

Good practice requires reverse polarity indicators on all AC-mains panels. It also suggests that the resistance of such indicators be at least 25,000 ohms in order that they do not bypass any isolation transformer or galvanic isolation-diodes installed in the shore-power circuit.

This two-lamp circuit consists of a green-neon lamp across the hot and neutral conductors and a red-neon lamp across neutral and ground. Proper polarity is indicated by just the green light alone. If the red light comes on, either alone or with the green, something is wrong.

To install the lamps, drill 5/16-inch holes in the distribution panel and press in.

Circuit

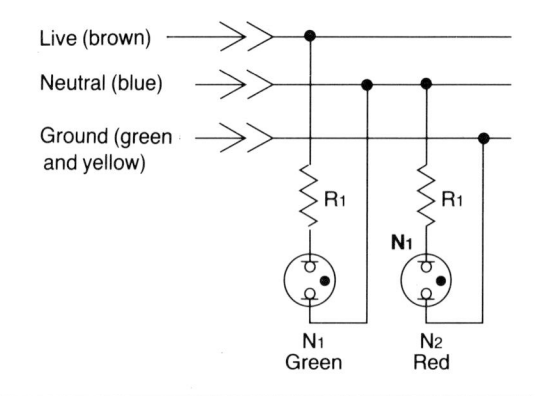

Components

Part	Description
N1	Green 120-volt neon lamp
N2	Red 120-volt neon lamp
R1	33k, 1/4-watt resistor

PROJECT 2
LED Panel Indicators

Many DC-distribution panels come only with circuit breakers or fuses, so it is difficult to tell at a glance whether a circuit is on or off. Others come with battery-draining incandescent lamps.

One of these low-current LED indicators can be installed on the output side of each circuit breaker and fuse to indicate, with a soft glow, when the circuit is on. The LED specified consumes only 0.0012 amp. Ten LEDs will consume only 0.3 Ah of battery power per 24 hours.

To install, drill press-fit holes in the panel adjacent to each fuse switch or circuit breaker. Press in the LED and solder the 10 kΩ resistor between the LED anode (see specification sheet for lead identification) and the hot terminal. Connect the LED cathode to the panel ground bus.

Circuit

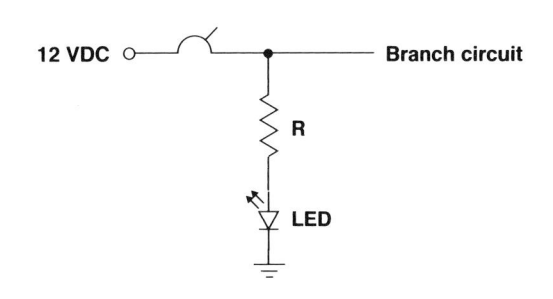

Components

Part	Description
R	10 kΩ, 1/4-watt resistor
LED	Red, T1-1/4 low-current LED

PROJECT 3
AC-Frequency Meter

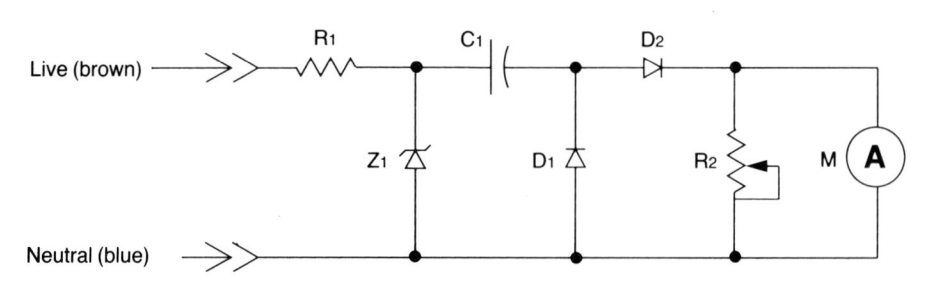

Good practice requires an AC-frequency meter on the AC-distribution panel fed by any onboard generator. The zener diode in this circuit clips incoming 120-volt-AC sine waves to 6.2-volt-DC square waves. Capacitor C1 differentiates the square waves into positive and negative pulses. Diode D1 shorts the negative pulses to ground, but diode D2 passes the positive pulses, which are then averaged by the inertia of the ammeter, M.

To calibrate the meter, connect the circuit to shore power, (60 hertz) and adjust R2 until M reads exactly 60 milliamps.

The meter can then be interpreted as frequency in hertz instead of milliamps.

Components

Part	Description
R1	100 kΩ, 1/2-watt resistor
R2	10 kΩ, 15-turn trimpot
C1	0.2-µF capacitor
D1	1n914 signal diode
Z1	6.2V zener diode
M	0 to 100-milliamp panel meter

Fun Weekend Projects

PROJECT 4
Small Battery Eliminator

If you are tired of replacing expensive batteries in your electronics, you can make a "battery" which will supply up to 1.5 amps at any voltage from 0- to 10-volts DC, drawing from your ship's battery. The 317T is an adjustable, three-terminal, integrated-circuit voltage regulator in a package smaller than a 10p piece.

To install, solder the circuit as shown, connect V_{in} to 12-volts DC and adjust trimpot R until V_{out} reads the desired voltage. Then connect V_{out} and Ground to the battery terminals of the electronic equipment.

You may wish to pack the circuit into a cardboard or plastic cylinder of the same dimensions as the battery you are replacing. An alternative is to wrap the circuit in foam and then stuff it into the battery slot.

If the 317T gets too hot to touch, mount it on the optional heat sink.

Circuit

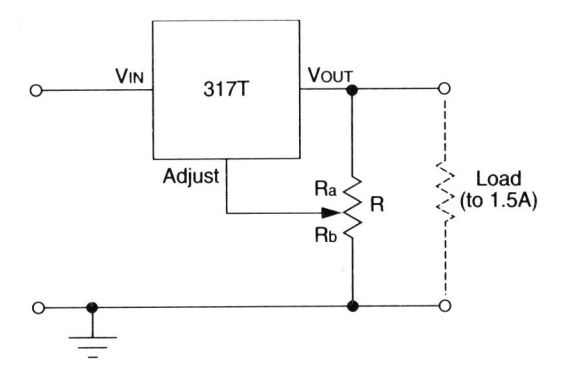

Components

Part	Description
317T	Adjustable voltage regulator
R	10 kΩ trimpot
*	Heat Sink (not shown)

PROJECT 5
Low-Voltage Alarm

In this circuit a 741 opamp compares the voltage of zener diode, Z_1, to a voltage determined by the ship's battery and the voltage divider, R_3 and R_4.

When the battery voltage falls below the preset lower-voltage limit, the voltage at the opamp's V_{in-} terminal drops below the zener 6.2 volts, and the output of the opamp rises to the battery voltage, lighting the LED. A 10 milliamp piezzo buzzer can replace the noiseless LED, if we change R_4 to 1 kΩ.

To set the battery low-voltage alarm point, monitor the battery voltage with a digital voltmeter. When the voltage reaches 12.00 volts, for example, adjust R_3 until the LED or buzzer just comes on.

A two-stage alarm can easily be constructed, which will give a visual LED warning at 50% discharge, for example, and a more dire audible warning at 75% discharge.

To construct, replace the 741 opamp with a 1458 dual opamp, feed the – input of the second opamp with a second R2/R3 voltage divider, and drive the piezo buzzer with the output of the second opamp. Calibrate the two set points as before, using a digital voltmeter to monitor battery voltage.

Circuit

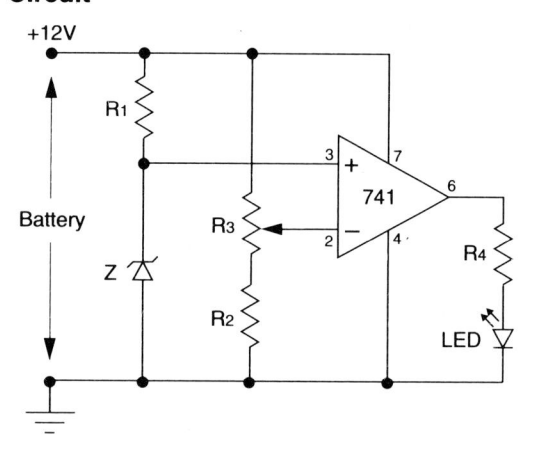

Components

Part	Description
R1	10 kΩ, 1/4-watt resistor
R2	1 kΩ, 1/4-watt resistor
R3	10 kΩ, 15-turn trimpot
R4	10 kΩ, 1/4-watt resistor
Z	1N4735, 6.2-volt zener diode
LED	Red, T1-1/4 low-current LED
741	741 operational amplifier

Fun Weekend Projects

PROJECT 6
Battery Monitor

The problem with monitoring battery voltage with an analog panel meter is that the normal 5% accuracy of the meter is equivalent to 50% of the battery's capacity. What is needed is an electronic magnifying glass to focus on the battery's 11.7 to 12.7-volt range.

In this circuit, a 317-T adjustable voltage regulator is used to provide a constant 11.70-volts-DC. The 0 to 1-volt-DC voltmeter reads the difference between the ship's battery voltage and the reference 11.70 volts. Assuming 12.70 and 11.70 volts represent 0 and 100% charge, 0 to 1 volt on the voltmeter represents 0 to 100% charge.

The 1.5-volt-DC alkaline cell boosts the regulator source so that the output can still deliver 11.7 volts, when the ship's battery is at 11.7 volts.

The 0 to 1-volt voltmeter can be replaced by R_{opt} and an ammeter, as shown in the component list.

Of course a digital voltmeter may be used, in lieu of the analog meter.

Circuit

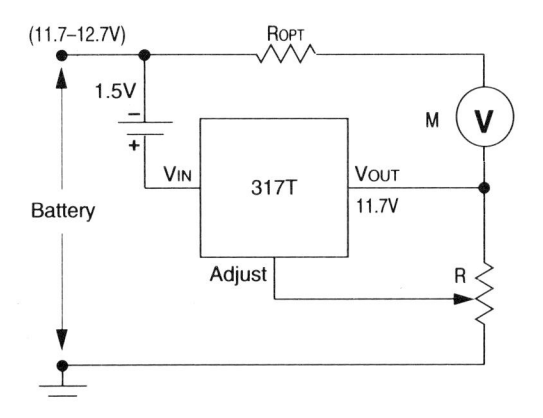

Components

Part	Description
317T	Adjustable voltage regulator
R	10 kΩ, 15-turn trimpot
M	0 to 1-volt DC meter
Ropt	10 kΩ resistor for 0 to 100-µA meter
"	1 kΩ resistor for 0 to 1-mA meter

PROJECT 7
Automatic Anchor Light

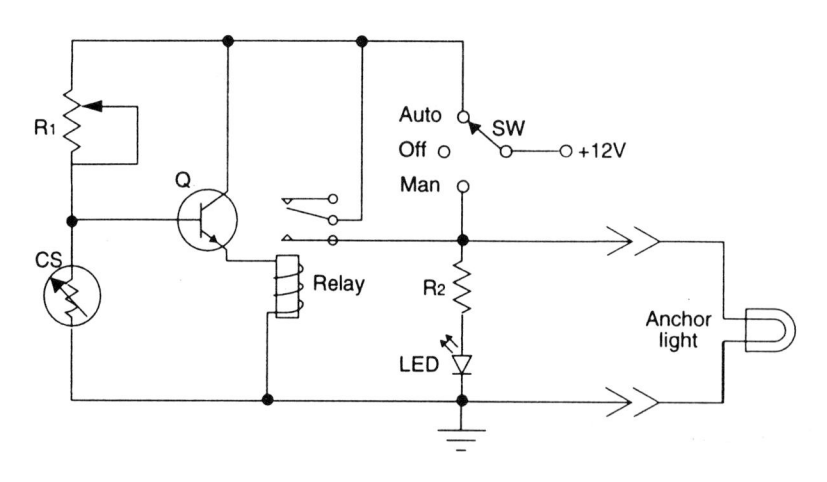

PROJECT 7
Automatic Anchor Light

The typical mast-top anchor light consumes 12 watts. Over a 12-hour period, it will drain 12 Ah from the battery. If you leave the boat unattended and leave the anchor light on (as you should), it will draw down the battery at 24 Ah per day!

This circuit saves battery power by automatically switching on at sunset and off a sunrise. At sunset, the resistance of the cadmium sulphide photoresistor increases, increasing the voltage to transistor, Q. The transistor provides the coil current to close the relay and feed 12 VDC to the anchor light.

The red LED indicates when the anchor light is switched on. A single-pole, three-position rotary switch allows selection between automatic, manual, and off modes.

Note that the cadium sulphide photoresistor must be placed so that it is not illuminated by the anchor light. Otherwise it will see the anchor light as the sun and cause the light to turn on and off rapidly.

Components

Part	Description
R1	10 kΩ trimpot
CS	Cadmium sulphide photoresistor
Q	2N2222 NPN transistor
Relay	12V. 320Ω, 10A, SPDT
SW	Switch, SPDT with center Off
LED	Red, low-current LED

Fun Weekend Projects

PROJECT 8
Cabin-Light Dimmer

Halogen cabin lamps are great for reading, but not very romantic for dining. Furthermore, dimming your cabin lights will save on battery power.

The heart of this circuit is the integrated-circuit 555 timer. The 555 runs as a multivibrator (digital oscillator) with its frequency determined by R_1, R_2, R_3, R_4 and C_1. Pin 3 of the 555 controls the gate of the MOSFET, Q, which supplies current to the cabin lamps in the form of square waves of modulated width.

The percentage of normal voltage supplying the lamps is equivalent to the percentage-on time of the pulses, which is controlled by adjusting trimpot R_2.

The dimmer circuit is switched in and out of the circuit by switch SW. Individual cabin lights can still be switched on and off with their own series-connected switches.

Since the life of the very expensive halogen lamps is extended markedly by reduction in supply voltage, you might consider leaving the dimmer circuit on all the time, set at the minimum power level required for the task at hand.

If the circuit load is more than 15 watts, check the operating temperature of the 555. If too hot to touch, attach a heat sink to the integrated circuit.

Circuit

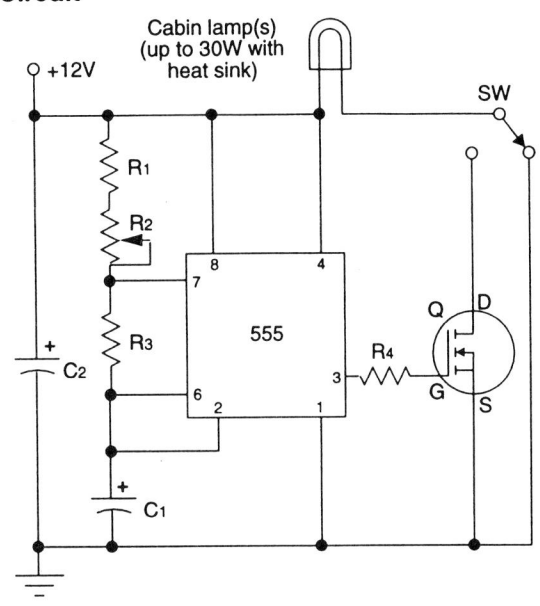

Components

Part	Description
R1	100 Ω, 1/4-watt resistor
R2	5 kΩ potentiometer
R3	1 kΩ, 1/4-watt resistor
R4	10 kΩ, 1/4-watt resistor
C1	.047 µF capacitor
C2	22µF capacitor
Q	IRF-510 power MOSFET
555	555 timer
SW	SPDT switch, center off

* Heat sink for Q (not shown)

PROJECT 9
Bilge-Water Alarm

Automatic bilge pump switches are notorious for failing. Although not usually dangerous, having bilge water rise above the cabin sole is not very good for the rugs or the joinery. This circuit gives an audible warning when the bilge water rises to the level of the normally dry probe.

The 741 opamp acts as a voltage comparator. The − input voltage is set at +6VCD by the voltage divider formed by R_2 and R_3. With a dry probe, the + input voltage is near 0 VDC, so the output of the 741 is near 0VDC.

With the probe immersed in water, however, the voltage at the + input rises to over 6 VDC, and the 741 output goes to 12VDC. Transistor, Q, boosts the 10 mA output of the 741 to drive the piezo transducer. R_4 prevents the + side of the probe from shorting to ground through the bilge water.

An inexpensive and convenient probe can be made from a section of television twin-lead with each conductor stripped back about one inch and tinned (soldered) to prevent corrosion. The probes should be mounted well above the normal bilge high-water level, so that they remain dry except when the regular bilge switch fails.

Circuit

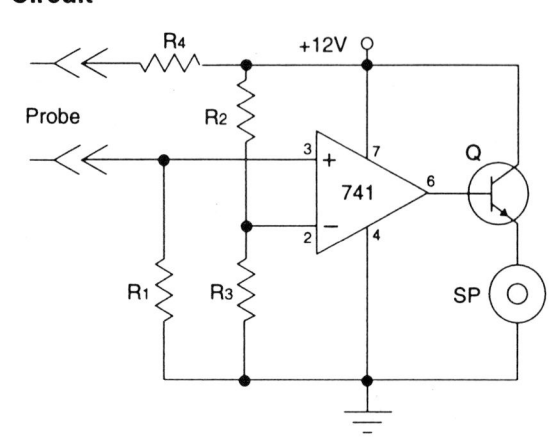

Components

Part	Description
R1	100 kΩ, 1/4-watt resistor
R2	100 kΩ, 1/4-watt resistor
R3	100 kΩ, 1/4-watt resistor
R4	10 kΩ, 1/4-watt resistor
Q	2N2222 NPN transistor
741	741 operational amplifier
SP	Piezo transducer
Probe	TV twin-lead antenna wire

PROJECT 10
Water Tank Indicator

Few things are more annoying than unexpectedly running out of water or having to lift deck hatches and unscrew access plates to check the level of water in your tanks. This circuit gives a visual warning when your water tank reaches a predetermined level.

The 741 opamp acts as a voltage comparator. The + input voltage is set by the voltage divider formed by trimpot R_2.

Run a length of television twin-lead antenna cable into your water tank from above. Strip about one inch of insulation from each of the two conductors and solder the exposed wire to prevent corrosion.

With the probe immersed in water, the voltage at the – input is near + 12-volts-DC. As soon as the water level drops below the probe leads, the resistance between the leads increases to near infinity and the – input voltage drops to zero. The opamp output rises to the supply voltage and lights the LED warning light.

Add a switch to the +12-volt-DC power lead if you want to turn the circuit on occasionally.

Circuit

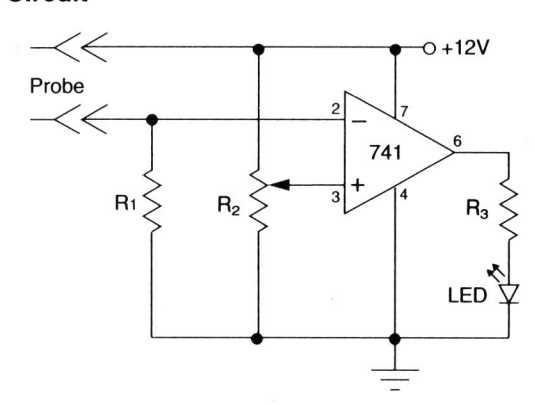

Components

Part	Description
R1	220 kΩ, 1/4-watt resistor
R2	100 kΩ trimpot
R3	10 kΩ, 1/4-watt resistor
LED	Red, low-power LED
741	741 operational amplifier

PROJECT 11
Boat Burglar Alarm

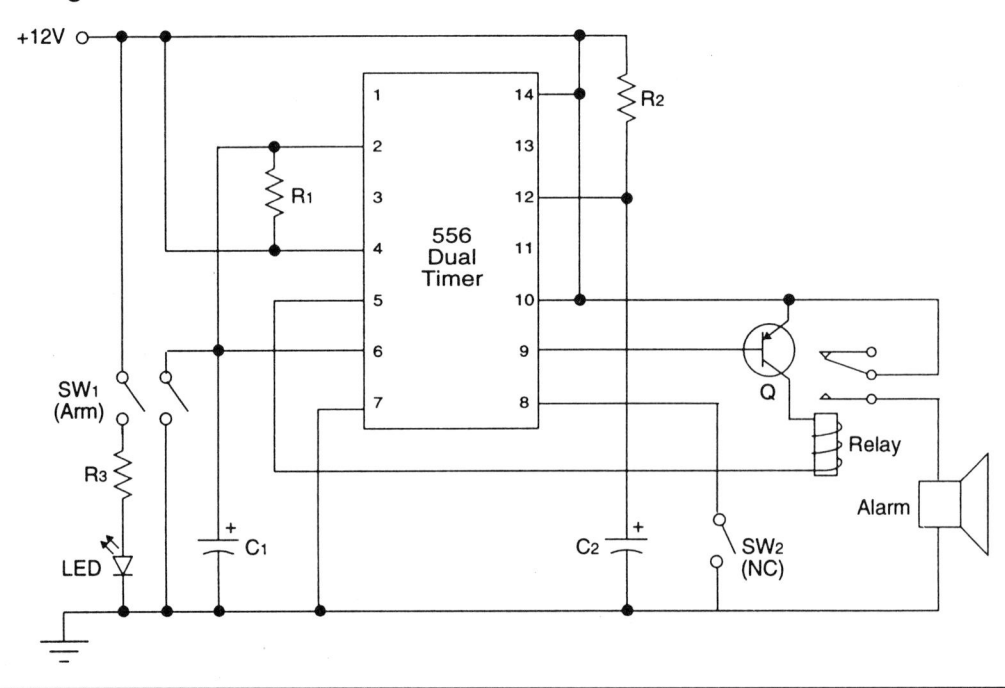

When switch SW_1 is closed, the LED lights up. At the same time, C_1 charges through R_1, allowing a safe interval of 10 seconds before the alarm is activated. This arming delay can be altered by changing the value of either R_1 or C_1. For example, doubling R_1 doubles the safe time from 10 to 20 seconds.

Switch SW_2 is the trigger for the alarm and may be one or several switches in series. Interrupting any one of the series switches will trigger the alarm after a 10 second delay. The alarm delay can also be modified by changing either R_2 or C_2.

Again, doubling either R_2 or C_2 doubles the duration of the alarm delay.

Components

Part	Description
R1	1 MΩ, 1/4-watt resistor
R2	1 MΩ, 1/4-watt resistor
R3	10 kΩ, 1/4-watt resistor
C1	10 µF, 35-volt capacitor
C2	10 µF, 35-volt capacitor
LED	Red, low-power LED
Q	MPS2907 PNP transistor
556	556 dual timer
SW1	Switch, DPDT, 6A
Alarm	Siren, 12-volt DC @ 0.5A

Fun Weekend Projects

PROJECT 12
Electronic Ship's Horn

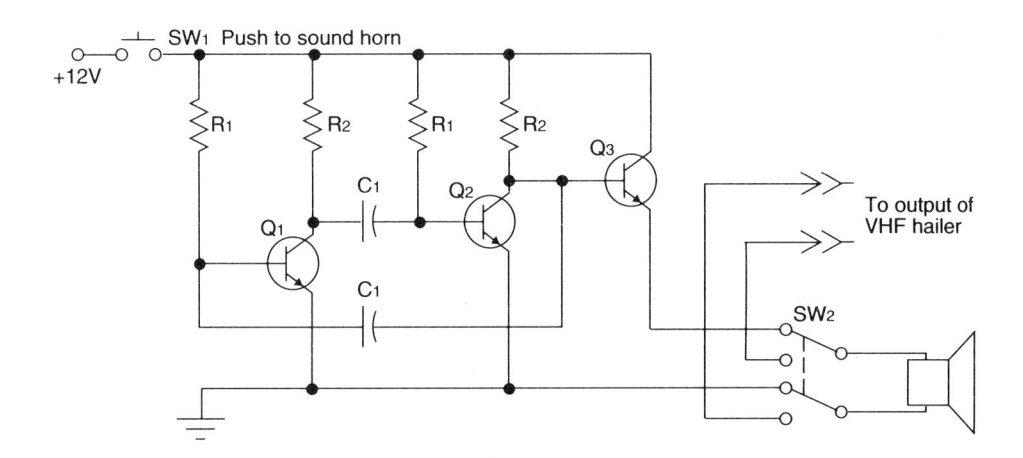

The circuit is a multivibrator (Q_1 and Q_2) with a frequency of $2\pi/R_1C_1 = 280$ hz. Transistor Q_3 boosts the current to drive the 8Ω, 40-watt speaker. Pushing the momentary contact switch, SW_1, sounds the horn.

Play with resistor(s) R_1 to achieve the pitch which is most pleasing to you, although 280 hz is close to the frequency of most commercial horns. A speaker with higher impedance can be used with an impedance-matching transformer.

Using switch SW_2, the speaker can be connected to the hailer output found in the rear of many VHF radios, allowing the speaker to be used as a bullhorn.

Components

Part	Description
R1(2)	100 kΩ, 1/4-watt resistor
R2(2)	1 kΩ, 1/4-watt resistor
C1(2)	0.22 µF capacitor
Q1	2N2222 NPN transistor
Q2	2N2222 NPN transistor
Q3	TIP-3055 NPN power transistor
SW1	Switch, momentary contact
SW2	Switch, DPDT, 10-amp
SP	Power horn, 8Ω, 40-watt

PROJECT 13
Fan Control for Refrigeration Compresser

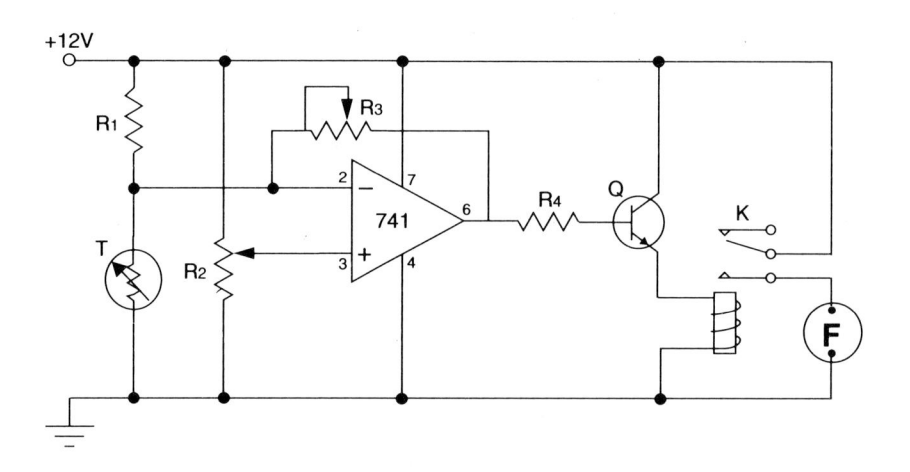

The efficiency of a refrigerator is affected greatly by the temperature of its condenser coil. Many small, 12-volt-DC boat compressors are located in warm or constricted spaces. Such condensers need fans to remove the heat from the coils.

This circuit uses a tiny thermistor, taped to the condenser tubing, to detect the need for air flow. The tape over the thermistor protects it from the direct flow of cool air, so that it truly measures coil temperature.

The opamp compares the voltages of two voltage dividers formed by R_1/T (- input) and R_2 (+ input). When the temperature of the thermistor rises above the setpoint, its resistance drops, the voltage at the negative input drops, and the output voltage of the inverting amplifier rises. Transistor Q boosts the opamp output current to close the relay and turn on the fan.

The temperature at which the fan comes on (the setpoint) is adjusted with trimpot R2. Trimpot R3 adjusts the gain of the amplifier and, thus, the difference between turn-on and turn-off temperatures.

Components

Part	Description
R1	10 kΩ, 1/4-watt resistor
R2	20 kΩ, 15-turn trimpot
R3	100 kΩ, 15-turn trimpot
R4	1 kΩ, 1/4-watt resistor
T	Thermistor, 10 kΩ @ 25C
Q	2N2222 NPN transistor
K	Relay, SPDT 12 volt-DC, 320Ω, 10 amp
741	741 operational amplifier

APPENDICES

A: Unit Conversions   302

B: European Standards   303

C: Circuit Symbols   304

D: Resistors   305

Unit conversions are provided in Appendix A to facilitate the conversion from English to Metric systems and back.

The new *European standards* are still in the process of being formulated. Appendix B compares U.S., U.K., and the new European color codes, as well as conductor cross-sections and ampacities.

For the reader's convenience, Appendix C repeats the *circuit symbols* found elsewhere in the book.

Appendix D lists all of the common *resistor* values and shows how to read the color code with which they are labelled.

Appendix A: Unit Conversions

Multiply	By	To Get	Multiply	By	To Get
Length			**Length**		
Inches	25.4	Millimeters	Millimeters	0.0394	Inches
Inches	2.54	Centimeters	Centimeters	0.3937	Inches
Inches	0.0254	Meters	Meters	39.37	Inches
Feet	30.48	Centimeters	Centimeters	0.0328	Feet
Feet	0.3048	Meters	Meters	3.281	Feet
Yards	0.9144	Meters	Meters	1.094	Yards
Miles	1.609	Kilometers	Kilometers	0.6215	Miles
Area			**Area**		
Inches^2	645.16	Millimeters^2	Millimeters^2	0.00155	Inches^2
Inches^2	6.4516	Centimeters^2	Centimeters^2	0.155	Inches^2
Feet^2	929.03	Centimeters^2	Centimeters^2	0.00108	Feet^2
Feet^2	0.0929	Meters^2	Meters^2	10.764	Feet^2
Yards^2	8361.3	Centimeters^2	Centimeters^2	0.00012	Yards^2
Yards^2	0.8361	Meters^2	Meters^2	1.196	Yards^2
Miles^2	2.59	Kilometers^2	Kilometers^2	0.3861	Miles^2
Volume			**Volume**		
Inches^3	16,387	Millimeters^3	Millimeters^3	6.1x10^{-05}	Inches^3
Inches^3	16.387	Centimeters^3	Centimeters^3	0.061	Inches^3
Feet^3	0.0283	Meters^3	Meters^3	35.33	Feet^3
Yards^3	0.7646	Meters^3	Meters^3	1.308	Yards^3
Energy			**Energy**		
Ergs	10^{-7}	Newton-meters	Newton-meters	10^7	Ergs
Joules	1	Newton-meters	Newton-meters	1	Joules
Joules	10^7	Ergs	Ergs	10^{-7}	Joules
Joules	0.2389	Calories	Calories	4.186	Joules
Joules	0.000948	BTUs	BTUs	1,055	Joules
Joules	0.7376	Foot-pounds	Foot-pounds	1.356	Joules
Calories	0.00397	BTUs	BTUs	252	Calories
Joules/sec	3.41	BTUs/hr	BTUs/hr	0.293	Joules/sec
BTUs/hr	252	Calories/hr	Calories/hr	0.00397	BTUs/hr
Horsepower	746	Watts	Watts	0.00134	Horsepower
F°	0.556	C°	C°	1.8	F°
°F	0.556(°F-32)	°C	°C	1.8(°C+32)	°F

Appendix B: European Standards

At the time of this writing, European wiring standards are in a state of flux. As every traveler knows, one must carry an adapter kit to use all of the various sockets in current use. ISO standards are now being developed that will probably be adopted by the EC. Until then, here is a little help.

AC Wiring Color Codes

Conductor	US 115VAC	US 230VAC	UK 240VAC (Old)	Europe 240VAC (New)
Ground	green or bare	green or bare	green or bare	green and yellow
Neutral	white	white	black	light blue
Live	black	black	red	brown
Live	NA	red	NA	NA

Comparison of Conductor Cross-Sections

Gauge AWG	Cross-sectional Area, mm² AWG	ISO	SAE	Ampacity, amps AWG	ISO
18	0.82	0.75	0.8	20	16
—	—	1.0	1.0	—	20
16	1.31	—	—	25	—
—	—	1.5	—	—	25
14	2.08	—	2.0	35	—
—	—	2.5	—	—	35
12	3.31	—	3.0	45	—
—	—	4.0	—	—	45
10	5.26	—	5.0	60	—
—	—	6.0	—	—	60
8	8.39	—	8.0	80	—
—	—	10.0	—	—	90
6	13.3	—	13.0	120	—
—	—	16.0	—	—	130
4	21.2	—	19.0	160	—
3	26.6	25.0	—	180	170
2	33.6	35.0	32.0	210	210
1	42.4	—	40.0	245	—
0	53.5	50.0	50.0	285	270
2/0	67.7	70.0	62.0	330	330
3/0	85.2	—	81.0	385	—
—	—	95.0	—	—	390
4/0	107	—	103	445	—

Appendix C: Circuit Symbols

Circuit Symbols

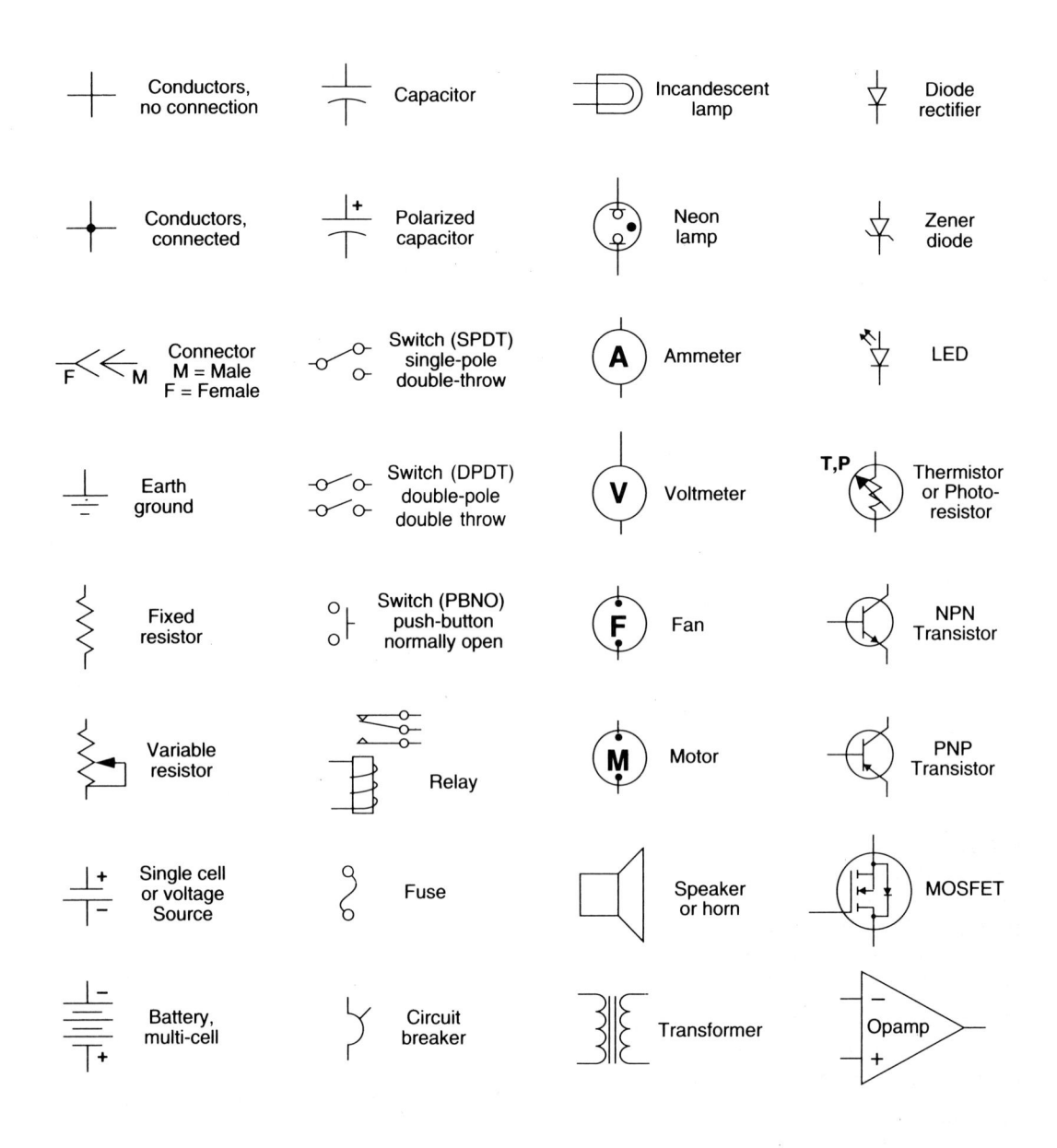

Conductors, no connection	Capacitor	Incandescent lamp	Diode rectifier
Conductors, connected	Polarized capacitor	Neon lamp	Zener diode
Connector M = Male F = Female	Switch (SPDT) single-pole double-throw	Ammeter	LED
Earth ground	Switch (DPDT) double-pole double throw	Voltmeter	Thermistor or Photo-resistor (T, P)
Fixed resistor	Switch (PBNO) push-button normally open	Fan	NPN Transistor
Variable resistor	Relay	Motor	PNP Transistor
Single cell or voltage Source	Fuse	Speaker or horn	MOSFET
Battery, multi-cell	Circuit breaker	Transformer	Opamp

Appendix D: Resistors

RESISTORS
Reading Resistor Values
Resistors are generally too small to allow the printing of identifying information. For this reason standard resistors are imprinted with color bands.

The figure below demystifies the color-code system for resistors.

Example: what is the resistance of a resistor with brown, red, orange, and silver bands?

Answer: 12,000 ± 10% Ω

There is also a BS1852 resistance code using numbers and letters:

0·47 Ω is marked R47   100 Ω is marked 100R
1 Ω is marked 1R0   1 kΩ is marked 1K0
4·7 Ω is marked 4R7   10 kΩ is marked 10K
47 Ω is marked 47R   10 M is marked 10M

After this is added a letter to indicate tolerance:
F = ±1%   G = ±2%   J = ±5%   K = ±10%
M = ±20%

Thus
R33M = 0.33 Ω ±20%   6K8DF = 6·8Ω ±1%
4R7K = 4·7 Ω ±10%   68KK = 68 kΩ ±10%
390RJ = 390 Ω ±5%   4M7M = MΩ ±20%

RESISTOR COLOR CODES

First significant digit
Second significant digit
Decimal multiplier
Tolerance:
  none = ± 20%
  silver = ±10%
  gold = ±5%

Band Color	Digit	Power of 10	Decimal Multiplier
Gold		10^{-1}	0.01
Silver		10^{-2}	0.1
Black	0	10^{0}	1
Brown	1	10^{1}	10
Red	2	10^{2}	100
Orange	3	10^{3}	1,000
Yellow	4	10^{4}	10,000
Green	5	10^{5}	100,000
Blue	6	10^{6}	1,000,000
Violet	7	10^{7}	10,000,000
Gray	8	10^{8}	100,000,000
White	9	10^{9}	1,000,000,000

RESISTOR SIZES
The electrical resistance of a resistor is not related to its size. Instead, resistor size is determined by the amount of power the resistor can safely dissipate in the form of heat.

Use the illustration at right to determine the size of the most common carbon-composition and carbon-film resistors.

Resistors with larger power ratings are labelled with both resistance and power.

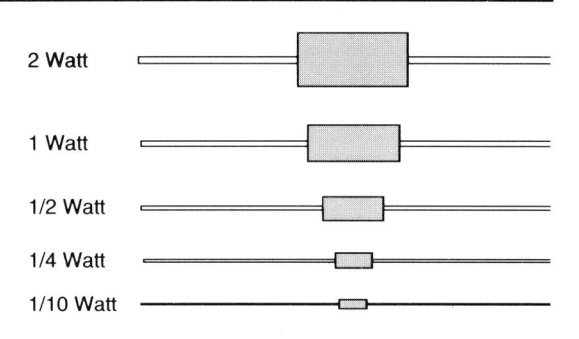

2 Watt
1 Watt
1/2 Watt
1/4 Watt
1/10 Watt

Appendix D: Resistors

Standard Resistance Values in Ohms

Bold values available only in 10% tolerance. All other values available in 5% tolerance. Values beginning with 10, 15, 22, 33, 47, and 68 also available in 20% tolerance.

First Band	Second Band	Gold	Black	Brown	Red	Third Band Orange	Yellow	Green	Blue
Brown	Black	1.0	10	100	1,000	10,000	100,000	1,000,000	10,000,000
Brown	Brown	1.1	11	110	1,100	11,000	110,000	1,100,000	11,000,000
Brown	Red	1.2	12	120	1,200	12,000	120,000	1,200,000	12,000,000
Brown	Orange	1.3	13	130	1,300	13,000	130,000	1,300,000	13,000,000
Brown	Green	1.5	15	**150**	1,500	15,000	150,000	1,500,000	15,000,000
Brown	Blue	1.6	16	160	1,600	16,000	160,000	1,600,000	16,000,000
Brown	Gray	1.8	18	**180**	1,800	18,000	180,000	1,800,000	18,000,000
Red	Black	2.0	20	200	2,000	20,000	200,000	2,000,000	20,000,000
Red	Red	2.2	22	**220**	2,200	22,000	220,000	2,200,000	22,000,000
Red	Yellow	2.4	24	240	2,400	24,000	240,000	2,400,000	
Red	Violet	2.7	27	**270**	2,700	27,000	270,000	2,700,000	
Orange	Black	3.0	30	300	3,000	30,000	300,000	3,000,000	
Orange	Orange	3.3	33	**330**	3,300	33,000	330,000	3,000,000	
Orange	Blue	3.6	36	360	3,600	36,000	360,000	3,600,000	
Orange	White	3.9	39	**390**	3,900	39,000	390,000	3,900,000	
Yellow	Orange	4.3	43	430	4,300	43,000	430,000	4,300,000	
Yellow	Violet	4.7	47	**470**	4,700	47,000	470,000	4,700,000	
Green	Brown	5.1	51	510	5,100	51,000	510,000	5,100,000	
Green	Blue	5.6	56	**560**	5,600	56,000	560,000	5,600,000	
Blue	Red	6.2	62	620	6,200	62,000	620,000	6,200,000	
Blue	Gray	6.8	68	**680**	6,800	68,000	680,000	6,800,000	
Violet	Green	7.5	75	750	7,500	75,000	750,000	7,500,000	
Gray	Red	8.2	82	**820**	8,200	82,000	820,000	8,200,000	
White	Brown	9.1	91	910	9,100	91,000	910,000	9,100,000	

Glossary

Air Terminal: a metal rod that terminates in a sharp point.

Alternating Current (AC): current which periodically reverses direction.

Ammeter: a meter connected in series with a circuit which measures the current flowing through the circuit.

Ampere: the unit of measure for electric current which equals one coulomb (6.24×10^{18}) of electrons passing a point per second.

Anode: a positively charged electrode or a metal molecule which, in an electrolyte, assumes a more positive charge than the one (cathode) with which it is coupled. A metal so charged tends to corrode.

Atom: the smallest quantity into which a chemical element can be divided and still maintain all of the qualities of that element.

Battery: a chemical apparatus which maintains a voltage between its terminals.

Battery Cold Cranking Rating: the discharge load in amperes which a battery at 0°F (-17.8°C) can deliver for 30 seconds and maintain a voltage of 1.2 volts per cell or higher.

Battery Reserve Capacity: the number of minutes a new fully charged battery at 80°F (26.7°C) can be discharged at 25 amperes and maintain a voltage of 1.75 volts or higher per cell (10.5 volts for a 12- volt battery or 5.25 volts for a 6-volt battery).

Bleeder Resistor: a resistor in the output of a power supply which removes the output voltage after the power supply is turned off.

Bonding: the electrical connection of the exposed, metallic, non-current carrying parts to the ground (negative) side of the direct current system.

Bonding Conductor: a normally noncurrent-carrying conductor used to connect the noncurrent-carrying metal parts of direct-current devices on the boat to the boat's bonding system.

Branch: a current path in a circuit.

Capacitance: the electrical size of a capacitor in farads. Equal to the amount of charge stored divided by the voltage across the capacitor.

Capacitor: a device that stores electrostatic charge when a voltage is applied.

Cathode: the more noble metal of an electrolytic cell which is negatively charged and tends to resist corrosion.

Cathodic Protection: reduction or prevention of corrosion of a metal by making it cathodic by the use of sacrificial anodes or impressed currents.

Cell: the smallest unit of a battery.

Chassis: the metal structure that supports the circuits and components of a piece of electronic equipment.

Choke: an inductor placed in series in a circuit to oppose changes in current.

Circuit: a complete electrical path from one terminal to the other of a voltage source.

Circuit Breaker: an automatic switch which opens when current exceeds the specified limit.

Coil: turns of wire that have inductance.

Common Bonding Conductor: an electrical conductor, usually running fore-and-aft, to which all equipment bonding conductors are connected.

Conductance: a measure of the ability to carry current. The inverse of resistance.

Conductor: any material that has little electrical resistance.

Controller: an automatic or manually operated device (in a controlled or regulated cathodic protection system) to regulate the flow of electric current for corrosion control.

Corrosion: the deterioration of a metal or alloy by chemical or electro-chemical reaction with its environment.

Coulomb: the unit of measurement of electrical charge. One coulomb equals 6.24×10^{18} electrons.

Couple: two dissimilar metals or alloys in electrical contact with each other that have different potentials and become anodes or cathodes when in common contact with an electrolyte. A couple may also be formed on the surface of the same metal.

Current: the flow of electrons through a material.

Current Density: for corrosion purposes the current per unit area of the anodes or cathodes expressed in amperes or milliamperes per square foot.

DC Ground Conductor: a current-carrying conductor connected to the side of the source which is intentionally maintained at boat ground potential.

Direct Current (DC): current that flows in one direction.

DC Grounding Conductor: a normally noncurrent-carrying conductor used to connect metallic noncurrent-carrying parts of direct current devices to the Engine Negative Terminal or its bus. Its purpose is to minimize stray current corrosion.

Double-Insulation System: an insulation system comprised of basic insulation and supplementary insulation. The two insulations are physically separated and so arranged that they are not simultaneously subjected to the same deteriorating influences (temperature, contaminants, and the like) to the same degree.

Driving Potential: voltage difference between the anode and the cathode of a couple.

Earth Ground: a point that is at the same potential or voltage as the local earth

Electrode: a conductive material through which electrical currents enter or leave an electrolyte.

Electrolysis: chemical changes in a solution or electrolyte due to the passage of electric current. This term is also loosely applied to corrosion processes. However, since the term refers to solution phenomena not to corrosion, its use to indicate corrosion should be discouraged.

Electrolyte: a liquid in which electrically charged ions render the liquid capable of conducting a current. Solutions of acids, bases and salts in water are electrolytes.

Electron: one of the subatomic particles with negative charge that surround the nucleus of an atom and determine its chemical properties.

Energy: the ability to do work. The unit Joule equals one watt for one second.

Engine Negative Terminal: the point on the engine at which the negative battery cable is connected.

Farad: the unit of capacitance. The size of a capacitor is one farad when it stores one coulomb of charge with one volt across its terminals.

Fuse: a conductive device which melts and breaks the circuit when current flow exceeds the rated amount.

Giga (G): prefix meaning 10^9 or one billion.

Galvanic Corrosion: the corrosion that occurs at the anode of a galvanic couple caused by the flow of ions from the anode to the cathode through an electrolyte.

Galvanic Isolator: a device installed in series with the grounding (green) conductor of the shore power cable to effectively block galvanic current flow but permit the passage of alternating current (AC). It is normally associated with the grounding (green) conductor.

Galvanic Series: a list of metals and alloys arranged in order of their potentials as measured in relation to a reference electrode when immersed in sea-water. The table of potentials is arranged with the anodic or least noble metals at one end and the cathodic or most noble metals at the other.

Ground: a surface or mass at the potential of the earth's surface, established at this potential by a conducting connection (intentional or accidental) with the earth, including any metal area which forms part of the wetted surface of the hull.

Grounded Conductor: a current-carrying conductor that is connected to the side of the source which is intentionally maintained at ground potential.

Grounding Conductor: a conductor not normally carrying current provided to connect the exposed metal enclosures of electric equipment to ground, the primary function of which is to minimize shock hazard to personnel.

Ground-Fault Circuit-Interrupter (GFCI): a device intended for the protection of personnel that functions to de-energize a circuit or portion thereof within an established period of time when a current to ground exceeds some predetermined value that is less than that required to operate the overcurrent protective device of the supply circuit.

Ground-Fault Protector (GFP): a device intended to protect equipment by interrupting the electric current to the load when a fault current to ground exceeds some predetermined value that is less than that required to operate the overcurrent protection device of that supply circuit.

Henry (H): the unit of inductance. A one-henry coil produces one volt when the rate of change of current through it is one ampere per second.

Horsepower: a measure of power equaling 746 watts.

Hot: any wire or point in a circuit that is not at ground voltage.

Ignition Protection: the design and construction of a device such that under design operating conditions:
 - it will not ignite a flammable hydrocarbon mixture surrounding the device when an ignition source causes an internal explosion, or
 - it is incapable of releasing sufficient electrical or thermal energy to ignite a hydrocarbon mixture, or
 - the source of the ignition is hermetically sealed.

Glossary

Impressed Current System: a cathodic protection system which utilizes a direct current source (usually with battery) to attain the required millivolt shift in the metallic parts to be protected.

Inductance: measure of the back voltage produced in a coil when current is changing. Unit is the henry.

Inductor: same as coil.

Insulator: any material which is used because of its great electrical resistance.

Isolator: a device installed in series with the grounding (green) conductor of the shore power cable to effectively block galvanic current (direct current (DC)) flow but permit the passage of alternating current (AC) to provide a path for ground fault currents.

Kilo (k): prefix meaning 10^3 or 1,000.

Leakage Resistance: the resistance (usually very high) across a device which is ideally a nonconductor.

Lightning Ground Plate: a means to conduct the electrical current from a boat's conductive elements to the water in which the boat floats. A separate lightning ground plate may be used or it may also serve other purposes.

Lightning Protective Mast: a conductive structure or if nonconductive, equipped with a conductive means and an air terminal.

Load: any device in a circuit which dissipates power.

Mega (M): prefix meaning 10^6 or one million.

Micro (μ): prefix meaning 10^{-6} or one millionth.

Milli (m): prefix meaning 10^{-3} or one thousanth.

Nano (n): prefix meaning 10^{-9} or one billionth.

Negative Ion: an atom with one or more extra electrons.

Ohm: the unit of electrical resistance.

Ohmmeter: a device that measures electrical resistance.

Ohm's Law: the mathematical relationship between current through and voltage across an element of a circuit.

Open Circuit: a break in a circuit path that prevents the flow of current.

Overcurrent Protection Device: a device, such as a fuse or circuit breaker, designed to interrupt the circuit when the current flow exceeds a predetermined value.

Panelboard: an assembly of devices for the purpose of controlling and/or distributing power on a boat. It may include devices such as circuit breakers, fuses, switches, instruments and indicators. Panelboards are intended to be installed in enclosures and may be accessible from the front or the rear.

Parallel Circuit: a circuit in which there is more than one path through which current can flow.

Pico (p): prefix meaning 10^{-12} or one million millionth.

Pigtails: external conductors that originate within the electrical component or appliance.

Polarity: the sign (+ or -) of a voltage.

Polarized System: a system in which the grounded and ungrounded conductors are connected in the same relation to all terminals or fixture leads on all devices in the circuit.

Positive Ion: an atom that has lost one or more electrons.

Potential Difference: the force that causes electrons and other charged objects to move. Same as electromotive force and voltage.

Power: the rate at which energy is used or converted. The unit, watt, equals one ampere through times one volt across.

Power Supply: a voltage source, not a battery, that supplies current at a fixed voltage to a circuit.

Reference Electrode: a metal and metallic-salt (silver-silver chloride for example) mixture in solution that will develop and maintain an accurate reference potential to which the potential of other metals immersed in the same electrolyte may be compared.

Reference Potential: the voltage difference between a reference electrode and a metal when they are immersed in the same electrolyte.

Resistance: opposition to electric current. The unit is the ohm, which equates to a voltage drop of one volt across a device through which one ampere of current is flowing.

Self-Limiting: a machine whose maximum output is restricted to a specified value by its magnetic and electrical characteristics.

Series Circuit: a circuit having only one path through which current can flow.

Sheath: a material used as a continuous protective covering, such as overlapping electrical tape, molded rubber, molded plastic, or flexible tubing, around one or more insulated conductors.

Shore-Power Inlet: the fitting designed for mounting on the boat, of a reverse-service type, requiring a female connector on the shore-power cable in order to make the electrical connection.

Short Circuit: a path, usually accidental, with little or no electrical resistance.

Shunt: a very low resistance device placed in series in a circuit to generate a small voltage in order to read the circuit current.

Solenoid: a relay used to switch heavy currents such as those in a starter motor.

Storage Battery: a connected group of cells, contained in a case, that by reversible chemical reactions converts chemical energy into electrical energy and may be recharged by passing a current through it in the opposite direction of the discharging current.

Stray Current Corrosion: corrosion that results when a current from a battery or other external electrical (AC or DC) source causes a metal in contact with an electrolyte to become anodic with respect to another metal in contact with the same electrolyte. Alternating current (AC) leakage may affect stray current corrosion.

Switch: a device used to open and close circuits.

Switchboard: an assembly of devices for the purpose of controlling and/or distributing power on a boat. It may include devices such as circuit breakers, fuses, switches, instruments and indicators. They are generally accessible from the rear as well as from the front and are not intended to be installed in cabinets.

Terminal: a point of connection to an electrical device.

Trip-Free Circuit Breaker: a thermal and/or magnetically operated overcurrent protection device, designed so that the resetting means cannot be manually held in to over-ride the current interrupting mechanism.

Ungrounded Conductor: a current-carrying conductor which is completely insulated from ground and connects the source of power to the utilization equipment. In direct current systems (DC), this conductor will be connected to the positive terminal of the battery. In alternating current systems (AC), this conductor will be connected to the "hot" side of the shore power system, or to the appropriate terminal of an on-board auxiliary generator.

Volt (V): the unit of voltage or potential difference.

Voltage Source: a device which supplies the voltage to a circuit.

Voltmeter: device for measuring voltage or potential difference between two points of a circuit.

Watertight: so constructed that moisture will not enter the enclosure.

Watt (W): unit of measurement of power. One watt is one ampere through times one volt across.

Weatherproof: constructed or protected so that exposure to the weather will not interfere with successful operation.

Zone of Protection: an essentially cone shaped space below a grounded air terminal or mast or overhead ground wire which is substantially immune to direct strokes of lightning.

Index

AC, 135–217; ABYC load calculations, 178; allowable amperage, 187; approved connectors, 192; approved wire and cable, 186; basics, 135; color code, 142; conductor identification, 142; conductor installation, 194; frequency meter, 292; galvanic protection, 201; ground-fault protection, 184; grounding, 141, 177; impedance, 147; main panelboard, 177; measuring, 146; over-current protection, 184; phase, 137; polarity, 149; polarity indicator, 177, 288; power factor, 138; sockets, 143, 193; safety, 140; three-phase, 138; transformations, 144; trouble-shooting, 147; voltages, 136; wiring standards, 171–217
Alarm: bilge, 296; burglar, 298
Allowable amperage for DC conductors, 111
Allowable voltage drop in conductors, 112
Alternators, 53–71; coil configurations, 60; controlling, 61; diodes and rectification, 56, 59; galley experiment, 54; isolating diode, 65; poles and coils, 55; powering regulator, 64; regulator, 62; regulator bypass, 67; troubleshooting, 68; type-P and type-N, 64
Ammeter: analog, 18; digital, 19
Amperage: allowable for conductors, 111
Ampere, André, 4
Anchor light: automatic control, 294; savings, 225
Antennas, 264-272; GPS, 271; location, 264; loran, 271; radar, 272; satnav, 271; SSB, 271; VHF, 269
Appliance power consumption, 154

Batteries, 29–51; BMEA standards, 51; box, 50; capacity vs. specific gravity, 37; capacity vs. voltage, 37; charge/discharge cycle, 32; charging characteristics, 41; charging recommendations, 42; chemical reaction, 31; condition monitor, 293; cost per kilowatt-hour, 46; discharge characteristics, 39; discharge ratings, 40; electrical model, 34; electrolyte corrections, 36; eliminator, 291; galley experiment, 30; installation, 50; life-cycles, 46; low-voltage alarm, 292; monitoring, 36; self-discharge, 35; series vs. parallel, 49; sizes, 44; sizing capacity to load, 45; specifications of popular models, 40; voltage vs. specific gravity, 37
Bilge alarm, 296
Bonding, 73-101; for corrosion protection, 86; for lightning protection, 78; common conductor, 76; conductors, 74; DC-system, 75; defined, 74; testing protection, 96; to bond or not to bond, 95
Burglar alarm, 298
Cabin-light dimmer, 295
Cathodic protection: general application, 98
Circuit breakers, 118
Circuit components, 280
Circuit symbols, 105, 304
Coaxial cable, 125, 165; adapters, 267; connectors, 266; installation, 266; moisture protection, 268
Conductors, 5; allowable amperage, 111; allowable voltage drop, 112; magnetic compass, 116; battery cables, 116; DC color code, 113; identification, 113; in bilge, 116; installation, 114; over-current protection, 116; support, 114
Connections, 120-124; making, 120; proper, 124; solder, 123; tools, 121; tensile strength, 123
Connectors: approved, 192; co-axial, 125
Conservation of electricity, 225–230; electronics, 229; fans, 229; lighting, 225; refrigeration, 225; typical power consumption, 230
Corrosion, 86–101; bonding, 86; cavitation erosion, 101; dezincification of brass, 99; galley experiment, 87; galvanic series table, 89; green AC-grounding wire, 201; stainless and aluminum, 100; stainless pitting, 100; stray-current, 92; zincs, 91
Costs per kilowatt-hour, 222
Coulomb, Charles, 4
Dalton, John, 4
DC, 3–132; ABYC load calculation method, 110; allowable amperage, 111; allowable voltage drop, 112; circuit concept, 5; conductor identification, 113; ignition protection, 127; measurements, 15; over-current protection, 116; wire type, 108; wiring diagrams, 104; wiring standards, 103-132
Democritus, 4
Dimmer: cabin light, 295
Do-it-yourself projects, 279-300
Electricity: discovery, 4; what is, 4
Electronics: installing, 263–277
Energy and power, 9
European standards, 303
Fan: refrigeration control, 300
Faraday, Michael, 4
Filtering electrical noise, 274
Frequency: U.S. and Europe, 136; meter, 290
Fuses, 119
Galvani, Luigi, 4
Galvanic protection: general

Index

application, 98; green AC-grounding wire, 201
Gauges: AWG, ISO, SAE, 303
Generators, 151–165; alternator-type, 167; armature-type, 165; frequency regulation, 168; purchasing, 170; troubleshooting, 169; voltage regulation, 168
GPS antennas, 271
Green wire and corrosion, 203
Ground-fault: devices, 143; protection, 184
Grounding: DC system, 76; AC system,141,177
Heat-shrink tubing, 123
Horn: ship's electronic, 299
Ignition protection, 127, 195
Impedance, 147
Impressed-current system, 91
Insulators, 5
Inverter, 151–164; battery charging, 163; efficiency, 162; schematic, 159; specifications, 160; switching, 164; waveform, 159
Isolation transformer, 205
Lamp: burned-out, 24; dimmer circuit, 295; fluorescent savings, 225; halogen savings, 225
LED panel indicators, 289
Lighting savings, 225
Lightning,78-85; ground connection, 82; interconnection of metallic masses, 83; protecting electronics, 84; protecting people, 85; safe path to ground, 82; zones of protection, 80
Loads: calculation of AC, 178; calculation of DC, 110; parallel, 7; series, 6; series/parallel, 7
Loran, 264, 271
Maxwell, James, 4
Multimeter: specifications, 20; use of, 26
Noise: electrical, 274-277; conducting audit, 274; curing, 274; filters, 274; shielding, 274
Oersted, Hans, 4
Ohm, Georg, 4

Ohm's Law, 5
Operational amplifiers, 286
Over-current protection, 116, 184; AC-main supply, 185; circuit breakers, 118; circuits requiring, 116; fuses, 119; location, 116; panelboards and switchboards, 117; unprotected length of supply conductors, 117
Polarity: AC, 149; indicator circuit, 290
Power, and energy, 9; factor, 138; supply, 145
Radar: antennas, 272; range, 272
Receivers: grounding, 273; installation, 273; power hook-up, 273
Rectification: diode, 57; full-wave, 58, 144; half-wave, 58, 144
Refrigeration: cooling load, 225; fan control circuit, 300; insulating box, 226; savings, 225
Resistors: color-code, 305; sizes, 305; values, 306
Reverse polarity: checking for, 149; indicator circuit, 289
RFI (see Noise)
Satnav antennas, 271
Shielding electrical noise, 274
Ship's-horn circuit, 299
Shore power, 172-176, 206-217; cable, 173; connectors, 174; transfer switch, 175; typical approved circuits, 206; inlet-warning sign, 175
Shunt: current, 147
Signal-to-noise ratio (SNR), 274
Solar panels, 231–244; electrical installation, 243; estimating daily output, 241; how they work, 234; interpreting specifications, 235; location options, 242; mechanical installation, 241; orientation to sun, 236
Solar power, 231–244; commercial panels, 233; is it for you, 232; production among cruisers, 232; rules for successful installation, 244
Solar radiation on surfaces, 237

Sources: parallel, 8; series, 8
SSB antennas, 271
Switch: finding defective, 25
Test-lead tips, 22
Testers: do-it-yourself, 21; troubleshooting with, 22
Thompson, Joseph, 4
Tools for wiring, 121
Transfer switch, 164, 175
Transformers: isolation, 144; step-down, 144
Transistors, 286
Transmitter: grounding, 273; installation, 273; power hookup, 273
Troubleshooting: AC, 147; generators, 169; noise, 274-277
Tubing: heat shrink, 123, 268
VHF: antennas, 269; range, 270
Volt-ohm meter (VOM): analog, 19; digital, 20
Volta, Allesandro, 4
Voltage: drop, 109; source, 6
Voltmeter: analog, 17; digital, 19
Water generators, 258
Water-tank indicator, 297
Wind machine, 245–258; electrical installation, 257; halyard-mount, 257; mechanical installation, 254; mizzen-mount, 254; outputs of commercial machines, 248; pole-mount, 254; specifications, 253
Wind power, 245–259; average amount in wind, 249; economics, 246; estimating average daily output, 252; is it for you, 246; production on cruising boats, 246; theory, 247; variation with height, 251
Wire: ampacity, 109; insulation, 108; stranding, 108; voltage drop, 109
Wiring diagrams, 104
Zincs, 86–99; general application of cathodic protection, 98; testing protection, 96